P9-CAF-351

CLB 1727
This edition published 1990 by CLB Publishing Inc,
Airport Business Center, 29 Kripes Road, East Granby, CT 06026

Printed and bound in Italy

ISBN 0 86283 791 X

Battlefields of THE CIVIL WAR

Text by

JAMES V. MURFIN

Introduced & Edited by

L. Edward Purcell

DESIGNED BY PHILIP CLUCAS

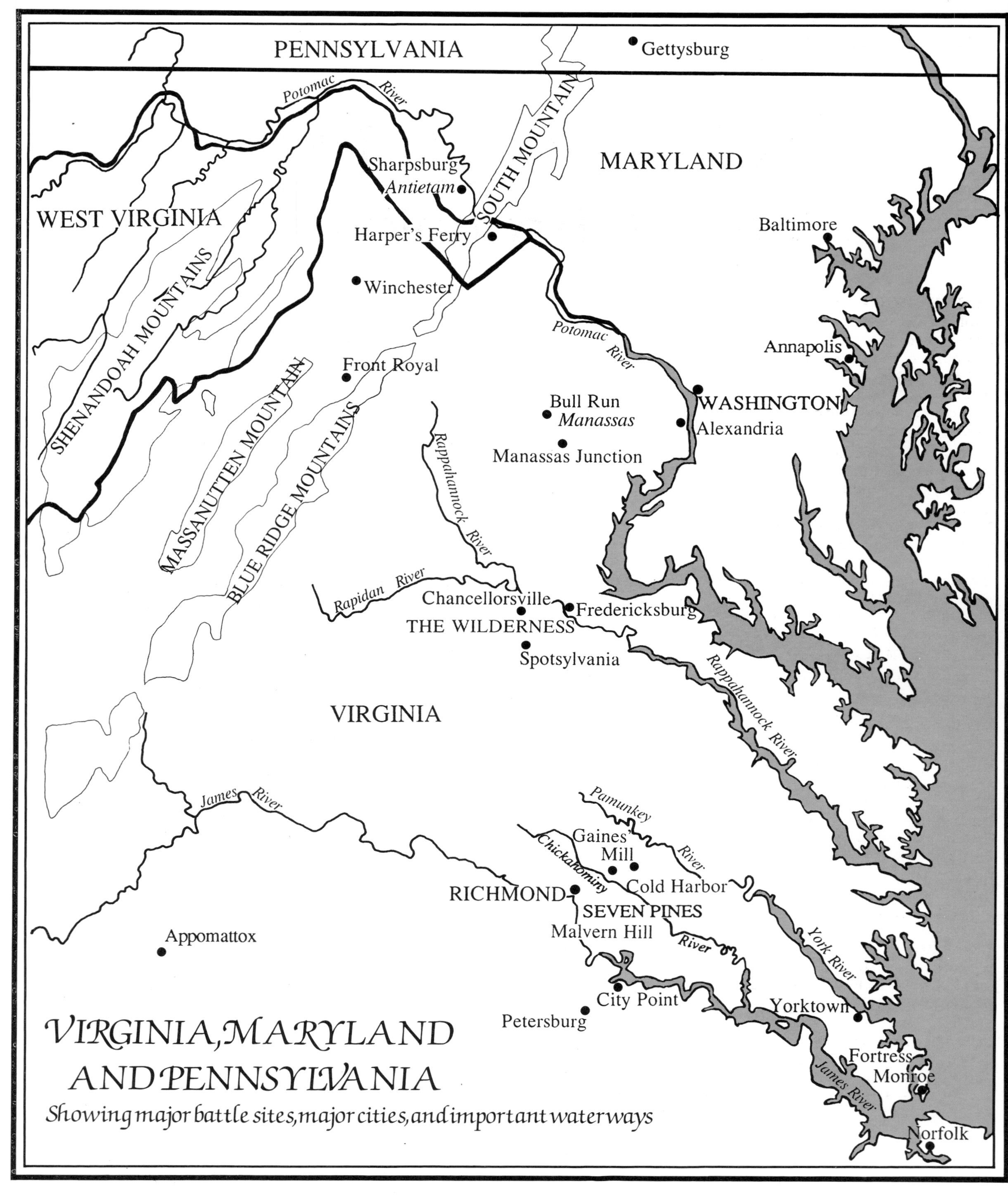
PENNSYLVANIA
Gettysburg
Potomac River
SOUTH MOUNTAIN
MARYLAND
Sharpsburg
Antietam
WEST VIRGINIA
Harper's Ferry
Baltimore
SHENANDOAH MOUNTAINS
Winchester
Potomac River
Annapolis
MASSANUTTEN MOUNTAIN
Front Royal
WASHINGTON
BLUE RIDGE MOUNTAINS
Bull Run
Manassas
Alexandria
Manassas Junction
Rappahannock River
Rapidan River
Chancellorsville
Fredericksburg
THE WILDERNESS
Spotsylvania
Rappahannock River
VIRGINIA
James River
Pamunkey River
Gaines' Mill
Chickahominy River
Cold Harbor
RICHMOND
SEVEN PINES
Malvern Hill
Appomattox
York River
City Point
Petersburg
Yorktown
Fortress Monroe
James River
Norfolk
VIRGINIA, MARYLAND AND PENNSYLVANIA
Showing major battle sites, major cities, and important waterways

CONTENTS and Chronology

INTRODUCTION

The Civil War was the most important conflict in American history. The causes and the continuing motives were stronger, more powerful, more compelling, and vastly more destructive than a foreign war could ever be.

Even though it is a well-worn cliché, this was truly a war of brother against brother, and therefore it was the most terrible possible conflict. The prolonged violence of the American Civil War was driven by the raw emotional energy of a domestic quarrel, which impelled the combatants in complicated ways toward battles filled with the intimate viciousness and the unflinching purpose that exist only when siblings are pitted against one another.

The results of these high emotions, when wedded to an emerging technology of killing power, were battles of inspiring grandeur and heartbreaking carnage.

For pure, terrible effect, few battles in history surpass those of the American Civil War, which was fought on a cusp between the ancient mode of face-to-face killing and modern, faceless slaughter. To recount the battles is to tell stories of hand-to-hand savagery, the ripping of bodies with bayonets and the smashing of skulls with clubbed muskets, as well as narratives of massive annihilation by superior technical firepower. The tales are by turn horrible and fascinating.

Valor was the common coin of the war, but at times it was minted from ignorance. Few generals on either side could quite grasp that defensive killing power had come to far surpass offensive potential. The legendary Stonewall Jackson was one who saw through to the core: ". . . my men had sometimes failed *to take* a position," he said at Fredericksburg, "but *to defend* one, never!"

Even the brilliant Lee and his able lieutenants – all of whom understood far better than their northern counterparts the power of prepared defensive positions – suffered occasional (and crucial) lapses in judgment. When deprived of Jackson's insight at Gettysburg, Lee succumbed to the seduction of the glorious assault.

Armies still fought in the 1860s with single-projectile weapons (not for another half-century did automatic firepower appear on the battlefields of France to teach anew the lesson of defensive superiority through even vaster carnage), but the invention of the Minie ball cartridge gave infantry a greatly increased power to hurt. Infantry fire was more rapid then in the days of the musket, considerably more accurate, and the large, low-velocity projectile inflicted terrible wounds. Even more crucial were improvements in artillery. Rifled cannon and the increased mobility of large caliber weapons made ordering infantry assaults a death sentence for thousands of men.

The major military lesson of the war, written in rivers of blood, was that well-placed, modern artillery and intrenched infantry could almost always destroy the most courageous attack. Firepower, even the relatively feeble firepower of the 1860s, was too deadly for the human spirit to endure.

An overall strategic view of the Civil War is crowded and complex. Because the two enemy capitals were only a few days' march apart, the conflict in the East ranged over the same territory again and again. Two or even three battles were fought on the same ground. Much of the Federal fumbling in the first years of the war (apart from the poor performance of the Union generals) flowed from Lincoln's keystone strategy of keeping at all times an army between Washington and any Confederate threat. And, the war could never cease until Richmond was taken. As Jefferson Davis wrote in 1863: "an advance against Richmond . . . in political if not military circles, was regarded as the objective point of the war."

So, battle raged again and again in Northern Virginia and Maryland, where the terrain of rivers, forests, mountains, and marshes created difficult, nasty campaigns.

In the West, great battles along the Mississippi and around Chattanooga and Atlanta produced huge butcher's bills and eventually deprived the Confederacy of the necessities of existence, for the Civil War also introduced the compelling power of total war – of war against the citizens and the economic base of the enemy.

The war opened with a polite, holiday-like battle of two standup armies at Manassas, presumed by both sides to settle the issue quickly and clearly. It ended four years later, only after Sherman's march destroyed the power of the Confederacy to make war. At the last, Grant realized no possible valor against the defenses of Richmond could have compelled Lee's appointment at Appomattox; the trail of twisted rail ties across Georgia did.

At the heart of the Civil War, however, not tactics nor technology nor even grand strategies were as important as the actions of individual men in blue and gray. The battlefields of the war were the arenas in which intense human drama was enacted again and again, sealing a nation broken asunder, to be made whole only through bloody sacrifice.

Abraham Lincoln. (University of Kentucky Photo Archives)

CHAPTER 1

PROLOGUE TO SUMTER

It was high noon, Monday, January 21, 1861. A tall, gaunt man rose from his desk in the United States Senate. The President recognized him at once as a hush spread over the crowded chamber. He looked out at his colleagues; every face turned to meet his eyes. There were 66 desks in the Senate; three of them were empty. The tall Senator knew that within the hour five more would be vacated and that one of those would be his. He also knew, as surely as he stood there, that before the trees blossomed in this beautiful city again, other desks would empty.

The man's name was Jefferson Davis; he was the senior Senator from Mississippi. Just 12 days before, his state had voted to secede from the Union; he could no longer wait and hope for a political miracle that would reverse this ominous news. It was time to bid his farewell.

"I rise, Mr. President," he began, "for the purpose of announcing to the Senate that I have satisfactory evidence that the State of Mississippi, by a solemn ordinance of her people in convention assembled, has declared her separation from the United States."

Davis was not well; a migraine headache spread across his eyes. He had had no sleep since the telegram from his governor. His voice was low at first, it faltered. To his wife, who sat in the gallery above, it soon "rang out melodiously clear, like a silver trumpet, to the extremest verge of the assembly."

"Under these circumstances, of course, my functions terminate here," Davis continued. "It has seemed to me proper, however, that I should appear in the Senate to announce that fact to my associates, and I will say but very little more."

Official Washington had expected Davis to resign days before. This morning they turned out early. By seven o'clock crowds were pushing toward the galleries. The "reporters" gallery was filled with the diplomatic corps and their families. Varina Davis wrote:

Curiosity and the expectation of an intellectual feast seemed to be the prevailing feeling, and I, who had come from a sleepless night, all through the watches of which war and its attendants, famine and bloodshed, had been predicted in despairing accents, looked on this festive crowd and wondered if they saw beyond the cold exterior of the orator – his deep depression, his desire for reconciliation, and his overweening love for the Union in whose cause he had bled, and to maintain which he was ready to sacrifice all but liberty and equality.

Jefferson Davis continued:

It is known to senators who have served with me here that I have for many years advocated, as an essential attribute of State sovereignty, the right of a State to secede from the Union. . . . If I had thought that Mississippi was acting without sufficient provocation . . . I should still, under my theory of government, because of my allegiance to the State of which I am a citizen, have been bound by her action.

We but thread in the paths of our fathers when we proclaim our independence and take the hazard . . . not in hostility to others, not to injure any section of the country, not even for our own pecuniary benefit, but from the high and solemn motive of defending and protecting the rights we inherited, and which it is our duty to transmit to our children.

"Unshed tears were in [his words] . . . ," Mrs. Davis wrote, "and a plea for peace permeated every tone. Every graceful gesture seemed to invite brotherly love. His manner suggested that of one who parts from his family, because even death were better than estrangement."

Davis looked at the empty desks and then at his fellow senators.

I see now around me some with whom I have served long. There have been points of collision; but whatever of offense there has been to me, I leave here. I carry with me no hostile remembrance. . . . I go hence unencumbered by the remembrance of any injury received, and having discharged the duty of making the only reparation in my power for any injury received.

The chamber was in absolute silence. Davis' eyes swept the rows of desks once more as he spoke his last words:

I am sure I feel no hostility to you, Senators from the North. I am sure there is not one of you, whatever sharp discussion there may have been between us, to whom I cannot now say, in the presence of God, I wish you well. . . . Mr. President and Senators, having made the announcement when the occasion seemed to me to require, it only remains for me to bid you a final farewell.

Davis sat down and buried his face in his hands. He had served his country well, as soldier, statesman, legislator, and now it had come to an end. Some said he wept; they looked from behind tears themselves as the emotional impact of his speech swept through the chamber. When he rose to leave, Davis' colleagues from Alabama and Florida joined him. Four states had now seceded from the Union; South Carolina was the first. Within less than five months, seven others had joined them: Georgia, Louisiana, Texas, Virginia, Arkansas, North Carolina, and Tennessee. And the man who had spoken so eloquently in the Senate that fateful day in January 1861, was chosen to head the Confederate States of America. The stage had been set.

The drama of America's Civil War had begun two centuries before, in 1619, when 20 black Africans were sold to colonists at Jamestown by a Dutch trader. Although these Africans were at first treated as indentured servants, it was not long before the slave traders saw the immense profit in dealing with human bodies in the Southern economy. In the ensuing decades, as the number of Africans shipped in to this country increased to the hundreds of thousands, slavery evolved into a legally sanctioned system, literally, in both the North and South. By 1800, various Northern states had passed laws abolishing slavery, such was the trend in thinking north of Virginia and Maryland, but in the South, where slaves had become inextricably woven into the economic and social ways of life, slavery remained absolutely legal, sanctioned, and supported in every possible way.

The chronology of slavery's development over the next 80 some years reads like an American history book:

July 1776: Thomas Jefferson's Declaration of Independence declares a "self-evident" truth "that all men are created equal."

1787: A constitutional convention in Philadelphia effectively sanctions slavery: (1) Fugitive slaves are to be returned to their owners; (2) Slave trade is to be permitted until 1808; and (3) For purposes of apportioning Congressional representatives on the basis of population, a slave is to be counted as 3/5 of a white person.

1787: Congress passes the Northwest Ordinance Act in which "there shall be neither slavery nor involuntary servitude" in the said territory – the future Ohio, Indiana, Illinois, Michigan, and Wisconsin.

December 1791: The Bill of Rights – first ten amendments to the Constitution – are put into effect saying nothing about the rights of black Americans.

October 1793: Eli Whitney invents the cotton gin, creating the need for more labor to produce cotton, thus the need for more slave labor in the South.

January 1808: The importation of new slaves into the United States is ended, but this does not end the buying and trading of slaves *within* the country, nor does it really end the smuggling of new slaves into the states.

January 1817: The American Colonization Society is founded to aid in settling freed slaves in Africa.

January-March 1820: Maine is admitted as a non-slave state; Missouri is admitted as a slave state; the combination bill is passed as the "Missouri Compromise," barring slavery in the rest of the Louisiana Purchase north of the 36° 30′ latitude.

May 1824: Congress passes a Protective Tariff Law satisfying the North but "discriminating against the South." The president of South Carolina College in Columbia asks: "Is it worth while to continue this Union of States, where the North demands to be our masters and we are required to be their tributaries?"

April-May 1828: Congress passes another Tariff Law creating high duties on raw materials for manufacturing. There are widespread protests throughout the South.

December 1828: South Carolina and Georgia legislatures adopt resolutions condemning the Tariff Act of 1828.

January 1831: William Lloyd Garrison, a radical abolitionist, begins publishing *The Liberator*, a newspaper dedicated to the abolition of slavery.

August 1831: Nat Turner, a radical slave preacher, leads an unsuccessful slave rebellion in Southampton County, Virginia.

July 1832: Congress passes another but more moderate Tariff Act; the South is still dissatisfied.

November 1832: South Carolina nullifies the Tariff Acts of 1828 and 1832 and prepares to secede if the federal government uses force.

January-March 1833: A last minute compromise bill passes the Congress cutting back tariffs; South Carolina suspends its nullification ordinance.

April 1836: Sam Houston defeats the Mexicans at the battle of San Jacinto, declares Texas independent, and demands annexation to the United States as a slave state.

June 1844: Antislavery forces convince a majority of the U.S. Senate that admitting Texas would lead to a confrontation between the North and South, thus the Texas Annexation Treaty is defeated.

May 1846: War with Mexico comes; Mexican forces attack a fort built by Gen. Zachary Taylor right on the border. Many of the soldiers and particularly officers who fight on both sides in the forthcoming Civil War would get their baptism of fire during this conflict.

February 1848: After nearly two years of fighting, the United States signs the Treaty of Guadalupe Hidalgo, ending the war with Mexico and receiving more than 500,000 square miles that include what will become California, Nevada, Utah, most of New Mexico and Arizona, and parts of Wyoming and Colorado. Texas is also conceded to the U.S. But the question of slavery in this new territory is open.

August 1848: President James Polk signs bill organizing the Oregon Territory without slavery.

November 1848: Gen. Zachary Taylor, hero of the Mexican War, and slaveholder, is elected president.

September-December 1849: California constitutional convention meets, prohibits slavery, and asks for admission to the union. Southern Congressmen balk and talk of secession.

July 1850: Taylor dies; Vice president Millard Fillmore assumes office.

September 1850: Congress adopts the Compromise of 1850 – admitting California as a free state; territories of Utah and New Mexico organized without restriction on slavery; Texas boundaries set without slavery restrictions; slave trade in the District of Columbia is abolished; new, stronger Fugitive Slave Act. President Millard Fillmore signs all the acts.

January 1854: Senator Stephen Douglas endorses a plan for "popular sovereignty," meaning that settlers in territories will be able to decide for themselves about slavery, effectively repealing the Missouri Compromise.

May 1854: The Congress passes Douglas' Kansas-Nebraska Act on the ground of popular sovereignty.

In May 1856, staunch abolitionist Charles Sumner of Massachusetts rose in the United States Senate and, with the Kansas situation as his subject, delivered a bitter attack on the South. Elderly Senator Andrew P. Butler of South Carolina was his target:

Before entering upon the argument, I must say something of a general character, particularly in response to what has fallen from Senators who raised themselves to eminence on this floor in championship of human wrongs. I mean the Senator from South Carolina [Butler] and the Senator from Illinois [Douglas], who, though unlike as Don Quixote and Sancho Panza, yet, like this couple, sally forth together in the same adventure. I regret much to miss the elder Senator from his seat, but the cause, against which he has run atilt, with such activity of animosity, demands that the opportunity of exposing him should not be lost; and it is for the cause that I speak. The Senator from South Carolina has read many books of chivalry and believes himself a chivalrous knight, with sentiments of honor and courage. Of course he has chosen a mistress to whom he has made his vows, and who, though ugly to others, is chaste in his sight – I mean the harlot, Slavery. For her, his tongue is always profuse in words. Let her be impeached in character, or any proposition made to shut her out from the extension of her wantonness, and no extravagance of manner or hardihood of assertion is then too great for this Senator. The frenzy of Don Quixote in behalf of his wench Dulcinea del Toboso, is all surpassed. The asserted rights of slavery, which shock equality of all kinds, are cloaked by a fantastic claim of equality. If the slave states cannot enjoy what, in mockery of the great fathers of the Republic, he misnames equality under the Constitution – in other words, the full power in the National Territories to compel fellow men to unpaid toil, to separate husband and wife, and to sell little children at the auction block – then, sir, the chivalric Senator will conduct the State of South Carolina out of the Union! Heroic knight! Exalted Senator! A second Moses come for a second exodus!

With regret I come again upon the Senator from South Carolina, who, omnipresent in this debate, overflowed with rage at the simple suggestion that Kansas had applied for admission as a state; and, with incoherent phrases, discharged the loose expectoration of his speech, now upon her representative and then upon her people. There was no extravagance of the ancient Parlimentary debate which he did not repeat; nor was there any possible deviation from truth which he did not make, with so much of passion, I am glad to add, as to save him from the suspicion of intentional aberration. But the Senator touches nothing which he does not disfigure – with error, sometimes of principle, sometimes of fact. He shows an incapacity of accuracy, whether in stating the Constitution or in stating the law, whether in the details of statistics or the diversions of scholarship. He cannot open his mouth, but out there flies a blunder. . . .

But it is against the people of Kansas that the sensibilities of the Senator are particularly aroused. Coming, as he announces, from a State – aye, sir, from South Carolina – he turns with lordly disgust from this newly-formed community, which he will not recognize even as "a body politic." Pray, sir, by what title does he indulge in this egotism? Has he read the history of "the State" which he represents? He cannot, surely, have forgotten its shameful imbecility from Slavery, confessed throughout the Revolution, followed by its more shameful assumptions for Slavery since. He cannot have forgotten its wretched persistence in the slave trade as the very apple of its eye, and the condition of its participation in the Union. He cannot have forgotten its Constitution, which is republican only in name, confirming power in the hands of the few and founding the qualifications of its legislators on "a settled freehold estate and ten negroes." And yet the Senator, to whom that "State" has in part committed the guardianship of its good name, instead of moving, with backward-treading steps, to cover its nakedness, rushed forward, in the very ecstacy of madness, to expose it, by provoking a comparison with Kansas. South Carolina is old: Kansas is young. . . . Were the whole history of South Carolina blotted out of existence, from its very beginning down to the day of its last election of the Senator to his present seat on this floor, civilization might lose – I do not say how little; but surely less than it has already gained by the example of Kansas, in its valiant struggle against oppression, and in the development of a new science of emigration. . . . Ah, sir, I tell the Senator that Kansas, welcomed as a Free State, will be a "ministering angel" to the Republic, when South Carolina, in the cloak of darkness which she hugs, lies howling."

On the day after Sumner gave his speech – he spoke on two separate days – he was sitting alone in the Senate chamber when Preston Brooks, a member of the House of

Representatives from South Carolina and a nephew of the man Sumner had insulted, walked in and without warning struck the Senator over the head with a cane until he collapsed. Brooks was hailed a hero in the South; tempers raged in the North.

On March 6, 1857, the Supreme Court handed down its decision in the case of *Dred Scott v. Sandford*; a majority declared that the Missouri Compromise of 1820 was unconstitutional. Scott was a black man whose owner took him from the slave state of Missouri into the free state of Illinois and territory north of the latitude 36° 30′ and then back to Missouri. Scott sued for his freedom, and the state Supreme Court overruled a lower court's decision in favor of Scott. Ultimately the United States Supreme Court ruled that Scott had never ceased to be a slave and so could not be considered a citizen with the right to sue in a federal court. The most far reaching impact of the decision came from the claim that the Congress had no right to deprive citizens of their property – such as slaves – anywhere within the United States.

As the country rapidly approached a major crisis over the slavery issue in 1858, Abraham Lincoln announced his candidacy for the United States Senate against Stephen Douglas with the following words: "A house divided against itself cannot stand. I believe this government cannot endure permanently half *slave* and half *free*. I do not expect the Union to be *dissolved* – I do not expect the house to fall – but I *do* expect it will cease to be divided." The campaign that followed echoed the critical issues the nation faced. Lincoln debated Douglas seven times; during the first debate at Ottawa, Illinois, August 21, Douglas stated his position:

We are told by Lincoln that he is utterly opposed to the Dred Scott decision and will not submit to it, for the reason that he says it deprives the negro of the rights and privileges of citizenship. That is the first and main reason which he assigns for his warfare on the Supreme Court of the United States and its decision. I ask you, are you in favor of conferring upon the negro the rights and privileges of citizenship? Do you desire to strike out of our state constitution that clause that keeps slaves and free negroes out of the state, and allow the free negroes to flow in and cover your prairies with black settlements?

Do you desire to turn this beautiful state into a free negro colony, in order that when Missouri abolishes slavery she can send one hundred thousand emancipated slaves into Illinois, to become citizens and voters, on an equality with yourselves? If you desire negro citizenship, if you desire to allow them to come into the state and settle with the white man, if you desire them to vote on an equality with yourselves, and to make them eligible to office, to serve on juries, and to adjudge your rights, then support Mr. Lincoln and the Black Republican party, who are in favor of the citizenship of the negro. For one, I am opposed to negro citizenship in any and every form. I believe this government was made on the white basis. I believe it was made by white men, for the benefit of white men and their prosperity for ever, and I am in favor of confining citizenship to white men, men of European birth and descent, instead of conferring it upon negroes, Indians and other inferior races. . . .

I do not hold that because the negro is our inferior that therefore he ought to be a slave. By no means can such a conclusion be drawn from what I have said. On the contrary, I hold that humanity and Christianity both require that the negro shall have and enjoy every right, every privilege, and every immunity consistent with the safety of the society in which he lives. On that point, I presume, there can be no diversity of opinion. You and I are bound to extend to our inferior and dependent every right, every privilege, every facility and immunity consistent with the public good. The question then arises, what rights and privileges are consistent with the public good? This is a question which each state and each territory must decide for itself – Illinois has decided it for herself. We have provided that the negro shall not be a slave, and we have also provided that he shall not be a citizen, but protect him in his civil rights, in his life, his person and his property, only depriving him of all political rights whatsoever, and refusing to put him on an equality with the white man. That policy of Illinois is satisfactory to the Democratic party and to me, and if it were to be the Republicans, there would then be no question upon the subject; but the Republicans say that he ought to be made a citizen, and when he becomes a citizen he becomes your equal, with all your rights and privileges. They assert the Dred Scott decision to be monstrous because it denies that the negro is or can be a citizen under the Constitution. Now, I hold that Illinois had a right to abolish and prohibit slavery as she did, and I hold that Kentucky has the same right to continue and protect slavery that Illinois had to abolish it. I hold that New York had as much right to abolish slavery as Virginia has to continue it, and that each and every state of this Union is a sovereign power, with the right to do as it pleases upon this question of slavery, and upon all its domestic institutions. Slavery is not the question which comes up in this controversy. There is a far more important one to you, and that is, what shall be done with the free negro? We have settled the slavery question as far as we are concerned; we have prohibited it in Illinois forever, and in doing so, I think we have done wisely, and there is no man in the state who would be more strenuous in his opposition to the introduction of slavery than I would; but when we settled it for ourselves, we exhausted all our power over that subject. We have done our whole duty and can do no more. We must leave each other and every other state to decide for itself the same question. . . .

Now, my friends, if we will only act conscientiously and rigidly upon this great principle of popular sovereignty which guarantees to each state and territory the right to do as it pleases on all things local and domestic instead of Congress interfering, we will continue at peace one with another.

Lincoln's position on the Negro differed little from that of Douglas. In the fourth debate at Charleston, September 18, Lincoln said:

Judge Douglas has said to you that he has not been able to get from me an answer to the question whether I am in favor of negro citizenship. So far as I know, the Judge never asked me the question before. He shall have no occasion to ever ask it again, for I tell him very frankly that I am not in favor of negro citizenship. This furnishes me an occasion for saying a few words upon the subject. I mentioned in a certain speech of mine which has been printed, that the Supreme Court had decided that a negro could not possibly be made a citizen, and without saying what was my ground of complaint in regard to that, or whether I had any ground of complaint, Judge Douglas has from that thing manufactured nearly every thing that he ever says about my disposition to produce an equality between the negroes and the white people. If any one will read my speech, he will find I mentioned that as one of the points decided in the course of the Supreme Court opinions, But I did not state what objection I had to it. But Judge Douglas tells the people what my objection was when I did not tell them myself. Now my opinion is that the different states have the power to make a negro a citizen under the Constitution of the United States if they choose. The Dred Scott decision decided that they have not that power. If the state of Illinois had that power I should be opposed to the exercise of it. That is all I have to say about it.

Three and a half weeks later, on October 13, when the two men debated in Quincy, Illinois, Lincoln said:

We have in this nation this element of domestic slavery. It is a matter of absolute certainty that it is a disturbing element. It is the opinion of all the great men who have expressed an opinion upon it, that it is a dangerous element. We keep up a controversy in regard to it. That controversy necessarily springs from difference of opinion, and if we can learn exactly – can reduce to the lowest elements – what that difference of opinion is, we perhaps shall be better prepared for discussing the different systems of policy that we would propose in regard to that disturbing element. I suggest that the difference of opinion, reduced to its lowest terms, is no other than the difference between the men who think slavery is wrong and those who do not think it is wrong. The Republican party think it wrong – we think it is a moral, a social and a political wrong. We think it is a wrong not confining itself merely to the persons or the states where it exists, but that it is a wrong in its tendency, to say the least, that extends itself to the existence of the whole nation. Because we think it wrong, we propose a course of policy that shall deal with it as a wrong. We deal with it as with any other wrong, in so far as we can prevent its growing any larger, and so deal with it that in the run of time there may be some promise of an end to it. We have a due regard to the actual presence of it amongst us and the difficulties of getting rid of it in any satisfactory way, and all the constitutional obligations thrown about it. I suppose that in reference both to its actual existence in the nation, and to our constitutional obligations, we have no right at all to disturb it in the states where it exists, and we profess that we have no more inclination to disturb it than we have the right to do it. We go further than that; we don't propose to disturb it where, in one instance, we think the Constitution would permit us. We think the Constitution would permit us to disturb it in the District of Columbia. Still we do not propose to do that, unless it should be in terms which I don't suppose the nation is very likely soon to agree to – the terms of making the emancipation gradual and compensating the unwilling owners. Where we suppose we have the constitutional right, we restrain ourselves in reference to the actual existence of the institution and the difficulties thrown about it. We also oppose it as an evil so far as it seeks to spread itself. We insist on the policy that shall restrict it to its present limit. We don't suppose that in doing this we violate anything due to the actual presence of the institution, or anything due to the constitutional guarantees thrown around it.

Lincoln lost the election. The Republican party received 125,430 votes to the Democrats 121,609, but in the Illinois legislature, where the Senatorial election really took place, the Douglas down-staters won 56 to 54, and the "little giant" was relected. The famous debates introduced Abraham Lincoln to the nation, however, and two years later he would use that recognition when he ran for the Presidency. Before he would come to Washington, however, another man would cross the American stage.

At Harper's Ferry, Virginia (now West Virginia), John Brown – considered by some a genius, by others a lunatic, by himself an abolitionist and a savior, and by all a radical – rented a farm near Harper's Ferry at the confluence of the Potomac and Shenandoah rivers, and from this base, on October 16, 1859, with a group of five blacks and 16 whites, including his sons, launched an attack against the federal arsenal.

Colonel Robert E. Lee led a force of United States Marines to capture Brown. Lee's report from Harpers Ferry:

On arriving here on the night of the 17th [October], I learned that a party of insurgents, about **11 p.m.** *on the 16th, had seized the watchmen stationed at the armory, arsenal, rifle factory and bridge across the Potomac, and taken possession of these points. They had dispatched six men, under one of their party, to arrest the principal citizens of the neighborhood and incite the negroes to join in the insurrection. The party took Colonel L. W. Washington from his bed about 1½ a.m. on the 17th, and brought him with four of his servants to this place. Mr. J. H. Allstadt and six of*

A broadside poster published by the Charleston (S.C.) *Mercury*, announcing the formal repudiation of the Union by the State of South Carolina in December 1860. (Library of Congress)

CHARLESTON

MERCURY

EXTRA:

Passed unanimously at 1.15 o'clock, P. M. December 20th, 1860.

AN ORDINANCE

To dissolve the Union between the State of South Carolina and other States united with her under the compact entitled "The Constitution of the United States of America."

We, the People of the State of South Carolina, in Convention assembled, do declare and ordain, and it is hereby declared and ordained,

That the Ordinance adopted by us in Convention, on the twenty-third day of May, in the year of our Lord one thousand seven hundred and eighty-eight, whereby the Constitution of the United States of America was ratified, and also, all Acts and parts of Acts of the General Assembly of this State, ratifying amendments of the said Constitution, are hereby repealed; and that the union now subsisting between South Carolina and other States, under the name of "The United States of America," is hereby dissolved.

THE

UNION

IS

DISSOLVED!

his servants were in the same manner seized about 3 a.m., and arms placed inthe hands of the negroes. As day advanced and the citizens of Harper's Ferry commenced their usual avocations, they were separately captured, to the number of forty, and confined in one room of the fire-engine house of the armory, which seems early to have been selected as a point of defense. . . .

I made preparations to attack the insurgents at daylight. But for the fear of sacrificing the lives of some of the gentlemen held by them as prisoners in a midnight assault, I should have ordered the attack at once. Their safety was the subject of painful consideration, and to prevent if possible jeopardizing their lives, I determined to summon the insurgents to surrender.

As soon after daylight as the arrangements were made, Lieutenant J. E. B. Stuart, 1st Cavalry, who had accompanied me from Washington as a staff officer, was dispatched under a flag with a written summons, as follows: "Colonel Lee, United States Army, commanding the troops sent by the President of the United States to suppress the insurrection at this place, demands the surrender of the persons in the armory buildings. If they will peaceably surrender themselves and restore the pillaged property, they shall be kept in safety to await the orders of the President. Colonel Lee represents to them, in all frankness, that it is impossible for them to escape; that the armory is surrounded on all sides by troops; and that if he is compelled to take them by force he can not answer for their safety."

Knowing the character of the insurgents, I did not expect the summons would be accepted. I had therefore . . . prepared a storming party of twelve Marines under their commander, Lieutenant Green, and had placed them close to the engine-house and secure from its fire. Three marines were furnished with sledgehammers to break in the doors, and the men were instructed how to distinguish our citizens from the insurgents, to attack with the bayonet, and not to injure the blacks detained in custody unless they resisted. Lieutenant Stuart was also directed not to receive from the insurgents any counter propositions. If they accepted the terms offered, they must immediately deliver their arms and release their prisoners. If they did not, he must, on leaving the engine-house, give me the signal. My object was, with a view of saving our citizens, to have as short an interval as possible between the summons and attack.

The summons, as I had anticipated, was rejected. At the concerted signal the storming party moved quickly to the door and commenced the attack. The fire-engines within the house had been placed by the besieged close to the doors. The doors were fastened by ropes, the spring of which prevented their being broken by the blows of the hammers. The men were therefore ordered to drop the hammers and to use as a battering-ram a heavy ladder, with which they dashed in a part of the door and gave admittance to the storming party. The fire of the insurgents up to this time had been harmless. At the threshold one Marine fell mortally wounded. The rest, led by Lieutenant Green and Major Russell, quickly ended the contest. The insurgents that resisted were bayoneted. Their leader, John Brown, was cut down by the sword of Lieutenant Green, and our citizens were protected by both officers and men. The whole was over in a few minutes. . . . The survivors of the expedition I have delivered into the hands of the marshal of the western district of Virginia and the sheriff of Jefferson County. They were escorted to Charlestown by a detachment of Marines. . . .

Brown was convicted of murder, conspiracy, and treason against the State of Virginia, and on the morning of December 2, 1859, was put to the gallows. David Hunter Strother wrote the following for *Harper's Weekly:*

He [Brown] was seated in a furniture waggon on his coffin with his arms tied down above the elbows, leaving the forearms free. The drivers with two others occupied the front seat while the jailer sat in the after part of the waggon. I stood with a group of half a dozen gentlemen near the steps of the scaffold when the prisoner was driven up. He wore the same seedy and dilapidated dress that he had at Harper's Ferry and during his trial, but his rough boots had given place to a pair of particoloured slippers and he wore a low crowned broad brimmed hat (the first time I had ever seen him with a hat). He had entirely recovered from his wounds and looked decidedly better & stronger than when I last saw him. As he neared the gibbet his face wore a grim & grisly smirk which, but for the solemnity of the occasion, might have suggested ideas of the ludicrous. He stepped from the waggon with surprising agility and walked hastily toward the scaffold pausing a moment as he passed our group to wave his pinioned arm & bid us good morning. . . . He mounted the steps of the scaffold with the same alacrity and there as if by previous arrangement, he immediately took off his hat and offered his neck for the halter which was as promptly adjusted my Mr. Avis the jailer. A white muslin cap or hood was then drawn over his face and the Sheriff not remembering that his eyes were covered requested him to advance to the platform. The prisoner replied in his usual tone, "You will have to guide me there."

The breeze disturbing the arrangement of the hood the Sheriff asked his assistant for a pin. Brown raised his hand and directed him to the collar of his coat where several old pins were quilted in. The Sheriff took the pin and completed his work.

He was accordingly led forward to the drop, the halter hooked to the beam, and the officers supposing that the execution was to follow immediately took leave of him. In doing so, the Sheriff enquired if he did not want a handkerchief to throw as a signal to cut the drop. Brown replied, "No, I don't care; I don't want you to keep me waiting unnecessarily."

These were his last words, spoken with that sharp nasal twang peculiar to him, but spoken quietly & civilly, without impatience or the slightest apparent emotion. In this position he stood for five minutes or more, while the troops that

composed the escort were wheeling into the positions assigned them. I stood within a few paces of him and watched narrowly during these trying moments to see if there was any indication of his giving way. I detected nothing of the sort. He had stiffened himself for the drop and waited motionless 'till it came.

During all these movements no sound was heard but the quick stern words of military command, & when these ceased a dead silence reigned. Col. Smith said to the Sheriff in a low voice, "We are ready." The civil officers descended from the scaffold. One who stood near me whispered earnestly, "He trembles, his knees are shaking." "You are mistaken," I replied, "It is the scaffold that shakes under the footsteps of the officers." The Sheriff struck the rope a sharp blow with a hatchet, the platform fell with a crash – a few convulsive struggles & a human soul had gone to judgement.

William Cullen Bryant wrote: "History, forgetting the errors of his judgement in the contemplation of his unfaltering courage, of his dignified and manly deportment in the face of death, and of the nobleness of his aims, will record his name among those of its martyrs and heroes."

Church bells rang throughout the North when Brown was hanged; his name was linked with sainthood. So was his name linked with the Republican Party, though most Republicans reprehended what Brown had done at Harpers Ferry.

John Brown had failed. He wanted to start a slave insurrection; he wanted to establish a "free state" in the southern Appalachians and from there spread a slave rebellion southward. But no slaves came to his call at Harpers Ferry. Instead the raid at Harpers Ferry spread alarm throughout the nation. Brown's eloquent defense during the trial convinced many Northerners that the abolition of slavery was a noble cause that required drastic, possibly violent action. His last prediction that "much bloodshed" would follow proved to be right. Although his violent tactics were not approved by many, Brown became something of a martyr, and his name was to be irrevocably linked with the beginnings of the Civil War.

On February 2 of the following year Senator Jefferson Davis introduced in the Senate a set of resolutions expressing the Southern extremist view: (1) no state had a right to interfere with the domestic institutions of other states; (2) any attack on slavery within the slave states was a violation of the Constitution; (3) it was the duty of the Senate to oppose all discriminatory measures against persons or property in the territories; (4) neither Congress nor a territorial legislature was in any way empowered to impair the right to hold slaves in the territories, and the federal government should extend all needful protection (i.e., a slave code) to slavery in the territories; (5) the territories might not decide on the question of slavery until admission to the Union; and (6) all the legislation interfering with the recovery of fugitive slaves was inimical to the constitutional compact.

The resolutions were adopted on May 24 and immediately set off an extensive debate on the constitutional and political questions of slavery. It did more; it widened the breach between the Northern and Southern wings of the Democratic party.

In October 1860, William Henry Gist, Governor of South Carolina, sent a letter by secret courier to several other governors of the cotton states. In it Gist sounded the death knell of the Union:

Executive Department

Unionville, S.C., Oct. 5, 1860

Dear Sir: The great probability, nay almost certainty, of Abraham Lincoln's election to the Presidency renders it important that there should be full and free interchange of opinion between the Executives of the Southern, and more especially of the Cotton, States, and while I unreservedly give you my views and the probable action of my State, I shall be much pleased to hear from you; that there may be concert of action, which is so essential to success. Although I will consider your communication confidential, and wish you so to consider mine so far as publishing in the newspapers is concerned, yet the information, of course, will be of no service to me unless I can submit it to reliable and leading men in consultation for the safety of our State and the South; and will only use it in this way. It is the desire of South Carolina that some other State should take the lead, or at least move simultaneously with her. She will unquestionably call a convention as soon as it is ascertained that a majority of the electors will support Lincoln. If a single State secedes, she will follow her. If no other State takes the lead, South Carolina will secede (in my opinion) alone, if she has any assurance that she will be soon followed by another or other States; otherwise it is doubtful. If you decide to call a convention upon the election of a majority of electors favorable to Lincoln, I desire to know the day you propose for the meeting, that we may call our convention to meet the same day, if possible. If your State will propose any other remedy, please inform me what it will probably be, and any other information you will be pleased to give me.

With great respect and consideration,

I am your, etc.

Wm. H. Gist

On February 27, Abraham Lincoln, Republican of Illinois, spoke before a distinguished audience at Cooper Union in New York City. He was virtually unknown in the East, but his words rang out across the land.

Lincoln refuted Douglas' "popular sovereignty" doctrine and examined Southern attitudes toward the North and the Republican party. Lincoln condemned Northern extremism and made an appeal for sectional understanding, but did not minimize the gravity of Southern disunionist threats and indicated that no compromise with principle on the slavery extension was possible.

The Democratic national nominating convention that met

in April in Charleston, South Carolina, formalized the devastating split in the party. The Southern Democrats, influenced by radicals, wanted a platform protecting slavery in the territories. The Douglas Democrats stood firm on the 1856 platform, which basically held to Supreme Court decisions and congressional nonintervention. Eight Southern states walked out and met on their own. The Douglas people adjourned to Baltimore and nominated Stephen A. Douglas, Illinois, for President, and Herschel V. Johnson, Georgia, for Vice-President. The Democrats that walked out at Charleston nominated their own: John C. Breckinridge, Kentucky, for President, Joseph Lane, Oregon, for Vice-President, on a platform that supported slavery in the territories, the admission of states into the Union on an equal footing with the rest, and the acquisition of Cuba. The Constitutional Union party nominated John Bell, Tennessee, and Edward Everett, Massachusetts.

The Republican National Convention met in Chicago on May 16, and nominated Abraham Lincoln for President on the third ballot. His running mate was Hannibal Hamlin. The platform was calculated to win the East as well as the West. It reaffirmed the principles of the Declaration of Independence, the Wilmot Proviso, and the right of each state to control its domestic institutions. It supported internal improvements, a railroad to the Pacific, a homestead law, and a liberal immigration policy. It condemned attempts to reopen the African slave trade and denied the authority of Congress or a territorial legislature to give legal status to slavery in the territories.

New York Tribune, Nov. 7, 1860, from Springfield, Illinois, by an anonymous correspondent:

About 9 o'clock last evening, when the returns began to tap in at the telegraph office, Mr. Lincoln, who had been notified beforehand, went over from the State House with a few friends, established himself comfortably near the instruments, and put himself into easy communication with the operators. The first fragments of intelligence were caught by the Superintendent as they ticked off at the tables, and, even before they could be recorded, were eagerly repeated and welcomed by all, for they came from the best counties in Illinois, and were full of good cheer. . . . Mr. Lincoln sat or reclined upon a sofa, while his companions mostly stood clustering around him. At length full sheets of returns were transcribed, and were taken apart, and were read aloud by Mr. Wilson – the listeners allowing no particle of good news to go by without their quick congratulations. . . .

There were four candidates for the office of sixteenth President of the United States. Mr. Lincoln was the Republican nominee; if he won, said the South, secession was certain. As the vote tallies began to trickle across the telegraph wires, it became apparent that the Republicans were the winners, but only by a small margin. Abraham Lincoln and his Vice Presidential candidate received 1,866,452 votes; Stephen Douglas, Illinois Democrat, and Herschel Johnson of Georgia, received 1,376,957; John C. Breckinridge, Southern Democrat of Kentucky, and Joseph Lane of Oregon, received 849,781; John Bell, Tennessee Constitutional Unionist, and Edward Everett of Massachusetts, received 588,879.

Mr. Lincoln received less than half of the popular vote; he was, in fact, a minority President. The electoral count was the most important, however, and here Lincoln had 180 votes, as opposed to Breckinridge's 72, Bell's 39, and Douglas' 12.

The *Tribune* article went on:

As the evening advanced, other excitements were afforded by batches of private messages which came rushing in, mostly addressed to Mr. Lincoln, but in some cases to Senator Trumbull, who had joined the company a little after the time of assembling. For these messages an active watch soon began to be kept, and the moment that one was lifted from the table, it would be clutched by some of the ardent news seekers, and sometimes, in the hurry and scramble, would be read by almost every person present before it reached him for whom it was intended. Whenever the information was of peculiarly gratifying character, as it often was, the documents would be taken out by some thoughful friend of the populace outside, and read aloud in the State House, or elsewhere, to large crowds which had met and were enjoying celebrations on the strength of their own convictions that the expected news would be sure to justify them. Occasionally, a line or two would come in with so much force of encouragement as to set the little group beside itself with elation. A confident declaration from Gen. S. Cameron, promising abundance of good things from Pennsylvania, produced a sensation that quite took away the composure of the telegraph manipulators; and some superb items which came just after Simeon Draper, setting aside all possibility of doubt as to New York, aroused demonstrations still more gleeful. There was just one person, however, who accepted everything with almost an immovable tranquility. Not that Mr. Lincoln undertook to conceal in the slightest degree the keen interest he felt in every new development; but, while he seemed to absorb it all with great satisfaction, the intelligence moved him to less energetic display of gratification than the others indulged in. He appeared, indeed, to be as fully alive to the smaller interests of some local districts, in which the fortunes of his friends were concerned, as to the wider and more universally important regions; and, in fact, his only departure from perfect quiet throughout the night was on hearing, just before he withdrew, of the complete success of the Republican ticket in his own precinct.

The States had spoken; the "Black Republican" had been elected. Two days later South Carolina Senators James Hammond and James Chestnut resigned their seats in the

Jefferson Davis, a native of Kentucky, former soldier, Cabinet officer, Congressman and U.S. Senator from Mississippi, was selected as the first and only President of the new Confederate States of America. (Library of Congress)

Congress and left for home. Almost immediately the South Carolina legislature called a convention of its people to discuss secession. All eyes turned toward Charleston.

There were three forts and several batteries in the Charleston harbor. Of the forts only Moultrie on the northeast side of the channel was garrisoned. Fort Sumter, in the middle of the channel, was unfinished. Captain (later General) Abner Doubleday described the scene:

To the South Carolinians, Fort Moultrie was almost a sacred spot, endeared by many precious historical associations, for the ancestors of most of the principal families had fought there in the Revolutionary War behind their hastily improvised ramparts of palmetto logs, and had gained a glorious victory over the British fleet in its first attempt to capture the city of Charleston.

The walls of the fort were twelve feet high. The constant action of the sea breeze had drifted an immense heap of sand against the front of the work, and another in the immediate vicinity. These sand hills dominated the parapet and made the fort untenable. Our force was pitifully small, even for a time of peace. It consisted of sixty-one enlisted men and seven officers, together with thirteen musicians; whereas the work called for a war garrison of 300 men.

Major Robert Anderson, the 55-year old career soldier in charge of the forts, was a Kentuckian by birth, a Virginian by ancestry, and pro-slavery in sentiment. At first it appeared he was an unlikely candidate for commander of the Charleston forts, but Anderson was loyal to the Union, and, it was said, "The Ten Commandments,' the Constitution of the United States, and the Army Regulations were his guides in life." Anderson was the ideal choice; he knew the people and he could be trusted to handle a potentially explosive situation with care. There was another reason. Doubleday described Anderson's arrival: "On November 21, 1860, our new commander, Major Robert Anderson, arrived and assumed command. He had a hereditary right to be there, for his father had distinguished himself in the Revolutionary War in defense of old Fort Moultrie and had been confined a long time as a prisoner in Charleston."

Several days after he arrived, Anderson reported to his commander in Washington:

In compliance with verbal instructions from the honorable Secretary of War, I have the honor to report that I have inspected the forts of the harbor. . . . At Fort Moultrie the Engineer, Captain Foster, is working very energetically on the outer defenses, which will, should nothing interfere to prevent, be finished and the guns mounted in two weeks. There are several sand hillocks within four hundred yards of our eastern wall, which offer admirable cover to approaching parties, and would be formidable points for sharpshooters. Two of them command our work. These I shall be compelled to level, at least sufficiently to render our position less insecure than it now is. When the outworks are completed, this fort, with its appropriate war garrison, will be capable of making a very handsome defense. . . . The garrison now in it is so weak as to invite an attack, which is openly and publicly threatened. We are about sixty, and have a line of rampart of 1,500 feet in length to defend. If beleaguered, as every man of the command must be either engaged or held on the alert, they will be exhausted and worn down in a few days and nights of such service as they would then have to undergo.

At Fort Sumter the guns of the lower tier of casemates will be mounted, the Engineer estimates, in about seventeen days. That fort is now ready for the comfortable accomodation of one company, and, indeed, for the temporary reception of its proper garrison. . . . This work is the key to the entrance of this harbor; its guns command this work [Moultrie], and could drive out its occupants. It [Sumter] should be garrisoned at once.

Castle Pinckney, a small casemated work, perfectly commanding the city of Charleston, is in excellent condition, with the exception of a few repairs, which will require the expenditure of about $500. . . . It is, in my opinion, essentially important that this castle should be immediately occupied by a garrison, say, of two officers and thirty men. The safety of our little garrison would be rendered more certain, and our fort would be more secure from an attack by such a holding of Castle Pinckney than it would be from guadrupling our force. The Charlestonians would not venture to attack this place when they knew that their city was at the mercy of the commander of Castle Pinckney. So important do I consider the holding of Castle Pinckney by the Government that I recommend, if the troops asked for cannot be sent at once, then I be authorized to place an Engineer detachment, consisting, say, of one officer, two masons, two carpenters, and twenty-six laborers, to make the repairs needed there. . . . If my force was not so small I would not hesitate to send a detachment at once to garrison that work. Fort Sumter and Castle Pinckney **must** *be garrisoned immediately if the Government determines to keep command of this harbor.*

I need not say how anxious I am – indeed, determined, so far as honor will permit – to avoid collision with the citizens of South Carolina. Nothing, however, will be better calculated to prevent bloodshed than our being found in such an attitude that it would be madness and folly to attack us. There is not so much of feverish excitement as there was last week, but that there is a settled determination to leave the Union, and to obtain possession of this work, is apparent to all. Castle Pinckney, being so near the city, and having no one in it but an ordnance sergeant, they regard as already in their possession. The clouds are threatening and the storm may break upon us at any moment. I do, then, most earnestly entreat that a re-enforcement be immediately sent to this garrison, and that at least two companies be sent at the same time to Fort Sumter and Castle Pinckney – half a company, under a judicious commander, sufficing, I think, for that latter work. I feel the full responsibility of making the above suggestions, because I firmly believe that as soon as the people of South Carolina learn that I have demanded re-enforcements, and that they have been ordered, they will occupy Castle Pinckney and attack this fort. It is therefore of vital importance that the troops embarked (say in war steamers) shall be designated for other duty. As we have no men who know anything about preparing ammunition, and our officers will be too much occupied to instruct them, I respectfully request that about half a dozen ordnance men, accustomed to the work of preparing fixed ammunition, be sent here, to be distributed at these forts. . . .

With these three works garrisoned as requested, and with a supply of ordnance stores, for which I shall send requisitions in a few days, I shall feel that, by the blessing of God, there may be a hope that no blood will be shed, and that South Carolina will not attempt to take these forts by force, but will resort to diplomacy to secure them. If we neglect, however, to strengthen ourselves, she will, unless these works are surrendered on their first demand, most assuredly immediatety attack us. I will thank the Department to give me special instructions, as my position here is rather a politico-military than a military one.

Anderson received a response from Washington early in December. It came from Adjutant General Samuel Cooper:

It is believed, from information thought to be reliable, that an attack will not be made on your command, and the Secretary [of War] has only to refer to his conversation with you, and to caution you that, should his convictions unhappily prove untrue, your actions must be such as to be free from the charge of initiating a collision. If attacked, you are, of course, expected to defend the trust committed to you to the best of your ability. The increase of the force under your command, however much to be desired, would, the Secretary thinks, judging from the recent excitement produced on account of an anticipated increase, as mentioned in your letter, but add to that excitement, and might lead to serious results.

Cooper's information was erroneous, of course, for secession was more than just talk. One man of obvious Southern sympathies, wrote that the "descendants of Marion, Sumter, & other revolutionary heroes" were worthy of their ancestors. "Every man able to bear a musket has joined a military company & is daily drilled. The merchants & their clerks, the lawyers, the mechanics & all classes of business men, after working all day for money to support their families, drill nearly half the night in order to be able to defend them."

Anderson knew the people of Charleston better than the politicians of Washington did; he repeated his warnings that the forts of Charleston were vulnerable to attack and that attack would come. Secretary of War Floyd sent a personal messenger; Major Don Carlos Buell, Assistant Adjutant General, came to Charleston. He counselled Anderson:

You are carefully to avoid every act which would needlessly tend to provoke aggression; and for that reason you are not, without evident and imminent necessity, to take up any position which could be construed into the assumption of a hostile attitude. But you are to hold possession of the forts in this harbor, and if attacked you are to defend yourself to the last extremity. The smallness of your force will not permit you, perhaps, to occupy more than one of the three forts, but an attack on or an attempt to take possession of any one of them will be regarded as an act of hostility, and you may then put your command into either of them which you may deem most proper to increase its power of resistance. You are also authorised to take similar steps whenever you have tangible evidence of a design to proceed to a hostile act.

Anderson occupied Fort Sumter the evening after Christmas Day, 1860. Doubleday narrated the journey across the harbor:

Anderson had been urged by several of us to remove his command to Fort Sumter, but he had invariably replied that he was especially assigned to Fort Moultrie and had no right to vacate it without orders.

Nevertheless, he had fully determined to make the change, and was merely awaiting a favorable opportunity.

In making his arrangements to cross over, Anderson acted with consummate prudence and ability. He only communicated his design to the staff officers whose co-operation was indispensable, and he waited until the moment of execution before he informed the others of his intention. On the last evening of our stay (December 26) I left my room to ask Major Anderson to take tea with us. He said quietly, "I have determined to evacuate this post immediately. I can allow you twenty minutes to form your company."

I dashed over to my quarters, told my wife to get ready immediately, and advised her to take refuge with some family outside. Then we took a sad and hasty leave of each other.

We silently made our way to a spot where the boats were hidden. There was not a human being in sight as we marched to the rendezvous. We found several boats intended for my company, and then we pushed rapidly to the fort. Noticing that one of the guard boats was approaching, we made a wide circuit to avoid it. As among my men there were a number of unskillful oarsmen, we made but slow progress, and it soon became evident that we would be overtaken in midchannel. The twilight had deepened, however, so that there was a fair chance for us to escape. While the steamer was yet afar off, I took my cap and threw open my coat to conceal the buttons. I also made the man take off their coats and use them to cover up their muskets. I hoped in this way we might pass for a party of laborers returning to the fort. The paddle wheels stopped within about a hundred yards of us; and to our great relief, after a slight scrutiny, the steamer kept on its way. Our men redoubled their efforts, and we soon arrived at our destination.

As we ascended the steps of the wharf, crowds of workmen rushed out to meet us, most of them wearing secession emblems. The majority called out angrily, "What are these soldiers doing here?" I at once charged my bayonets, drove the tumultuous mass inside the fort and the disloyal workmen were shipped off to the mainland.

Major Anderson thought it best to give some solemnity to the occasion. The band played "The Star Spangled Banner," the troops presented arms, and our chaplain offered up a fervent supplication, invoking the blessing of Heaven upon our small command and the cause we represent.

"Anderson has united the Cotton States," was the table talk in Charleston, Mary Boykin Chestnut wrote in her diary. "Those who want a row are in high glee. Those who dread it are glum and thoughtful. The talk is: 'Fort Sumter must be taken, and it is one of the strongest forts.'"

Dr. Samuel Wylie Crawford, the New England surgeon assigned to Anderson's command, presented a rather bleak picture of Sumter:

When occupied by Major Anderson's command on the night of December 26, 1860, Fort Sumter was in no condition for defense. There were but three 24-pounders mounted on the uppermost tier. The second tier was wholly incomplete and without embrasures [gun openings]. There was but one gun, and that for experimental purposes, yet mounted on that tier. On the lower tier, eleven 32–pounders had been mounted. The barracks for the men were unfinished, but the officers' quarters were completed and were occupied by the garrison. A large number of wooden structures crowded the parade [ground], while all over it lay sand and rough masonry, besides sixty guns with their carriages and 5,600 shot and shell. The main entrance was closed by double gates secured by bars, they were insecure and weak.

On the thirteenth of December, all communication with the city was cut off, and no supplies of any description allowed to go to the fort, the governor having declined to change or modify his order. Storm and rain now set in. For several days the fort was enveloped in fog, and under its cover and concealment work was pushed rapidly on. Major Anderson considered that in a week he would be fully prepared for any attack that might be made.

Meantime, increased activity was visible in the harbor. Small steamers with troops and laborers were passing to and fro. Men and materials were landed on Morris Island, and preparations made for remounting the guns at Fort Moultrieand strengthening its parapet toward Fort Sumter. The harbor lights on Sullivan's and Morris Islands were put out on the night of the twentieth of December, leaving the one upon Sumter and that upon the lightship in the offing the only lights in the harbor.

By taking possession of Forts Moltrie and Castle Pinckney, which were Federal property but which the Washington government had failed to garrison, South Carolina had now committed an act which could have been construed into one of war, had [President] Buchanan so decided. He still entertained the hope, however, that open hostilities could somehow be avoided.

Nevertheless, he now tried to do what could have been done without any difficulties earlier – strengthen Major Anderson's force and provision it. On December 30, 1860, General Scott requested and obtained permission to dispatch 200 to 300 men to Fort Sumter with arms, ammunition and supplies.

And so, 1860 came to an end.

CHAPTER 2
1861

As January 1861 dawned over the land, the North numbered 23 states and seven territories with a population of 22,000,000 people. The South consisted of 11 states with a population of 9,000,000, some 3,500,000 of which were black slaves. The North had 4,000,000 men eligible for military service; the South had 1,140,000 eligible males between the ages of 15 and 40. The economy of both sections of the country was likewise divided – the North was varied and industrial; the South had a one-crop agrarian economy, cotton, cultivated and harvested primarily by slave labor. The North raised many more food crops than the South; its manufacturing capacity was five times and its available work force ten times more powerful. The North had 70 percent of the nation's railroad mileage and 96 percent of its railway equipment, and 81 percent of the nation's bank deposits were in Northern banks.

What all of this meant to the most casual observer was that the North had the virtually unlimited capacity to wage war, while the South would be hard pressed even to get started, much less catch up. Nearly all the country's weapons factories were in the North. The South would immediately begin purchasing war materials from foreign nations, but the North's ability to blockade Southern ports would simply cripple both the war effort and the economy. The game of chess, so often seen on the battlefield, began before the first shots were fired.

Of course, not all circumstances gave the North the advantage. To those who viewed military leadership as the most crucial element in the build-up of tensions in 1860-61, the Gods clearly favored the South. An inordinate number of West Point graduates came from the Southern states, and all but a handful immediately defected, including the man many would regard as the ultimate leader, Robert E. Lee. Too, a huge number of the United States Navy – 200 officers – came from the South, and returned to form a Confederate navy. And when it came to volunteers, Southern men responded with a spirit that surpassed that of the colonists in 1776. As the war moved on and the productivity of the South and the Confederate government fell apart, perhaps the one thread that kept the armies on the battlefield was that remarkable spirit of the Confederate soldier.

This was how things looked in January 1861, as the inevitable conflict rapidly approached.

Dr. Samuel Crawford described the arrival of *Star of the West* to supply Fort Sumter:

The general in chief was satisfied that the movement could be made with the ***Star of the West*** *without exciting suspicion. The ship was to clear for New Orleans without formal notice and as if for her regular trip. The provisions necessary were to be bought on the ship's account, so that no public agency should be used. The arms and ammunition were to be put on board the next day. Major Anderson was also informed by letter of the character and composition of the expedition on the day it sailed, and special instructions were communicated to him that, if fire be opened upon any vessel bringing reinforcements or supplies within reach of his guns, "they may be employed to silence such fire"; and he was also to act in like manner in case his fort was fired upon.*

On the morning of January 5, 1861, the ***Star of the West*** *sailed with 250 troops on board and pursued her course toward Charleston. The weather was fine, and a skilled pilot accompanied the ship. At 1:30 on the morning of the ninth she arrived off the Charleston bar. She groped in the dark until near dawn, when the solitary light at Sumter became visible. Checking her course, she steamed slowly along under careful soundings, until she arrived off the mainship channel, where she hove to, to await the dawn.*

When opposite to a group of houses near the shore, a red palmetto flag was seen, and immediately and without warning a gun battery opened upon the ship. The battery was concealed amid the sand hills, and its existence had been unsuspected. Its first shot had been fired across the bow of the ship which, nevertheless, continued on its course, when a rapid and continuous fire was opened by the battery. The firing was wild and unskillful, but one spent shot struck the ship aft near the rudder, while another struck just aft the port channels, about two feet above the water line, passing through one of the guards. As soon as the battery had opened fire, a large garrison flag was run up at the fore of the vessel, lowered and again run up as a signal to Major Anderson.

The ***Star of the West*** *had now almost passed the battery and continued her course against a strong ebb tide, up the main ship channel. She would soon be within range of the guns of Fort Moultrie, then distant about one and a half miles. Seeing her approach, the commanding officer of that work opened at long range with four columbiads and two 32-pounders, the shots falling wildly and in all directions. Fort Sumter was silent. It was then determined, both by the officer in command of the troops and the captain of the ship, that it was impossible to reach Fort Sumter. Had she continued upon her course, she must have exposed her broadside to the direct* *and close fire of the entire battery of Fort Moultrie, whose fire would have been, in all probability, fatal.*

Lessening her speed, she turned around, lowered her flag and, putting on all steam, headed down the channel for the bar. The strong tide carried the ship swiftly out of range.

Major Anderson thought that General Scott would not send troops except by a vessel of war, and no arrangements had been made in anticipation of such a contingency as that with which he was suddenly confronted. He was excited and uncertain about what to do. The steamer had hoisted and lowered the national flag, when the writer reported to Major Anderson that she was naming signals, but our halyards had become twisted and the flag could not be used. A lieutenant called the attention of Major Anderson to Fort Moultrie and suggested firing on the battery. Major Anderson seemed for a moment to acquiesce. Then, seeing the **Star of the West** *turn, he said, "Hold on, do not fire."*

The flag of the country had been fired on under our very guns, and no helping hand had been extended.

On February 4, two significant conventions were called – a peace convention in Washington at the urging of Virginia, and a convention of seceding states in Montgomery, Alabama. The first failed to find any compromise to saving the Union; the second drafted a constitution, and on February 9 elected Jefferson Davis as provisional President of the Confederacy, Alexander Stephens as provisional Vice-President. Two days later, Abraham Lincoln left Springfield, Illinois for Washington. That night, from the balcony of his hotel, the President-elect of the United States said:

The words "coercion" and "invasion" are in great use about these days. Suppose we were simply to try, if we can, and ascertain what is the meaning of these words. Let us get, if we can, the exact definition of these words – not from dictionaries, but from the men who constantly repeat them – what things they mean to express by the words. What, then, is "coercion"? What is "invasion"? Would the marching of an army into South Carolina, for instance, without the consent of her people, and in hostility against them, be coercion or invasion? I very frankly say, I think it would be invasion, and it would be coercion too, if the people of that country were forced to submit. But if the government, for instance, but simply insists upon holding its own forts, retaking those forts which belong to it, or even the withdrawal of the mails from those portions of the country where the mails themselves are habitually violated; would any or all of these things be coercion? Do the lovers of the Union contend that they will resist coercion or invading a State? If they do, then it occurs to me that the means for the preservation of the Union they do greatly love, in their own estimation, is of a very thin and airy character. If sick, they would consider the little pills of the homeopathist as already too large for them to swallow. In their view the Union, as a family relation, would not be anything like a regular marriage at all, but only as a sort of free-love arrangement – to be maintained on what that sect calls passionate attraction. But, my friends, enough of this.

What is the particular sacredness of a State? I speak not of that position which is given to a State in and by the Constitution of the United States, for that all of us agree to – we abide by; but that position assumed, that a state can carry with it out of the Union that which it holds in sacredness by virtue of its connection with the Union. I am speaking of that assumed right of a State, as a primary principle, that the Constitution should rule all that is less than itself, and ruin all that is bigger than itself. But, I ask, wherein does consist that right? If a State, in one instance, and a county in another, should be equal in extent of territory, and equal in the number of people, wherein is the right? By what principle of original right is it that one-fiftieth or one-ninetieth of a great nation, by calling themselves a State, have the right to break up and ruin that nation as a matter of original principle? . . . I am deciding nothing, but simply giving something for you to reflect upon; and, with having said this much . . . I thank you again for this magnificent welcome, and bid you an affectionate farewell.

Jefferson Davis was little qualified to lead the beleaguered South in any kind of war. Though he had graduated from West Point (in the same class with Robert E. Lee) and had seen some action in the Black Hawk Indian War of 1832, he had never become an experienced soldier. He had resigned from the army and had become a planter in Mississippi, where, as was typical of his social status, he identified with the Southern plantation mentality – slavery, pride in home state, and a feeling that the South must be allowed to choose its own political future.

On February 9, 1861, Davis was elected President of the Confederacy. Nine days later he was inaugurated in Montgomery, Alabama. The Charleston *Mercury* reported his arrival:

President Davis' trip from Jackson, Mississippi, to Montgomery, was one continuous ovation. He made no less than twenty-five speeches upon the route, returning thanks for complimentary greetings from crowds of ladies and gentlemen. There were military demonstrations, salutes of cannon, &c., at the various depots.

The Committee of Reception, appointed by the Southern Congress, and also the Committee appointed by the Montgomery authorities, met President Davis about 80 miles from the city and formally welcomed him. Two fine companies from Columbus, Ga., formed an escort to Opelika. The **cortege** *reached Montgomery Friday night at ten o'clock. Salvos of artillery greeted his approach, and a very large crowd assembled at the depot, hailing his appearance with tremendous cheering. President Davis, returning thanks, said that he was proud to receive the congratulations and hospitality of the people of Alabama. He briefly reviewed the present position of the South. The time for compromise, he said, had passed, and our only hope was in a determined maintenance of our position, and to make all who oppose us smell Southern powder and feel Southern steel. If coercion should be persisted in, he had no doubt as to*

Ft. Sumter in Charleston harbor received the first blows of the war. South Carolina militia opened fire on the lightly provisioned and garrisoned federal fort on April 12, 1861. Four years of conflict lay ahead. (Library of Congress)

the result. We would maintain our right to self–government at all hazards. We ask nothing, want nothing, and will have no complications. If other States should desire to join our Confederation, they can freely come on our terms. Our separation from the old Union is complete. NO COMPROMISE; NO RECONSTRUCTION CAN BE NOW ENTERTAINED.

Two days later, Jefferson Davis stood on the portico of Alabama's state capitol and to the cheers of thousands of onlookers, took his oath of office as President of the Confederate States of America. He spoke to a wild, cheering throng:

The right solemnly claimed at the birth of the United States, and which has been solemnly affirmed and reaffirmed in the Bill of Rights of the States subsequently admitted into the Union of 1789, undeniably recognizes in the people the power to resume the authority delegated for the purposes of government. Thus the sovereign States here represented have proceeded to form this Confederacy; and it is by abuse of language that their act has been denominated as revolution. They formed a new alliance, but within each State its government has remained; so that the rights of person and property have not been disturbed. The agent through which they communicated with foreign nations is changed, but this does not necessarily interrupt their international relations. Sustained by the consciousness that the transition from the former Union to the present Confederacy has not proceeded from a disregard on our part of just obligations, or any failure to perform every constitutional duty, moved by no interest or passion to invade the rights of others, anxious to cultivate peace and commerce with all nations, if we may not hope to avoid war, we may at least expect that posterity will acquit us of having needlessly engaged in it. Doubly justified by the absence of wrong on our part and by wanton aggression on the part of others, there can be no cause to doubt that the courage and patriotism of the people of the

Confederate States will be found equal to any measure of defense which their honor and security may require. . . .

We have entered upon the career of independence, and it must be inflexibly pursued. Through many years of controversy with our late associates of the Northern States, we have vainly endeavored to secure tranquillity and obtain respect for the rights to which we were entitled. As a necessity, not a choice, we have resorted to the remedy of separation, and henceforth our energies must be directed to the conduct of our own affairs and the perpetuity of the Confederacy which we have formed. If a just perception of mutual interest shall permit us peaceably to pursue our separate political career, my most earnest desire will have been fulfilled. But if this be denied to us and the integrity of our territory and jurisdiction be assailed, it will but remain for us with firm resolve to appeal to arms and invoke the blessing of Providence on a just cause. . . .

As a consequence of our new condition and relations and with a view to meet anticipated wants, it will be necessary to provide for the speedy and efficient organization of branches of the Executive department having special charge of foreign intercourse, finance, military affairs, and the postal service. For purposes of defense, the Confederate States may, under ordinary circumstances, rely mainly upon the militia; but it is deemed advisable, in the present condition of affairs, that there should be a well-instructed and disciplined army, more numerous than would usually be required on a peace establishment. I also suggest that, for the protection of our harbors and commerce on the high seas, a navy adapted to those objects will be required.

It is joyous in the midst of perilous times to look around upon a people united in heart, where one purpose of high resolve animates and actuates the whole; where the sacrifices to be made are not weighed in the balance against honor and right and equality. Obstacles may retard, but they cannot long prevent, the progress of a movement sanctified by its justice and sustained by a virtuous people. Reverently let us invoke the God of our fathers to guide and protect us in our efforts to perpetuate the principles which by His blessing they were able to vindicate, establish, and transmit to their posterity. With the continuance of His favor ever gratefully acknowledged, we may hopefully look forward to success, to peace, and to prosperity.

Mr. Lincoln's arrival in Washington was far from uneventful. A reporter for the *New York Times* filed this dispatch from Harrisburg, Pennsylvania, February 23:

Abraham Lincoln, the President-elect of the United States, is safe in the capital of the nation. By the admirable arrangement of General Scott, the country has been spared the lasting disgrace which would have been fastened indelibly upon it had Mr. Lincoln been murdered upon his journey thither, as he would have been had he followed the programme as announced in the papers and gone by the Northern Central Railroad to Baltimore.

On Thursday night after he had retired, Mr. Lincoln was aroused and informed that a stranger desired to see him on a matter of life and death. He declined to admit him unless he gave his name, which he at once did, and such prestige did the name carry that while Mr. Lincoln was yet disrobed he granted an interview to the caller.

A prolonged conversation elicited the fact that an organized body of men had determined that Mr. Lincoln should not be inaugurated; and that he should never leave the city of Baltimore alive, if, indeed, he ever entered it.

The list of names of the conspirators presented a most astonishing array of persons high in Southern confidence, and some whose fame is not confined to this country alone.

Statesmen laid the plan, bankers indorsed it, and adventurers were to carry it into effect. As they understood, Mr. Lincoln was to leave Harrisburg at nine o'clock this morning by special train, the idea was, if possible, to throw the cars from the road at some point where they would rush down a steep embankment and destroy in a moment the lives of all on board. In case of failure of this project, their plan was to surround the carriage on the way from depot to depot in Baltimore, and to assassinate him with dagger or pistol shot.

So authentic was the source from which the information was obtained that Mr. Lincoln, after counselling with his friends, was compelled to make arrangements which would enable him to subvert the plans of his enemies.

Greatly to the annoyance of the thousands who desired to call on him last night, he declined giving a reception. The final council was held at eight o'clock.

Mr. Lincoln did not want to yield, and Colonel Sumner actually cried with indignation; but Mrs. Lincoln, seconded by Mr. Judd and Mr. Lincoln's original informant, insisted upon it, and ***at nine o'clock Mr. Lincoln left on a special train****. He wore a Scotch plaid cap and a very long military cloak, so that he was entirely unrecognizable. Accompanied by Superintendent Lewis and one friend, he started, while all the town, with the exception of Mrs. Lincoln, Colonel Sumner, Mr. Judd, and two reporters who were sworn to secrecy, supposed him to be asleep.*

The telegraph wires were put beyond reach of anyone who might desire to use them.

At one o'clock the fact was whispered from one to another, and it soon became the theme of most excited conversation. Many thought it a very injudicious move, while others regarded it as a stroke of great merit.

The special train leaves with the original party, including the ***Times*** *correspondence, at nine o'clock.*

Several weeks later, on March 4, Abraham Lincoln stood on the east portico of the Capitol in Washington and spoke to the people of the entire nation. His words were more precisely directed to the South:

That there are persons in one section or another who seek to destroy the Union at all events, and are glad of any pretext to do it, I will neither affirm nor deny; but if there be such, I need address no word to them. To those, however, who really love the Union, may I not speak?

Before entering upon so grave a matter as the destruction of our national fabric, with all its benefits, its memories, and its hopes, would it not be wise to ascertain precisely why we do it? Will you hazard so desperate a step, while there is any possibility that any portion of the ills you fly from, have no real existence? Will you, while the certain ills you fly to, are greater than all the real ones you fly from? Will you risk the commission of so fearful a mistake?

All profess to be content in the Union, if all constitutional rights can be maintained. Is it true, then, that any right, plainly written in the Constitution, has been denied? I think not. Happily the human mind is so constituted that no party can reach to the audacity of doing this. . . . All the vital rights of minorities, and of individuals, are so plainly assured to them, by affirmations and negations, guarantees and prohibitions in the Constitution, that controversies never arise concerning them. But no organic law can ever be framed with a provision specifically applicable to every question which may occur in practical administration. No foresight can anticipate, nor any document of reasonable length contain express provisions for all possible questions. Shall fugitives from labor be surrendered by national or by state authority? The Constitution does not expressly say. **May** *Congress prohibit slavery in the territories? The Constitution does not expressly say.* **Must** *Congress protect slavery in the territories? The Constitution does not expressly say.*

From questions of this class spring all our constitutional controversies, and we divide upon them into majorities and minorities. If the minority will not acquiesce, the majority must, or the government must cease. There is no other alternative; for continuing the government is acquiescence on one side or the other. If the minority, is such case, will secede rather than acquiesce, they make a precedent which, in turn, will divide and ruin them, whenever a majority refuses to be controlled by such minority. For instance, why may not any portion of a new confederacy, a year or two hence, arbitrarily secede again, precisely as portions of the present Union now claim to secede from it? All who cherish disunion sentiments are now being educated to the exact temper of doing this. Is there such perfect identity of interests among the States to compose a new Union, as to produce harmony only, and prevent renewed secession?

Plainly, the central idea of secession is the essence of anarchy. A majority, held in restraint by constitutional checks and limitations, and always changing easily, with deliberate changes of popular opinions and sentiments, is the true sovereign of a free people. Whoever rejects it does, of necessity, fly to anarchy or to despotism. Unanimity is impossible; the rule of a minority, as a permanent arrangement, is wholly inadmissible; so that, rejecting the majority principle, anarchy, or despotism in some form, is all that is left. . . .

Physically speaking, we cannot separate. We cannot remove our respective sections from each other, nor build an impassable wall between them. A husband and wife may be divorced, and go out of the presence, and beyond the reach of each other; but the different parts of our country cannot do this. They cannot but remain face to face; and intercourse, either amicable or hostile, must continue between them. Is it possible then to make that intercourse more advantageous, or more satisfactory, **after** *separation than* **before**? *Can aliens make treaties easier than friends can make laws? Can treaties be more faithfully enforced between aliens, than laws can among friends? Suppose you go to war, you cannot fight always; and when, after much loss on both sides, and no gain on either, you cease fighting, the identical old questions, as to terms of intercourse, are again upon you.*

My countrymen, one and all, think calmly and **well**, *upon this whole subject. Nothing valuable can be lost by taking time. If there be an object to* **hurry** *any of you, in hot haste, to a step which you would never take* **deliberately**, *that object will be frustrated by taking time; but no good object can be frustrated by it. Such of you as are now dissatisfied, will have the old Constitution unimpaired, and, on the sensitive point, the laws of your own framing under it; while the new administration will have no immediate power, if it would, to change either. If it were admitted that you who are dissatisfied, hold the right side in the dispute, there still is no single good reason for precipitate action. Intelligence, patriotism, Christianity, and a firm reliance on Him who has never yet forsaken this favored land, are still competent to adjust, in the best way, all our present difficulty.*

In **your** *hands, my dissatisfied fellow countrymen, and not in* **mine**, *is the momentous issue of civil war. The government will not assail* **you**. *You can have no conflict without being yourselves the aggressors.* **You** *have no oath registered in Heaven to destroy the government, while* **I** *shall have the most solemn one to "preserve, protect and defend it."*

I am loath to close. We are not enemies, but friends. We must not be enemies. Though passion may have strained, it must not break our bonds of affection. The mystic chords of memory, stretching from every battle-field, and patriot grave, to every living heart and hearthstone, all over this broad land, will yet swell the chorus of the Union, when again touched, as surely they will be, by the better angels of our nature.

Lincoln went to his office in the White House for the first time on March 5, where he found, according to his secretaries, John Nicolay and John Hay, "a disheartening, almost disastrous, beginning for the Administration." The President had only just appointed his cabinet – they had not even taken office – when he was informed by General Winfield Scott that Fort Sumter would have to be either reinforced immediately or abandoned.

"Evacuation seems almost inevitable," Scott said, "and in this view our distinguished Chief Engineer (Brigadier Totten) concurs – if indeed the worn-out garrison be not assaulted and carried in the present week."

Fort Sumter was now the target of fire from the very land it was designed to protect from an enemy entering the harbor. It could be hit from any of the surrounding batteries, and, in the best estimates from the military, probably would not survive. Advice came from both the navy, who felt the batteries could be run and the fort provisioned, and the army, who believed Sumter was doomed without an army of twenty thousand and a bloody battle. Lincoln sought word from all his cabinet, but there was division among them. Attorney General Edward Bates:

The President has required my opinion, in writing, upon the following question: "Assuming it to be possible now to provision Fort Sumter, under all the circumstances, is to wise to attempt it?"

This is not a question of lawful right nor physical risk, but of prudence and patriotism. The right in my mind is unquestionable, and I have no doubt at all that the government has the power and means not only to provision the fort, but also, if the exigency required, to man it so as to make it impregnable.

The wisdom of the act must be tested by the value of the object to be gained and by the hazard to be encountered in the enterprise. The object to be gained by the supply of provisions is not to strengthen the fortress, so as to command the harbor and enforce the laws, but only to prolong the labors and privations of the brave little garrison that has so long held it. The possession of the fort as we now hold it does not enable us to collect the revenue or enforce the laws of commerce and navigation. It may indeed involve a point of honor or a point of pride, but I do not see any great national interest involved in the bare fact of holding the fort, as we now hold it – and to hold it at all we must supply it with provisions. It seems to me that we may in humanity and patriotism safely waive the point of pride.

I am unwilling at this moment to do any act which may have the semblance of beginning a civil war, the terrible consequences of which would, I think, find no parallel in modern times.

For these reasons I am willing to evacuate Fort Sumter.

Mrs. Chestnut's diary:

March 31, 1861*. General Beauregard called. He is in command here and the hero of the hour. That is, he is believed to be capable of great things. A hero worshiper was struck dumb because I said: "So far, he has only been a captain of artillery or engineers or something." I did not see him. Mrs. Wigfall did and reproached my laziness in not coming out.*

Last Sunday at church beheld one of the peculiar local sights, old Negro mammies going up to communion in their white turbans and kneeling devoutly around the rail.

The morning papers say Mr. Chestnut made the best shot on the island at target practice. No war yet, thank God. Likewise they tell me Mr. Chestnut has made a capital speech in the convention.

Not one word of what is going on now. "Out of the fullness of the heart the mouth speakest," says the Psalmist. Not so here. Our hearts are in doleful dumps, but we are as gay, as madly jolly, as sailors who break into the strong-room when the ship is going down. At first in our great agony we were out alone. We longed for some of our big brothers to come out and help us. Well, they are out, too, and now it is Fort Sumter and that ill-advised Anderson. There stands Fort Sumter, ***en evidence****, and thereby hangs peace or war.*

It was at the cabinet meeting of March 29 that Lincoln decided to send a relief expedition to land provisions; the ships would land neither men or munitions unless the fort was attacked while they were there. On April 6, the White House sent a message to the new governor of South Carolina, Francis W. Pickens, and informed him of the impending action. Three days later the expedition sailed from New York.

Charleston had been waiting for the fuse to be lit, so taut were the military nerves of the organized Confederate forces. When the Lincoln telegram was received in Charleston, it set the city and the Confederate government awhirl. When Robert Toombs, the Confederate Secretary of State was shown the message, he said, "The firing upon that fort will inaugurate a civil war greater than any the world has yet seen . . ."

The Secretary of War, L.P. Walker, sent a message to Brigadier General Pierre Gustave Toutant Beauregard, recently resigned from the U.S. Army, in command at Charleston. "If you have no doubt of the authorized character of the agent who communicated to you the intention of the Washington government to supply Fort Sumter by force," it read, "you will at once demand its evacuation and, if this is refused, proceed in such manner as you may determine to reduce it."

Dr. Crawford described the Confederate action:

Shortly after noon on the eleventh of April a boat flying a white flag pushed off from a wharf in Charleston and made its way down the harbor toward Fort Sumter. In her stern sat three men. They were: Colonel James Chestnut, recently United States Senator from South Carolina; Captain Stephens D. Lee, a graduate of West Point, who had resigned his commission in the United States Army; and Lieutenant Colonel A.R. Chisolm, an aide-de-camp and representative of the governor of the state. At half-past three the boat arrived at Fort Sumter, and its occupants were at once conducted to the guardroom, where they were met by Major Anderson in person. They bore a communication from the Confederate general to Major Anderson demanding the evacuation of the work.

I am ordered by the Government of the Confederate States [the message read] to demand the evacuation of Fort Sumter. My aides, Colonel Chestnut and Captain Lee, are authorized to make such a demand of you. All proper facilities will be afforded for the removal of yourself and command, together with company arms and property, and all private property, to any post in the United States which you may select. The flag which you have upheld so long and with so much fortitude, under the most trying circumstances, may be saluted by you on taking it down.

Anderson at once summoned his officers [Crawford cont-

Ft. Sumter as seen from the South Carolina shore batteries. The garrison, under Maj. Robert Anderson, surrendered within a few hours. (Library of Congress)

inued], *and submitted to them the demand of the Confederate general.*

The session lasted for an hour, when the following response was made by Major Anderson and handed to the messengers:

General: I have the honor to acknowledge the receipt of your communication demanding the evacuation of this fort, and to say, in reply thereto, that it is a demand with which I regret that my sense of honor, and of my obligations to my Government, prevent my compliance. Thanking you for the fair, manly, and courteous terms proposed, and for the high compliment paid me, I am, general, very respectfully, your obedient servant.

Beauregard:

In consequence of the verbal observation made by you to my aides, Messrs. Chestnut and Lee, in relation to the condition of your supplies and that you would in a few days be starved out if our guns did not batter you to pieces, or words to that effect, and desiring no useless effusion of blood, I communicated both the verbal observations and your written answer to my communication to my Government.

If you will state the time at which you will evacuate Fort Sumter, and agree that in the mean time you will not use your guns against us unless ours shall be employed against Fort Sumter, we will abstain from opening fire upon you. Colonel Chestnut and Captain Lee are authorized by me to enter into such an agreement with you. You are, therefore, requested to communicate to them an open answer.

Anderson:

General: I have the honor to acknowledge the receipt by Colonel Chestnut of your second communication of the 11th instant, and to state in reply that, cordially uniting with you in the desire to avoid the useless effusion of blood, I will, if provided with the proper and necessary means of transportation, evacuate Fort Sumter by noon on the 15th instant, and that I will not in the meantime open my fires upon your forces unless compelled to do so by some hostile act against this fort or the flag of my government, by the forces under your command, or by some portion of them, or by the perpetration of some act showing a hostile intention on your part against this fort or the flag it bears, should I not receive prior to that time controlling instructions from my government or additional supplies.

Anderson's reply was not acceptable to the Confederates. At 3:30 a.m. on April 12, Colonel Chestnut and Captain Lee handed Anderson the following note and then quickly departed: "Sir: By authority of Brigadier General Beauregard, commanding the provisional forces of the Confederate States, we have the honor to notify you that he will open fire of his batteries on Fort Sumter in one hour from this time."

Anderson immediately put his men on alert. They were not to open fire until daylight and then only "slowly and carefully." "I do not pretend to go to sleep," wrote Mrs. Chestnut. "How can I? If Anderson does not accept terms at four, the orders are, he shall be fired upon. I count four, St Michael's bells chime out and I begin to hope. At half-past four the heavy booming of cannon. I sprang out of bed, and on my knees prostrate I prayed as I never prayed before."

General Beauregard:

The peaceful stillness of the night was broken just before dawn. From Fort Johnson's mortar battery, at 4:30 A.M., April 12, 1861, issued the first – and, as many thought, the too-long-deferred – signal shell of the war. It was fired, not by Mr. Edmund Ruffin, of Virginia, as has been erroneously believed, but by George St. James, of South Carolina, to whom Captain Stephen D. Lee issued the order. It sped aloft, with crashing noise, in the very center of the parade.

Thus was "reveille" sounded in Charleston and its harbor on this eventful morning. In an instant all was bustle and activity. Not an absentee was reported at roll call. The citizens poured down to the battery and the wharves, and women and children crowded each window of the houses overlooking the sea – rapt spectators of the scene. At ten minutes before five o'clock, all the batteries and mortars which encircled the grim fortress were in full play against it.

Round after round had already been fired; and yet, for nearly two hours, not a shot in response had come from Fort Sumter. Had Major Anderson been taken by surprise? Or was it that, certain of his ability to pass unscathed through the onslaught thus made upon him, it mattered not how soon or how late he committed his flag? At last, however, near seven o'clock, the United States flag having previously been raised, the sound of a gun, not ours, was distinctly heard. Sumter had taken up the gage of battle, and Cummings Point had first attracted its attention. It was almost a relief to our troops - for gallantry ever admires gallantry, and a worthy foe disdains one who makes no resistance.

Captain Doubleday, at the fort:

The first shot came from the mortar battery at Fort Johnson. Almost immediately afterward a ball from Cummings Point lodged in the magazine wall. In a moment the firing burst forth in one continuous roar, and large patches of both the exterior and interior masonry began to crumble and fall in all directions.

Nineteen batteries were now hammering at us, and the balls and shells from the 10-inch columbiads, accompanied by shells from the 13-inch mortars which constantly bombarded us, made us feel that the war had commenced in earnest.

When it was broad daylight. I went down to breakfast. I found the officers already assembled at one of the long tables in the mess hall. Our party was calm and even somewhat merry. We had retained one colored man to wait on us. He was a spruce-looking mulatto from Charleston, now completely demoralized. He leaned back against the wall, almost white with fear, his eyes closed and his whole expression one of perfect despair. Our meal was not very sumptuous. It consisted of pork and water, but Dr. Crawford triumphantly brought forth a little farina, which he had found in a corner of the hospital.

When this frugal repast was over, my company was told off in three details for firing purposes.

In aiming the first gun fired against the Rebellion I had no feeling of self-reproach, for I fully believed that the contest had been inevitable. My first shot bounded off from the sloping roof of the battery opposite without producing any apparent effect. It seemed useless to attempt to silence the guns there, for our metal was not heavy enough to batter the work down.

Assistant Surgeon Crawford, having no sick in hospital, volunteered to take command of one of the detachments, and I soon heard his guns on the opposite side of the fort echoing my own. They attacked Fort Moultrie with greater vigor. Our firing became regular, and was answered from the Rebel guns which encircled us on four sides of the pentagon upon which the fort was built. The other side faced the open sea. Showers of balls and shells poured into the fort in one incessant stream. When the immense mortar shells, after sailing high in the air, came down in a vertical direction and buried themselves in the parade ground, their explosion shook the fort like an earthquake.

Mrs. Chestnut:

There was a sound of stir all over the house, pattering of feet in the corridors. All seemed hurrying one way. I put on my double-gown and a shawl and went, too. It was to the housetop. The shells were bursting. In the dark I heard a man say, "Waste of ammunition." I knew my husband was rowing about in a boat somewhere in that dark bay, and that the shells were roofing it over, bursting toward the fort. If Anderson was obstinate, Colonel Chestnut was to open fire. Certainly fire had begun. The regular roar of the cannon, there it was. And who could tell what each volley accomplished of death and destruction?

The women were wild there on the housetop.

Prayers came from them, and imprecations from the men. And then a shell would light up the scene. Tonight they say the forces are to attempt to land. We watched up there, and everybody wondered that Fort Sumter did not fire a shot.

Beauregard:

The action was now general and was so maintained throughout the day, with vigor on both sides. Our guns were served with admirable spirit, and the accuracy of our range was made evident by the clouds of dust . . .

Dr. Crawford:

All of the woodwork was in flames. The officers, seizing the axes that were available, exerted themselves in cutting away whatever woodwork was accessible. It soon became evident that the magazine with its 300 barrels of powder was in danger of the flames, and every man that could be spared was placed upon the duty of removing the powder, toward which fire was gradually progressing, now separated from the magazine by only one set of quarters. Not a third of the barrels could be removed; so thick was the cloud of smoke and burning cinders, that penetrated everywhere, that a cause of serious danger arose from the exposed condition of the powder taken from the magazine, and Major Anderson ordered that all but five barrels be thrown into the sea.

The men, almost suffocated as the south wind carried the cloud of hot smoke and cinders into the casemates, threw themselves upon the ground and covered their faces with wet cloths, or rushed to the embrasures, where the occasional draught made it possible to breathe. The enemy maintained his increased fire. The nine-inch shells which had been filled, and located in different parts of the work, to be used as grenades in repelling an assault, now exploded from time to time as the fire spread, adding greatly to the danger and destruction.

A large number had been placed in the towers on the spiral staircase of granite. They exploded, completely destroying these structures at the west gorge angle, as well as the interior of the other. It was at this moment that the writer, in obedience to Anderson's orders, had ascended to the parapet to report any movement of the fleet. It was with the greatest difficulty that he could make his way amid the destruction and reach the parapet at all. The fleet had made no movement.

The magazines were not closed, when a shot from the enemy's batteries "passed through the intervening shield, struck the door, and bent the lock in such a way that it could not be opened again."

The scene was well nigh indescribable. . . . The enemy's fire from his mortars and gun batteries had been so increased that there was scarcely an appreciable moment that shot and shell were not searching the work. The flames of the burning quarters were still spreading, shooting upward amid the dense smoke as heavy masses of brick and masonry crumbled, and fell with loud noise. All of the woodwork had now been consumed. The heavy gates at the entrance of the work, as well as the planking of the windows on the gorge, were gone, leaving access to the fort easy and almost unobstructed.

Beauregard:

The engagement was continued with unceasing vigor until nightfall, although Sumter's fire had evidently slackened before that time.

During the whole night which followed, in spite of rain and darkness, our batteries continued playing upon the fort with unvarying effect, but the shots were fired at longer intervals, in obedience to orders. It was estimated that over 2,500 shot and shell struck the fort during the first twenty-four hours.

It was expected that the Federal fleet would arrive that night and might attempt to throw troops, ammunition and supplies into Fort Sumter. To guard against such an untoward event, the keenest watchfulness was observed at our beach batteries and by the forces on Morris and Sullivan's islands. The details of men at the Drummond lights were also on the alert and ready at a moment's notice to illuminate the channels; while our cruising vessels actively patrolled the outer harbor. . . .

The fleet that had sailed from New York arrived during the morning of the 13th, but they remained "spectators off the bar." "The presence of the fleet outside the bar, now visible to all," wrote General Beauregard, "no doubt inspired both officers and men of the garrison with additional courage and a renewed spirit of endurance. Major Anderson with his officers and men did hold out; their flag was flying on the twelfth of April, and again on the thirteenth; and they were fighting in all earnest. The fleet outside thought proper, nevertheless, to abstain from all participation in the engagement."

Mrs. Chestnut's diary continued an expression of the homefront:

***April 13, 1861**. Nobody has been hurt at all. How gay we were last night. Reaction after the dread of all the slaughter we thought those dreadful cannon were making. Not even a battery worse for wear. Fort Sumter has been on fire. Anderson has not yet silenced any of our guns. So the aides will, with swords and red sashes by way of uniform, tell us. But the sound of those guns make regular meals impossible. None of us go to table. Tea trays pervade the corridors going everywhere. Some of the anxious hearts lie on their beds and moan in solitary misery. Mrs. Wigfall and I solace ourselves with tea in my room. These women have all a satisfying faith. "God is on our side," they say. When we are shut in, Mrs. Wigfall and I ask, "Why?" "Of course, he hates the yankees," we are told.*

Not by one word or look can we detect any change in the demeanor of our Negro servants. Lawrence sits at our door, sleepy and respectful, and profoundly indifferent. So are they all, but they carry it too far. You could not tell they even heard the awful roar going on in the bay though it has been dinning in their ears night and day. People talk before them as if they were chairs and tables. They make no sign, Are they stolidly stupid? Or wiser that we are? Silent and strong, biding their time?

The war steamers are still there, outside the bar. And there are people who thought the Charleston bar "no good" to Charleston. The bar is the silent partner, or sleeping partner, and in this fray it is doing us yeoman service.

Beauregard, April 13th:

At about 8:00 A.M. on April 13, in the thickest of the bombardment, a thin smoke was observable, curling up from Fort Sumter. It grew denser and denser as it steadily rose in the air; and it soon became apparent that the barracks of the fort had been set on fire by forty rounds of red-hot shot, thrown from an 8-inch columbiad at Fort Moultrie. This sight increased the vigor of our attack; both officers and men feeling now that the garrison would soon be brought to terms. In spite, however, of this new and terrible element against which it had to contend, the fort still responded to the fire of our batteries, though at long and irregular intervals only.

Appreciating the critical position of the enemy, and carried away by their own enthusiasm, our troops, mounting the parapets in their front, cheered Major Anderson at each successive discharge that came from the fort, deriding and hooting, the while, what to them seemed the timorous inaction of the fleet outside the bar.

Matters had evidently reached a crisis for the men within the walls of Sumter. Fearing that some terrible calamity might befall them, and being informed that the United States flag no longer floated over the fort, I immediately dispatched three of my aides with offers of assistance to Major Anderson, who thanked me for my courtesy but declined to accept aid. Before the aides could get to the fort, the United States flag, which had not been hauled down, as we supposed, but had fallen from the effects of a shot, was hoisted anew.

Dr. Crawford:

The Confederate general had noticed the absence of the flag and the burning of the quarters and had sent officers to offer assistance. Anderson declined and determined to reopen his batteries. But he was persuaded to postpone any such action until General Beauregard could be advised of the terms to which he must consent. Meantime, he reduced to writing the terms upon which he would evacuate the fort and sent them to General Beauregard by Captain S.D. Lee, one of the aides.

The formal and final terms agreed to were presented to Anderson by some messengers from General Beauregard at 7:00 P.M., April 13, in regard to which Anderson expressed his gratification; and it was arranged that he should leave in the morning, after communicating with the fleet, but that he must be responsible for the fort in the meantime, as otherwise four companies of artillery would be ordered there. The fort was a scene of ruin and destruction. For thirty-four hours it had sustained a bombardment from seventeen 10-inch mortars and heavy guns, well placed and well served. The quarters and barracks were in ruins. The main gates and the planking of the windows on the gorge were gone; the magazines closed and surrounded by smoldering flames and burning ashes; the provisions exhausted; much of the engineering work destroyed and the cartridge gone.

With only four barrels of powder available, the command at last yielded to the inevitable.

Beauregard:

The flag over Fort Sumter at last was lowered, and a white flag substituted for it. The contest was over. Major Anderson had acknowledged his defeat.

While final arrangements were being made for the withdrawal of the garrison, and before it was effected, I ordered a company of Regulars with two fire engines from Sullivan's Island, to repair to Fort Sumter, to put out the conflagration which, not entirely subdued, had broken out afresh. This was a harder task than was at first supposed. The two engines proven insufficient, and others had to be brought from Charleston with additional firemen. It was only toward dawn that the fire was at last brought under control, and the powder magazine secured from explosion.

Owing to unavoidable delays resulting from the state of confusion existing in the fort, its formal transfer to our troops did not take place until four o'clock in the afternoon on Sunday, the fourteenth of April. At that hour Major Anderson and his command marched out of the work, and we entered it, taking final possession. Then it was that, amid deafening cheers and with an enthusiastic salute from the guns of all the batteries around the harbor, the Confederate and the Palmetto flags were hoisted side by side on the damaged ramparts of the fort.

Mrs. Chestnut:

***April 15**. I did not know that one could live through such days of excitement. Someone called: "Come out! There is a crowd coming." A mob it was, indeed, but it was headed by Colonels Chestnut and Manning. The crowds was shouting and showing these two as messengers of good news. They were escorted to Beauregard's headquarters. Fort Sumter had surrendered!*

Within 24 hours after Fort Sumter was surrendered, President Lincoln issued a proclamation that would, in effect, declare war on the Confederate States of America. Calm and composed to his secretaries, the President did what he had to do. Nicolay and Hay narrate:

In the forenoon (of the 15th). . . Lincoln and his Cabinet, together with sundry military officers, were at the Executive Mansion, giving final shape to the details of the action the Government had decided to take. A proclamation, drafted by himself, copied on the spot by his secretary, was concurred

Young Private Edwin F. Jemison, Company C, 2nd Louisiana Infantry, like many of his comrades, sat for a studio portrait before he went off to war. He was killed during the summer of 1862. (Library of Congress)

in by his Cabinet, signed, and sent to the State Department to be sealed, filed, and copied for publication in the next morning's newspapers.

The document bears the date April 15 (Monday), but was made and signed on Sunday. This proclamation, by authority of the Act of 1795, called into service seventy-five thousand militia for three months, and convened Congress in extra session on the coming 4th of July. It commanded treasonable combinations to disperse within twenty days, and announced that the first object of this military force was to repossess the forts and places seized from the Union.

News of Fort Sumter traveled fast. Theodore Upson, an Indiana farm boy, wrote:

Father and I were husking out some corn. We could not finish before it wintered up. When William Cory came across the field (he had been down after the Mail) he was excited and said, "Jonathan the Rebs have fired upon and taken Fort Sumter." Father got white and couldn't say a word.

William said, "The President will soon fix them. He has called for 75,000 men and is going to blockade their ports, and just as soon as those fellows find out that the North means business they will get down off their high horse."

Father said little. We did not finish the corn and drove to the barn. Father left me to unload and put out the team and went to the house. After I had finished I went in to dinner. Mother said, "What is the matter with Father?" He had gone right upstairs. I told her what we had heard. She went to him. After a while they came down. Father looked ten years older. We sat down to the table. Grandma wanted to know what was the trouble. Father told her and she began to cry. "Oh my poor children in the South! Now they will suffer! God knows how they will suffer! I knew it would come! Jonathan I told you it would come!"

"They can come here and stay," said Father.

"No they will not do that. There is their home. There they will stay. Oh to think that I should have lived to see the day when Brother should rise against Brother."

She and Mother were crying and I lit out for the barn. I do hate to see women cry.

John D. Billings, Massachusetts:

War, that much talked-of, much dreaded calamity, was at last upon us. Could it really be so? We would not believe it; and yet daily happenings forced the unwelcome conclusions upon us.

The Governor of Massachusetts has told the militia to hold themselves in readiness to respond to a call by the President, or else resign, and this order caused the more timid to withdraw from the militia at once. A great many more would have withdrawn had they not been restrained by pride and the lingering hope that there would be no war after all. This was the final test of the militiamen's actual courage and thirst for glory, and a severe one it proved, for at this eleventh hour there was another falling out along the line. But the moment a man's declination for further service was made known, he was hooted at for his cowardice, and for a time his existence was made quite unpleasant in his own immediate neighborhood.

Possessing an average amount of the fire and enthusiasm of youth, I asked my father's consent to go, but he would not give ear to any such "nonsense," and, having been brought up to obey his orders, although of military age (eighteen years), I did not enter the service in the first rally.

The methods by which these regiments were raised were various. In 1861 a common way was for someone who had been in the regular army to take the initiative and circulate an enlistment paper for signatures. His chances were pretty good for obtaining a commission as its captain.

War meetings were designed to stir lagging enthusiasm. Musicians and orators blew themselves red in the face with their windy efforts. Choirs sang "Red, White, and Blue" and "Rallied 'Round the Flag" till too hoarse for further endeavor. The old veteran soldier of 1812 was trotted out and worked for all he was worth, and an occasional Mexican War veteran would air his nonchalance at grim-visaged war. At proper intervals the enlistment roll would be presented for signatures. There was generally one old fellow present who, upon slight provocation, would yell like a hyena and declare his readiness to shoulder his musket and go, if he wasn't so old, while his staid and half-fearful consort would pull violently at his coattails to repress his unreasonable effervescence ere it assumed more dangerous proportions. There there was a patriotic maiden lady who kept a flag or a handkerchief waving with only the rarest and briefest of intervals, who "would go in a minute if she was a man." Besides these there was usually a man who said he would enlist if fifty others did likewise, when he well understood that such a number could not be obtained. And there was one more often found present who, when challenged to sign, would agree to, ***provided*** *that A or B (men of wealth) would put down* ***their*** *names.*

Sometimes the patriotism of such a gathering would be wrought up so intensely by waving banners, martial and vocal music and burning eloquence, that a town's quota would be filled in less than an hour. It needed only the first man to step forward, put down his name, be patted on the back, placed upon the platform and cheered to the echo as the hero of the hour, when a second, a third, a fourth would follow, and at last a perfect stampede set in to sign the enlistment roll. A frenzy of enthusiasm would take possession of the meeting. The complete intoxication of such excitement, like intoxication from liquor, left some of its victims (especially if the fathers of families), on the following day, with sober thoughts to wrestle with; but Pride, that tyrannical master, rarely let them turn back.

After enlistment, what? The responsibility of the citizen for himself ceased. From then on Uncle Sam had him in charge.

The impact of Lincoln's proclamation on a Southern enlistee:

In the first place let me observe, that prior to the proclamation of April 1961, in which President Lincoln warned us "to disperse to our home in (twenty). . . days," there were many who fondly expected that common sense would rule in the councils of the North, and that the Government would not force a war upon their "brethren" of the South. We were all mistaken; and when the proclamation was read on the bulletin boards of the telegraph offices, crowds perused the document with roars of laughter.

At the first whispers of war among these excited crowds, a hundred youths repaired to a lawyer's office, drew up a muster-roll, inscribed their names for twelve months' service, and began drilling in a concert hall. Subscriptions for arms and accoutrements began to pour in, and an emmissary was dispatched Northwards post haste to get these requisites. Many among us having studied at military or semi-military colleges, the details of infantry drill were perfectly understood, so that squads were quickly placed at the command of striplings. Muskets, formerly used for holiday parades, were immediately appropriated. Banners of costly material were made by clubs of patriotic young ladies, and delivered to the companies with appropriate speeches; the men on such occasions swearing that they would perish rather than desert the flag thus consecrated.

The States responded to Mr. Lincoln's call immediately: Governor Morton of Indiana: ". . . I tender to you for the defense of the nation and to uphold the authority of the Government 10,000 men." And so it went. Ohio, 13 regiments; Michigan, 50,000 men; Massachusetts, four regiments; Illinois, 40 companies – "Our people burn with patriotism," telegraphed Governor Richard Yates, "and all parties show the same alacrity to stand by the Government and the laws of the country."

Kentucky was a border state. Governor Beriah Magoffin responded to Mr. Lincoln: "I say emphatically Kentucky will furnish no troops for the wicked purpose of subduing her sister Southern States." Nor would North Carolina. Governor John Ellis said, "I regard the levy of troops made by the Administration for the purpose of subjugating the States of the South as in violation of the Constitution and a gross usurpation of power. I can be no party to this wicked violation of the laws of the country and to this war upon the liberties of a free people. You can get no troops from North Carolina."

Newspapers in the North reported:

Milwaukee, Wisconsin, April 16: "An immense meeting was held at the Chamber of Commerce last night. Men of all parties participated and the excitement was very great. The feeling is unanimous for asserting the authority of the Government, and crowds of men are offering their services to the Adjutant General. Three Volunteer Rifle Companies were formed yesterday."

Cincinnati, Ohio, April 16: "The merchants have stopped shipping goods to the South."

And in the South:

Richmond, Virginia, April 16: "The Richmond *Whig* hauled down the Stars and Stripes this afternoon, and ran up the flag of Virginia."

New Orleans, Louisiana, April 16: "Lincoln's war proclamation was received with no astonishment. Everybody is highly pleased and the people are resolved to maintain their position at all hazards. Two more volunteer companies left today for Pensacola, and the rest will probably remain to defend the city. Volunteer regiments are forming throughout the state."

Montgomery, Alabama, April 16: "The people here are delighted that the uncertainty is at an end, and that we are now entirely justified in driving the invaders from our soil. No one feels a particle of doubt as to the result, and the only regret is that President Lincoln does not head the expedition. . . . The Cabinet were in council this afternoon. Mr. Lincoln's proclamation was read amid bursts of laughter."

On April 17, a Virginia convention voted 103 to 46 to secede. Former President John Tyler, native Virginian, addressed that convention, and later wrote to his second wife, a native of New York:

Well, my dearest one, Virginia has severed her connection with the Northern hive of abolitionists, and takes her stand as a sovereign and independent State. By a large vote she decided on yesterday, at about three o'clock, to resume the powers she had granted to the Federal government, and to stand before the world clothed in the full vestments of sovereignty. The die is thus cast, and her future in the hands of the god of battle. The contest into which we enter is one full of peril, but there is a spirit abroad in Virginia which cannot be crushed until the life of the last man is trampled out. The numbers opposed to us are immense; but twelve thousand Grecians conquered the whole power of Xerxes at Marathon, and our fathers, a mere handful, overcame the enormous power of Great Britain.

The North seems to be thoroughly united against us. The ***Herald*** *and the* ***Express*** *both give way and rally the hosts against us. Things have gone to that point in Philadelphia that no one is safe in the expression of a Southern sentiment. . . . At Washington a system of martial law must have been established. The report is that persons are not permitted to pass through the city to the South. . . .*

Robert E. Lee was offered command of the Union armies. Forty eight hours after he turned it down on April 18, he wrote to his brother:

The question which was the subject of my earnest consultation with you on the 18th inst. has in my own mind been decided. After the most anxious inquiry as to the correct course for me to pursue, I concluded to resign, and sent in my resignation this morning. I wished to wait till the Ordinance of Secession should be acted on by the people of Virginia; but war seems to have commenced, and I am liable at any time to be ordered on duty which I could not conscientiously perform. To save me from such a position, and to prevent the necessity of resigning under orders, I had to act at once, and before I could see you again on the subject, as I had wished. I am now a private citizen, and have no ambition than to remain at home. Save in defense of my native State, I have no

desire ever again to draw my sword.

Another man, graduate of West Point, veteran of the Mexican War, and, not unlike Lee, a family man, wrote to his father on April 21 from Galena, Illinois. His name was Ulysses S. Grant:

We are now in the midst of trying times when every one must be for or against his country, and show his colors too, by his every act. Having been educated for such an emergency, at the expense of the Government, I feel that it has upon me superior claims, such claims as no ordinary motives of self-interest can surmount. I do not wish to act hastily or unadvisedly in the matter, and as there are more than enough to respond to the first call of the President, I have not yet offered myself. I have promised, and am giving all the assistance I can in organizing the company whose services have been accepted from this place. I have promised further to go with them to the State capital, and if I can be of sevice to the Governor in organizing his state troops to do so. What I now ask is your approval of the course I am taking, or advice in the matter. A letter written this week will reach me in Springfield. I have not time to write to you but a hasty line, for, though Sunday as it is, we are all busy here. In a few minutes I shall be engaged in directing tailors in the style and trim of uniforms for our men.

Whatever may have been my political opinions before, I have but one sentiment now. That is, we have a Government, and laws and a flag, and they must be sustained. There are but two parties now, traitors and patriots, and I want hereafter to be ranked with the latter, and I trust, the stronger party. I do not know but you may be placed in an awkward position, and a dangerous one pecuniarily, but costs cannot now be counted. My advice would be to leave where you are if you are not safe with the views you entertain. I would never stultify my opinion for the sake of a little security. . . .

Thomas Jonathan Jackson, also a graduate of West Point and veteran of the Mexican War, was professor of artillery tactics and natural philosophy at the Virginia Military Institute in Lexington. Mrs. Jackson:

About the dawn of that Sabbath morning, April 21st, our door-bell rang, and the order came that Major Jackson should bring the cadets to Richmond ***immediately.*** *Without waiting for breakfast, he repaired at once to the Institute, to make arrangements as speedily as possible for marching, but finding that several hours of preparation would necessarily be required, he appointed the hour for starting at one o'clock p.m. He sent a message to his pastor, Dr. White, requesting him to come to the barracks and offer a prayer with the command before its departure. All the morning he was engaged at the Institute, allowing himself only a short time to return to his home about eleven o'clock, when he took a hurried breakfast, and completed a few necessary preparations for his journey. Then, in the privacy of our chamber, he took his Bible and read that beautiful chapter in Corinthians beginning with the sublime hope of the resurrection – "For we know that if our earthly house of this tabernacle be dissolved, we have a building of God, a house not made with hands, eternal in the heavens"; and then, kneeling down, he committed himself and her whom he loved to the protecting care of his Father in heaven. . . .*

When Dr. White went to the Institute to hold the short religious service which Major Jackson requested, the latter told him the command would march precisely at one o'clock, and the minister, knowing his punctuality, made it a point to close the service at a quarter before one. Everything was then in readiness, and after waiting a few moments an officer approached Major Jackson and said: "Major, everything is now ready. May we not set out?" The only reply he made was to point to the dial-plate of the barracks clock, and not until the hand pointed to the hour of one was his voice heard to ring out the order, "Forward, march!"

An unidentified volunteer, one of the 75,000 who answered President Lincoln's call to defend the Union in 1861. (Library of Congress)

A Southern farmer:

Not far from us lived a family, father and two sons. The father was among the first to volunteer in the Southern Army and fight for his "rights," although he was utterly impecunious, having no Negroes or much of anything else. He was captured, paroled and sent home until exchanged. The Federal Army came near, and his two sons, then at man's estate, went down to the Union camp to see how things looked. They met friends there and were bountifully fed upon crackers and coffee. This last was a luxury of which they had long been deprived. They actually enlisted to get plenty of coffee and grub. When the old man heard of this performance, he started for the camp to get his sons out of the scrape. He got in, got some of that good coffee, enlisted for the war and fought it through with his two sons on the Union side.

Edward Dicey, a liberal English journalist:

Surely no nation in the world has gone through such a baptism of war as the people of the United States underwent in one short year's time. With the men of the Revolution the memories of the revolutionary wars had died out. Two generations had passed away to whom war was little more than a name. The Mexican campaign was rather a military demonstration than an actual war, and the sixteen years which had elapsed since its termination form a long period in the life of a nation whose whole existence has not completed its first century. Twenty months ago there were not more than 12,000 soldiers in a country of 31,000,000. A soldier was as rare an object throughout America as in one of our country hamlets. I recollect a Northern lady telling me that, till within a year before, she could not recall the name of a single person whom she had ever known in the army, and that now she had sixty friends and relatives who were serving in the war; and her case was by no means an uncommon one.

CHAPTER TWO - 1861

Once in four years, on the fourth of March, two or three thousand troops were collected in Washington to add to the pomp of the Presidential inauguration; and this was the one military pageant the country had to boast of. Almost in a day this state of things passed away. Our English critics were so fond of repeating what the North could not do – how it could not fight, nor raise money, nor conquer the South – that they omitted to mention what the North **had** *done. There was no need to go farther than my windows at Washington to see the immensity of the war. It was curious to me to watch the troops as they came marching past. Whether they were regulars or volunteers, it was hard for the unprofessional critic to discern; for all were clad alike, in the same dull, grey-blue overcoats, and most of the few regular regiments were filled with such raw recruits that the difference between volunteer and regular was not a marked one.*

Of course it was easy enough to pick faults in the aspect of such troops. As each regiment marched, or rather waded through the dense slush and mud which covered the roads, you could observe many inaccuracies of military attire. One man would have his trousers rolled up almost to his knees; another would wear them tucked inside his boots; and a third would appear with one leg of his trousers hanging down, and the other gathered tightly up. It was not unfrequent, too, to see an officer with his epaulettes sewed on to a common plain frock-coat. Then there was a slouching gait about the men, not soldierlike to English eyes. They used to turn their heads round when on parade, with an indifference to rule which would drive an old drill-sergeant out of his senses. There was an absence, also, of precision in the march. The men kept in step; but I always was at a loss to discover how they ever managed to do so. The system of march, it is true, was copied rather from the French than the English or Austrian fashion; but still it was something very different from the orderly disorder of a Zouave march. That all these, and a score of similar irregularities, are faults, no one – an American least of all – would deny. But there are two sides to the picture.

One thing is certain, that there is no physical degeneracy about a race which could produce such regiments as those which formed the army of the Potomac. Men of high stature and burly frames were rare, except in the Kentucky troops; but, on the other hand, small, stunted men were almost unknown. I have seen the armies of most European countries; and I have no hesitation in saying that, as far as the average raw material of the rank and file is concerned, the American army is the finest.

The officers are, undoubtedly, the weak point of the system. They have not the military air, the self-possession which long habit of command alone can give; while the footing of equality on which they inevitably stand with the volunteer privates, deprives them of the esprit de corps belonging to a ruling class. Still they are active, energetic, and constantly with their troops.

Wonderfully well equipped too, at this period of the war, were both officers and men. Their clothing was substantial and fitted easily, their arms were good, and the military arrangements were as perfect as money alone could make them.

It was remarkable to me how rapidly the new recruits fell into the habits of military service. I have seen a Pennsylvanian regiment, raised chiefly from the mechanics of Philadelphia, which, six weeks after its formation, was, in my eyes, equal to the average of our best-trained volunteer corps, as far as marching and drill-exercise went. Indeed, I often asked myself what it was that made the Northern volunteer troops look, as a rule, so much more soldier-like than our own. I suppose the reason is, that across the Atlantic there was actual war, and that at home there was at most only a parade. I have no doubt that, in the event of civil war or invasion, England would raise a million volunteers as rapidly as America has done – more rapidly she could not; and that, when fighting had once begun, there would only be too much of grim earnestness about our soldiering; but it is not want of patriotism to say that the American volunteers looked to me more businesslike than our own. At the scene of war itself there was no playing at soldiering. No gaudy uniforms or crack companies, no distinction of classes. From every part of the North; from the ports of New York and Boston; from the homesteads of New England; from the mines of Pennsylvania and the factories of Pittsburgh; from the shores of the great lakes; from the Mississippi valley; and from the far-away Texan prairies, these men had come to fight for the Union. It is idle to talk of their being attracted by the pay alone. Large as it is, the pay of thirteen dollars a month is only two dollars more than the ordinary pay of privates in the Federal army during peace times. Thirteen shillings a week is poor pay for a labouring man in America, even with board, especially during the war, when the wages of unskilled labour amounted to from twenty to thirty shillings a week. . . .

The bulk of the native volunteers consisted of men who had given up good situations in order to enlist, and who had families to support at home; and for such men the additional pay was not an adequate inducement to incur the dangers and hardships of war. Of course, wherever there is an army, the scum of the population will always be gathered together; but the average morale and character of the couple of hundred thousand troops collected round Washington was extremely good. There was very little outward drunkenness, and less brawling about the streets than if half a dozen English militia regiments had been quartered there. The number of papers purchased daily by the common soldiers, and the amount of letters which they sent through the military post, was astonishing to a foreigner, though less strange when you considered that every man in that army, with the exception of a few recent immigrants, could both read and write. The ministers, also, of the different sects, who went out on the Sundays to preach to the troops, found no difficulty in obtaining large and attentive audiences.

In June, William Howard Russell, a London news reporter arrived at the foot of Chicksaw Bluffs on the Mississippi, where the Confederate Camp Randolph was located:

On looking out of my cabin window this morning I found the steamer fast alongside a small wharf, above which rose, to the height of 150 feet, at an angle of forty-five degrees, a rugged bluff. The wharf was covered with commissariat stores and ammunition. Three heavy guns, which some men were endeavoring to sling to rude bullock carts, in a manner defiant of all the laws of gravitation, seemed likely to go slap into the water at every moment; but of the many big fellows lounging about, not one gave a hand to the working party. At the height of fifty feet above the level of the river two earthworks had been rudely erected.

A number of the soldiers, under the notion that they were washing themselves, were swimming about in a backwater of the great river, regardless of catfish, mud and fever.

After breakfast we mounted the cart-horse chargers which were waiting to receive us. It is scarcely worth while to describe the works. Certainly, a more extraordinary maze could not be conceived in the dreams of a sick engineer. They were so ingeniously made as to prevent the troops engaged in their defense from resisting the enemy's attacks, or getting away from them when assailants had got inside.

The general ordered some practice to be made with round shot down the river. An old 42-pound carronade was loaded with some difficulty and pointed at a tree about 1,700 yards distant. I ventured to say, "I think, General, the smoke will prevent your seeing the shot." To which the general replied, "No, sir," in a tone which indicated "I beg you to understand I have been wounded in Mexico and know all about this kind of thing."

"Fire!" The string was pulled, and out of the touchhole popped a piece of metal with a little chirrup. "Darn these friction tubes! I prefer the linstock and match," quoth one of the staff, "but the general will have us use friction tubes." Tube No. 2, however, did explode, but where the ball went no one could say, as the smoke drifted right into our eyes.

Slowly winding for some distance up the steep road in a blazing sun, we proceeded through the tents which were scattered in small groups on the wooded plateau above the river. The tents were of the small ridge-pole pattern, six men to each, many of whom, from their exposure to the sun and from the badness of the water, had already been laid up with illness.

By order of the general some 700 or 800 men were formed into line for inspection. Many were in their short sleeves, and the awkwardness with which they handled their arms showed that, however good they might be as shots, they were bad at manual platoon exercises; but such great strapping fellows, that as I walked down the ranks there were few whose shoulders were not above the level of my head. They were armed with old pattern percussion muskets, no two clad alike, many very badly shod, few with knapsacks but all provided with a tin water flask and a blanket.

From the quartermaster general I heard that each man had a daily ration of ¾ lb. to 1¼ lb of meat and a sufficiency of bread, sugar, coffee and rice; however, these military Olivers asked for more. Neither whick nor tobacco was served out to them, which to such heavy consumers of both must have proved a source of dissatisfaction. The officers were plain planters, merchants, lawyers and the like – energetic, determined men, but utterly ignorant of the most rudimentary parts of military science.

Having gone down the lines of these motley companies, the general addressed them in a harangue in which he expatiated on their patriotism on their courage and the atrocity of the enemy, in an old farrago of military and political subjects. But when he wound up by assuring them, "When the hour of danger comes I will be with you," the effect was by no means equal to his expectations. The men did not seem to care much whether the general would be with them or not at that moment; and, indeed, he did not give one an idea that he would contribute much to the demands of resistance.

We returned to the steamer and proceeded onward to another landing, protected by a battery, where we were received by a guard dressed in uniform, who turned out with some appearance of soldierly smartness. The general told me the corps was composed of gentlemen planters and farmers. They had all clad themselves, and came from the best families in the state of Tennessee.

On returning to the boats the band struck up the "Marseillaise" and "Dixie Land." In the afternoon we returned to Memphis.

Massachusetts was the first of the states to respond to Lincoln's call to arms. The Sixth Massachusetts militia left Boston on April 17 by train for Washington. John W. Hanson:

Orders were. . . given to the band, to confine their music to tunes that would not be likely to give offense, especially avoiding the popular air, "Dixie." Quartermaster Munroe distributed twenty rounds of ball cartridges; and Col. Jones went through the cars, issuing an order, that the regiment should march across Baltimore in column of sections. The regiment here loaded and capped their rifles. As soon as the cars reached the station, the engine was unshackled, horses were hitched to the cars, and they were drawn rapidly away. . . .

Some slight demonstrations were made on one or two of the cars containing the fifth and sixth companies; but nothing like an attack was made until the seventh car started. . . . It was attacked by clubs, paving-stones, and other missiles. The men were very anxious to fire on their assailants; but Maj. Watson forbade them, until they should be attacked by fire-arms. One or two soldiers were wounded by paving-stones and bricks; and at length one man's thumb was shot, when, holding the wounded hand up to the major, he asked leave to fire in return. Orders were then given to lie on the bottom of the car and load, and rising, to fire from the windows at will. These orders were promptly obeyed. . . .

Moving with as much rapidity as possible, and receiving an occasional musket or pistol shot, or a shower of rocks and bricks, the car reached the main body of the regiment. . . .

Four companies marched:

Capt. Follansbee. . . took the command. There were but about two hundred and twenty on the column; and the mob soon reached ten thousand, at least. The air was filled with yells, oaths, taunts, all sorts of missiles, and soon pistol and musket shots; and Capt. Follansbee gave the order to fire at will. But few of the crows were on the front of the column, but they pressed on the flank and rear more and more furiously. At one of the bridges in Pratt Street, a formidable barricade, with cannon to sweep the streets, not quite ready for service, had been arranged. Here the mob supposed that the column would be obliged to halt; but Capt. Follansbee ordered his command to scale the barricade. Before the ruffians could follow over the bridge, or run around to intercept them, the soldiers had succeeded in getting quite a distance up Pratt Street. . . . Cheers for "Jeff Davis," and for "South Carolina, and the South;" all sorts of insulting language, – such as "Dig your graves!" – "You can pray, but you cannot fight!" and the like, – were heard; but the little battalion went steadily ahead, with no thought of turning back.

As the gallant detachment passed along Pratt Street, pistols and guns were fired at them from the windows and doors of stores and houses; and our boys, getting a little accustomed to the strange circumstances in which they were placed, loaded their guns as they marched, dragging them between their feet, and, whenever they saw a hostile demonstration, they took as good aim as they could, and fired. There was no platoon firing whatever. At one place, at an upper window, a man was in the act of firing, when a rifle ball suggested to him the propriety of desisting, and he came headlong to the sidewalk. And thus the men, whose rare good fortune it was to contribute the first instalment of blood to pay the price of our redemption, hurried along their way. They were hampered by their orders to fire as little as possible; they were anxious to get to the capital, even then supposed to be in danger; they were separated from the larger part of the regiment, and knew not where their comrades were; and thus assaulted on each side, and by all sorts of weapons and missiles, they kept on their way, loading and firing at will, marching the entire distance, – a mile and a half – bearing several of their wounded with them, and reached the station, and joined the rest of the regiment.

Seeing the train about to start, the mob ran on ahead, and placed telegraph poles, anchors, etc., on the track. The train moved a short distance and stopped; a rail had been removed; it was replaced, and the cars went on; stopped again, the road was repaired, and the train went on again; stopped again, and the conductor reported to the colonel that it was impossible to proceed, that the regimnent must **march** *to Washington. Col. James replied, "We are ticketed through, and are going in these cars. If you or the engineer cannot run the train, we have plenty of men who can. If you need protection or assistance, you shall have it; but we go through."*

The crowd went for some miles out, as far as Jackson Bridge, near Chinkapin Hill, and the police followed, removing obstructions; and at several places shots were exchanged. At length, they reached the Relay House, where the double tracks ended, and where they waited for hours – and long hours they were – for a train from Washington that had the right of way; and at length started again, reaching Washington late in the afternoon.

The Sixth Massachusetts moved into Washington, a city of bedlam.

John G. Nicolay:

Washington took on the aspect of a city under siege. The supplies of flour and grain in the Georgetown mills were seized. Business was suspended, stores were closed and locked, the streets remained empty save for hurrying patrols. At the first news of burned railroad bridges and attacks on troops, all transient dwellers in Washington wanted to go home – and the desire was not lessened by a rumor that every able-bodied male might be impressed for the town's defense. On Monday the 22nd several hundred clerks in the government departments gave way to their southern sympathies and resigned their offices. Certain military and naval officers did likewise. One was Commodore Franklin Buchanan, who turned over the Washington Navy Yard with its ships and stores and priceless machinery to Commodore Dahlgren and departed, leaving him with scarcely enough marines to keep watch against possible incendiaries. Another was Captain John B. Magruder, who commanded a battery upon which General Scott had placed much reliance for the defense of the city. No case of desertion gave the President greater pain. "Only three days ago," he said, "Magruder came voluntarily to me in this room, and with his own lips, and in my presence, repeated over and over again, his asseverations and protestations of loyalty."

The President had his emotions well under control. In the presence of others he gave little sign of the anxiety he was enduring, but on the 23rd, one of the days of darkest gloom, after the business of the day was over and he thought himself alone, one of the White House staff, passing the open door of the Executive Office, saw him pacing the floor, then pause and look wistfully out of the window in the direction from which help was expected, and heard him exclaim: "Why don't they come? Why don't they come!" Next day, when they still had not come, and he was talking to the wounded men of the Sixth Massachusetts, he spoke with an irony that only the intensest feeling could wring from him: "I begin to believe that there is no North. The Seventh Regiment is a myth. Rhode Island is another. You are the only real thing."

But the Seventh New York arrived two days later. Lincoln's secretaries described that day:

Those who were in the Federal capital that Thursday, April 25, will never, during their lives, forget the event. . . . As

The first serious engagement of the Civil War was at Manassas, Va., near the banks of the Bull Run River. The federal army marched out from Washington, D.C., expecting a quick, decisive victory. Instead, Confederate forces routed the Union Army and served notice of a protracted conflict. Alfred R. Waud, who recorded this charge by the Rhode Island Brigade and the New York 71st Regiment against a Southern artillery battery, became one of the foremost battlefield artists of the War. Like his colleagues in the field, he made pencil and wash drawings to be later engraved and printed in Northern newspapers and magazines. (Library of Congress)

soon as the arrival was known, an immense crowd gathered at the depot to obtain ocular evidence that relief had at length reached the city. Promptly debarking and forming, the Seventh marched up Pennsylvania Avenue to the White House. As they passed up the magnificent street, with their well-formed ranks, their exact military step, their soldierly bearing, their gayly floating flags, and the inspiring music of their splendid regimental band, they seemed to sweep all thought of danger and all taint of treason out of that great national thoroughfare and out of every human heart in the Federal city. The presence of this single regiment seemed to turn the scales of fate. Cheer upon cheer greeted them, windows were thrown up, houses opened, the population came forth upon the streets as for a holiday. It was an epoch in American history. For the first time, the combined spirit and power of Liberty entered the nation's capital.

MANASSAS

Only one hundred miles separated the capitals of the Union and the Confederacy, Washington and Richmond. Between them lay four rivers – the Potomac, the Rappahannock, the York, and the James. Immediately on the outskirts of Washington, just across the Potomac, was the old colonial town of Alexandria. Twenty five or so miles further south and some miles to the west was the important railroad center of Manassas Junction.

During the early spring of 1861, both governments assembled armies to defend their capitals – the Federal government in and around Washington, the Confederate government to the north at Manassas and at Winchester. General P.G.T. Beauregard, hero of Charleston and Fort Sumter, commanded 22,000 men at Manassas; General Joseph E. Johnston commanded 11,000 at Winchester in the Shenandoah Valley. General Winfield Scott, old veteran of two wars, about to retire, had assembled 35,000 men at Centreville under General Irvin McDowell. The stage for war had been set.

The first casualties came at Alexandria across the Potomac. Southern sympathizer, Mrs. Julia Brockenbrough McGuire wrote:

Fairfax C.H., May 25. – The day of suspense is at an end. Alexandria and its environs, including, I greatly fear, our home, are in the hands of the enemy. Yesterday morning, at an early hour, as I was in my pantry, putting up refreshments for the barracks preparatory to a ride to Alexandria, the door was suddenly thrown open by a servant, looking wild with excitement, exclaiming, "Oh, madam, do you know?" "Know what, Henry?" "Alexandria is filled with Yankees." "Are you sure, Henry?" said I, trembling in every limb. "Sure, madam! I saw them myself. Before I got up I heard soldiers rushing by the door; went out, and saw our men going to the cars."

"Did they get off?" I asked, afraid to hear the answer. "Oh, yes, the cars went off full of them, and some marched out, and then I went to King Street, and saw such crowds of Yankees coming in! They came down the turnpike, and some came down the river; and presently I heard such noise and confusion, and they said they were fighting, so I came home as fast as I could."

I lost no time in seeking Mr.—, who hurried out to hear the truth of the story. He soon met Dr.—, who was bearing off one of the editors in his buggy. He more than confirmed Henry's report, and gave an account of the tragedy at the Marshall House. Poor Jackson (the proprietor) had always said that the Confederate flag which floated from the top of his house should never be taken down but over his dead body. It was known that he was a devoted patriot, but his friends had amused themselves at this rash speech. He was suddenly aroused by the noise of men rushing by his room-door, ran to the window, and seeing at once what was going on, he seized his gun, his wife trying in vain to stop him; as he reached the passage he saw Colonel Ellsworth coming from the third story, waving the flag. As he passed Jackson he said, "I have a trophy." Jackson immediately raised his gun, and in an instant Ellsworth fell dead. One of the party immediately killed poor Jackson. The Federals then proceeded down the street, taking possession of public houses, etc. I am mortified to write that a party of our cavalry, thirty-five in number, was captured. It can scarcely be accounted for. It is said that the Federals notified the authorities in Alexandria that they would enter the city at eight, and the captain was so credulous as to believe them. Poor fellow, he is now a prisoner, but it will be a lesson to him and to our troops generally. Jackson leaves a wife and children. I know the country will take care of them. He is the first martyr. I shudder to think how many more there may be.

But the North also had a martyr; the man who had taken the first Confederate flag, Colonel Elmer Ellsworth. Lincoln wrote to his parents:

My dear Sir and Madam: In the untimely loss of your noble son, our affliction here, is scarcely less than your own. So much of promised usefulness to one's country, and of bright hopes for one's self and friends, have rarely been so suddenly dashed, as in his fall. In size, in years, and in youthful appearance, a boy only, his power to command men, was surpassingly great. This power, combined with a fine intellect, an indomitable energy, and a taste altogether military, constituted in him, as seemed to me, the best natural talent, in that department, I ever saw. But yet he was singularly modest and deferential in social intercourse. My acquaintance with him began less than two years ago; yet through the latter half of the intervening period, it was as intimate as the disparity of our ages, and my engrossing engagements, would permit. To me, he appeared to have no indulgences or pastimes; and I never heard him utter a profane, or an intemperate word. What was conclusive of his good heart, he never forgot his parents. The honors he labored for so laudably, and, in the sad end, so gallantly gave his life, he meant for them, no less than for himself.

In the hope that it may be no intrusion upon the sacredness of your sorrow, I have ventured to address you this tribute to the memory of my young friend, and your brave and early fallen child.

May God give you that consolation which is beyond all earthly power. Sincerely your friend in a common affliction – A. Lincoln.

On May 23, General Joseph E. Johnston took command of Confederate troops at Harpers Ferry, and, a few days later, moved them to Winchester, Virginia, to guard the pathway to the Shenandoah Valley from General Robert Patterson's Federal troops at Chambersburg, Pennsylvania. While all of this did not go unnoticed, there were other things on Northern minds. "Forward to Richmond," wrote the *New*

York Tribune. "The Rebel Congress must not be allowed to meet there on the 20th of July! By that date the place must be held by the National Army!" To take Richmond, if indeed the Federal government thought it wise, meant first taking Manassas and the concentrated Confederate army there. General Irvin McDowell submitted a plan:

The Secession forces at Manassas Junction and its dependencies are supposed to amount at this time to –

Infantry 23,000
Cavalry 1,500
Artillery 500

We cannot count on keeping secret our intention to overthrow this force. Even if the many parties intrusted with the knowledge of the plan should not disclose or discover it, the necessary preliminary measures for such an expedition would betray it, and they are alive and well informed as to every movement, however slight, we make. They have, moreover, been expecting us to attack their position, and have been preparing for it. When it becomes known positively we are about to march, and they learn in what strength, they will be obliged to call in their disposable forces from all quarters, for they will not be able, if closely pressed, to get away by railroad before we can reach them. If General J. E. Johnston's force is kept engaged by Major-General Patterson, and Major-General Butler occupies the force now in his vicinity, I think they will not be able to bring up more than ten thousand men. So we must calculate on having to do with about thirty-five thousand men. . . .

Jefferson Davis:

Already the Northern officer in charge had evacuated Harper's Ferry, after having attempted to destroy the public buildings there. His report says: "I gave the order to apply the torch. In three minutes or less, both of the arsenal buildings, containing nearly fifteen thousand stand of arms, together with the carpenter's shop, which was at the upper end of a long and connected series of workshops of the armory proper, were in a blaze. There is every reason for believeing the destruction was complete." Mr. Simon Cameron, the Secretary of War, on April 22d replied to his report in these words: "I am directed by the President of the United States to communicate to you, and through you to the officers and men under your command at Harper's Ferry Armory, the approbation of the Government of your and their judicious conduct there, and to tender you and them the thanks of the Government for the same." At the same time the ship-yard at Norfolk was abandoned after an attempt to destroy it. About midnight of April 20th, a fire was started in the yard, which continued to increase, and before daylight the work of destruction extended to two immense ship-houses, one of which contained the entire frame of a seventy-four-gun ship, and to the long ranges of stores and offices on each side of the entrance. The great ship Pennsylvania was burned, and the frigates Merrimac and Columbus, and the Delaware, Raritan, Plymouth, and Germantown were sunk. A vast amount of machinery, valuable engines, small-arms, and chronometers, was broken up and rendered entirely useless. The value of the property destroyed was estimated at several millions of dollars.

This property thus destroyed had been accumulated and constructed with laborious care and skillful ingenuity during a course of years to fulfill one of the objects of the Constitution, which was expressed in these words, "To provide for the common defense." It had belonged to all the States in common, and to each one equally with the others. If the confederate States were still members of the Union, as the President of the United States asserted, where can he find a justification of these acts?

In explanation of his policy to the Commissioners sent to him by the Virginia State Convention, he said, referring to his inaugural address, "As I then and therein said, I now repeat, the power confided in me will be used to hold, occupy, and possess property and places belonging to the Government." Yet he tendered the thanks of the Government to those who applied the torch to destroy this property belonging, as he regarded it, to the Government.

How unreasonable, how blind with rage must have been that administration of affairs which so quickly brought the Government to the necessity of destroying its own mean of defense in order, as it publicly declared, "to maintain its life"! It would seem as if the passions that rule the savage had taken possession of the authorities at the United States capital! In the conflagrations of vast structures, the wanton destruction of public property, and still more in the issue of **lettres de cachet** *by the Secretary of State, who boasted of the power of his little bell over the personal liberties of the citizen, the people saw, or might have seen, the rapid strides toward despotism made under the mask of preserving the Union. Yet these and similar measures were tolerated because the sectional hate dominated in the Northern States over the higher motives of constitutional and moral obligation.*

Leaving small garrisons in the defensive works, I propose to move against Manassas with a force of thirty-five thousand of all arms, organized into three columns, with a reserve of ten thousand. One column to move from Falls Church or Vienna (preferably the latter), to go between Fairfax Court-House and Centreville, and, in connection with another column moving by the Little River turnpike, cut off or drive in (the former, if possible) the enemy's advanced posts. The third column to move by the Orange and Alexandria Railroad, and leaving as large a force as may be necessary to aid in rebuilding it, to push on with the remainder to join the first and second columns.

The enemy is said to have batteries in position at several places in his front, and defensive works on Bull Run and Manassas Junction. I do not propose that these batteries be attacked, for I think they may all be turned. Bull Run, I am told, is fordable at most any place. After uniting the columns this side of it, I propose to attack the main position by turning it, if possible, so as to cut off communications by rail with the

South, or threaten to do so sufficiently to force the enemy to leave his intrenchments to guard them; if necessary, and I find it can be done with safety, to move a force as far as Bristoe, to destroy the bridge at that place.

On July 16, in a house quite near the White House, a Confederate spy delivered a message to a woman, who in turn wrote a message in code to General Beauregard at Manassas. While Federal troops prepared to march that day, Beauregard was reading: "Order issued for McDowell to march upon Manassas tonight."

Warren Lee Goss, of the 2nd Massachusetts, left his camp that night:

Our regiment was camped near Alexandria, and the whole of us grew impatient to end the war and get home. I tell you, we were glad when we were told to get ready for a march.

They gave us rations of salt junk, hardtack, sugar and coffee. Each man carried his rubber and woolen blanket, forty rounds of cartridges, a canteen, his gun and equipments and most of us a patent drinking tube. I hadn't been on the march an hour before I realized that it might not be such fun, after all. There was a 32-pound gun mooring on the road, with sixteen or eighteen horses to pull it. Finally, two or three companies were detailed to help the horses. The weather was scorching hot, but the most trying thing was the jerky way they marched us. Sometimes they'd double-quick us, and again they'd keep us standing in the road waiting in the hot sun for half an hour, then start us ahead again a little way, then halt us again, and so on. The first day we marched until after sundown, and when we halted for the night we were the tiredest crowd of men I ever saw.

The next day was the seventeenth of July. I was hungry, so I stopped at a house and asked if they would sell me something to eat. There were three Negro girls, a white woman and her daughter in the house. The white folks were proud and unaccommodating. They said the Yankees had stolen everything – all their "truck," as they called it; but when I took a handful of silver change they brought me a cold Johnnycake and some chicken. As I was leaving the house, the daughter said; "You'n Yanks are right pert just now, but you'ns'll come back soon a right smart quicker than yer'r going, I reckon!"

We marched helter-skelter nearly all night without orders to stop until, just before daylight, we halted near a little building they called a church.

The first gun of the fight I heard was when we were eight or ten miles from Centreville, on the afternoon of the eighteenth of July, the day of the engagement at Blackburn's Ford. We were hurried up at double-quick and marched in the direction of the firing until we reached Centreville, about seven o'clock that night. Very early on the morning of the twenty-first we marched through Centreville. Near Cub Run we saw carriages and barouches which contained civilians. We thought it wasn't a bad idea to have the great men from Washington come out to see us thrash the Rebs.

Beauregard:

Soon after the conflict in Charleston Harbor, I was called to Richmond, which had become the Confederate seat of Government, and was directed to "assume command of the Confederate troops on the Alexandria line." Arriving at Manassas Junction, I took command on the second of June, 1861.

Although the position was strategically of commanding importance, the terrain was unfavorable. Its strategic value was that, being close to the Federal capital, it held in observation the chief enemy army then being assembled by General McDowell for a movement against Richmond. We had a railway approach in our rear for the accumulation of reinforcements, while another (the Manassas Gap) railway gave rapid communications with the fertile valley of the Shenandoah. But on the other hand, Bull Run, a pretty stream, was of little or no defensive strength, for it abounded in fords.

At the time of my arrival, a Confederate army under General Joseph E. Johnston was at Harpers Ferry, in a position from which he was speedily forced to retire, however, by a Federal army under the veteran General Robert Patterson. On my right flank a Confederate force of some 2,500 men under General T.H. Holmes occupied the position of Aquia Creek on the Lower Potomac. I was anxiously aware that the sole military advantage of the moment of the Confederates was that of holding the **interior lines***. On the Federal side were all material advantages: superior numbers, decidedly better arms and equipment, and a small but incomparable body of Regular infantry as well as Regular field artillery of the highest class.*

Happily, arrangements had been made which enabled me to receive regularly, from private persons at the Federal capital, most accurate information. I was almost as well advised of the strength of the hostile army in front as its own commander.

A former clerk in one of the departments in Washington had volunteered to bring me the latest information of the military and political situation. With no more delay than the writing in cipher by Mrs. Greenhow, a Southern sympathizer, of the words "Order issued for McDowell to march upon Manassas tonight," my agent was carried in a buggy with a relay of horses down the eastern shore of the Potomac. The momentous dispatch was in my hands between eight and nine o'clock that night. Within half an hour my outpost commanders were directed at the first evidence of the enemy in their front to fall back to positions already prescribed. I next suggested to President Davis that the Army of the Shenandoah should be ordered to reinforce me – a suggestion that was at once heeded. General Johnston was induced to join me; and to facilitate that movement I hastened to accumulate all possible railway transport at the eastern foot of the Blue Ridge, to which Johnston's troops directed their march.

It seemed, however, as though the deferred attempt at concentration was to go for naught, for on the morning of the eighteenth the Federal forces were massed around Centreville, only three miles from Mitchell's Ford, and soon were seen advancing upon the roads leading to that and Blackburn's Ford. My order of battle, issued in the night of the seventeenth, contemplated an offensive return, particularly from the strong brigades on the right and right center.

Our success in the first limited collision between McDowell's forces and mine was of decisive importance, by so increasing General McDowell's caution as to give time for the arrival of some of General Johnston's forces. But while on the nineteenth I was awaiting a renewed attack by the Federal army, I received a telegram from Richmond urging me to withdraw my call on General Johnston on account of the supposed impracticability of the concentration. As this was not an order and left me technically free, I preferred to keep both the situation and the responsibility, being resolved to take the offensive myself.

The Federal artillery opened in front on both fords, and the infantry, while demonstrating in front of Mitchell's Ford, endeavored to ford a passage at Blackburn's. The Federals, after several attempts to ford a passage, met a final repulse and retreated. The contest lapsed into an artillery duel in which the Washington Artillery of New Orleans won credit against the renowned batteries of the United States Regular Army. A comical effect of this artillery fight was the destruction of the dinner of myself and staff by a Federal shell that fell into the fire place of my headquarters at the McLean House.

General McDowell, fortunately for my plans, spent the nineteenth and twentieth in reconnaissances; meanwhile, General Johnston brought 8,340 men from the Shenandoah Valley, with twenty guns, and General Holmes 1,265 rank and file, with six pieces of artillery, came from Aquia Creek. My force now mustered 29,188 rank and file and fifty-five guns.

McDowell opened battle Sunday, July 21, by attacking the Confederate left. Beauregard:

The firing on the left began to increase so intensely as to indicate a severe attack, whereupon General Johnston said that he would go personally to that quarter.

After weighing attentively the firing, which seemed rapidly and heavily increasing, it appeared to me that the troops on the right would be unable to get into position before the Federal offensive should have made too much progress on our left, and that it would be better to abandon it altogether, maintaining only a strong demonstration so as to detain the enemy in front of our right and center, and hurry up all available reenforcements – including the reserves that were to have moved upon Centreville – to our left and fight the battle out in that quarter. Communicating this view to General Johnston, who approved it (giving his advice, as he said, for what it was worth, as he was not acquainted with the country), I ordered Ewell, Jones, and Longstreet to make a strong demonstration all along their front on the other side of the Run, and ordered the reserves below our position . . . to move swiftly to the left. General Johnston and I now set out at full speed for the point of conflict. We arrived there just as Bee's troops, after giving way, were fleeing in disorder behind the height in rear of the Stone Bridge. They had come around between the base of the hill and the Stone Bridge into a shallow ravine which ran up to a point on the crest where Jackson had already formed his brigade along the edge of the woods. We found the commanders resolutely stemming the further flight of the routed forces, but vainly endeavoring to restore order, and our own efforts were as futile. Every segment of the line we succeeded in forming was again dissolved while another was being formed; more than two thousand men were shouting each some suggestion to his neighbor, their voices mingling with the noise of the shells hurtling through the trees overhead. It was at this moment that General Bee used the famous expression, "Look at Jackson's brigade! It stands there like a stone wall" – a name that passed from the brigade to its immortal commander. The disorder seemed irretrievable, but happily the thought came to me that if their colors were planted out to the front the men might rally on them, and I gave the order to carry the standards forward some forty yards, which was promptly executed by the regimental officers, thus drawing the common eye of the troops. They now received easily the orders to advance and form the line of their colors, which they obeyed with a general movement; and as General Johnston and myself rode forward shortly afterward with the colors of the 4th Alabama by our side, the line that had fought all morning, and had fled, routed and disordered, now advanced again into position as steadily as veterans.

Jefferson Davis came to the battlefield:

On reaching the railroad junction, I found a large number of men, bearing the usual evidence of those who leave the field of battle under a panic. They crowded around the train with fearful stories of a defeat of our army. The railroad conductor announced his decision that the railroad train should proceed no farther. Looking among those who were about us for one whose demeanor gave reason to expect from him a collected answer, I selected one whose gray beard and calm face gave best assurance. He, however, could furnish no encouragement. Our line, he said, was broken, all was confusion, the army routed, and the battle lost. I asked for Generals Johnston and Beauregard; he said they were on the field when he left it. I returned to the conductor and told him that I must go on; that the railroad was the only means by which I could proceed, and that, until I reached the headquarters, I could not get a horse to ride to the field where the battle was raging. He finally consented to detach the locomotive from the train, and, for my accommodation, to run it as far as the army headquarters.

At the headquarters we found the Quartermaster-General, W.L. Cabell, and the Adjutant-General, Jordan, of General Beauregard's staff, who courteously agreed to furnish us horses, and also to show us the route. While the horses were being prepared, Colonel Jordan took occasion to advise my aide-de-camp, Colonel Davis, of the hazard of going to the field, and the impropriety of such exposure on my part. The horses were after a time reported ready, and we started to the field. The stragglers soon became numerous, and warnings as to the fate which awaited us if we advanced were not only frequent but evidently sincere.

There were, however, many who turned back, and the wounded generally cheered upon meeting us. I well remember one, a mere stripling, who, supported on the shoulders of a man, who was bearing him to the rear, took off his cap and waved it with a cheer, that showed within that slender form beat the heart of a hero – breathed a spirit that would dare the labors of Hercules.

As we advanced, the storm of the battle was rolling westward, and its fury became more faint. When I met General Johnston, who was upon a hill which commanded a general view of the field of the afternoon's operations, and inquired of him as to the state of affairs, he replied that we had won the battle.

Thomas Jonathan Jackson, who at Manassas was christened "Stonewall," wrote to his wife on July 23:

My Precious Pet, – Yesterday we fought a great battle and gained a great victory, for which all the glory is due to ***God alone****. Although under a heavy fire for several continuous hours, I received only one wound, the breaking of the longest finger of my left hand; but the doctor says the finger can be saved. It was broken about midway between the hand and knuckle, the ball passing on the side next the forefinger. Had it struck the centre, I should have lost the finger. My horse was wounded, but not killed. Your coat got an ugly wound near the hip, but my servant, who is very handy, has so far repaired it that it doesn't show very much. My preservation was entirely due, as was the glorious victory, to our God, to whom be all the honor, praise and glory. The battle was the hardest that I have ever been in, but not near so hot in its fire. I commanded the centre more particularly, though one of my regiments extended to the right for some distance. There were other commanders on my right and left. Whilst great credit is due to other parts of our gallant army, God made my brigade more instrumental than any other in repulsing the main attack. This is for your information only – say nothing about it. Let others speak praise, not myself.*

Within days following Manassas, George Brinton McClellan received a telegram from Washington. It read: "Circumstances make your presence here necessary. . . come hither without delay." Five days after the tragedy at Manassas Junction, on July 21, 1861, McClellan arrived in Washington. Within 48 hours he had assumed command of the Potomac Department of the Federal army.

George McClellan would become one of the most controversial generals in all the Civil War; he was not totally unknown in these early days, having graduated from West Point and served with Lee, Beauregard, Johnston, and Winfield Scott in the war with Mexico. He was no stranger to Lincoln either, for as chief engineer for the Illinois Central Railroad, McClellan had hired Lincoln as an attorney for the company.

At the outbreak of hostilities, McClellan was president of the Ohio and Mississippi Railroad, at the age of 36, living in Cincinnati. He was appointed a major general of Ohio volunteers and in a matter of weeks the same rank in the regular army. The campaign in western Virginia was more a series of contacts with Confederates which, when reported to Washington, elevated McClellan's stock in the War Department, and gave him much more credit then he deserved. But he was the only general with victories of any sort, and, therefore, Lincoln's logical choice to gather some order out of utter chaos.

McClellan wrote in one of his first reports:

I found no army to command; a mere collection of regiments cowering on the banks of the Potomac, some perfectly raw, others dispirited by the recent defeat. I found no preparations whatever for defence, not even to the extent of putting the troops in military positions. Not a regiment was properly encamped, not a single avenue of approach guarded. All was chaos, and the streets, hotels, and bar-rooms were filled with drunken officers and men absent from their regiments without leave – a perfect pandemonium. A determined attack would doubtless have carried Arlington Heights and placed the city at the mercy of a battery of rifled guns.

McClellan's lights burned long into the night. His perseverance astounded all of Washington. From dawn to sunset he drove himself with a force unlike any seen in the military for years. Slowly the army began to catch the "McClellan fever." Within a matter of weeks a new and exciting drama unfolded along the Potomac. Veterans of Manassas were aligned with new recruits and then organized into provisional brigades. New commanders were chosen as divisions gradually took shape. A new army was born, the name for which McClellan himself chose: "I saw the absolute necessity of giving a name to the mass of troops under my command, in order to inspire them with *esprit de corps*; I therefore proposed to call my command 'The Army of the Potomac.'"

Russell of the *London Times* wrote on September 2, 1861: "Never perhaps has a finer body of men in all respects of *physique* been assembled by any power in the world, and there is no reason why their *morale* should not be improved so as to equal that of the best troops in Europe." Russell's statement was no exaggeration. What he had seen was a great transformation, a regeneration of the military forces of the United States. McClellan had started with little – "a collection of undisciplined, ill-officered, and uninstructed men, who were, as a rule, much demoralized by defeat and ready to run at the first shot." He ended with the finest army ever seen on the North American continent. This, and little else, would forever be to his credit.

"No one has denied that McClellan was a marvelous organizer," wrote the Comte de Paris, who served for a period as the general's aide-de-camp:

His military bearing breathed a spirit of frankness, benevolence, and firmness. His look was piercing, his voice gentle, his temper equable, his word of command clear and definite. His encouragement was most affectionate, his reprimand couched in terms of perfect politeness. Discreet.

Four officers of the federal First Brigade Horse Artillery take their ease in camp early in the war, near Brandy Station, Va. (Library of Congress)

as a military or political chief should be, he was slow in bestowing his confidence; but once given, it was never withdrawn. Himself perfectly loyal to his friends, he knew how to inspire others with an absolute devotion.

On July 27, and again on August 9, McClellan made an amazing confession to his wife:

I find myself in a new and strange position here: President, cabinet, Gen. Scott, and all deferring to me. By some strange operation of magic, I seem to have become the power of the land. . . . I receive letter after letter, have conversation after conversation, calling on me to save the nation, alluding to the presidency, dictatorship, etc. As I hope one day to be united with you for ever in heaven, I have no such aspiration. I would cheerfully take the dictatorship and agree to lay down my life when the country is saved. . . . I feel that God has placed a great work in my hands.

A few days later, McClellan wrote: "I have Washington perfectly quiet now. . . . I have restored order very completely already." And indeed he had, but the honeymoon did not last long. Soon the signs of strain between army headquarters and the various departments of the government began to show. "Little Mac" obviously wanted Scott's job of commanding all the armies and was determined not to "respect anything that (was) in the way." The old general had a great deal of respect for McClellan when the war started. Mac had served him well in the Mexican war, and Scott subsequently watched his career carefully. But now McClellan was vying for the top post. His rows with Scott started early and friction grew with each passing day. "The old general always comes in the way," McClellan wrote. "He understands nothing, appreciates nothing. I have to fight my way against him. He is the most dangerous antagonist I have."

The agitation between Scott and McClellan increased until, under pressure from the White House and the War Department, the aged Scott finally retired from the army. On the first day of November 1861, McClellan assumed command of all Federal forces. But by this time the pressure was on McClellan. He had the Army of the Potomac and now he had all the armies. The public began to wonder why he had not taken to the field. The weather was good, the roads were dry, the army was well trained, well supplied, well fed; the army was 168,000 strong, a 35-mile ring of fortifications surrounded Washington. McClellan had written his wife in August: "I handed to the President tonight a carefully considered plan for conducting the war on a large scale. . . . I shall carry this thing on *en grande* and crush the rebels in our campaign . . ." McClellan's retort to his critics: "Let those who criticise me for the delay in creating an army and its material point out an instance when so much has been done with the same means in so short a time."

In the Fall of 1861 the Confederate forces at Manassas numbered at the most 41,000 men "capable of going into battle." Allan Pinkerton, head of a private detective agency employed by McClellan, estimated 100,000 Southern troops. McClellan believed him and made no attempt to reconnoiter with his own scouts. He thus established for the record one major fault on which historians would dwell for a century.

On August 8, the general wrote to Scott: "I am induced to believe that the enemy has at least 100,000 men in front of us . . . with that force at my disposal, I would attack the positions on the other side of the Potomac and at the same time cross the river above the city in force." The Confederates were thinking the same thing. On October 1, General Joseph E. Johnston, now in command at Manassas, told Jefferson Davis that had he 19,000 more men as good as the 41,000 on duty, along with the necessary transportation and ammunition, he could "cross the Potomac and carry the war into the enemy's country."

But as the days went by, McClellan's estimate of Confederate strength grew. Later, in October, he wrote to the Secretary of War: "As you are aware, all the information we have from spies, prisoners, etc., agrees in showing that the enemy have a force on the Potomac not less than 150,000 strong, well drilled and equipped, ably commanded, and strongly intrenched."

And so 1861 came to an end. The Confederates were at Manassas. McClellan remained in Washington.

CHAPTER 3

1862

The new year came and still the Army of the Potomac did not move. "On to Richmond," the newspapers again cried. The weather was mild and the roads dry. "What is such weather *for,* if not for fighting?" asked an artillery officer. Horace Greeley, editor of the New York *Tribune:*

The loyal masses – awed by the obloquy heaped on those falsely accused of having caused the disaster at Bull Run by their ignorant impatience amd precipitancy – stood in silent expectation. They still kept raising regiment after regiment, battery after battery, and hurrying them forward to the all-ingulfing Army of the Potomac, to be in time for the decided movement that must be just at hand – but the torrent was there drowned in a lake of Lethean stagnation. First, we were waiting for reenforcements – which was most reasonable; then, for the requisite drilling and fitting for service – which was just as helpful to the Rebels as to us; then for the leaves to fall – so as to facilitate military movements in a country so wooded and broken as Virginia; then, for cannon – whereof we had already more than 200 first-rate field pieces in Virginia, ready for instant service; and so the long, bright Autumn, and the colder but still favorable December, wore heavily away and saw nothing of moment attempted. Even the Rebel batteries obstructing the lower Potomac were not so much as menaced – the Navy laying the blame on the Army; the Army throwing it back on the Navy – probably both right, or, rather, both wrong; but the next result was nothing done; until the daily repetition of the sterotyped telegraphic bulletin, "All quiet on the Potomac" – which had at first been received with satisfaction; afterward with complacency; at length evoked a broad and general roar of disdainful merriment.

McClellan was commander of all the Federal armies; his obsession was with the Army of the Potomac; his immediate concern was with what faced him across the Potomac River. This would be his folly and haunt him the rest of his days.

Exactly why McClellan relied so heavily on Pinkerton's reports can never be adequately explained. Southern prisoners, escaped Federal prisoners, and Northern citizens trapped behind the lines and then permitted to return to Washington, all confirmed much lower figures for the Confederate army. At least two newspapers, *Harper's Weekly* and the Washington *National Republican*, reported by the end of September that the Rebel force numbered 60,000 troops. That "the total force of the enemy in Virginia does not exceed 100,000 men," one reporter wrote, "is as certain as it can be made by anything short of an actual count." By this date the Army of the Potomac had at least 85,000 men available for advance into the field.

To McClellan, at least, the Army of the Potomac was outnumbered and the general was being plagued with what he called "a set of men to deal with unscrupulous and false." He added that "if possible they will throw whatever blame there is on my shoulders . . . I can't move without more means. . . . the enemy have from three to four times my force; . . . I . . . only wish to save my country, and find the incapables around me will not permit it."

Although the Young Napoleon was growing increasingly weary of Lincoln as his superior ("I am becoming daily more disgusted with this administration – perfectly sick of it."), the Commander in Chief seemed to have "absolute confidence" in the general. Lincoln supported McClellan's repeated delays. "You shall have your own way," the President had told McClellan. And in a December message to the Congress, Lincoln publicly defended the selection of McClellan to head the armies: "It is a fortunate circumstance that neither in council nor country was there, as far as I know, any difference of opinion as to the proper person to be selected . . . there is . . . hope there will be given him, the confidence, and cordial support thus, by fair implication, promised, and without which, he cannot, with so full efficiency, serve the country."

While defending McClellan publicly, however, Lincoln was privately very disturbed. It had become painfully evident that the general had not plans for any offensive action. "I will hold McClellan's horse if he will only bring us success," said the President. Although he was ever mindful of the importance of defending Washington and was determined not to let it rest unmanned, Lincoln wanted McClellan to take to the field before the bad weather of winter arrived. There was still time if he hurried. Therefore, early in December, Lincoln, more to prod McClellan than anything else, submitted a plan of attack on the Confederate forces at Manassas. The general quickly rejected Mr. Lincoln's ideas and replied that he had "actively turned toward another plan of campaign" that he did not think "at all anticipated by the enemy. . ." He told the President nothing more. This was the first inkling of McClellan's forthcoming Urbana plan, which could place him between the enemy at Manassas and the Confederate capital at Richmond. But while the general still kicked it around in his mind, the rains came and winter compounded his problems.

For the first time McClellan had a legitimate excuse for staying in camp. Then he came down with typhoid fever. All military plans in the Eastern theatre came to a complete standstill. Not a single concrete blueprint for action had been proposed since McClellan had come to Washington six months earlier.

On January 27, 1862, Lincoln wrote General War Order No. 1, directing that a general movement of all Federal forces, both army and navy, be made against the Confederates by February 22. The order itself was absurd. Military orders are simply not written a full month in advance of execution with complete disregard for interim events. Lincoln knew this and was severely ridiculed for it, but he had ulterior motives. Pressure on the White House was overwhelming. McClellan was now out of his sickbed, his illness not as severe as Lincoln had thought. How else could he move McClellan into action without openly breaking his publicly stated confidence?

Maria Lydig Daly, wife of a prominent judge, wrote in her diary on January 29, 1862, that "the rebel army. . . threatens Washington, and still hopes to take it, whilst over three hundred thousand soldiers lie opposite them, idle and well-fed, with full pay, their families supported by public charity, their officers spending their time reveling, flirting, and drinking." Mrs. Daly recorded the rumors circulating Washington society: "McClellan, they now say, is incapable, and is striving after the Presidency. . . . It will not be worth having soon."

Years later McClellan defended these accusations when he wrote:

They committed a grave error in supposing me to be politically ambitious and I thinking that I looked forward to military success as a means of reaching the presidential chair. At the same time they knew if I achieved marked success my influence would necessarily be very great throughout the country – an influence which I should certainly have used for the good of the whole country, and not for that of any party at the nation's expense.

The order itself seemed to have little if any effect on McClellan. He responded with a cordial letter of acceptance to the President and then immediately launched another plan of attack on Richmond, this time between the York and James rivers on what was known as the Peninsula.

Neither Stanton nor Lincoln was overly enthusiastic about the proposals. Yet, once again the President consented, this time with certain conditions. Washington could not be left unguarded, nor could Manassas, now that it was in Federal control. McClellan must see to that before he left. Stanton's message to McClellan showed his impatience: "Move the remainder of the force down the Potomac, choosing a new

The capture of Ft. Donelson on the Kentucky-Tennessee border by Gen. U.S. Grant gave the Union its first major victory in February 1862. A portion of the battle is shown in this engraving, based on a painting. (Library of Congress)

base at Fortress Monroe, or anywhere between here and there; or at all events, move the remainder of the army at once in pursuit of the enemy by some route." Few times in the history of this country has a general taken to the field with such wholesale mistrust from his superiors.

The first regiments of the Army of the Potomac began their amphibious movement from Alexandria on March 17. They would establish their supply base around April 1 at Fortress Monroe, which was still held by Federal forces. McClellan himself was anxious to get started. He left Alexandria on April 1 after a brief interview with the President, who had come to see him off. The general made no attempt to assure Lincoln that he was following his orders to leave Washington secure. It was not until after he had departed that a message arrived at the War Department indicating the arrangements he had made. McClellan stated that he had left 73,456 men to guard the capital. In this total he had included those troops at Manassas and surrounding areas, some 35,000 of which were in the Shenandoah Valley, and those actually scattered along the Potomac and in Washington. He had counted men twice, counted non-existing regiments which he proposed calling up, and counted forces already moved to other areas. After his letter had been deciphered and appraisals made by the War Department, it appeared that only 19,000 men were in a position to actually defend the city.

Had McClellan deliberately disobeyed Lincoln's orders? It looked as though he had. Thoughts of treason again entered Lincoln's mind.

At the time this dangerous situation was realized, two corps were still in Alexandria awaiting departure for the Peninsula. Lincoln ordered one, the First Corps under Irvin McDowell, to remain, giving the city an additional 30,000 men. McClellan protested, stating that he was beginning to meet the enemy head on and that he needed all the troops he could get. He was "outnumbered" again. Lincoln, suppressing his anger and sidestepping pressure from Congress and the War Department to bring McClellan back on charges of treason and conspiracy, wrote the general a kind but firm letter on April 9:

Your dispatches complaining that you are not properly sustained, while they do not offend me, do pain me very much. After you left, I ascertained that less than twenty thousand unorganized men, without a single field battery, were all you designed to be left for the defence of Washington. My explicit order that Washington should . . . be left entirely secure, had been neglected. It was precisely this that drove me to detain McDowell.

The President concluded with a very polite suggestion that the general move at once and without any complaints. It had overtones of irritation and warning:

And, once more let me tell you, it is indispensable to **you** *that you strike a blow. I am powerless to help this. You will do me the justice to remember I always insisted that going down the Bay in search of a field, instead of fighting at or near Manassas, was only shifting, and not surmounting, a difficulty – that we would find the same enemy, and the same or equal intrenchments, at either place. The country will not fail to note – is now noting – that the present hesitation to move upon an intrenched enemy, is but the story of Manassas repeated.*

I beg to assure you that I have never written you, or spoken to you, in greater kindness of feeling than now, now with a fuller purpose to sustain you, so far as in my most anxious judgement, I consistently can. **But you must act.**

McClellan's relationship with the White House and the War Department grew steadily worse. The next few months would reveal, as far as the President was concerned, the difference between McClellan the fighting man and McClellan the administrator, and they would clearly show how empty his victories in western Virginia had been, if, indeed, anyone by this time considered them victories at all. McClellan's supporters would later argue that the general had done the best he could on the Peninsula under existing circumstances, but McClellan's best was simply not good enough for the President and his Secretary of War.

Despite his anxiety for a decisive victory and his apprehensions at sending the army so far from Washington, Lincoln continued to suppress a strong anti-McClellan movement in the administration. McClellan failed to recognize this, or perhaps he did not want to recognize it. The benevolent yet firm attitude with which Lincoln wrote the letter of April 9 completely escaped the general's eye for reality, as had all other sincere attempts to prod him into action. McClellan knew for a fact that Stanton had come to dislike him intensely. Without stopping to consider the opportunities Lincoln had offered him, he blindly assumed the President was also conspiring against him.

On April 11, McClellan wrote of his woes to his wife Ellen:

Don't worry about the wretches [in Washington]; they have done nearly their worst, and can't do much more. I am sure that I will win in the end, in spite of their rascality. History will present a sad record of these traitors who are willing to sacrifice the country and its army for personal spite and personal aims. The people will soon understand the whole matter.

There can be no doubt of McClellan's loyalty to the Union. At the same time there is no doubt of Lincoln's loyalty. The general should have seen this and given the President his due. He should also have known, certainly after six months, that Lincoln was his mentor and the only thin thread binding him to his army. Instead he wrote to his wife:

They [Lincoln and his cabinet] are determined to ruin me in any event and by any means: first, by endeavoring to force me into premature movements [Lincoln's insistence on a drive on Manassas], knowing that a failure would end my military career; afterwards by witholding the means necessary to achieve success [Lincoln's withdrawal of McDowell's corps to defend Washington]. They determined that I should not succeed, and carried out their determinations only too well and at a fearful sacrifice of blood, time and treasure.

Harpers Ferry (these pages), in West Virginia since 1863, lies at the meeting of the Shenandoah and Potomac rivers and was a strategic prize during much of the Civil War. It was also the site of radical John Brown's famous pre-war raid in October 1859. Brown seized the town with its armory and arsenal in hopes of raising a slave rebellion. He barricaded his small force in the engine house (facing page). Ironically, the U.S. government sent troops under Army Col. Robert E. Lee to capture Brown. The engine house was successfully stormed and Brown captured by an assault force led by Lt. J.E.B. Stuart.

The first shots of conflict struck Ft. Sumter (these pages) in Charleston Harbor early on the morning of April 12, 1861. After its capture by the Confederates, the fort withstood several determined efforts by Federal forces to retake the commanding position, and it remained in Southern hands until the War's end. The impressive structure still shows the marks of repeated bombardment and was armed with large-caliber, rifled Parrot guns, now on display.

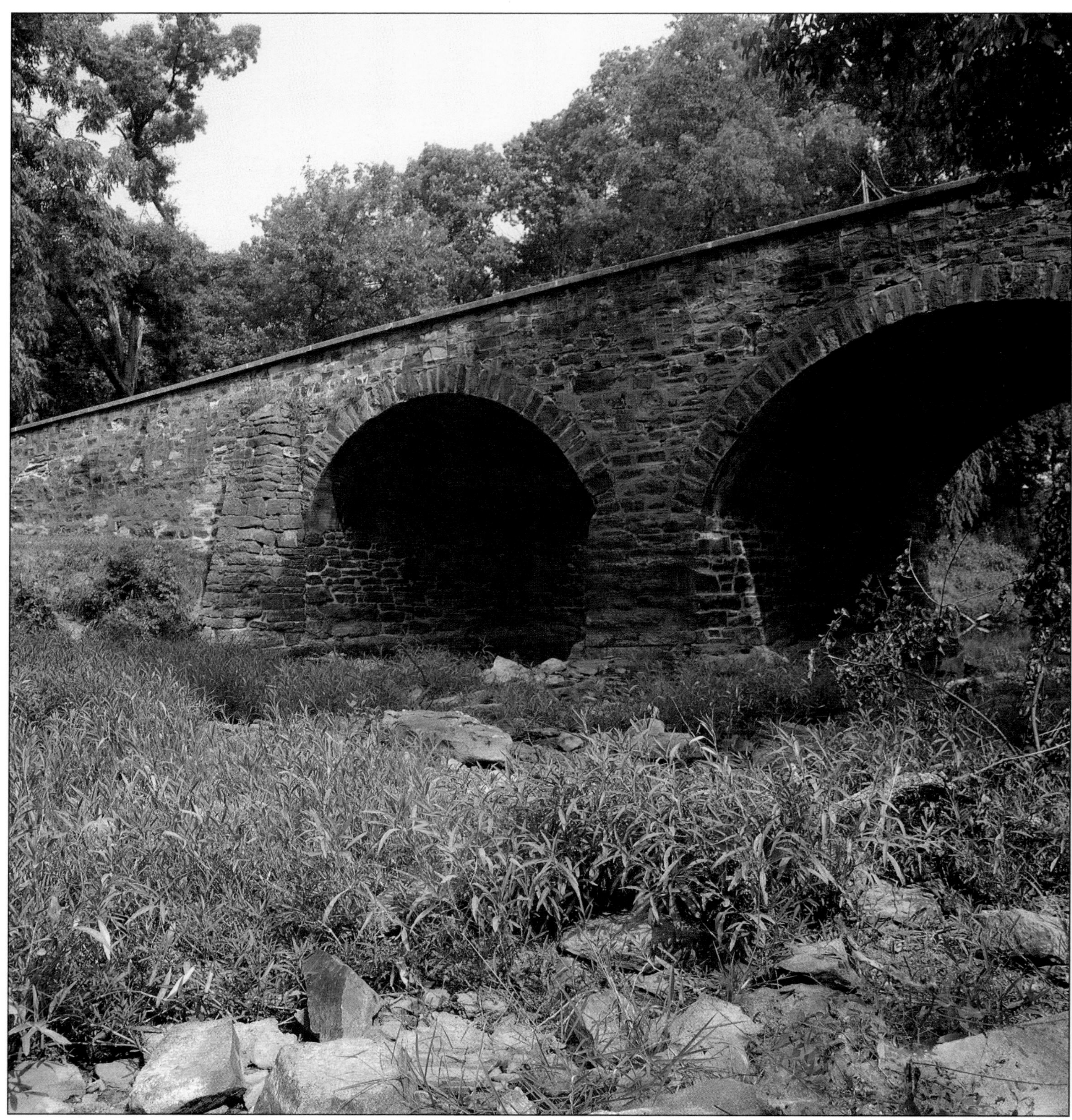

Two battles were fought at Manassas, Virginia, nearly a year apart. In July 1861, the Union Army hoped to open the road to Richmond. The Federals began the battle near the Stone Bridge across Bull Run Creek (facing page and below). Much of the first day's fighting swirled around artillery positions on Henry Hill (right), finally held by Confederate Gen. Thomas Jackson. The Henry House was captured by the Confederates.

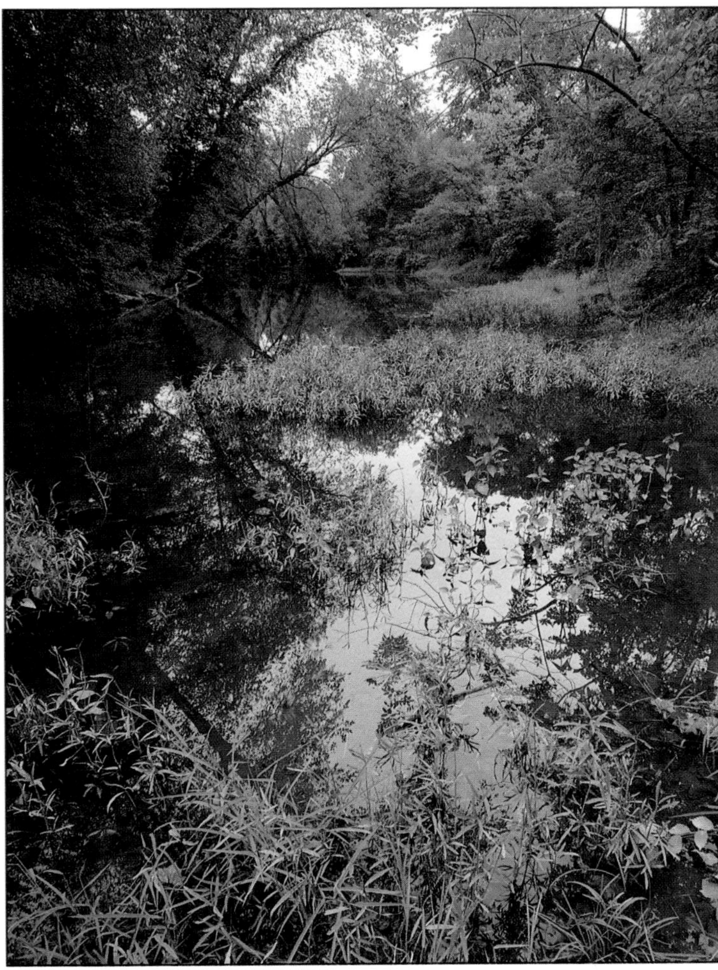

First Manassas was a disheartening defeat for the Union. The Battle of Second Manassas in 1862 was also a Confederate triumph. The Stone House (right) stood in the middle of the battlefield and served as a hospital, miraculously surviving both battles. The eastern theatre of operations moved back and forth over the same territory throughout the four years of war, and several places in Virginia and Maryland – like Manassas – were fought over more than once.

The Union cause fared better in the West than in Virginia and Maryland. The major goal of the Federals was to clear the western rivers of Confederate strongholds. So long as the South held the transportation waterways, it could fight on indefinitely. Two important points on the Tennessee and Cumberland Rivers, Ft. Henry and Ft. Donelson, were the first targets of a joint water and land campaign under Gen. Ullyses S. Grant and naval Flag Officer Andrew Foote. Lightly-held Ft. Henry fell easily in February 1862. The Confederates fought hard at reinforced Ft. Donelson (these pages). Foote's fleet was repulsed by powerful river batteries (above). Grant was more successful, and forced Confederate commander Gen. Simon Bolivar Buckner, his close friend before the War, to accept the famous demand for "unconditional surrender." Cut off from support, Buckner had no choice, despite the inherent strength of his defenses. He met Grant at the Dover Hotel (facing page top left) and capitulated.

A Confederate monument (top right) is now part of the extensive military park at Ft. Donelson, which also offers demonstrations of musketry (right). The victory at Donelson was the first major triumph for the Union, elevating Grant into the public eye and setting the pattern for the eventual wresting of the western river system from the grasp of the Confederacy. The Union's strategy of combined river and land campaigns proved successful in the long run.

The Battle of Shiloh (or Pittsburgh Landing) cost 23,000 casualties in two days of fighting and nearly secured the Confederacy's western front. The brilliant Southern commander Albert Sidney Johnston surprised Grant's army in camp with its back to the Tennessee River while the Union commander was waiting for Gen. Buell's army to join him. The Confederates pushed Grant's men into desperate positions, but the Federals held. Soldiers from both sides colored Bloody Pond (facing page bottom) with their wounds. Union resistance stiffened at the Sunken Road (facing page top center) and gave Grant time to reorganize. The Confederates effectively used massed artillery (above) to batter their opponents, who just evaded disaster. At the height of the first day's fighting, Johnston was struck and slowly bled to death from the neglected wound. He expired under a tree (facing page top left) on the battlefield. Strengthened by the arrival of reinforcements, Grant lashed out on the second day and the Confederates were forced to retreat. Left: the George Cabin, and (facing page top right) a Confederate monument, both in Shiloh National Military Park.

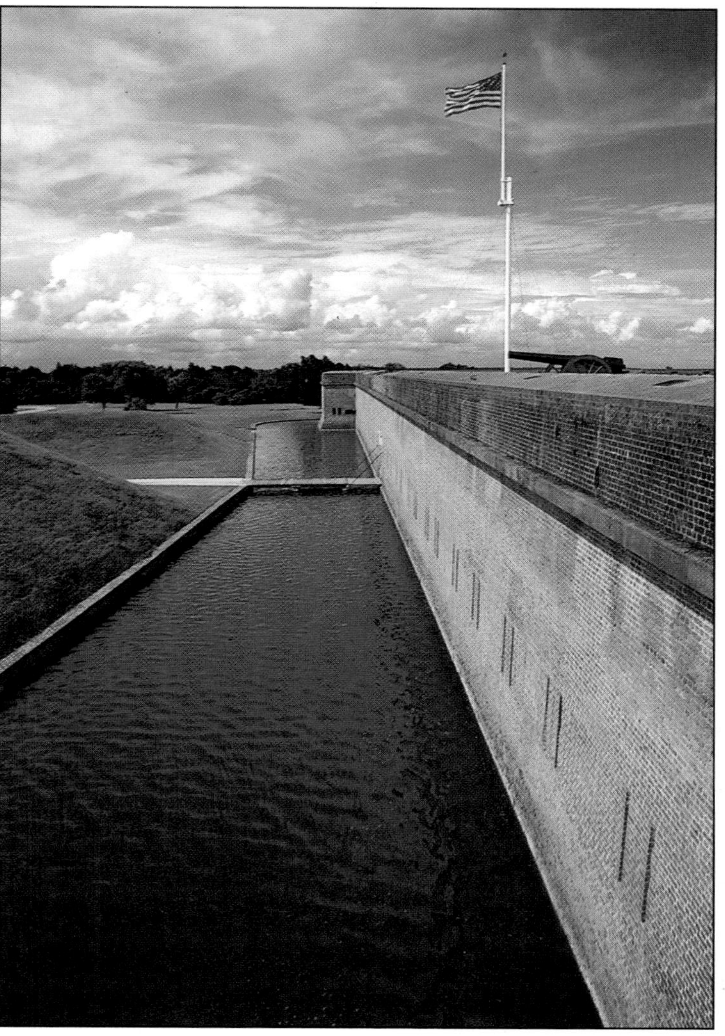

Combined Union naval and land forces tried to strangle the South's economy with a blockade and the capture of key Atlantic coast ports such as Ft. Pulaski (these pages), a massive brick fort commanding the water approaches to Savannah, Georgia, from an island in the river. Thought to be impregnable, the fortress was reduced by a 30-hour bombardment from new-style heavy guns and mortars in April 1862 and surrendered, sealing off Savannah as a Confederate port.

The fiercest struggles at Antietam took place around a small Dunker church (right). Ripe grain in a 40-acre patch, "The Cornfield," was clipped to ground level by musket balls. Both sides attacked and counterattacked, leaving hundreds of soldiers dead or dying before the sun was even well up. Entire regiments were reduced to a dozen survivors within minutes. A fresh Union attack near the church was smashed by Confederate artillery. By midday the fighting had moved southward toward the creek. The Union assault came up against a slightly sunken road called Bloody Lane, filled with Confederate troops. Wave after wave of advancing infantry were swept away until finally the Southern defenders were overrun. A Union flanking maneuver threatened Lee's main position on high ground, but troops under hapless Ambrose Burnside failed to take a key stone bridge across the creek (above) until too late. Toward the end of the day, fresh Southern troops under A.P. Hill arrived and struck the Union flank, throwing it back and ending the bloodiest day of the War. Lee withdrew across the Potomac to Virginia – undefeated but his invasion stymied.

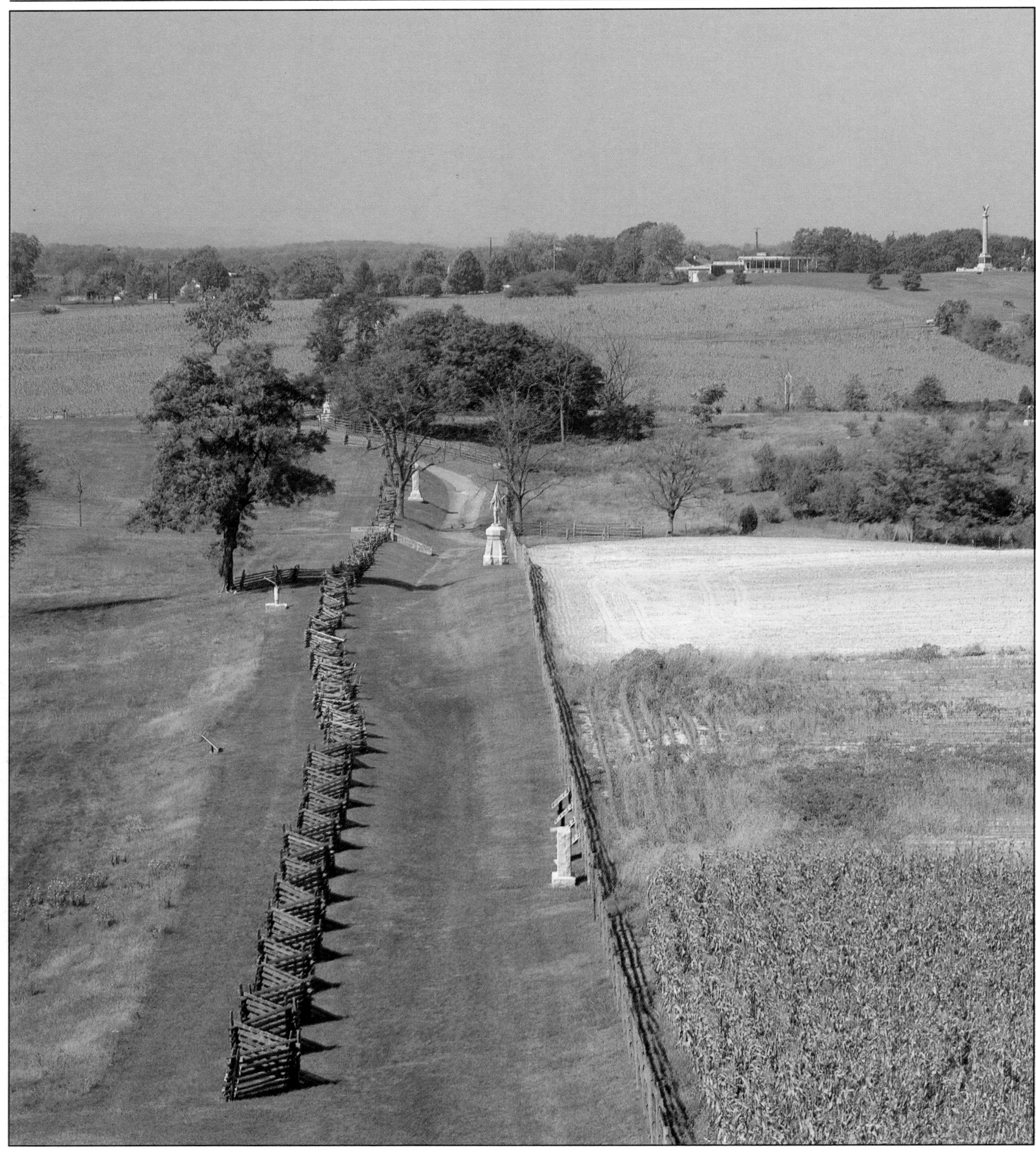

After he launched the Peninsula Campaign, seldom did McClellan speak of the President in anything but disparaging terms. He referred to Lincoln as the "original Gorilla" and added: "What a specimen to be at the head of our affairs now!" A.K. McClure, Lincoln's friend and confident, wrote: "McClellan [did] both himself and Lincoln the gravest injustice. I am quite sure that the two men of all the nation who most desired McClellan's success in the field were Lincoln and McClellan themselves."

On January 14, President Lincoln made a most important change in his administration. Simon Cameron, inefficient Secretary of War, was replaced by Edwin McMasters Stanton, brilliant lawyer of some renown, energetic, outspoken, a man who liked and demanded power, and a Democrat, a man to be reckoned with. McClellan, regarded as a prominent member of the Democratic party, would now have at least one friend in the administration, or so he thought. Between Stanton's appointment and his actual occupation of office, he had gone to McClellan's home with a proposition that he would not accept the office unless the general was certain that he could make some valuable contribution.

McClellan consented, although he was highly perturbed at Lincoln for making the appointment without consulting him first. Exactly why Stanton went to McClellan is unknown, for he embodied precisely what McClellan opposed. Where the general was against any interference with military affairs by civilians, Stanton had an intense dislike for professionally trained soldiers. He would, in ensuing months, become one of McClellan's bitterest enemies. That evening, however, Stanton played one of his best roles. "He said that acceptance would involve very great personal sacrifices on his part, and that the only possible inducement would be that he might have it in his power to aid me in the work of putting down the rebellion; that he was willing to devote all his time, intellect, and energy to my assistance, and that together, we would soon bring the war to an end. If I wished him to accept he would do so, but only on my account . . ."

In late January, McClellan showed the first signs of his Urbana plan to the War Department. Stanton told him to take it directly to the President, which McClellan did. The general advocated an amphibious movement down the Potomac and through the Chesapeake Bay, to Urbana at the mouth of the Rapahannock River, where he would establish a base and from there a direct line to Richmond. This not only would pull the potentially dangerous Confederate army away from the fringes of Washington, but it would employ the easiest possible method of supplying his army, via naval routes, the York River, and then by rail from West Point to Richmond. Last, McClellan announced, this plan would "gain a decisive victory which [would] end the war."

Lincoln wasted no time in disapproving the plan. He immediately repeated his order for the Army of the Potomac to move on Manassas not later than February 22. McClellan was panic-stricken at the thought of the overwhelming odds facing him, and he begged Lincoln to reconsider his Urbana scheme. After much soul-searching, and much against his better judgement, the President finally relented. McClellan felt so much better that for the first time in months he had some nice things to say about Lincoln. But the President was obsessed with a fear for the safety of Washington. While McClellan was sailing away on his adventure, the success of which Lincoln doubted, the Rebels might launch a full-scale attack against the capital. Lincoln had made a serious mistake in not forcing McClellan to attack Manassas and clean out the thorn that was in his side. The more he thought about it, the more it pained him that he had not insisted. Finally, on March 8, the President summoned the general to the White House to discuss "a very ugly matter."

Rumors had been circulating throughout official Washington that McClelllan was deliberately leaving the city to the Rebels, "that my plan of campaign was. . . conceived with the traitorous intent of removing its defenders from Washington, and thus giving over to the enemy the capital and the government, thus left defenceless."

Only McClellan's account of his meeting with Lincoln remains. In this he quotes the President as saying that it looked "much like treason" to him. The general was enraged. "I arose, and, in a manner perhaps not altogether decorous towards the chief magistrate, desired that he should retract the expression, telling him that I could permit no one to couple the word treason with my name." Lincoln assured him that it was only rumor and that he himself did not believe it to be an act of treason. Nonetheless, McClellan insisted on proving to the President that there was no basis to the stories by laying out detailed plans for the Richmond campaign, the first time that he had done so. Again the President reluctantly approved; but to put a check on McClellan, he issued an order placing the 12 new divisions of the army into four corps commanded by four senior officers, all of whom outranked McClellan, and several of whom were older and who resented the young commander.

On top of all of McClellan's problems, the Confederates gave him the real setback. The day following his session with the President, the general was informed that the Rebels had evacuated their camp at Manassas and repaired to a position behind the Rappahannock. This forced a cancellation of the Urbana plan. In a rush of blind fury, McClellan ordered an immediate advance and occupation of the enemy's site. In so doing, he nearly ended his career. It not only appeared foolish, moving so rapidly into an evacuated area after months of delays, but once there, it was apparent to all that the total number of the enemy's forces was far less than everyone had been led to believe. Now the suspicions about "Little Mac" began to gain impetus. It would be recalled that he had done this same thing in western Virginia. Correspondents sent back stories telling of a camp which could not have supported more than 60,000 troops, and reports were offered second hand that the Confederates themselves had stated these figures. To hide his embarrassment, McClellan rebuked the papers for trifling "with the reputation of an army" and deluding the country with "gross understatements of the number of the enemy." Rather than question Pinkerton's figures, he remained loyal to the original report.

(It is significant to note that though McClellan's memoirs were written years later, when, in retrospect, the Pinkerton figures appeared totally ridiculous, he still failed through quite obvious intentions to give the true picture. Not once did he alter, even through footnotes, any facts or figures, which by that time were contradictive of common knowledge. Nor did the editors, who on several occasions defended the general's statements, attempt to make corrections.)

This series of events left Lincoln little choice but to issue his War Order No. 3: "Major General McClellan having personally taken the field at the head of the Army of the Potomac, until otherwise ordered, he is relieved from the command of the other Military departments, he retaining command of the Department of the Potomac."

There immediately sprang up two schools of thought on the significance of this order. It was obvious that Lincoln had taken about all he could take. The pressure from the War Department to remove the general from command, coupled with his increasing anxieties for some definitive military actions in the East, forced him into a decision that was long overdue. On the other hand, the order had stated "until otherwise ordered," which clearly meant to McClellan supporters, as it did to the general himself, that this was only temporary and that it had been done because McClellan, being in the field with the Army of the Potomac, could not direct overall operations of all the commands.

But it was with a troubled heart, mindful of enemies, seen and unseen, that McClellan early in April set about his operations on that peninsula of land between the York and James Rivers. General Peter S. Michie, West Point instructor and biographer of McClellan, commented: "General McClellan had now arrived at the most critical point of his career as a commander of an army – but for the first time, the real enemy and real war." He could take Yorktown easily with the 50,000 men he had available on landing; yet he must move rapidly, for Johnston would be advancing southward from his position near Culpeper to reinforce the small force under Maj. Gen. John Magruder. However, McClellan did not move fast enough. Magruder had set up a line of about 11,000 men across the Peninsula from Yorktown, behind the Warwick River, to the James, a distance of about 14 miles. McClellan knew, at least at first, that he outnumbered the Confederates, but Magruder pulled a Confederate stunt that triggered McClellan's old malady. The young Confederate general, fully aware of his weak position (he hardly had enough to man the lines), and knowing that it would be days before reinforcements could arrive, began shifting his units back and forth in full view of Federal pickets. The deception had its intended effect. The Pinkerton boys worked overtime and came up with a report that startled McClellan. Had an attack been inaugurated immediately, the defenses would have been broken, but McClellan was "outnumbered" again. He settled back for a long siege, which was actually what he preferred anyway.

On April 6, Lincoln telegraphed his general: "I think you better break the enemies' line. . . at once." That night McClellan wrote his wife: "I was much tempted to reply that he had better come and do it himself." The siege continued. By the 17th, Johnston had arrived from the North, taken overall command and swelled the ranks to 55,000. He wrote to Robert E. Lee, then serving in the capacity of military advisor to Jefferson Davis: "No one but McClellan would have hesitated to attack." It seemed that the Confederates knew McClellan as well, if not better, than did Washington.

General Joseph E. Johnston:

It was ascertained, about the fifth of April, that the Federal army was marching from Fort Monroe toward Yorktown. The President was convinced that the entire army was then on the Peninsula. He therefore directed me to make defensive arrangements.

General J. Bankhead Magruder was in charge of our troops in the Lower Peninsula. That officer had estimated the importance of at least delaying the invaders until an army capable of coping with them could be formed, meanwhile opposing them with about one tenth of their number. This judicious course saved Richmond.

I hastened back to Richmond to see the President. Instead of delaying the Federal army, I proposed that it should be encountered in front of Richmond by one quite as numerous, formed by uniting all the available forces in the Carolinas, Georgia and Norfolk. This great army, surprising that of the United States by an attack when it was expecting to besiege Richmond, would be almost certain to win, and the enemy, defeated a hundred times from Fort Monroe, their place of refuge, could scarcely escape destruction. Such a victory would decide not only the campaign, but the war.

The President, who had heard me with apparent interest, replied that the question was so important that he would hear it fully discussed before making his decision and desired me to meet General George W. Randolph (Secretary of War) and General Lee in his office at an appointed time for the purpose; at my suggestion, he authorized me to invite Major Generals Gustavus W. Smith and James Longstreet to the conference.

In the discussion that followed, General Randolph objected to the plan proposed because it included at least the temporary abandonment of Norfolk, which would involve the probable loss of the materials for many vessels of war. General Lee opposed it because he thought that the withdrawal from South Carolina and Georgia of any considerable number of troops would expose the important seaports of Charleston and Savannah to the danger of capture. He thought, too, that the Peninsula had excellent fields of battle for a small army contending with a great one. General Longstreet took little part, which I attributed to his deafness. I maintained that all to be accomplished, by any success attainable on the Peninsula, would be to delay the enemy two or three weeks in his march to Richmond, and that

The meeting of the Confederate ironclad *Virginia* (called the *Merrimac* in the North) and the innovative but untested Union *Monitor* on March 9, 1862 at Hampton Roads off Norfolk, Va., was the most storied naval engagement of the War. This engraving was based on a sketch by a sergeant of New York Volunteers who witnessed the battle. (Library of Congress)

success would soon give us back everything temporarily abandoned to achieve it.

At 1:00 a.m. the President announced his decision in favor of General Lee's opinion.

During the four-week seige of Yorktown, the Federal forces grew as additional units of the Army of the Potomac arrived by water at Fortress Monroe. At this point, after a full month of build-up, a Federal thrust at Johnston would surely have netted great results; but the Confederates, ever mindful of the odds and not wishing to be caught, pulled back to Williamsburg on May 5. When McClellan marched, he repeated his Manassas "victory." The Rebels had evacuated. Lincoln would be reminded of his message of April 9. He had told the general then that the country would not fail to note "that the present hesitation to move upon an entrenched enemy is but the story of Manassas repeated."

The President and Stanton visited the Peninsula immediately after the army occupied Yorktown. McClellan could not, or would not, see them. He was busy – busy sizing up the results of the battle at Williamsburg which had inflicted rather serious damages on the Union right wing that had followed Johnston's withdrawal. Although the official party from Washington remained behind the Federal lines for six days, McClellan continued to busy himself with an amphibious movement up the York River from Yorktown to West Point. Lincoln returned to Washington without talking to his general.

By May 25, McClellan was on the Chickahominy River, about seven miles from Richmond, and he was extremely nervous. According to his intelligence, the Confederate forces then numbered 200,000 troops. Exactly how Pinkerton established such a fantastic figure is unknown. He was 130,000 men from the truth. McClellan pleaded with Washington for more troops. Anyone would do, even McDowell, on whom he blamed the withdrawal of the First Corps from his army. Lincoln replied that he would aid the army in every way he could and that he would send McDowell by land to join the forces at Richmond, thus keeping a sizable army between the two capitals and preventing any Confederate surprise thrust at Washington. But McDowell never got under way.

Joseph E. Johnston:

After reaching the Chickahominy, a river which separates

the peninsula into a northern and southern section, General McClellan's troops advanced very slowly. Three corps were on and above the railroad on the north side of the river, and two below it, south of the river and on the Williamsburg Road. The latter, after crossing the stream at Bottom's Bridge on the twenty-second, apparently remained stationary for several days, constructing a line of entrenchments two miles in advance of the bridge. I hoped that their advance would give us an opportunity to make a successful attack upon these two corps, by increasing the interval between them and the larger portion of their army remaining beyond the Chickahominy.

McClellan to his wife:

May 15, 1862. *Another wet, horrid day! It rained a little yesterday morning, more in the afternoon, much during the night, and has been amusing itself in the same manner very persistently all day. I had expected to move headquarters to White House today, but this weather has put the roads in such condition that I cannot do it. I think the blows the Rebels have lately received ought to break them up; but one can do no more than speculate. Still raining hard and dismally.*

May 16. *Have just arrived over horrid roads. No further movement possible until they improve. The house is where Washington's courtship took place and where he resided when first married. I do not permit it to be occupied by anyone, nor the grounds around. It is a beautiful spot directly on the banks of the Pamunkey.*

May 17. *I am pushing on the advanced guard and reconnaissance in various directions. We gain some ground every day; but our progress has been slow on account of the execrable nature of the roads, as well as their extreme narrowness and fewness in number. I am very sorry that we could not have advanced more rapidly; my only consolation is that it has been impossible. Just think of its requiring forty-eight hours to move two divisions with their trains five miles! Nothing could be much worse than that. The fastest way to move in wet weather is not to move at all.*

A Confederate war clerk by the name of Jones watched the developments:

May 26. *General Lee is strengthening the army. Every day additional regiments are coming. We are now so strong that no one fears the result when the great battle takes place. McClellan has delayed too long, and he is doomed to defeat.*

May 27. *More troops came in last night and were marched to the camp at once, so that the Yankees will know nothing of it.*

May 29. *More troops are marching into the city, and General Lee has them sent out in such manner and at such times as to elude the observations of even the spies.*

May 31. *Everybody is upon the tiptoe of expectation. It has been announced (in the streets!) that a battle would take place this day, and hundreds of men, women and children repaired to the hills to listen and possibly see the firing. The great storm day before yesterday, it is supposed, has so swollen the Chickahominy as to prevent McClellan's left wing from retreating, and reinforcements from being sent to its relief. The time is well chosen by General Johnston for the attack, but it was bad policy to let it be known where and when it would be made; for, no doubt, McClellan was advised of our plans an hour or so after they were promulgated in the streets. Whose fault is this? Johnston could hardly be responsible for it, because he is very reticent and appreciates the importance of keeping his purposes concealed from the enemy. Surely none of his subordinates divulged the secret, for none but generals of divisions knew it.*

May 31. *The President took an affectionate leave of General Johnston, and General Lee held his hand a long time and admonished him to take care of his life. There was no necessity of him to endanger it. This General Johnston, I believe, has had the misfortune to be wounded in most of his battles.*

The French Prince de Joinwille, on McClellan's staff during the Peninsula Campaign, and Jefferson Davis, President of the Confederacy, who saw some of the fighting, described the battles of Seven Pines and Fair Oaks.

Davis:

In the forenoon of the thirty-first of May, riding out on the New Bridge Road, I heard firing in the direction of Seven Pines. The enemy had constructed redoubts, with long lines of rifle pits covered by abatis, from below Bottom's Bridge to within less than two miles of New Bridge, and had constructed bridges to connect his forces on the north and south sides of the Chickahominy. The left of his forces on the south side was thrown forward from the river; the right was on its bank and covered by its slope. Our main force was on the right flank of our position. There were small tracts of cleared land, but most of the ground was wooded and much of it so covered with water as seriously to embarrass the movement of troops.

When we reached the left of our line, our men had driven the enemy from his advanced encampment, and he had fallen back behind an open field to the bank of the river where, in a dense wood, was concealed an infantry line with artillery in position. Soon after our arrival, General Johnston, who had gone farther to the right where the conflict was expected and whither reinforcements from the left were marching, was brought back severely wounded and was removed from the field.

Our troops on the left made vigorous assaults under most disadvantageous circumstances, but were each time repulsed with heavy loss.

The rain during the night of the thirtieth had swollen the Chickahominy; it was rising when the Battle of Seven Pines was fought, but had not reached such height as to prevent the enemy from using his bridges; consequently, General Edwin

V. Sumner, during the engagement, brought over his corps as a reinforcement. With the true instinct of the soldier to march upon fire, when the sound of the battle reached him, he formed his corps and stood under arms waiting for an order to advance. He came too soon for us and, but for his forethought and promptitude, he would have arrived too late for his friends. It may be granted that his presence saved the left wing of the Federal army from defeat.

De Joinville:

At the moment it was attacked, the Federal army occupied a position having the form of a V. The base of the V was at the Bottom's Bridge near where the railroad crosses the Chickahominy. The left arm stretched toward Richmond; it was composed of four divisions echeloned, one behind the other, between Fair Oaks and Savage's stations, and encamped in the woods on both sides of the road. The other arm of the V, the right, followed the left bank of the river. Between the two arms of the V flowed the Chickahominy. Three or four bridges had been undertaken, only one of which was serviceable on the thirty-first of May. It had been built by General Sumner, and saved the army that day from disaster.

It was against the left wing of the army that every effort of the enemy was directed. That wing had its outposts at Fair Oaks Station and at a place called Seven Pines, on the Williamsburg Road. There the Federals had thrown up a redoubt in a clearing.

The pickets and sentries were violently driven in; the woods which surround Fair Oaks and Seven Pines were filled with clouds of the enemy. The troops rushed to arms and fought in desperation; but their adversaries' forces constantly increased, and their losses did not stop them. The redoubt of the Seven Pines was surrounded, and its defenders died bravely. In vain Generals E.D. Keyes and H.M. Naglee exhausted themselves in a thousand efforts to keep their soldiers together; they were not listened to.

S.P. Heintzelman rushed to the rescue with his two divisions. Philip Kearny arrived in good time to re-establish the fight. Hiram G. Berry's brigade advanced firm as a wall into the midst of the disordered mass which wandered over the battlefield and did more by its example than the most powerful reinforcements. About a mile of ground had been lost, fifteen pieces of cannon, the camp of the division of the advanced guard, that of General Silas Casey; but then we held our own. A sort of line of battle was formed across the woods, perpendicularly to the road and railroad, and there the repeated assaults of the enemy's masses were resisted. The left could not be turned, where the White Oak Swamp was, an impassable morass; but the right might be surrounded. At that very moment a strong column of Confederates was directed against that side. If it succeeded in interposing between Bottom's Bridge and the Federal troops, the entire left wing was lost; but precisely at this moment – at six o'clock in the evening – General Sumner, who had succeeded in passing the Chickahominy over the bridge constructed by his troops, arrived suddenly on the left flank of the column with which the enemy was endeavoring to cut off Heintzelman and Keyes.

He planted in the clearing a battery which he had succeeded in bringing with him. The discharging of these pieces made terrible havoc in the opposing ranks. In vain he rushed on it himself; nothing could shake the Federals who, at nightfall, valiantly led by General Sumner in person, threw themselves upon the enemy at the point of the bayonet and drove him furiously, with frightful slaughter and fear, back as far as Fair Oaks Station.

Night put an end to the combat.

De Joinville on the second day:

At the earliest dawn of June 1 the combat was resumed with great fury. The enemy came on in a body, but without order or method, and rushed upon the Federals, who, knowing that they were inferior in numbers and without hope of being supported, did not attempt to do more than resist and hold their ground. They fought with fierce determination on both sides, without any noise, without any cries, and whenever they were too hard pressed they made a charge with the bayonet. The artillery, placed on the eminences in the rear, fired shells over the combatants.

Toward midday the fire gradually diminished, then ceased. The enemy retreated, but the Federals were not in a position to pursue them. No one knew then what a loss the Southerners had suffered in the person of their commander, General Johnston, who was severely wounded. It was due to his absence, in a great measure, that the attacks against the Federal army in the morning were unskillful. When the firing ceased at midday the Confederates retreated in a state of inextricable confusion. The North had lost 5,000 men, the South at least 8,000, but the results were as barren on one side as on the other.

The battle was a draw, if anything; its most important result was bringing Robert E. Lee to the field as a commander.

Davis:

General R.E. Lee was now in immediate command and thenceforward directed the movements of the army in front of Richmond. Laborious and exact in details as he was vigilant and comprehensive in grand strategy, a power, with which the public had not credited him, soon became manifest in all that makes an army a rapid, accurate, compact machine, with responsive motion in all its parts.

On the next morning, June 1, he took command of the troops. During the night our forces on the left had fallen back from their position at the close of the previous day's battle, but those on the right remained in the one they had gained, and some combats occurred there between the opposing forces.

Both combatants claimed the victory. The withdrawal of the Confederate forces on the day after the battle from the ground on which it was fought certainly gives color to the claim of the enemy, though that was really the result of a policy much broader that the occupation of the field of Seven Pines.

Our army now was in line in front of Richmond, but without entrenchments. General Lee immediately commenced the construction of an earthwork for a battery on our left flank and a line of entrenchment to the right, necessarily feeble because of our deficiency in tools. It seemed to be the intention of the enemy to assail Richmond by regular approaches, which our numerical inferiority and want of engineer troops, as well as the deficiency of proper utensils, made it improbable that we should be able to resist.

McDowell had received his orders to join McClellan on May 26 and should have been there before Seven Pines, but his corps did not leave, and for very good reasons. Major Sidney W. Thaxter explained:

The crew of the *Monitor* lounges on deck in July 1862. The ship later sank in heavy seas, but its design was reproduced effectively by the Union in later versions, known generically as "monitors." (Library of Congress)

Early in May 1862 the line of operations of the Union armies in Virginia extended from the James River, a few miles below Richmond, to the Blue Ridge, with a heavy force in the Shenandoah Valley. This line was held on the left by General McClellan with about 100,000 fine troops; in the center by General McDowell with about 40,000 troops; and on the right by General Nathaniel P. Banks with a movable force of about 15,000 men. McClellan had come to a halt before the Confederate Army of Northern Virginia, which covered Richmond and was ready to oppose his further progress. McClellan was calling for reinforcements, and the government had unwillingly determined upon moving McDowell down to join McClellan's right wing and transfer a part of Banks's force from the Shenandoah Valley to that of McDowell. This concentration of Union forces against the army under General Johnston was what the Rebel government feared, and what it bent its energies to prevent.

The position of the Rebel armies was as follows: the Army of Northern Virginia of about 75,000 troops under General J.E. Johnston was within the entrenchments of Richmond; 15,000 troops under General R.H. Anderson were observing McDowell; 8,000 men under General R.S. Ewell stood near Gordonsville, ready to reinforce the army of General Johnston at Richmond or move to the support of Stonewall Jackson, who with about 8,000 troops was encamped at Swift Run Gap, threatening the flank of General Banks if he should continue his movement up the Valley; lastly, about 4,000 men under General Edward Johnson, a few miles west of Staunton, opposed the advance of General John C. Fremont who had two small brigades under R.H. Milroy and Robert C. Schenck. While awaiting developments, Jackson proposed to General Lee (who was at this time general in chief with headquarters at Richmond) a bold plan of campaign, which was approved and immediately put in execution. This plan was to attack Milroy and Schenck, then move speedily back into the Shenandoah Valley, take up the army of General Ewell and drive Banks down the Valley. This plan would at least neutralize McDowell, if it did not result in bringing him into the Valley; further progress by McClellan's army would be stopped and the pressure upon General Johnston relieved.

In conforming with this plan, Jackson marched rapidly to the village of McDowell, about twenty miles west of Staunton. Here the brigade under Milroy was encountered, and the next day, May 8, a fierce and sanguinary engagement took place. During the night the Union forces withdrew from the field. Jackson immediately retraced his steps and turned down the Valley toward Harrisonburg, sending word to Ewell to join him. The united forces of the three commands were about 18,000 men. Banks had been stripped of the larger part of his troops, and his force of about 8,000 men was entrenched at Strasburg, with the design of holding the lower Valley. Jackson, instead of going straight down the Valley and attacking Banks in front, turned off at New Market. The first news that Banks had that Jackson was on his flank, and threatening his rear, came from frightened fugitives. His trains and infantry were immediately put on the pike to Winchester; but Jackson struck his column, threw it into utter confusion and made large captures of wagons, men, horses and material. Banks, however, reached Winchester with his army somewhat broken, but not demoralized, and the next morning continued his retreat to the Potomac and, crossing over, found safety on the Maryland shore.

As the result of these operations, Milroy and Schenck were now beaten, Banks's army was routed, the fertile Valley of Virginia cleared of Union troops, Harpers Ferry in danger, and Maryland and Washington threatened. In addition Washington was thrown into alarm and trepidation; McDowell's movements to connect with McClellan was suspended; he was ordered to move 20,000 men into the Valley to cut off Jackson, while Fremont with his whole force was ordered into the Valley at Harrisonburg for the same purpose. The whole plan of Union operations had been completely upset, and confusion reigned from one end of the line to the other. At no time during the war was there such dismay in the North. The government at Washington appealed to the states nearest the scene of action for help. The governors of Pennsylvania, New York, and Massachusetts issued stirring appeals, the militia was called upon for services.

General Jackson himself seems to have been the only one who had not lost his head. He kept his army from May 26 to May 30 threatening Harpers Ferry and an invasion of Maryland; and gathering up the immense spoils of men and material, he moved the main body of his troops on May 30 up the Valley, reaching Strasburg on the thirty-first. He was none too soon, for the advance of McDowell's troops under Shields had already crossed the Blue Ridge and had appeared at Front Royal, a distance of twelve miles from Strasburg.

Fremont, on the other side, was distant with his advance only ten miles. Two brigades of Jackson's forces had been left in front of Harpers Ferry with orders to march on the 31st and join the main body. Their distance from Strasburg was over 50 miles, and Jackson with his troops must keep the road open until they joined him. So, sending a part of General Ewell's division to check the advance of Fremont, with the remainder Jackson held on at Strasburg.

The night of the 31st brought the two rear brigades to Strasburg after an extraordinary march of 36 miles. Our admiration at the perfect knowledge Jackson had of the movements of the Union armies, the unexampled celerity with which he moved, the adroit manner in which he slipped through the net that had been spread to catch him, was only equalled by the shame and indignation which we felt that so much incompetency was shown on the part of our own generals.

Having started his wagon train with the spoils of his brief campaign, Jackson withdrew his army up the Valley. General Shields, instead of joining Fremont at Strasburg and pressing Jackson with their united forces, turned down the Luray Valley with the hope of crossing the south branch of the Shenandoah and defeated Shield's purpose. Fremont's pursuit resulted in no engagement of any importance until the main body of Jackson's army had reached Port Republic, where the two valleys unite. Here Jackson formed the daring plan of fighting his pursuers in detail. He directed General

Ewell to oppose General Fremont, while he held Port Republic. General Ewell formed his line of battle at Cross Keys, about halfway between Port Republic and Harrisonburg, and in a sharp fight forced Fremont from the field. The following day Jackson, leaving a small force to repress Fremont, crossed the river at Port Republic, attacked the leading brigades of Shields and drove them in confusion down the Valley with large losses in killed and wounded and prisoners. Fremont came up on the opposite side of the river in time to hear the last guns of the battle and to find that the bridge had been destroyed and that he had lost his game.

Thus was finished this brilliant campaign of a little more than a month in which Jackson's army had marched more than 250 miles, fought four pitched battles and had captured more than 4,000 prisoners, guns, wagons, and immense military supplies.

McClellan complained about McDowell's troops being withdrawn to chase Jackson:

Had McDowell's corps effected its promised junction, we might have turned the headwaters of the Chickahominy and attacked Richmond from the north and northwest, while we preserved our line of supply from West Point; but with the force actually left at my disposal such an attempt would simply have exposed the Army of the Potomac to destruction in detail and the total loss of its communications. The country in which we operated could supply nothing and, with our communications cut, nothing but starvation awaited us.

All the information obtained indicated that the enemy occupied all the approaches to Richmond from the east, and that he intended to dispute every step of our advance beyond the Chickahominy on our left and to resist the passage of the stream opposite our right. Strong entrenchments had been constructed around the city. Up to this time I had had every reason to expect that McDowell would commence his march from Fredericksburg on the morning of May 26, and it was only during the evening of the twenty-fourth that I had received from the President a telegram announcing the suspension of his movement. The order for the co-operation of McDowell was only suspended, not revoked; and therefore it was necessary to retain a portion of the army on the northern bank of the Chickahominy; I could not make any serious movement on the southern bank until the communications between the two parts of the army were firmly and securely established by strong and sufficiently numerous bridges.

In view of the peculiar character of the Chickahominy, and the liability to sudden inundations, it became necessary to construct eleven bridges, all long and difficult, with extensive logway approaches, and often built under fire.

THE SEVEN DAYS

On June 15, Stonewall Jackson rode into Fair Oaks and Robert E. Lee's headquarters. Dàniel Harvey Hill, his brother-in-law, was relieved to see him. Hill:

We went together into General Lee's office. General Jackson declined refreshments, courteously tendered by General Lee, but drank a glass of milk. Soon after, Generals Longstreet and A.P. Hill came in, and General Lee, closing the door, told us that he had determined to attack the Federal right wing and had selected our four commands to execute the movement. He told us that he had sent Whiting's division to re-enforce Jackson, and that at his instance the Richmond papers had reported that large re-enforcements had been sent to Jackson "with a view to clearing out the Valley of Virginia and exposing Washington." He believed that General McClellan received the Richmond papers regularly, and he [Lee] knew of the nervous apprehensions concerning Washington. He then said that he would retire to another room . . . and would leave us to arrange the details among ourselves. The main point on his mind seemed to be that the crossings of the Chickahominy should be covered by Jackson's advance down the left bank, so that the other three divisions might not suffer in making a forced passage.

During the absence of General Lee, Longstreet said to Jackson: "As you have the longest march to make, and are likely to meet opposition, you had better fix the time for the attack to begin."

Jackson replied: "Daylight of the 26th."

Longstreet then said: "You will encounter Federal cavalry and roads blocked by felled timber, if nothing more formidable; ought you not to give yourself more time?

When General Lee returned, he ordered A.P. Hill to cross at Meadow Hill, Longstreet at Mechanicsville Bridge, and me to follow Longstreet. The conference broke up about nightfall. . . .

What would be called the Seven Days battle opened ominously for Lee. Jackson and A.P. Hill were late in their march, and D.H. Hill suffered a terrible beating from Federal guns. McClellan had anticipated the attack. Cincinnati *Commercial* reporter, William Bickman, wrote:

. . . The fight opened with artillery, at long range, but the enemy, finally discovering our superiority in this arm, foreshortened the range, and came into close conflict. He was evidently provoked at his own inefficiency, since his shells were not destructive in our intrenchments, while our gunners played upon his exposed ranks with fearful effect. The fight seemed to increase in fury as it progressed, and it finally became the most terrific artillery combat of the war. I had been accustomed for months to the incessant roar of heavy guns, but until that period I had failed to comprehend the terrible sublimity of a great battle with field pieces. The uproar was incessant and deafening for hours. At times it seemed as if fifty guns exploded simultaneously, and then ran off at intervals into splendid file-firing, if I may apply infantry descriptive terms to cannonading. But no language can describe its awful grandeur. The enemy at last essayed a combined movement. Powerful bodies of troops plunged into the valley to charge our lines, but our men, securely posted, swept them away ruthlessly. Again and again the

desperate fellows were pushed at the breastworks, only to be more cruelly slaughtered than before. Meantime our force had been strengthened by Griffin's brigade, which increased the volume of infantry fire, and Martindale's brigade came up to be ready for emergencies. At dark it was evident the rebels had enough, much more than they bargained for.

Their infantry fire had entirely subsided, and it was obvious that they were withdrawing under cover of their artillery. Our own batteries which had opened in full cry at the start, had not slackened an instant. Comprehending the situation fully now, the cannoneers plied themselves with tremendous energy to punish the retreating foe. We have no sure means to determine how many were slaughtered, but prisoners who were in the fight, and an intelligent contraband who escaped from Richmond the next day, and who was all over the field, are confident that three thousand fell. Our own loss was eighty killed and less than one hundred and fifty wounded. The conduct of our troops was admirable, and the gallantry of the officers conspicuous. Gen. McClellan was not in the battle, but was at Gen. Porter's headquarters until it terminated.

Jefferson Davis:

Not until 3:00 P.M. on June 26 did A.P. Hill begin to move. Then he crossed the river and advanced upon Mechanicsville. After a sharp conflict he drove the enemy from his entrenchments and forced him to take refuge in his works, on the left bank of Beaver Dam, about a mile distant. This position was naturally strong, the banks of the creek in front being high and almost perpendicular, and the approach to it was over open fields commanded by the fire of artillery and infantry under cover on the opposite side. The difficulty of crossing the stream had been increased by felling the fringe of woods on its banks and destroying the bridges. Jackson was expected to pass Beaver Dam above and turn the enemy's right, so General Hill made no direct attack. Longstreet and D.H. Hill crossed the Mechanicsville Bridge as soon as it was uncovered and could be repaired, but it was late before they reached the north bank of the Chickahominy. The troops were unable in the growing darkness to overcome the obstructions and were withdrawn. The engagement ceased about 9:00 P.M.

General McClellan's position was regarded at this time as extremely critical. If he concentrated on the left or northern bank of the Chickahominy, he abandoned the attempt to capture Richmond and risked a retreat upon White House and Yorktown, where he had no reserves or reason to expect further support. If he moved to the right bank of the river, he risked the loss of his communications with White House, whence his supplies were drawn by railroad.

It would almost seem as if the Government of the United States anticipated, at this period, the failure of McClellan's expedition. On June 27 President Lincoln issued an order creating the Army of Virginia to consist of the forces of Fremont, in their Mountain Department; of Banks, in their Shenandoah Department; and of McDowell, at Fredericksburg. The command of this army was assigned to Major General John Pope. This cut off all reinforcements from McDowell to McClellan.

The battle was renewed at dawn on June 27 and continued with animation about two hours, during which the passage of Beaver Dam Creek was attempted and our troops forced their way to its banks, where their progress was arrested by the nature of the stream and the resistance encountered. They maintained their position while preparations were being made to cross at another point nearer the Chickahominy. Before these were completed, Jackson crossed Beaver Dam above, and the enemy abandoned his entrenchments and retired rapidy down the river, destroying a great deal of property, but leaving much in his deserted camps.

Pressing on toward the York River Railroad, A.P. Hill, who was in advance, reached the vicinity of New Cold Harbor about 2:00 P.M., where he encountered the foe and soon became hotly engaged. The arrival of Jackson on our left was momentarily expected, and it was supposed that his approach would cause the extension of the opposing line in that direction. Under this impression, Longstreet was held back until this movement should commence. Hill's single division met this large force with the impetuous courage for which that officer and his troops were distinguished. They drove it back and assailed it in its strong position on the ridge. The battle raged fiercely and with varying fortune more than two hours.

When Jackson arrived, his right division took position on the left of Longstreet. At the same time, D.H. Hill formed on our extreme left, and, after a short but bloody conflict, forced his way through the morass and obstructions, and drove the foe from the woods on the opposite side. The lines being now complete, a general advance from right to left was ordered. The enemy was driven to the first line of breastworks, over which our impetuous column dashed up to the entrenchments on the crest. These were quickly stormed, fourteen pieces of artillery captured and the foe driven into the field beyond. Fresh troops came to his support, and he endeavored repeatedly to rally, but in vain. He was forced back with great slaughter until he reached the woods on the banks of the Chickahominy, and night put an end to the pursuit. Our troops remained in undisturbed possession of the field.

On the morning of the twenty-eight it was ascertained that none of the enemy remained in our front north of the Chickahominy.

George Williams, soldier in the 5th New York Volunteers and a war correspondent, wrote of his experiences at Gaines' Mill:

My regiment formed part of the right wing under Fitz-John Porter. On the afternoon of June 26 the camps were startled by a sudden roll of musketry, and the cry, "We are attacked!" ran through the tents. A terrific burst of artillery and musket firing broke out towards the ravine called Beaver Dam. The attacking force was evidently a strong one, for the fusillade of small arms increased in volume and instensity every moment, and our artillery now began pouring in a deadly fire of shell and solid shot. As we moved up into position, I could see Sykes's regulars pushing forward through a hollow, and it seemed quite certain that we would soon receive our share of the assault.

Our colonel indulged in a grim bit of humor. "Attention, battalion!" he shouted. "Parade rest!"

The order was promptly obeyed, though the men laughed to see the regiment thus put through holiday maneuvers in sight of the enemy. Our colonel's coolness, however, had its intended effect, for other moving columns stiffened up and passed on in excellent shape to the position assigned them.

At that instant the regulars opened a fierce volley, and we began to see the head of the attacking force. Like a swarm of angry bees, the Confederates poured out of the woods and engaged the regulars, who soon found themselves outnumbered. They stubbornly held to their own ground, however, until a battery galloped up and, rapidly unlimbering, opened on Sykes's line with solid shot.

Here came our colonel's opportunity. As yet we had not fired a bullet; and, though the men no longer stood at their absurd parade rest, the line was as steady as if on review. Dismounting, the colonel waved his hat over his head, shouting, "Forward! Double quick!"

With a cheer every man sprang forward on the run. The battery was scarcely six hundred yards away; and, as we dashed through the standing grain, the left gun was suddenly wheeled about for the purpose of giving us a round of grape. As the gunner withdrew his ramrod and stepped back to his position by the wheel, our colonel yelled out an order to lie down, at the same moment throwing himelf flat upon the ground. We followed his example by instinct and the next instant the air above us was full of whistling missiles. Scarcely had the report of the gun thundered in our ears when I saw our colors rise from among the wheat stalks; then the regiment resumed its headlong career.

Before the piece could be reloaded, we were among the gunners and had it in our possession. Our fellows having been instructed in the use of artillery, several of them seized the gun and, slinging it round, sent a charge of grape into the body of Confederate infantry coming up to support their battery. A deadly volley of musketry was their reply, and I saw men falling all around me. We were for the moment in a perilous position, but our wild dash had disconcerted the battery and checked its fire, thus enabling the regulars to advance, which they soon did in splendid order.

But the battle was not yet over. The troops on our right were rapidly falling back; and soon after the regulars came up, showing that a general retreat of the entire right wing had really commenced. Then orders came for our brigade to move on. Just at that moment a column of our cavalry dashed across the plain and disappeared amid the smoke. Forgetting for the time that my regiment was in motion, I stood still and watched the result of this last despairing charge. In a few minutes a broken band of horsemen came flying back with ten or twenty riderless animals among them. As they galloped past, I also saw that three pieces of a battery were being abandoned for want of horses to drag them off.

Night came, and we maneuvered to and fro, sometimes on firm, solid ground, sometimes in treacherous swamps. None knew precisely where we were, or where we were going. The miserable roads were choked with cannon, ambulances and wagons; sometimes we were compelled to abandon a gun as it sank almost out of sight. Even the infantry found it difficult to gain a firm footing; and, for my own part, I was soon covered with mud and sand.

Just then, a bright light suddenly shot up into the sky. "What can that be?" exclaimed a corporal.

"It must be the stores on fire at White House," I replied. The flames grew brighter and brighter, until the horizon was red with angry light. It was serious business for us, because the destruction of our stores was proof of the critical position of the army.

Orders came for our corps to cross the Chickahominy River. We were to keep the column in motion; no man being permitted to halt on the bridge even for an instant. For four long hours the troops pressed on, the trains holding the center of the road. With a few torches to define the outlines of the bridge, we stood there, urging on the laggards, or lending a helping hand to some half-wrecked vehicle. Wagons, cannon, pontoons and ambulances, artillery, cavalry and infantry all pushed on pell-mell, with that painful haste incident to a retreat.

As the first faint streaks of dawn reddened the treetops, the last division came up at a swinging gait. Scarcely had the rear guard reached the other bank of the river when the engineers began destroying the bridge. We were all safely across, and the army was once more reunited. But we had left our dead and wounded behind us, the ground where they fell being strewn with abandoned weapons.

The night of the 26th, a Prussian officer on the Confederate side recorded the following:

Although I . . . could scarcely keep in the saddle, so great was my fatigue, I hastened with one of my aides to that quarter of the field where the struggle had raged the most fiercely. The scene of ruin was horrible. Whole ranks of the enemy lay prone where they had stood at the beginning of the battle. The number of wounded was fearful, too, and the groans and imploring cries for help that rose on all sides had, in the obscurity of the night, a ghastly effect that froze the blood in one's veins. Although I had been upon so many battle-fields in Italy and Hungary, never had my vision beheld such a spectacle of human destruction.

The preparations for the transportation of the wounded were too trifling, and the force detailed for that purpose was either too feeble in numbers or had no proper knowledge of its duties. Even the medical corps had, by the terrors of the situation, been rendered incapable of attending to the

The Confederate General Albert Sidney Johnston caught Grant's army in camp near Shiloh, Tennessee (also known as Pittsburg Landing) and nearly snatched victory from the unprepared Union forces. A regiment of Wisconsin volunteers is shown in this engraving at the start of a charge against artillery. (Library of Congress)

wounded with zeal and efficiency. With inconceivable exertion I at length succeeded, with the assistance of some humane officers, in bringing about some kind of order amid this frightful confusion. By the happiest chance, I found some Union ambulances, had all our men who could drive and knew the way pressed into service, and set to work to get the wounded into Richmond. A most heart-rending task it was; for often the poor sufferer would expire just as we were about to extend him succor.

By midnight we had got the first train ready. It consisted of sixty wagons, with two hundred seriously wounded. I cautiously and slowly conducted this train with success to the city. The first hospital reached I was met with refusal. "All full," was the reply to my inquiry. "Forward to the next hospital," was my word of command. "All full," was again the answer. Just then a friend said to me that if I would wait he might be able to help me, as he would have a neighboring tenement, used as a tobacco warehouse, prepared for a hospital. So I had to make up my mind to wait there an hour and a half in the street with my dying charges. I did my best to supply the poor fellows with water, tea, and other refresh-

Henry Lovie, another of the famed battlefield artists, labeled this sketch the "last charge" of Grant's forces at Shiloh. The handwritten notes were instructions to the engraver at *Leslie's Illustrated.* (Library of Congress)

ments, so as to alleviate their sufferings in some degree; but the late hour of the night and the agitation of the city prevented me from putting my design into more than half execution.

At length the so-called hospital was ready; but I could scarcely believe my eyes when I saw the dismal hole offered me by that name. There, in open lofts, without windows or doors, a few planks nailed together were to be the beds of the unfortunate defenders of our country. During those days of fate the soldier had endured all things – hunger, thirst, heat. Nothing could rob him of his courage, his indifference to death, and now he lay there wounded to the death at the door of his friends, whose property he had defended, for those welfare he had exposed his life; and these friends turn him away to an open barn, where, without dressing for his wounds or any care, he is left to perish.

And yet this city had a population of forty thousand souls, had churches admirably adapted to conversion into hospitals, had clergymen in numbers; but neither the doors of the churches opened, nor were the ministers of the gospel there to sweeten the last moments of the dying soldier. Sad and dispirited, I gave the order to carry in the wounded, cast one more glance at that house of death and horror, and then swung myself into my saddle and fled, with a quiet oath on my lips, back to my regiment.

Confederate Lt. Col. Evander McIvor Law, whose brigade was involved in the fighting on the afternoon of June 27, wrote:

By 5 o'clock the battle was in full progress all along the line. Longstreet's and A.P. Hill's men were attacking in the most determined manner, but were met with a courage as obstinate as their own. After each bloody repulse the Confederates only waited long enough to reform their shattered lines or to bring up their supports, when they would again return to the assault. Besides the terrific fire in their front, a battery of heavy guns on the south side of the Chickahominy were in full play on their right flank. There was no opportunity for manoeuvering or flank attacks. The enemy was directly in front and could only be reached in that direction. If he could not be driven out before night it would be the equivalent to a Confederate disaster, and would involve the failure of General Lee's whole plan for the relief of Richmond. It was a critical moment for the Confederates.

When Gen. William Henry "Little Billy" Whiting came to A.P. Hill's support, Law was an observer and wrote:

As we moved forward to the firing we could see the straggling Confederate line lying behind a gentle ridge that ran across the field parallel to the Federal position... Passing over the scattering line of Confederates on the ridge, we broke into a trot down the slope toward the Federal works. Men fell like leaves in the autumn wind; the Federal artillery tore gaps in the ranks at every step; the ground in the rear of the advancing column was strewn thickly with the dead and wounded. Not a gun was fired by us in reply; there was no confusion and not a step faltered as the two gray lines swept silently and swiftly on; the pace became more rapid every moment; when within thirty yards of the ravine, and the men could see the desperate nature of the work in hand, a wild yell answered the roar of Federal musketry and they rushed for the works. The Confederates were within ten paces of them when the Federals in the front line broke cover and, leaving their log breastworks, swarmed up the hill in their rear, carrying away their second line with them in their rout.... Anderson's brigade, till then in reserve, passed through on their right and led the way for Longstreet's division; while on the left the roll of musketry receded toward the Chickahominy, and the cheering of the victorious Confederates announced that Jackson, Ewell and D.H. Hill were sweeping that part of the field.

New York Tribune reporter Sam Wilkeson was on the field. His account is classic:

A motley mob started pell-mell for the bridges.... Scores of gallant officers endeavored to rally and re-form the stragglers, but in vain; while many officers forgot the pride of their shoulder-straps and the honor of their manhood and herded with the sneaks and cowards.... The scene was one not to be forgotten. Scores of riderless, terrified horses dashing in every direction; thick flying bullets singing by, admonishing of danger; every minute a man struck down; wagons and ambulances and cannon blocking the way; wounded men limping and groaning and bleeding amid the throng; officers and civilians denouncing and reasoning and entreating, and being insensibly borne along with the mass; the sublime cannonading, the clouds of battlesmoke and the sun just disappearing, large and blood-red – I can not picture it, but I see it and always shall.

George McClellan, in a long series of blunt and insubordinate letters to Washington, wrote the following to the Secretary of War, a man he now considered one of his many enemies. It is one of the most astounding documents of the war and one which, in any other society, indeed in any other American war, would have caused the immediate cashiering of the author:

Headquarters, Army of the Potomac,

Savage's Station, June 28, 1862, 12.20 a.m.

Hon. E.M. Stanton, Secretary of War:

I now know the full history of the day. On this side of the river (the right bank) we repulsed several strong attacks. On the left bank our men did all that men could do, all that soldiers could accomplish, but they were overwhelmed by vastly superior numbers, even after I brought my last reserves into action. The loss on both sides is terrible. I believe it will prove to be the most desperate battle of the war. The sad remnants of my men behave as men. Those battalions who fought most bravely and suffered most are still in the best order. My regulars were superb, and I count upon what are left to turn another battle in company with their gallant comrades of the volunteers. Had I twenty thousand, or even ten thousand, fresh troops to use to-morrow, I could take Richmond; but I have not a man in reserve, and shall be glad to cover my retreat and save the material and **personnel** *of the army.*

If we have lost the day we have yet preserved our honor, and no one need blush for the Army of the Potomac. I have lost this battle because my force was too small.

I again repeat that I am not responsible for this, and I say it with the earnestness of a general who feels in his heart the loss of every brave man who has been needlessly sacrificed to-day. I still hope to retrieve our fortunes; but to do this the government must view the matter in the same earnest light that I do. You must send me very large reinforcements, and send them at once. I shall draw back to this side of the Chickahominy, and think I can withdraw all our material. Please understand that in this battle we have lost nothing but men, and those the best we have.

In addition to what I have already said, I only wish to say to the President that I think he is wrong in regarding me as ungenerous when I said that my force was too weak. I merely intimated a truth which to-day has been too plainly proved. If, at this instant, I could dispose of ten thousand fresh men, I could gain the victory to-morrow.

I know that a few thousand more men would have changed this battle from a defeat to a victory. As it is, the government must not and cannot hold me responsible for the result.

I feel too earnestly to-night. I have seen too many dead

and wounded comrades to feel otherwise than that the government has not sustained this army. If you do not do so now the game is lost.

If I save this army now, I tell you plainly that I owe no thanks to you or to any other persons in Washington.

You have done your best to sacrifice this army.

G.B. McClellan

David Homer Bates, manager of the War Department telegraph office, received McClellan's message. "Such language was insubordinate, and might fairly be held to be treasonable," he wrote. "When it reached the War Department, William S. Sanford, military supervisor of telegrams, directed that the last two lines be omitted before it was delivered to the Secretary of War and the President."

"In other countries, under strict military rules," Bates observed, "officers could be court-martialed and shot for a lesser offense." And Bates was right. But neither Lincoln nor Stanton ever saw the last few lines.

As the Seven Days' Battles moved on, William Bickman reported for the Cincinnati *Commercial* in some of the finest writing of the war:

*Saturday [June 28] . . . loomed upon us hotly and cheerlessly. Until nine o'clock not the sound of a hostile gun disturbed the dread silence. The profound stillness of morning became so oppressive that the dull report of a musket on the borders would have been comparative happiness. About nine o'clock this anxiety was relieved by an awful cannonade opened upon Smith's position from two forts in Garnett's field, a battery at Fitz-John Porter's old position, and another below it, on the left bank of the Chickahominy, raking his intrenchments and compelling him to abandon the strongest natural position on our whole line. The fire was terrible. I can describe its lines fairly by comparing it with the right lines and angles of a chess-board. Smith fell back to the woods, a few hundred yards, and threw up breastworks out of range. The enemy, content with his success, ceased firing, and quiet was not disturbed again that day. The silence of the enemy was explained to me that night by a negro slave, who had escaped from his master at headquarters in Richmond. He said a despatch had been sent by Jackson to Magruder, who remained in command in front of Richmond, expressed thus: "***Be quiet. Every thing is working as well as we could desire!***" *Ominous words!*

I now proceeded to Savage station. I shall not attempt to describe the sombre picture of gloom, confusion and distress, which oppressed me there. I found officers endeavoring to fight off the true meaning. Anxiety at headquarters was too apparent to one who had studied that branch of the army too sharply to be deluded by thin masks. Other external signs were demonstrative. The wretched spectacle of mangled men from yesterday's battle, prone upon the lawn, around the hospital, the wearied, haggard, and smoke-begrimed faces of men who had fought, were concomitants of every battle-field, yet they formed the sombre coloring of the ominous picture before me. Then there were hundreds who had straggled from the field, sprawled upon every space where there was a shadow of a leaf to protect them from a broiling sun; a hurry and tumult of wagons and artillery trains, endless almost, rushing down the roads towards the new base, moving with a sort of orderly confusion, almost as distressing as panic itself. But I venture that few of all that hastening throng, excepting old officers, understood the misfortune. Strange to say, that even then, almost eleven o'clock, communication with White House by railroad and telegraph was uninterrupted, but soon after eleven the wires suddenly ceased to vibrate intelligibly.

From headquarters I passed along our lines. The troops still stood at the breastworks ready for battle; but it was evident they had begun to inquire into the situation. Some apprehensive officers had caught a hint of the mysteries which prevailed. The trains were ordered to move, troops to hold themselves in readiness to march at any moment. So passed that day, dreadful in its moral attributes as a day of pestilence, and when night closed upon the dreary scene, the enterprise had fully begun. Endless streams of artillery-trains, wagons, and funereal ambulances poured down the roads from all the camps, and plunged into the narrow funnel which was our only hope of escape. And now the exquisite truth flashed upon me. It was absolutely necessary, for the salvation of the army and the cause, that our wounded and mangled braves, who lay moaning in physical agony in our hospitals, should be **deserted** *and left in the hands of the enemy.*

From Savage Station, Bickman reported:

The advance column and all that mighty train had now been swallowed in the maw of the dreary forest. It swept onward, onward, fast and furious like an avalanche. Every hour of silence behind was ominous, but hours were precious to us. Pioneer bands were rushing along in front, clearing and repairing our single road; reconnaissance officers were seeking new routes for a haven of rest and safety. The enemy was in the rear pressing on with fearful power. He **could press down flankward to our front**, *cutting off our retreat. Would such be our fate? The vanguard had passed White Oak bridge and had risen to a fine defensive post, flanked by White Oak swamps, where part of the train at least could rest. How sadly the feeble ones needed it, those who having suspected their friends were about to abandon them, trusted rather to the strength of fear to lead them to safety, than to the fate which might await them at the hands of the foe. But the march was orderly as upon any less urgent day, only swifter – and marvellous, too, it seemed that such caravans of wagons, artillery, horsemen, soldiers, camp-followers, and all, should press through that narrow road with so little confusion.*

Two miles beyond the bridge the column suddenly halted. A tremor thrilled along the line. A moment more, and the dull boom of a cannon and its echoing shell fell grimly upon our ears. Were we beleaguered? An hour later, and there was an onimous roar behind. The enemy was thundering on our rear. I know that the moment was painful to many, but no soldier's heart seemed to shrink from the desperate shock. Back and forth dashed hot riders. Messengers here, orders here, **composure and decision where it should be**, *with determination to wrest triumph from the jaws of disaster. As yet every thing had prospered, and at noon a brighter ray flashed athwart our dreary horizon. Averill – our dashing "Ashby" – had moved with the vanguard, met eight companies of rebel cavalry, charged them, routed them, pursued them miles beyond our reach, and returned in triumph with sixty prisoners and horses, leaving nine dead foes on the field. He explained it modestly, but I saw old generals thank him for the gallant exploit – not the first of his youthful career. Gen. Keyes had sent a section of artillery with the vanguard, Averill's cavalry escorting it. The rebels charged at the guns, not perceiving our cavalry, which was screened by thickets. The artillery gave them shell and canister, which checked their mad career. Averill charged, and horse, rider and all were in one red burial blend. Dead horses are scattered over that field, and dead men lie under the shadows of the forests. We lost but one brave trooper.*

George Williams described the retreat:

Then we began our memorable march to the James River. For seven weary days we fought from early dawn until far into the night, marching from the right to the left, each corps and division going into action after traversing in turn the interior line of the army. Battle after battle was fought, until we ceased counting the engagements. We struggled through swamps and waded swollen streams as we charged one position after another. Amidst a hellish confusion of sounds we fought on; we marched and countermarched, hardened in feeling, vengeful at heart, fighting with the courage born of despair. At length, our corps emerged from the woods, and we found ourselves in a broad, open field of standing wheat.

"The James River! The James!" shouted hundreds of voices, the welcome cry being taken up and repeated again and again.

It was indeed the James and, as we moved across the field, I could see the gunboats lying in the stream. Soon after, we had halted for camp.

Col. W.W.H. Davis commanded the 104th Pennsylvania Volunteers. His account of the army's retreat is chilling:

McClellan having lost all hope of assistance from McDowell, resolved to change his base to the James River. Every energy was bent toward making the movement a success. Cars were loaded with provisions and ammunition at White House and run to Savage's Station to the last moment; and all the wagons were loaded and sent up. On the day and night of the twenty-eighth the supply and baggage trains were withdrawn from Savage's Station and sent off toward the James.

The road was crowded with wagons, and the march necessarily slow. Our brigade crossed the White Oak Swamp some time after midnight and bivouacked on the rising ground.

The enemy pushed after us immediately and were close in our rear. Our engineers had hardly destroyed the swamp bridge and retired before his skirmishers came up to reconnoiter. For several hours only the swamp divided the opposing forces. Without a note of warning, the enemy suddenly ran his artillery forward from behind the opposite hills and opened several batteries on our army while the men were lounging on the grass eating their dinner. The shock was so sudden that everybody seemed stunned for a moment. One division broke for the wood – the officers leaving their horses tied to the trees in the open field – but was rallied again. The teamsters were threatened with instant death if they drove faster than a walk, and guards were placed at short intervals along the road to prevent a stampede. A New York regiment broke and was leaving the field when it was charged with the bayonet by another regiment and stopped. Our guns had been placed in battery and soon thundered at the enemy in reply. The distance was hardly a mile, and they had our exact range. It was one of the most furious cannonades of the war and continued through the day. The infantry was obliged to endure this severe shelling that hot afternoon without an opportunity to reply, an ordeal more trying than any other to a soldier. Some of the batteries had to fill their ammunition chest three times, so rapid was the firing. The men serving the batteries were almost worn out, and one faithful gunner stood to his piece until he was entirely deaf. The enemy made repeated efforts to cross the swamp while this cannonading was going on, but in each case was prevented. An Irish camp woman, belonging to a New York regiment, made herself quite conspicuous during the action. She remained close to the side of her husband, and refused to retire to a place of security. Occasionally she would notice some fellow sneaking to the rear, when she would run after him, seize him by the nape of the neck and place him in the ranks again, calling him a "dirty, cowardly spaldeen," and other choice epithets. The flying shells had no terrors for her. During the hottest of the cannonade this courageous woman walked fearlessly about among the troops, encouraging them to stand up to their work. Her only weapon, offensive or defensive, was a large umbrella she carried under her arm. About the middle of the afternoon, heavy firing was heard on the left where our troops were fighting the enemy at Glendale. He had succeeded in crossing the swamp higher up, and was making an effort to fall upon our rear. This firing, so close on our left, caused considerable alarm, for should the enemy succeed in his attack, it would enable him to cut off our retreat. A brigade was sent off to reinforce our troops. Our commander became so much interested in the progress of events in that quarter toward evening that he rode in that direction to endeavor to obtain information. In a short time he returned at a gallop, shouting as he came up, "All's right; we've repulsed them."

Those who were with the rear guard that night at the White Oak Swamp crossing will long remember it. The situation was extremely critical. There was not a sentinel between the two armies to announce the approach of the enemy. Our two guns threw an occasional shell to give notice that we still occupied the ground.

It was now two o'clock on the morning of the first of July and the march was commenced. We did not know what road to take. Those whose business it was to know the route taken by the retreating army had remained on the ground all day without informing themselves. The head of the column was directed toward the right, contrary to the conviction of the most intelligent officers present, and the troops took the direct route for the enemy. After marching some distance they passed the pickets of another portion of our army and were again outside the Federal lines. The road was filled with stragglers coming from the field of Glendale. They were much demoralized, and many had thrown away their arms.

The regiments made the march to the rear at as rapid a gait as the men could make. Part of the time, they moved in a slow trot – as near a "double-quick" as their fatigued bodies would permit. The column was overtaken by a mounted officer, who advised them to "hurry up," as the enemy was not far off and was expected to make an attack when daylight appeared. Scarcely a word was spoken, except now and then a whispered command to the men to "close up." The road was still filled with stragglers, through which our men had to force their way – and it was often with much difficulty our wearied fellows could be prevented from mingling with the throng of fugitives going the same way. Several of the officers and men were really too sick to march, and all their physical strength was taxed to keep up with the command.

The condition of the roads the last two days had been such that the trains were got through with much difficulty. Many wagons were abandoned and destroyed, and a number were unloaded to enable the mules to draw them empty. Every kind of baggage was thrown into the mud. Officers' trunks were broken open and rifled of their contents by soldiers who were too much fatigued to carry their knapsacks, but who could bear a few pounds of plunder. Cases of expensive surgical instruments were cast away, to be picked up by the first party that claimed them. At one point where the mud was too deep for the men to cross the road, a crossing was made of mattresses taken from a hospital wagon. In this manner thousands of dollars' worth of valuable and useful baggage was destroyed.

Gen. Fitz-John Porter wrote of the battle at Malvern Hill:

This new position was better adapted for a defensive battle than any with which we had been favored. It was elevated, and protected on each flank by small streams or swamps; while the woods in front were marshy, and the timber so thick that artillery could not be brought up; even troops moved with difficulty. The ground in front was sloping, and over it our artillery and infantry, themselves protected by the crest and ridges, had clear sweep for their fire.

About 3 o'clock on Monday, June 30, the enemy advanced and opened fire. In return the rapid fire of our artillery was opened upon them, smashing one battery to pieces, silencing another, and driving back their infantry and cavalry. The gun-boats in the James made apparent their welcome presence and gave good support by bringing their heavy guns to bear on the enemy.

Our forces lay on their arms during the night, awaiting the attack expected on the following day. About 10 a.m. the enemy began feeling for us along our line. Until nearly one o'clock our infantry were resting, waiting for the moment when, the enemy advancing, would render it necessary to expose themselves. An ominous silence now intervened until about 5:30 o'clock, when the enemy opened with artillery from nearly the whole front, and soon afterward pressed forward his infantry, first on one side, and then on the other, or on both. As if moved by reckless disregard of life, with a determination to capture our army or destroy it by driving us into the river, regiment after regiment, and brigade after brigade, rushed at our batteries; but the artillery mowed them down with shrapnel, grape and canister, while our infantry, witholding their fire until the enemy were within short range, scattered the remnants of their columns.

The sight became one of the most interesting imaginable. The havoc made by the bursting shells was fearful to behold. The courage of our men was fully tried. The safety of the army was felt to be at stake. Determined to finish the contest. I pushed on into the woods held by the enemy. I sent messages to the commanding General, expressing the hope that we should hold the ground we occupied, but within an hour I received orders to withdraw and move to Harrison's Landing.

Thus ended the memorable "Seven Days" battles. Each antagonist accomplished the result for which he has aimed: one insuring the temporary relief of Richmond; the other gaining security on the north bank of the James from whence it could renew the contest successfully.

July 1. A Confederate officer wrote of the last day of the Peninsula Campaign:

The gray of morning was just beginning to appear upon the horizon when the roar of artillery was once more heard. A battery which, during the night, Gen. Anderson had placed nearer to the hostile lines was instantly noticed by the enemy and vigorously attacked by his field-pieces. Every shot struck, and the fragments were hurled in all directions. Of the twelve pieces in the battery five were quickly dismounted and the teams half destroyed, yet the commanding officer held his post. In the meanwhile our columns had formed without having tasted any strengthening or nourishing refreshment. Exhausted by the fatigues of the preceding days, they fairly reeled on their feet, yet not a man shrank back from duty. At length, as the sun rose in splendor, and we could better distinguish the enemy's position, an involuntary exclamation escaped me, for it was evident to me, from the denser ranks he exhibited, that McClellan had been considerably reinforced during the night, and could

Major General George McClellan (fourth from right) was twice the controversial commander of Union forces. He posed for this photo with his staff during the Virginia campaign in March 1862. (Library of Congress)

therefore withdraw his worn-out troops from the foremost lines, and have an easy struggle with fresh men against our famished and exhausted force.

Gen. Lee, convinced of the perilous position of affairs, at once issued orders to Stonewall Jackson to cover the retreat in case the army should be compelled to fall back, and directions were sent to Richmond to get all the public property ready for immediate removal. Then the divisions of Hill, Longstreet, Anderson, Cobb, and Whitcomb were ordered to storm the enemy's works.

And now again commenced one of the most desperate combats that ever took place in any war. The loss on our side was absolutely frightful. McClellan, observing the devastation his artillery was making among our troops, called up a division of reserves, and overwhelmed us with a terrific rain of musketry. His masses pressed forward, step by step, nearer and nearer, until at length some companies of ours threw their arms away and fled. McClellan availed himself of this panic, and ordered a flank movement of his cavalry. Quick as thought, Anderson placed himself at the head of our horse, and led three regiments to the charge. Their onset was magnificent. Our Texans burst with ringing huzzas into the ranks of the foe, who, without even giving us time to try our sabres, turned to the right-about; but here, too, the hostile field-pieces prevented further success, and we had to draw back from before that crushing fire.

The enemy, noticing our confusion, now advanced with the cry, "Onward to Richmond!" Yes, along the whole hostile front rang the shout, "Onward to Richmond!" Many old soldiers who had served in distant Missouri and on the plains of Arkansas wept in the bitterness of their souls like children. Of what avail had it been to us that our best blood had flowed for six long days? – of what avail all our unceasing and exhaustless endurance? Every thing, every thing seemed lost, and a general depression came over all our hearts. Batteries dashed past in headlong flight; ammunition, hospital, and supply wagons rushed along, and swept the troops away with them from the battle-field. In vain the most frantic exertion, entreaty, and self-sacrifice of the staff-officers. The troops had lost their foothold, and all was over with the Southern Confederacy.

Warclerk Jones summed up the day:

The serpent has been killed, though its tail still exhibits some spasmodic motions. It will die, so far as the Peninsula is concerned, after sunset, or when it thunders.

The commanding general neither sleeps nor slumbers. Already [July 4] the process of reorganizing Jackson's corps has been commenced for a blow at or near the enemy's capital. Let Lincoln beware the hour of retribution.

The diary of a Southern lady expressed the people's joy at the results of the campaign:

Richmond is disenthralled – the only Yankees there are in the "Libby" and the other prisons. The gunboats are rushing up and down the river, shelling the trees on the banks, afraid to approach Drewry's Bluff. The Northern papers and Congress are making every effort to find out to whom the fault of their late reverses is to be traced. Our people think that their whole army might have been captured but for the dilatoriness of some of our generals.

McClellan and his "Grand Army" are on the James River, enjoying mosquitoes and bilious fever. The weather is excessively hot. I dare say the Yankees find the "Sunny South" all that their most fervid imaginations ever depicted it, particularly on the marshes. So may it be, until the whole army melts with fervent heat.

THE CLASH BETWEEN THE MONITOR AND THE MERRIMAC

Gideon Welles, Lincoln's Secretary of the Navy, had the task of refurbishing the United States fleet in order effectively to carry out planned blockades of Confederate ports. Welles, in his much-heralded memoirs, related the beginnings of one of the most important innovations in naval history, the ironclad:

The Navy of the United States, at the commencement of Mr. Lincoln's administration, was wholly destitute of ironclad steamers, but the attention of Congress was invited thereto, and an act was passed on the third of August, 1861, placing at the disposal of the Navy Department one and a half million dollars. A board of naval officers was appointed to receive and report upon plans which might be submitted within twenty-five days.

Before the time limit expired, I went to Hartford. While I was there, a model was laid before me, invented by John Ericsson, for a turreted vessel, or floating battery, which impressed me favorably. I directed that the model be submitted to the Board for examination and report.

A contract for this vessel which, when built, would be called the **Monitor**, *by his request, was made and signed on the fourth of October, 1861. It was stipulated that she should be ready for sea in one hundred days.*

Unfortunately, there was delay on the part of the contractors, and she was not turned over to the Government until the third of March.

The **Merrimac**, *a vessel then under construction by the Confederates, was being clothed with iron armor when the contract for the* **Monitor** *was made. We, of course, felt great solicitude, not lessened by the fact that extraordinary pains were taken by them to keep secret from us their labors. Their efforts to withhold information, though rigid, were not wholly successful, for we contrived to get occasional vague intelligence of the work as it progressed. When the contract for the* **Monitor** *was made, in October, with a primary condition that she should be ready for sea in one hundred days, the Navy Department intended that she should proceed up the Elizabeth River to the Navy Yard at Norfolk, place herself opposite the dry dock and the* **Merrimac**. *This was* **our** *secret. The* **Monitor** *could easily have done what was required, for her appearance at Norfolk would have been a surprise. But the hundred days expired, weeks passed on and the Monitor was not ready.*

The South had no navy and little resources to construct one in time to counter any Union moves. It would have been a hopeless situation had not a stroke of extraordinary good fortune fallen into the Confederacy's lap. A report from *Harper's Weekly* detailed how the Confederacy "acquired a navy:"

The great naval station at Portsmouth near Norfolk, Virginia, was the most enviable place south of New York for the purpose to which it was appropriate. In April 1861, twelve vessels of war of various sizes were lying there, from the **Pennsylvania**, *a four-decker of 120 guns, to the brig* **Dolphin** *of four. Among them was the sloop of war* **Cumberland** *and the* **Merrimac**, *the latter a steam frigate of forty guns which had been launched in 1855.*

The place was entirely without protection; no measures had been taken against an attack. Commodore McCauley, in command of the yard, only was directed on April 10, to use "extreme vigilance and circumspection."

On April 12, Fort Sumter was fired on, and at last Commodore McCauley gave orders to lose no time in loading the **Merrimac**, *the* **Plymouth**, *the* **Dolphin** *and the* **Germantown** *with the more valuable ordnance and in putting these vessels in a position to be moved at any moment. The* **Cumberland** *was placed so as to command Portsmouth, the Navy Yard and Norfolk. This was not done until April 17, the day on which the ordinance of secession was passed at Richmond.*

Union horse artillery on the move near Fair Oaks, Va. The inconclusive battle fought there in the spring of 1862 was one part of McClellan's several tepid campaigns to take the Confederate capital of Richmond. (Library of Congress)

A large number of the naval officers were from slave states, and the people of Norfolk were among the bitterest secessionists. They openly declared that, if the government attempted to move any of the ships, they would attack immediately. Commodore McCauley allowed his junior officers to persuade him that delay would be prudent. On the eighteenth, they resigned their commissions. McCauley's eyes were at last opened but only to see his peril and utter helplessness. He then decided to scuttle all the vessels except the ***Cumberland****.*

The dry dock was mined, and combustibles were scattered through the scuttled ships. The roar of the flames, as they devoured the work of years and the wealth of a nation, was heard far and wide. The loyal officers and men took ship on the ***Pawnee*** *and the* ***Cumberland****.*

When the flames had subsided, it was found that little

harm had been done to the yard and the ships, all of which were seaworthy. Even the **Plymouth** *and the* **Merrimac** *eventually were raised and made serviceable. And that was how the Confederacy acquired a navy.*

The *Merrimac*, now in the possession of the South, presented some hope not only for the beginnings of a navy, but for some defense against the *Monitor*, rumors of which had been circulating for months. The *New York Tribune* gave the story of how the old *Merrimac* became the Confederate *Virginia*:

There was much discussion at one time of the question as to whom, the credit for the plans of the **Merrimac** *belonged. It finally was generally conceded, however, that her origin and perfection were due to Commander John M. Brooke of the Confederate Navy; and the terrible banded rifle gun and bolt she used was his undisputed invention.*

When the United States warship **Merrimac**, *by Commodore McCauley's orders, had been scuttled and partly sunk in Norfolk Harbor, only her rigging and upper works were burned, her hull being saved by a speedy submersion. After she had been plugged, pumped out and raised, her hull was cut down nearly to the water's edge; then a sloping roof of heavy timber, strongly and thoroughly plated with railroad iron, rose from two feet below the waterline to about ten feet above, the ends and sides being alike and thoroughly shielded. A false bow was added, and beyond this projected a strong iron beak. Thoroughly shotproof, she was armed with ten seven-inch rifled Brooke guns; and so, having been largely refitted from the spoils of the deserted Navy Yard, she became the cheapest and most formidable naval engine of destruction that the world had ever seen.*

Much wonder had the good people of Norfolk expressed in their frequent visits to the strange-looking, turtle structure. It was the **Merrimac**, *which the Confederates had rechristened the* **Virginia**. *Day by day she slowly grew; and at length, after weary waiting, took on her armament; then her crew was picked carefully from eager volunteers. Her captain, Commodore Franklin Buchanan, took his place, and all was ready for the trial.*

March 8, 1862, the *Merrimac* steamed out of the Norfolk harbor to attempt to break the Federal blockade. Lt. Israel N. Stiles, of an Indiana Regiment reported from shore:

I was at that time an officer of the 20th Indiana Volunteer Infantry, stationed at one of the fortified camps guarding Hampton Roads. On the eighth of March, at about 1:00 P.M., the long roll sounded, and the cry ran through the camp, "The **Merrimac** *is coming." She was now about five or six miles away and looked very much like a house submerged to the eaves, borne onward by a flood. We had been expecting her for some weeks. We had heavy guns commanding our fort; and we thought we were ready to receive her becomingly. Near by and at anchor were two of our largest sailing frigates, the* **Congress** *and* **Cumberland**, *carrying fifty and thirty guns respectively. They also were ready, prepared as well as wooden ships could be, to contend with an ironclad. A few miles away were the Union frigates* **Minnesota**, **Roanoke**, *and* **St. Lawrence** *and several gunboats.*

The **Merrimac** *moved very slowly, accompanied by the* **Beaufort** *and* **Raleigh**, *two small boats carrying one gun each. Not until she fired her first gun was there any outward sign of life on board, or of any armament, although she bore a crew of 300 and carried ten heavy guns. She had practically no visible deck; her crew were somewhere under her roof but out of sight; her gun ports were covered by hinged lids, which were raised only when her guns were brought forward for firing and closed when they were withdrawn. She moved directly for the* **Cumberland**, *which had cleared for action when the enemy was first sighted, and for the last half hour had been ready with every man at his post. On her way she passed the* **Congress** *on her starboard side, and within easy range. The latter greeted her with a terrific broadside, to which the* **Merrimac** *responded but kept on her course. Soon she came within range of the shore batteries, which opened upon her, and a minute or two later the thirty guns of the* **Cumberland** *were doing their duty. Many of the shots struck her, but they rebounded from her sides like marbles thrown against a brick wall. Approaching the* **Cumberland**, *she fired her bow gun and struck her at full speed on her port bow, delivering another shot at the same time. The blow opened an immense hole in the frigate, and the force of it was so great that the* **Merrimac's** *iron prow, or beak, was wrenched off as she withdrew and was left sticking in the side of the ship. The two shots which were delivered from her bow gun had been terribly destructive. One entered the* **Cumberland's** *port, killing or wounding every man at one of her guns; the other raked her gun deck from one end to the other. Withdrawing from the frigate, the* **Merrimac** *steamed slowly up the river and, turning, chose her own position, from which she delivered broadside after broadside into the now sinking ship, and then changing her position, raked her fore and aft with shell and grape.*

Meantime the shore batteries had kept up their fire, while the **Congress** *had been towed up into position and with her thirty guns pounded away at the iron monster. It was plain to us on shore that all combined were not a match for her. This must have been plain to the officers and men of the* **Cumberland** *as well; yet, with their ship sinking under them, they continued the fight with a courage and desperation which is recorded in no other naval battle. It was stated at that time that while her bow guns were under water, those in the after part of the ship were made to do double duty. Her commander was called upon to surrender; he refused, and his men cheered him. Still she sank, and the men were ordered to save themselves by swimming ashore. The water closed over her with her flag still flying.*

While the **Merrimac** *was occupied with the* **Cumberland**, *three Confederate steamers – the* **Patrick Henry**, **Jamestown** *and* **Teaser** *– had come down the James River, and with the two gunboats* **Beaufort** *and* **Raleigh** *had already engaged the* **Congress**. *On our side, the screw frigate*

***Minnesota** had worked her way from the fort, but had grounded a mile and a half way. For half an hour or more the **Merrimac** alternated her attentions between the **Congress** and the **Minnesota**. Owing to her great draught of water, the **Merrimac** could not get near enough to the latter to do much damage, but she chose her own position, and the utter destruction of the **Congress** became only a question of time. She had repeatedly been set on fire; her decks were covered with the dead and wounded; and the loss of life (including that of her commander) had been very great. She was run ashore, head on, and not long after hoisted the white flag. Two tugs were sent by the enemy alongside the **Congress** to take possession and to remove the prisoners, but a sharp fire of artillery and small arms from the shore drove them off. Captain Reed raised a question of military law: "Since the ship has surrendered, has not the enemy the right to take possession of her?" The question was answered by General Joseph K. Mansfield in one of the shortest and most conclusive opinions on record. "I know the damned ship has surrendered," said he, "but **we** haven't." That settled it. During the firing, Commander Buchanan of the **Merrimac** received a wound which disabled him from further participation in the fight. Being unable to take possession of the frigate, the ironclad again opened fire upon her – this time with incendiary shot – and the ship was soon on fire in several places*

*It was now nearly dark, and the **Merrimac** hauled off. She had received no substantial injury and had demonstrated her ability to sink any wooden ship which might dare cope with her. Indeed, it looked that night as if the entire fleet would be wholly at her mercy on the morrow. The crew of the **Congress**, such as were able, had escaped, and during the early hours of the evening the wounded had been brought ashore. They and those of the **Cumberland** filled the little hospital. Officers and men gathered around those brave fellows and listened with moistened eyes to their accounts of the fight. One gunner, who had had both legs shot away just before the **Cumberland** sank, hobbled several steps on his bloody stumps and seized the lanyard that he might fire one more shot. An officer of the **Congress**, who had both arms shot away, cried out, "Back to your guns, boys! Give 'em hell! Hurrah for the old flag!"*

I found one poor fellow, the surface of whose body was burned from head to heel. "I am all right," said he. "I have no pain. I shall get along." His sensory nerves are destroyed," said the surgeon to me; "he will not live five hours." And so it proved.

*The **Congress** continued to burn, her loaded guns discharging as the fire reached them, until about 1:00 a.m. When the fire reached her magazine, she blew up with a tremendous roar and with a shock so great that many of us on shore were prostrated, although we had retired to what we considered a safe distance. We were not sleepy that night.*

Gideon Welles described the absolute panic created in Washington by the mere thought of the ***Merrimac*** sailing up the Potomac. Secretary of War Stanton, in particular, was horrified at the possibility and was certain that it would happen:

*On Sunday morning, the ninth of March, Mr. Peter H. Watson, Assistant Secretary of War, hastily entered with a telegram from General John E. Wool at Fort Monroe, stating that the **Merrimac** had destroyed the **Cumberland** and **Congress**. Apprehensions were expressed by General Wool that the remaining vessels would be made victims the following day, and the fort itself was in danger, for the **Merrimac** was impenetrable and could take what position she pleased for assault. I had scarcely read the telegram when a message from the President requested my immediate attendance at the Executive Mansion. The Secretary of War, on receiving General Wool's telegram, had gone instantly to the President, and at the same time sent messages to other Cabinet officers. I went at once to the White House. Mr. Seward and Mr. Chase, with Mr. Stanton, were already there, had read the telegram and were discussing the intelligence in much alarm. Each inquired what had been, and what could be done to meet and check this formidable monster which in a single brief visit had made such devastation and would, herself uninjured, repeat her destructive visit with still greater havoc, probably, while we were in council. The Admiralty, appealed to for help, was unable to issue a reassuring statement, which tended to increase the panic.*

*I stated that our **Monitor**, which had left New York on Thursday, should have reached Hampton Roads on Saturday, and my main reliance was upon her.*

Mr. Stanton was terribly excited and walked the room in great agitation. Mr. Seward, usually buoyant and self-reliant, overwhelmed with the intelligence, was greatly depressed, as, indeed, were all the members.

*"The **Merrimac**," said Stanton, "will change the whole character of the war; she will destroy every naval vessel; she will lay all the cities on the seaboard under contribution. Likely her first move will be to come up the Potomac and disperse Congress, destroy the Capitol and public buildings. I will notify the governors and municipal authorities in the North to take instant measures to protect their harbors." He had no doubt, he said, "that the monster was at this moment on her way to Washington," and, looking out of the window, which commanded a view of the Potomac for many miles, he added, "Not unlikely we shall have a shell or cannon ball from one of her guns in the White House before we leave this room." I told the President that the **Merrimac** could not, with her heavy armor, cross the Kettle Bottom Shoals. This was a relief. I questioned the propriety of sending abroad panic missives, and said it was doubtful whether the **Merrimac** armor would venture outside of the Capes.*

*"What," asked Stanton, "is the size and strength of this **Monitor**? How many guns does she carry?" When I replied two, but of large caliber, he turned away with a look of mingled amazement, contempt and distress.*

On the evening of that memorable Sunday, Stanton

proceeded to state that he had advised the governors of the Northern States and the mayors of some cities to place rafts of timber and other obstructions at the mouths of their harbors. He had also directed the purchase of all the boats that could be procured in Washington, Georgetown and Alexandria, which were being laden with stone and earth, with a view of sinking them, in order to prevent the ascension of the **Merrimac** *up the Potomac. He did procure a fleet of some sixty canal boats, which were laden, but Mr. Lincoln forbade that they should be sunk until it was known that the* **Merrimac** *really was approaching.*

Stiles, again on shore, witnessed one of the great events of the Civil War:

Before morning we heard of the arrival of "Ericsson's Battery." It is a floating battery," said our surgeon, "lying very low in the water, with its guns enclosed in a revolving turret." He was well up in the details of the construction and had great confidence in the thing.

Morning came, and with it came into view the great hull of the **Minnesota**, *also the* **Merrimac** *and her attendants, the* **Yorktown** *and the* **Patrick Henry**. *Alongside the* **Minnesota** *lay "Ericsson's Battery," a most insignificant-looking thing, a "cheese-box on a raft." The* **Merrimac** *and her companions were stationary and seemed to be in consultation. At seven o'clock a plan seemed to have been adopted, and the* **Merrimac** *steamed in the direction of the* **Minnesota**. *She was followed in the distance by the* **Yorktown** *and the* **Patrick Henry**, *which were crowded with troops. The* **Minnesota** *was still hard aground, and the* **Merrimac** *evidently counted upon disposing of her as she had done with the* **Cumberland** *and* **Congress** *the day before; but now a lion was in her path. The* **Monitor** *had steamed around the bow of the* **Minnesota** *and like another David, marched out to meet this Goliath. At 8:10 o'clock the fire opened, and the first shot was fired by the* **Merrimac** *at the* **Minnesota**. *The next shot was from the* **Monitor**, *which struck the* **Merrimac** *near her water line but with little effect. The ironclads now came very near together – as it seemed to us on shore, less than one hundred feet apart – and the firing was very rapid. Occasionally the* **Merrimac** *varied the entertainment by a few shots at the* **Minnesota** *and, as often as the position would enable her to do so, the frigate would give her a broadside. Frequently the* **Merrimac** *would try to ram her little antagonist; but the ease with which the latter was handled enabled her to avoid a direct shock. In turn, the* **Monitor** *attempted to disable her enemy's screw, but without success. In vain the* **Merrimac** *tried to work her way up to close quarters with the* **Minnesota;** *the* **Monitor** *would not consent. The shores, which were but a few miles apart, were lined with Union and Confederate soldiers, and the ramparts of the fort and the rigging of the ships at anchor were also crowded with witnesses of the fight.*

At ten o'clock no perceptible damage had been sustained by either of the contestants. With her ten guns the **Merrimac** *was able to return two or three shots for every one she received. She had no solid shot, as she had expected to meet only wooden ships. Twenty-one in all of her shells struck the* **Monitor**, *but without doing any injury that needed repairing. The* **Merrimac** *presented a large mark, and during the last two hours of the fight nearly every shot of the* **Monitor** *struck her. Her armor was broken in several places, and in three instances, when two or more shots had struck the same place, the wood backing was badly shattered. As the fight continued, nearly all of the smaller craft ventured near enough to fire a few shots and, when at one time the batteries at Sewell's Point joined in, the soldiers declared that there was "music by the entire band." The fight continued till 12:15, when the* **Merrimac** *quit and steamed toward Norfolk. The commander of the* **Monitor** *wanted to follow her but was prevented by orders from the flag officer, who thought the risk too great. The official report of the* **Merrimac** *says: "Our loss is two killed and nineteen wounded. The stern is twisted, and the ship leaks. We have lost the prow, starboard anchor, all the boats; the armor is somewhat damaged, the steampipe and smokestack both riddled, and the muzzles of two guns shot away."*

The **Merrimac** *came down to the old fighting-ground on two or three occasions afterward and dared the* **Monitor** *to fight her single-handed. The* **Monitor** *refused to meet her, except in waters where the whole Union fleet could have pounced upon her. The* **Monitor** *was the only vessel that could possibly cope with her, and should some mishap befall her, the rest of the fleet would be wholly at the* **Merrimac's** *mercy.*

Samuel Lewis was a member of the *Monitor's* crew:

The **Monitor** *was a little bit the strangest craft I had ever seen; nothing but a few inches of deck above the water line, her big, round tower in the center and the pilot house at the end. We had confidence in her, though, from the start, for the little ship looked somehow like she meant business, and it didn't take us long to learn the ropes. The crew were exactly sixty strong, with the pilot.*

Our first sight of the **Merrimac** *was around the Rip Raps. She had been described to us and there was no mistaking her long, slanting, rakish outlines. I guess she took us for some kind of a water tank. You can see surprise in a ship just as you can see it in a human being, and there was surprise all over the* **Merrimac**. *She fired a shot across us, but Captain Worden, our commander, said, "Wait till you get close, boys, and then let her have it."*

In a moment the ball had opened. Our guns were so low down that it was practically point-blank firing. At first the **Merrimac** *was evidently trying hard to put a shell into the*

Steel-eyed Captain William Caleb Brown of the Rough and Ready Guards, 14th North Carolina Regiment. Of such men the fabled Confederate armies were formed – tough, resolute, skilled, and ably lead. (Library of Congress)

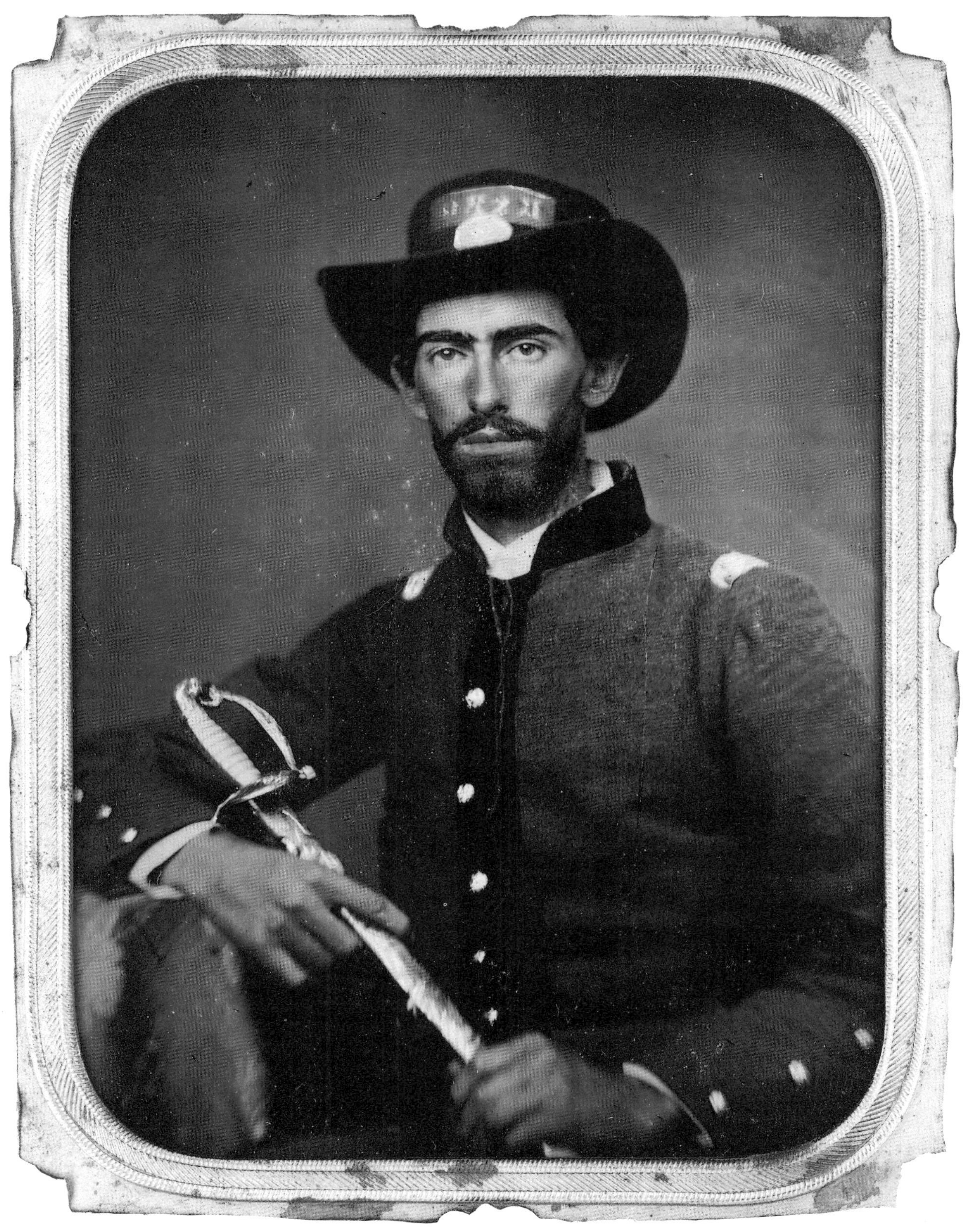

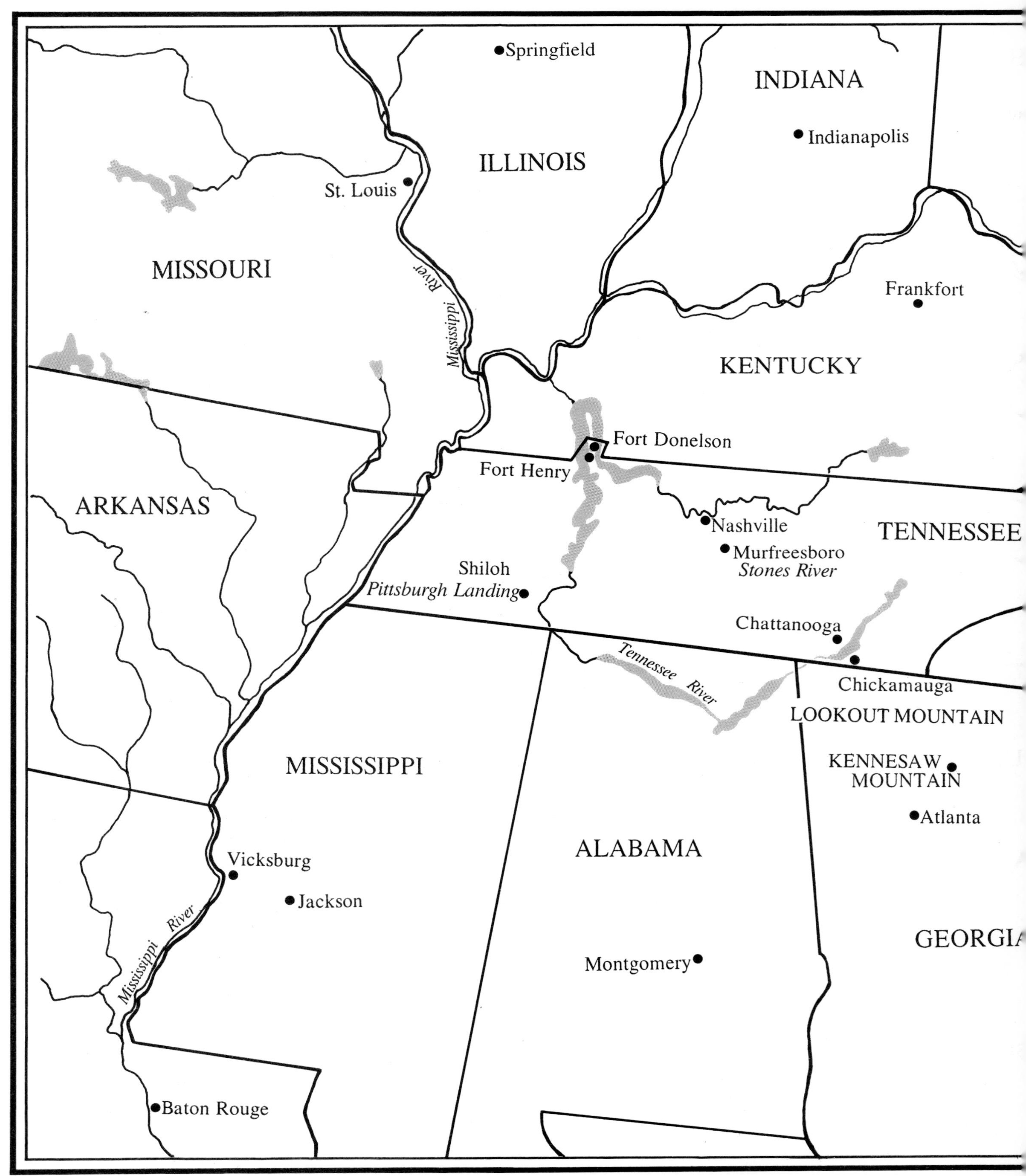

Springfield
INDIANA
Indianapolis
ILLINOIS
St. Louis
MISSOURI
Mississippi River
Frankfort
KENTUCKY
Fort Donelson
Fort Henry
ARKANSAS
Nashville
TENNESSEE
Murfreesboro
Stones River
Shiloh
Pittsburgh Landing
Chattanooga
Tennessee River
Chickamauga
LOOKOUT MOUNTAIN
KENNESAW MOUNTAIN
MISSISSIPPI
Atlanta
ALABAMA
Vicksburg
Jackson
Mississippi River
GEORGIA
Montgomery
Baton Rouge

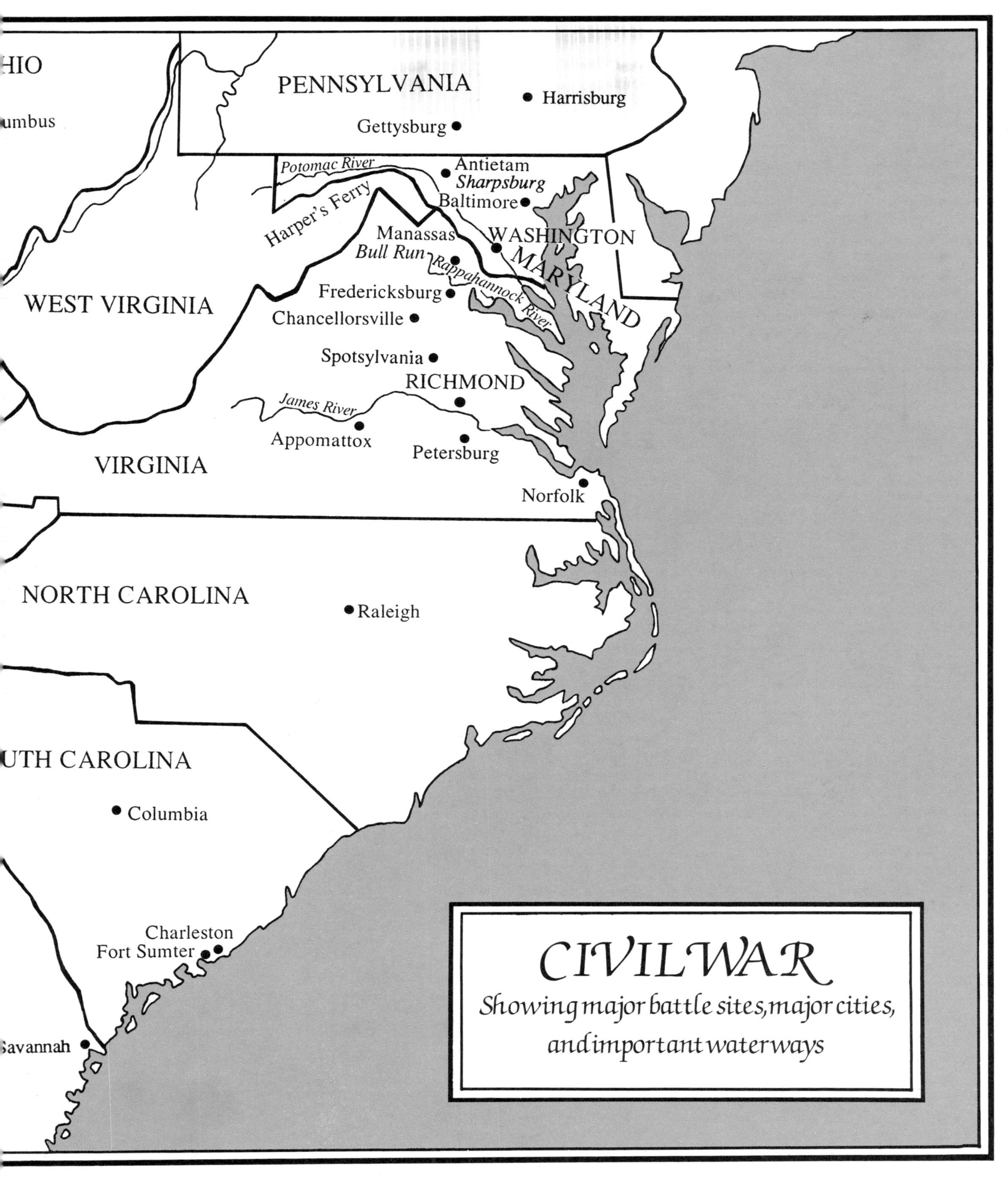
HIO
umbus
PENNSYLVANIA
Harrisburg
Gettysburg
Potomac River
Antietam
Sharpsburg
Baltimore
Harper's Ferry
Manassas
Bull Run
WASHINGTON
MARYLAND
Rappahannock River
Fredericksburg
WEST VIRGINIA
Chancellorsville
Spotsylvania
RICHMOND
James River
Appomattox
Petersburg
VIRGINIA
Norfolk
NORTH CAROLINA
Raleigh
UTH CAROLINA
Columbia
Charleston
Fort Sumter
Savannah
CIVIL WAR
Showing major battle sites, major cities, and important waterways

turret. That was impossible, however, for two reasons. The portholes were protected by heavy iron pendulums that fell of their own weight over the openings as soon as the muzzles of the guns were taken out, and when the guns were loaded they were put out at the far side, away from the ***Merrimac****.*

The din inside the turret was something terrific. The noise of every solid ball that hit fell upon our ears with a crash that deafened us. About that time an unexpected danger developed. The plates of the turret were fastened on with iron bolts and screwheads on the inside. These screwheads began to fly off from the concussion of the shots. Several of the men were badly bruised by them, and had anybody been hit in the face or eyes they would have been done for. Luckily this did not take place.

The immense volume of smoke made maneuvering very difficult, and at times we had hard work telling where the enemy was. Twice she tried to ram us, but we got out of the way. We looked for an attack by a boarding party and had a supply of hand grenades ready to throw out of the turret if one succeeded in gaining the deck.

The gun I served had just been pulled in and the pendulum dropped when a ball struck it a few inches from the head. The shock was so fearful that I dropped over like a dead man, and the next thing I knew I was in the cabin with the doctor bathing my head. I soon recovered enough to go up again. Meantime the ***Merrimac*** *had concentrated her fire upon the pilot house, giving up the turret as a bad job, and I think made an effort or two to get close and board us. I do not think that a boarding party could have been successful, even had they reached the deck, because they couldn't have penetrated the interior. There was but one hatch, and that had been closed and barred on the inside before the engagement.*

The ***Merrimac*** *turned tail after a little over four hours of fighting. The enthusiasm of our men was at fever heat.*

Next day we were the heroes of the hour. The Presidential party came down with a lot of ladies, and they cheered and toasted us to the echo. The troops about the fortress all felt so proud over the victory that they started a contribution of one dollar each for the crew of the ***Monitor****. The sum they raised was sent to Washington, but for some reason Congress objected, and it was never distributed.*

Stiles:

On the tenth of May, 1862, the enemy abandoned Norfolk, on the eleventh they blew up the ***Merrimac****, and on the twelfth we marched in. We talked with one of the engineers who had charge of the repairs. He stated to us that a shot from the* ***Monitor*** *had so "shivered her timbers that she never afterward could be made seaworthy. Her officers knew it when they went out and dared the* ***Monitor*** *to fight her. It was a case of pure bluff; we didn't hold a single pair."*

The commander of the *Monitor*, J.P. Bankhead:

The ***Monitor*** *left Hampton Roads, in tow of the United States Steamer* ***Rhode Island,*** *on the twenty-ninth of December, 1862, at 2:30 P.M., wind light at southwest, weather clear and pleasant.*

At 5:00 A.M., we began to experience a swell from the southward, with a slight increase of the wind, the sea breaking over the pilot house forward and striking the base of the turret, but not with sufficient force to break it. Speed at this time about five knots; ascertained from the engineer that the bilge-pumps kept her perfectly free. Felt no apprehension at the time. At 7:30 the wind increased in strength, position at this time about fifteen miles south of Cape Hatteras. At 8:00 P.M., the sea commenced to rise very rapidly, causing the vessel to plunge heavily, competely submerged the pilot house, and washing over and into the turret, and at times into the blower-pipes. Signalized several times to the ***Rhode Island*** *to stop. The engineer reported that it would be necessary to start the centrifugal pump. About 10:30 P.M., finding the water gaining rapidly upon us, I determined to make the preconcerted signal of distress, which was immediately answered by the* ***Rhode Island****. I requested her commander to send boats to take off the crew. Finding that the heavy steam cable used to tow the* ***Monitor*** *rendered the vessel more unmanageable while hanging slack to her bow, and being under the absolute necessity of working the engines to keep the pumps going, I ordered it to be cut, and ran down close under the lee of the* ***Rhode Island****, at times almost touching her. At 11:30 my engines worked slowly, and all the pumps in full play, but water gaining rapidly, sea very heavy. Finding the vessel filling rapidly and the deck on a level with the water, I ordered all left on board, about twenty-five or thirty men, to get into two boats which were then approaching us. The boats approached very cautiously, as the sea was breaking upon our now submerged deck with great violence, washing several men overboard. Feeling that I had done everything in my power to save the vessel and crew, I jumped into the already deeply laden boat and left the* ***Monitor****, whose heavy, sluggish motion gave evidence that she could float but a short time longer. Shortly after we reached the* ***Rhode Island*** *she disappeared.*

Before closing I must testify to the coolness, prompt obedience and absence of any approach to panic on the part of the officers and, with but few exceptions on the part of the crew, many of whom were at sea the first time and (it must be admitted) under circumstances that were calculated to appall the boldest heart.

ULYSSES S. GRANT AND THE MISSISSIPPI

THE FALL OF FORTS HENRY AND DONELSON

A man by the name of Ulysses Simpson Grant came upon the scene late in 1861. Veteran of the war with Mexico, he had resigned his captain's commission in 1854 and, at the beginning of the Civil War, was a clerk in the town of Galena.

Illinois. In June 1861, he was appointed colonel of an Illinois regiment. By the time Dr. John H. Brinton wrote the following description, Grant had been advanced to brigadier general. He was destined to be the general who would later bring an end to the hostilities, and, for whatever reasons, Brinton seemed to sense the greatness that would befall this plain and unassuming man:

Of the many who have written of Grant, made speeches about him, applauded him and flattered him, few, very few, watched him and studied him as I did. From the very first he attracted me, and I felt very soon, and indeed wrote home, that the man had come who would finish this war, should he have the chance.

I first saw General Grant in Cairo at a dinner table. I was introduced to him and received a friendly nod from him. On the same evening I went into the bank. Behind the counter, the general and his assistant adjutant general, John A. Rawlins, or Captain Rawlins, as he was then, were seated at a little round table. I fancy that I wanted to write a letter, for I remember that the general kindly asked me to sit down and continued his work with Rawlins. I had a good opportunity to observe him and did so very closely. He was then a very different looking man from the General Grant, or the President, of after days.

As I first saw him, he was a very short, small, rather spare man with full beard and mustache. His beard was a little long, very much longer than he afterwards wore it, unkempt and irregular, and of a sandy, tawny shade. His hair matched his beard, and at a first glance he seemed to be a very ordinary sort of a man, indeed, one below the average in most respects. But as I sat and watched him then, and many an hour afterward, I found that his face grew upon me. His eyes were gentle with a kind expression, and thoughtful. He did not, as a rule, speak a great deal. At that time he seemed to be very much occupied indeed with the work of the hour. He worked slowly, every now and then stopping and taking his pipe out of his mouth.

But this reminds me that I have not yet spoken of his pipe. The man in after days became so thoroughly identified with the cigar that people could scarcely believe that he was once an assiduous smoker of the pipe. Well, the pipe which he first used was a meerschaum with a curved stem eight or ten inches long, which allowed the pipe to hang down. He smoked steadily and slowly and evidently greatly enjoyed his tobacco.

Grant's chief concern were the three rivers that flowed through the heart of the Confederacy: the Mississippi, the Cumberland and the Tennessee. He wrote:

The enemy at this time occupied a line running from the Mississippi River at Columbus to Bowling Green and Mill Springs, Kentucky. Each of these positions was strongly fortified, as were also points on the Tennessee and Cumberland rivers. The work on the Tennessee was called Fort Henry, and that on the Cumberland Fort Donelson, at which points the two rivers approached within eleven miles of each other. These positions were of immense importance to the enemy and, of course, correspondingly important for us to possess ourselves of. With Fort Henry in our hands, we had a navigable stream open to us up to Muscle Shoals in Alabama. Fort Donelson was the gate to Nashville – a place of great military and political importance. These two points in our possession, the enemy would necessarily be thrown back to the boundary of the Cotton States.

As a result of an exploratory expedition, General C.F. Smith, one of my subordinate officers, reported that he thought it practicable to capture Fort Henry. This report confirmed views I had previously held, that the true line of operations for us was up the Tennessee and Cumberland rivers.

Flag Officer Andrew Hull Foote commanded the little fleet of gunboats then in the neighborhood of Cairo and, though in another branch of the service, was subject to the same command. He and I agreed perfectly as to the feasibility of the campaign up the Tennessee.

Dr. Brinton's astute description of Grant continued:

I had been in charge of the general hospitals of the District of Cairo; General Grant was away, and General John A. McClernand commanded in his absence. One of the latter's orders was to this effect: "That all able-bodied men in the hospitals in the district should be returned to their command, irrespective of the hospital duties they were performing." The order was clearly illegal, but apart from this, its execution would have instantly paralyzed the whole hospital department of the entire District of Cairo. I accordingly instructed my surgeons to disobey it, and by my own endorsement disputed its validity. General Grant on his return sent for me, showed me my rebellious order, and added, "Doctor, this is a very serious business." My answer to him was, "General, when you entrusted to me, as your medical director, the care of the invalids of your command, you said to me, 'Doctor, take care of my sick and wounded to the best of your ability, don't bother over regulations.' Now, General," I added, "I have done this to the best of my ability. If I have done right, you will support me; if I have done wrong, you know what to do with me."

The general looked at me a moment, took a paper, and put on it the endorsement which lives in my memory: "The object of having a Medical Director is that he shall be supreme in his own department. The decision of Surgeon Brinton is sustained."

I think that my veneration for his character and my strong personal affection for him dated from that interview. I doubt if another officer of his rank in the army would have so supported a medical officer under like circumstances.

The President of the Confederacy, keenly aware of what each of the three rivers meant to the South, explained the fortifications:

When the State of Tennessee seceded, measures were immediately adopted to occupy and fortify all the strong points on the Mississippi, such as Memphis, Fort Randolph,

Fort Pillow and Island No. 10. As it was our purpose not to construct defenses for the Cumberland and Tennessee rivers on Kentucky territory, they were located within the borders of Tennessee. On these were commenced the construction of Fort Donelson on the west of the Cumberland and Fort Henry on the east side of the Tennessee, about twelve miles apart. The latter stood on the lowlands adjacent to the river above high-water mark; being just below a bend in the river and at the head of a straight stretch of two miles, it commanded the river for that distance.

Fort Donelson was placed on high ground; and with the plunging fire from its batteries was more effective against ironclads brought to attack it on the water side. But on the land side it was not equally strong and required extensive outworks and a considerable force to resist an attack in that quarter.

Grant's departmental commander was Major General Henry Wager Halleck, who would later be called to Washington to command all the armies. Now he was in command at St. Louis and Grant had to defer to him:

On January 6, 1862, I had asked permission of General Halleck . . . to go to see him at St. Louis. My object was to lay before him my plan of campaign against Fort Henry. Now that my views had been confirmed by so able a general as C.F. Smith, I renewed my request to go to St. Louis on what I deemed important military business. The leave was granted, but not graciously. I was received with so little cordiality that I perhaps stated the object of my visit with less clearness than I might have done, and I had not uttered many sentences before I was cut short as if my plan was preposterous. I returned to Cairo very much crestfallen.

On January 28, notwithstanding the rebuff I had received, I renewed the suggestion that "If permitted, I could take and hold Fort Henry on the Tennessee." This time I was backed by Flag Officer Foote, who sent a similar dispatch. On January 29 I wrote fully in support of the proposition. On February 1 I received instructions from department headquarters to move upon Fort Henry. On February 2 the expedition started.

Jefferson Davis:

On February 2 General Grant started from Cairo with 17,000 men on transports. Flag Officer Foote accompanied him with seven gunboats. On the fourth the landing of the troops commenced three miles or more below Fort Henry. General Grant took command on the east bank with the main column, while General Charles F. Smith, with two brigades of some five to six thousand men, landed on the left bank, with orders to take the earthworks opposite Fort Henry known as Fort Heiman. On the fifth, landing was completed, and the attack was made on the next day.

The forces of General Lloyd Tilghman, who was in command at Fort Henry, were about 3,400 men. On the fifth he intended to dispute Grant's advance by land, but on the sixth, before the attack by the gunboats, he abandoned hope of a successful defense and made arrangements for the escape of his main body to Fort Donelson, while the guns of Fort Henry should engage the gunboats. He ordered Colonel Heiman to withdraw the command to Fort Donelson, while he himself would obtain the necessary delay for the movement by standing a bombardment in Fort Henry. For this purpose he retained his heavy artillery company – seventy-five men – to work the guns, a number unequal to the strain and labor of the defense.

Noon was the time fixed for the attack; but Grant, impeded by the overflow of water and unwilling to expose his men to the heavy guns of the fort, held them back to wait the results of the gunboat attack. In the meantime the Confederate troops were in retreat. Four ironclads, mounting forty-eight heavy guns, approached and took position within six hundred yards of the fort, firing as they advanced. About half a mile behind these came three unarmored gunboats, mounting twenty-seven heavy guns, which took a more distant position and kept up a bombardment of shells that fell within the works. Some four hundred of the formidable missiles of the ironclad boats were also thrown into the fort.

The officers and men inside were not slow to repond, and as many as fifty-nine of their shots were counted as striking the gunboats. On the ironclad **Essex** *a cannon ball ranged her whole length; another shot, passing through the boiler, caused an explosion that scalded her commander and many of the seamen and soldiers on board.*

Five minutes after the fight began, the 24-pounder rifled gun, one of the most formidable in the fort, burst, disabling every man at the piece. Then a shell exploded at the muzzle of one of the 32-pounders, ruining the gun and killing or wounding all the men who served it. About the same moment a premature discharge occurred at one of the 42-pounder guns, killing three men and seriously injuring others. The 10-inch columbiad, the only gun able to match the artillery of the assailants, was next rendered useless by a priming wire that was jammed and broken in the vent. An heroic blacksmith labored for a long time to remove it, under the full fire of the enemy, but in vain. The men became exhausted and lost confidence; and Tilghman, seeing this, in person served a 32-pounder for some fifteen minutes. Though but four of his guns were disabled, six stood idle for want of artillerists, and but two were replying to the enemy. After an engagement of two hours and ten minutes he ceased firing and lowered his flag.

Our casualties were five killed and sixteen wounded; those of the enemy were sixty-three of all kinds. Twelve officers and sixty-three noncommissioned officers and

Robert E. Lee, who had been a military advisor to Jefferson Davis, assumed command of Confederate forces in the field on June 1, 1862. For the ensuing three years, he dealt the Union defeat after defeat, usually against large odds and with increasingly inadequate supplies and support. Blessed with gifted lieutenants, Lee stands head and shoulders above all other generals in American history. (Library of Congress)

privates were surrendered with the fort. The Tennessee River was thus open, and a base by short lines was established against Fort Donelson.

Grant moved against Fort Donelson forthwith:

I informed the department commander of our success at Fort Henry, and that on the eighth I would take Fort Donelson. But the rain continued to fall so heavily that the roads became impassable for artillery and wagon trains. Then, too, it would not have been prudent to proceed without the gunboats.

On the day after the fall of Fort Henry, I took my staff and made a reconnaissance to within about a mile of the outer line of works at Donelson. I had known one of its commanders, General Gideon J. Pillow, in Mexico, and judged that with any force, no matter how small, I could march up to within gunshot of any entrenchments he was given to hold. I knew that John B. Floyd was in high command, but he was no soldier, and I judged that he would yield to Pillow's pretensions.

Fort Donelson embraced about one hundred acres of land and stood on high ground, some if it as much as a hundred feet above the Cumberland. Strong protection to the heavy guns in the water batteries had been obtained by cutting away places for them in the bluff. To the west there was a line of rifle pits some two miles back from the river at the farthest point. The ground inside and outside of this entrenched line was very broken and generally wooded. The trees outside of the rifle pits had been cut down for a considerable way out and had been felled so that their tops lay outwards from the entrenchments. The limbs had been trimmed and pointed and thus formed an abatis in front of the greater part of the line.

General Halleck commenced his efforts to get reinforcements to me immediately on my departure from Cairo. I was very impatient to get to Fort Donelson, because I knew the importance of the place to the enemy and supposed he would reinforce it rapidly. I felt that 15,000 men on the eighth would be more effective than 50,000 a month later. I asked. . . Foote, therefore, to order his gunboats still about Cairo to proceed up the Cumberland River and not to wait.

I started from Fort Henry with 15,000 men and the advance arrived in front of the enemy by noon. That afternoon and the next day were spent in making the investment as complete as possible. General Smith occupied our left. McClernand was on the right and covered the roads running south and southwest from Dover. Our line was generally along the crest of ridges. The greatest suffering was from want of shelter. It would not do to allow campfires except out of sight of the enemy. In the march over from Fort Henry numbers of the men had thrown away their blankets and overcoats. There was therefore much discomfort and suffering.

Dr. Brinton's continued narrative describes the march:

General Grant and his staff remained at Fort Henry until about February 12. Two roads led from Fort Henry to Fort Donelson; the army moved along both, the cavalry watching the space between, so as not to allow any of the enemy to escape us. I rode near the General on my black horse, a strong, powerful beast which I had bought at Cairo. I could hardly keep him back; he particularly and persistently would pass the General who rode his old favorite stallion "Jack." Finally, he very good-naturedly said to me, "Doctor, I believe I command this army, and I think I'll go first."

We marched in battle order, ready for action. The actual luggage of the staff was represented by a few collars, a comb and brush and such toilet articles, contained in a small satchel belonging to me. General Grant had only a toothbrush in his waistcoat pocket, and I supplied him with a clean white collar. Of whiskey or liquor, of which so much has been said, there was not one drop, except that in my pocket, an 8-ounce flask, which I was especially requested by the General to keep only for medical purposes, and I was further instructed by him not to furnish a drink under any pretext to any member of the staff, except when necessary in my professional judgment.

We occupied the headquarters house on the afternoon of February 12, and here we remained until after the capture of Fort Donelson. The kitchen had in it a double feather bed, and this was occupied by the General. Some small rooms in the other parts of the house were crowded by other members of the staff. I think for one night the General slept somewhere else than the kitchen, but came down because of the bed and the warmer temperature.

On the thirteenth I was busy fixing my hospitals and doing the best I could. The whole of this day was employed in establishing the positions of our forces and in strengthening their lines. We threw up no breastworks but depended upon the natural strength of the ground and its "lay" for our protection, should the enemy attempt any sortie. However, the idea of a sortie never entered General Grant's head, or if it did, it found no lodgment there. His ideas were fixed, that the enemy would stay inside their works and not readily venture out.

The taking of Fort Donelson was much more difficult than Grant had imagined. His report was quite frank and honest:

Until the arrival of Lew Wallace on the fourteenth, the National forces, composed of but 15,000 men, without entrenchments, confronted an entrenched army of 21,000, without conflict further than what was brought on by ourselves. Only one gunboat had arrived. There was no actual fighting except once, on the thirteenth, in front of McClernand's command. That general had undertaken to capture a battery of the enemy which was annoying his men. Without orders or authority he sent three regiments to make the assault. The battery was in the main line of the enemy, which was defended by his whole army. Of course the assault was a failure, and the loss on our side was great for the number of men engaged.

During the night of the thirteenth Flag Officer Foote arrived with the ironclads **St. Louis, Louisville**, *and* **Pittsburgh**, *and the wooden gunboats* **Tyler** *and*

***Conestoga**. Wallace, whom I had ordered over from Fort Henry, also arrived about the same time. His new division was assigned to the center, giving the two flanking divisions an opportunity to close up and form a stronger line.*

The plan was for the troops to hold the enemy within his lines while the gunboats should attack the water batteries at close quarters and silence his guns, if possible. By three in the afternoon of the fourteenth Flag Officer Foote advanced upon the water batteries with his entire fleet. After coming in range of the batteries the advance was slow, but a constant fire was delivered from every gun that could be brought to bear upon the fort. The leading boat got within a very short distance of the water battery, not further off, I think, than two hundred yards, and I soon saw one and then another of them dropping down the river, visibly disabled. Then the whole fleet followed, and the engagement closed for the day. The gunboat which. . . Foote was on, besides having been hit about sixty times, several of the shots passing through near the water line, had a shot enter the pilothouse, which killed the pilot, carried away the wheel and wounded the Flag Officer himself. The tiller ropes of another vessel were carried away and she, too, dropped helplessly back. Two others had their pilothouses so injured that they scarcely formed a protection to the men at the wheel.

The enemy was jubilant when they saw the disabled vessels dropping down the river entirely out of control of the men on board. The sun went down on the night of February 14, 1862, leaving the army confronting Fort Donelson anything but comforted over the prospects. The weather had turned intensely cold; the men were without tents. Two of the strongest of our gunboats had been disabled, presumably beyond the possibility of rendering any present assistance. I retired this night, not knowing but that I would have to entrench my position and bring up tents for the men or build huts under the cover of the hills.

Jesse Young was but a boy doing duty with the Federal army. He wrote in *What a Boy Saw in the Army*, published in 1894, the following description of the gunboat attack on Donelson:

The gunboats carefully steamed around the bend and maneuvered into position. Before they were ready to commence operations I noticed a puff of smoke appear at a certain point in one of the embankments. In a moment afterward I heard a boom and a terrible screech which filled the air.

*The leading boat returned the fire, that boat being the **St. Louis** under Flag Officer Foote. In a moment the **Louisville** also was in action, and then the other ironclads of the fleet, the **Carondelet** and the **Pittsburgh**, followed at some distance downstream by the wooden gunboats, the **Tyler** and the **Conestoga**.*

When each boat arrived at the proper post, it delivered its fire and then circled around to reload and give the other boats opportunity to deliver their broadsides. Once in a while a solid shot from the fort would strike an iron-plated ship, make a deep dent in its armor and then glance off with a terrific splashing into the water. Then a shell would burst just over the deck, sending a perfect storm of iron hailstones down on the metal plates.

*At the very height of the engagement I saw a well-aimed bombshell enter the porthole of the **Carondelet**, exploding just within the opening, dismantling a cannon and wounding a dozen or more men. Through the din and confusion of the conflict there could be distinguished the officers' voices giving command to the gunners, the cries of the wounded and the battering and hammering of the detail of men who at once were set to work to clear away the wreck which had been made by the shell, so as to get the decks ready for action again. Thick and fast came the shots and bombs from the batteries, crashing on the iron plates, skipping across the waves, going clean through the smokestacks, tearing down the rigging; but still the lucky Commodore Foote kept his flagship, the **St. Louis**, in the forefront of the fight, and kept signaling to the others what to do. He had been severely wounded in the ankle, but he would not leave the field without doing all that he, with his fleet, might achieve toward capturing the fort.*

*After an hour and a half of this sort of work a couple of the boats, the flagship **St. Louis**, and the **Louisville**, were noticed to be in trouble. They moved wildly and falteringly hither and thither, and it was seen that the officers could not manage them. The signals soon told the fleet what was wrong; the steering apparatus of both boats was out of gear, the pilothouse of the **St. Louis** had been almost destroyed by round shot, and the machinery injured so that the ships could not be maneuvered and soon began to drift helplessly down the stream. The loss of these two disabled ships so weakened the fleet that it was soon found necessary to suspend the gunboat attack.*

One issue was decided by this engagement: Fort Donelson could not be taken, as Fort Henry had been, by an attack on the water front by the fleet. It would need more than a mere bombardment by cannon and mortar to conquer and capture it. The land forces would have to try their powers at it. The works would have to be stormed by the infantry.

Lew Wallace, whose military career was less than distinguished, would become famous some years later as the author of the extremely popular novel *Ben Hur*. In February 1862, as a Union general, he was called up from Fort Henry to assist in the attack on Donelson. His reporting style showed some signs of his future career:

Fort Henry had been surrendered on February 6. On February 10 an orderly crossed the river with a note for me, sealed, informal, but very interesting. There would be, it said, a meeting of general officers at headquarters next day. Time – two o'clock, afternoon. My presence was desired.

This, I saw, meant a council of war. How often had I read of such affairs in books of war! Now I was to see one and have a voice in it.

*General Grant had his headquarters on the steamboat **Tigress**. Not an armed sentinel could be seen on the landing*

COL. BURNSID

or on the vessel. I found my own way into the ladies' cabin. General Grant was there, and Rawlins, his adjutant general, sat at the table. I also recall the presence of Generals Charles F. Smith and John A. McClernand. It struck me that the company were in icy binding; probably because, like myself, they were mostly new to the business. Our uniforms and swords, worn in compliance with etiquette, may have had something to do with the frigidity of the occasion.

After a little, General Grant stepped to the table and said ever so quietly, "The question for consideration, gentlemen, is whether we shall march against Fort Donelson or wait for reinforcements. I should like to have your views." He looked first at General Smith – we were all standing – and Smith replied, "There is every reason why we should move without the loss of a day." General McClernand, taking the sign next, drew out a lengthy paper and read it. He, too, was in favor of going at once; then, as if in haste, Grant turned to me, nodding, and said, "Let us go, by all means; the sooner the better. We will set out immediately. Orders will be sent you. Get your commands ready."

That the opinions submitted had any influence with Grant is hardly supposable. There is evidence that he had already determined upon the movement.

Preparations for the attack on Donelson are described by Jefferson Davis:

The plan of operations for the next day [February 15] was determined by the Confederate generals about midnight [the 14th]. The whole of the left wing of the army except eight regiments was to move out of the trenches, attack, turn and drive the enemy's right until the Wynne's Ferry Road, which led to Charlotte through good country, was cleared and an exit thus secured.

The troops, moving in the small hours of the night over the icy and broken roads, which wound through the obstructed area of defense, made slow progress and delayed the projected operations. At 4:00 a.m. on the fifteenth Pillow's troops were ready, except one brigade, which came late into action. By six o'clock Colonel William E. Baldwin's brigade was engaged with the enemy, only two or three hundred yards front his lines, and the bloody contest of the day began. At one o'clock the enemy's right was doubled back. The Wynne's Ferry Road was cleared, and it only remained for the Confederates to do one of two things: the first was to seize the golden moment and, adhering to the original purpose and plan of the sortie, move off rapidly by the route laid open by such strenuous efforts and so much bloodshed; the other depended on the inspiration of a mastermind, which should

Officers of the 1st Rhode Island Volunteers with their colonel, Ambrose Burnside, in the first year of the War. Burnside, he of the famous whiskers, was a capable commander up to a point. When elevated to high command, however, he was a disaster. (Library of Congress) *complete the partial victory by the utter rout and destruction of the enemy.*

Grant's narrative details the battle:

On the morning of the fifteenth, the day chosen by the Confederates for their sortie, before it was yet broad day, a messenger from Flag Officer Foote, who was suffering from a painful wound, handed me a note expressing a desire to see me on the flagship. I directed my adjutant general to notify each of the division commanders of my absence and instruct them to do nothing to bring on an engagement until they received further orders, but to hold their positions.

When I left to visit . . . Foote I had no idea that there would be an engagement on land unless I brought it on myself.

Just as I landed from my visit to the flag officer,' I met Captain Hillyer of my staff, white with fear, not for his personal safety but for the safety of the National troops. He said the enemy had come out of his lines in full force and attacked and scattered McClernand's division which was in full retreat. The attack had been made on the National right.

Dr. Brinton:

One of my hospitals, that nearest to the Southern lines, was in a ravine, within sight of the hostile troops. It happened that some heavy skirmishing took place on the thirteenth, chiefly along General McClernand's front, our right. Indeed it was more than skirmishing, for a time in fact a very lively fight. During this, a good many wounded found their way to this particular hospital, and not only wounded, but many, a great many fainthearted ones, who disgracefully sought the hospital precinct as a shelter. This congregation hourly increased, and I began after a time to feel anxious lest the enemy, noticing so many stragglers, might sweep down and make capture of both hurt and unhurt. The hospital had only its sacred character to defend it, and this was being debased by the gathering crowd. Then, too, most of our hospital stores, I mean the reserve supplies, were here, and I did not wish them to fall into the enemy's hands. So I went to General Grant and explained to him the exposed position of the hospital. His answer was, "Yes, Doctor, I see, but they will **not** *come and capture you." And back I went to the hospital. Yet things went from bad to worse. Again I saw the general. Again I told him my fears, and again heard his answer, as before, "They will not come."*

As the peril increased still more, I sought him a third time, and after saying all I could, I asked him, "Am I exaggerating the risk of the loss of the medical stores of your army?" The general heard me as he always did, most patiently, and replied, "No, Doctor, you are right, but, Doctor, they won't do it; they are not thinking of anything, except holding their position."

General Wallace:

I now was at the head of a division of seven regiments, the total of which I roughly estimated at 6,000 men. I formed the center of the line of investment, with General McClernand on my right and General Smith on my left.

"You will hold your position to prevent escape of the Confederates without assuming the aggressive" – that was the order of the day.

The morning of the fifteenth crawled up the eastern sky as a turtle in its first appearance after hibernation crawls up a steep bank. An unusual sound off to the right front of my position attracted me. I listened. The sound broke at a jump into what was easily recognizable as a burst of musketry. What was it?

"What do you think of it?" I asked my officers. One of them thought it was McClernand assaulting the works.

"No," I replied, "the fort is here, more to our front."

Then another officer said, "The Johnnies are out pitching into McClernand." In a little while guns joined in.

"There! That settles it," I said. "Get out your horses. It looks as if we are to have it in boatloads today."

The noise over at the right had swollen in volume until it bore likeness to a distant train of empty cars rushing over a creaking bridge. But my orders were to keep my place, letting come what might.

The situation was very trying. Questions thronged in on me, all the output of imagination, but not less confusing on that account.

What, for instance, if the enemy had received reinforcements from Nashville in the night, making him once more superior to us in numbers? What if the demonstration at the moment going on over in McClernand's zone of investment were but a feint, leaving me or General Smith on my left the object of an impending attack?

The noise kept grinding on without lull or intermission; an hour – two hours – would it never end? The suspense became tortuous. At last a horseman galloped up from the rear. "I am from General McClernand," he said, "sent to ask assistance of you. The whole Rebel force in the fort massed against him in the night. Our ammunition is giving out. We are losing ground."

I dispatched a lieutenant to Grant's headquarters for permission to help McClernand. This was about eight o'clock. In good time my aide returned and reported General Grant on board the gunboat **St. Louis***, in conference with Flag Officer Foote. Nobody at headquarters felt authorized to act on my request. The battle, meantime, roared on.*

After a while a second messenger came from General McClernand, a gray-haired man in uniform. His news could hardly be worse, and he spoke with tears in his eyes.

"Our right flank is turned," he said. "The regiments are being crowded back on the center. We are using ammunition taken from the dead and wounded. The whole army is in danger."

My impulse had been to send help at the first asking; that impulse was now seconded by judgment. Disaster to the first division meant that if that division were rolled back on me, a panic might ensue. In the absence of the commanding general, the responsibility was mine. I said, "Tell General McClernand that I will send him my first brigade with Colonel Charles Cruft." Cruft acted promptly, and moved off through the woods under direction of a guide.

Shortly afterward Captain Rawlins came out to me, and I gave him an account of the messengers from General McClernand, and of what I had done with Cruft. While we talked, stragglers from the fight appeared coming on the run up a half-defined road. We scarcely noticed the fugitives, so much more were we drawn by the noise behind them. That grew in volume, being a compound of shouts and yells, mixed with the rattle of wheels and the rataplan and throbbing rumble of hoofs in undertone.

I called to an orderly, "Ride and see what all that flurry means." A suspicion of the truth broke through my wonder.

Then, as Rawlins and I sat waiting, an officer mounted and bareheaded and wild-eyed, rode madly up the road and past us, crying in shrill repetition, "We're cut to pieces!"

Now I had never seen a case of panic so perfectly defined, and it was curious, even impressive. Rawlins, however, was not disposed to view the spectacle philosophically. Jerking a revolver from his holster, he would have shot the frantic wretch had I not caught his hand. He remonstrated with me viciously, but the orderly came back at full speed and with an ominous look on his face.

"What is it?" I asked.

And he said, "The road back there is jammed with wagons, and men afoot and on horseback, all coming toward us. On the plains we would call it a stampede."

We looked at each other – Rawlins and I – and there was no need of further question. The first division was in full retreat.

"What are you going to do?" he asked.

"There's but one thing I can do."

"What is that?"

"Get this brigade out of the way. If those fellows strike my people, they will communicate the panic."

"Where will you go?"

"To take that way – "pointing to the rear – "is to retreat and carry the panic to General Smith; so I'll go up this road toward the enemy."

Then, at my word, the drummers beat the long roll. The men took arms. "By the right flank, file left!" And out in columns of companies they went.

I gave an instant to the coming mob and, believing from the sound that there would be time to get the last of my regiments clear of it and of contagion, I called my staff and hastened forward.

The firing seemed right of us, not fifty paces away. I noticed it extending rapidly, despite the undergrowth. Instead of advancing in line of battle, the enemy had marched up the cramped road in files of four, and, meeting us unexpectedly, were trying to deploy. It was a tactical mistake with a terrible penalty in payment. All we had to do was to ply them with fire. Colonel John M. Thayer had then got the 1st Nebraska and the 58th Illinois in line, the former next the road on the right. I gave him a sign. He spoke to Colonel William D. McCord, of the 1st Nebraska. I saw their muskets rise and fall steadily as if on a parade ground. A volley – and smoke – and after that constant fire at will as fast as skilled men could load.

Then Colonel William B. Woods arrived and, without slackening speed, wheeled his first section into battery right across the road. I heard him shout, "Grape now. Double-shot them, boys!" He could not see the foemen, I knew. But why look for them; was not their fire sufficient? Almost before the wheels were stationary his guns opened; a moment more and I lost sight of guns and men in a deepening cloud of smoke. The gallant fellows were doing the right thing.

The fight was now set, and we were on the defensive. For three-quarters of an hour it went on. The Confederate artillery, having to fire uphill, was of no service. Their shot and shell flew over the trees. I would not be understood as speaking lightly of the Confederates. The struggle on their part was to get into line, and in that they were persistent to obstinacy. Twice they quit, then returned to the trial. A third time repelled, they went back to stay. From a height Colonel Cruft saw them retreat pell-mell into their works.

The success, it may as well be admitted, more than gratified me. With a brigade thrust between it and its over-confident pursuers, I had been instrumental in relieving the first division from an imminent peril. Next day, Captain William S. Hillyer, aide-de-camp, sent me a note saying, "I speak advisedly. God bless you! You did save the day on the right!"

Grant:

I saw everything favorable for us along the line of our left and center. On the right I saw the men standing in knots talking in the most excited manner. No officer seemed to be giving any directions. The soldiers had their muskets but no ammunition, while there were tons of it close at hand. I heard some of the men say that the enemy had come out with knapsacks and haversacks filled with rations. They seemed to think this indicated a determination on his part to stay out and fight just as long as the provisions held out.

The enemy had come out in full force to cut his way out and make his escape. McClernand's division had had to bear the brunt of the attack from this combined force. When the men found themselves without ammunition, they could not stand up against troops who seemed to have plenty of it. But most of the men, as they were not pursued, only fell back out of range of the fire of the enemy. I turned to Colonel J.D. Webster of my staff, who was with me, and said, "Some of our men are pretty badly demoralized; however, the enemy must be more so, for he had attempted to force his way out but has fallen back; the one who attacks first now will be victorious." I determined to make the assault at once on our left. It was clear to my mind that if our attack could be made on the left, before the enemy could redistribute his forces along the line, we would find but little opposition except from the intervening abatis.

We rode to General Smith's quarters, where I explained the situation to him. The general was off in an incredibly short

Headquarters of the Union Army of the Potomac at Cumberland Landing, Va., on the Pamunky River in May 1862. McClellan's Peninsular Campaign ended in failure after the Battle of Seven Pines and the Seven Days Battles, and he was relieved of command. He was restored two months later. (Library of Congress)

time, going in advance himself to keep his men from firing while they were working their way through the abatis. The outer line of rifle pits was passed, and during the night of the fifteenth General Smith, with much of his division, bivouacked within the line of the enemy. There was now no doubt but that the Confederates must surrender or be captured the next day.

Jefferson Davis:

Of the two alternatives after his successful sortie – to march for Nashville or turn against the demoralized Union forces and try to destroy them – the Confederate commander tried neither. A fatal policy was suddenly but dubiously adopted, and not carried out. For seven hours the Confederate battalions had been pushing over rough ground and through thick timber, at each step meeting fresh troops massed, where the discomfited regiments rallied. Hence the vigor of assault slackened, though the wearied troops were still ready and competent to continue their onward movement. Fresh regiments, over 3,000 men, had then not fired a musket.

General Simon B. Buckner, third in command, had halted, according to the preconcerted plan, to allow the army to pass out by the opened road and to cover the retreat.

At this point of the fight, General Pillow heard of (or saw) preparations by General C.F. Smith for an assault on the Confederate right. He ordered the regiments which had been engaged to return to the trenches and instructed Buckner to hasten to defend the imperiled point. Buckner refused to obey and, after receiving reiterated orders, started to find General Floyd, who at that moment had joined them. He urged upon Floyd the necessity of carrying out the original plan of evacuation. Floyd assented to this view and told Buckner to stand fast until he would see Pillow. He then rode back and saw

Pillow and, hearing his arguments, yielded to them. Floyd simply says that he found the retreat movement so nearly executed that it was necessary to complete it. Accordingly, Buckner was recalled. In the meantime, Pillow's right brigades were retiring to their places in the trenches, under orders from the commanders.

The conflict on the left soon ended. Three hundred prisoners, 5,000 stands of small arms, six guns and other spoils of victory had been won by our forces. But the enemy, cautiously advancing, gradually recovered most of his lost ground. It was about 4:00 P.M. when the assault on the right was made by General C.F. Smith. The enemy succeeded in carrying the advanced work which General Buckner considered the key to his position.

After nightfall a consultation of the commanding officers was held. After a consideration of the question in all its aspects, it was decided that a surrender was inevitable and that to accomplish its objects it must be made before the assault, which was expected at daylight.

The decision to surrender having been made, it remained to determine by whom it should be made. Generals Floyd and Pillow declared they would not surrender and become prisoners; the duty was therefore allotted to General Buckner. Floyd said, "General Buckner, if I place you in command, will you allow me to draw out my brigade?" General Buckner replied, "Yes, provided you do so before the enemy acts upon my communication." General Pillow, regarding this as a mere technical form by which the command was to be conveyed to Buckner, then said, "I pass it." Buckner assumed the command, sent for a bugler to sound the parley, for pen, ink and paper, and opened negotiations for surrender. General Pillow advised Colonel N.B. Forrest, who was present, to go out with his cavalry regiment and any others he could take with him through the overflow.

Dr. Brinton:

The enemy had made their unsuccessful sortie on the fifteenth. As I happened to be in our kitchen bedroom in the afterpart of the day, I heard General Grant give orders to aide-de-camp Captain Hillyer to get ready to go to the nearest point of telegraph and send a dispatch to General Halleck, informing him that "Fort Donelson would surrender on the following morning." When I was alone with the general I said to him, "General, was it not a little dangerous to send so positive a message as to what the enemy will do tomorrow? Suppose he doesn't do it?" "Doctor," said the general to me, "he **will** *do it. I rode over the field this afternoon and examined some of the dead bodies of his men; their knapsacks, as well as their haversacks, were full of food; they were fighting to get away, and now that they have failed they will surrender. I knew Generals Buckner and Pillow in Mexico and they will do as I have said."*

The night was inclement. General Grant slept at his headquarters in the feather bed in the kitchen, and I was curled up on the floor. Early, very early, an orderly entered, ushering in General C.F. Smith, who seemed half-frozen. He walked at once to the open fire on the hearth, for a moment warmed his feet, then turned his back to the fire, facing General Grant who had slipped out of bed and was quickly drawing on his outer clothes. "There's something for you to read, General Grant," said Smith, handing him a letter. I can almost see General Smith now, erect, manly, every inch a soldier, standing in front of the fire, twisting his long white mustache. "What answer shall I send to this, General Smith?" asked Grant. Those were his actual words. Then he gave a short laugh and, drawing a piece of paper, letter size and of rather poor quality, began to write. In a short time, certainly not many minutes, he finished and read aloud, as if to General Smith but really so that we understrappers could all hear, his famous "unconditional surrender" letter.

Grant's account of the surrender:

Before daylight General Smith brought to me a letter from General Buckner asking for terms. To this I responded as follows.

"Sir:

"Yours of this date, proposing armistice and appointment of Commissioners to settle terms of capitulation, is just received. No terms except an unconditional and immediate surrender can be accepted. I propose to move immediately upon your work.

"Your obedient servant,

"U.S. Grant.

To this I received the following reply:

"Headquarters, Dover, Tennessee,
"February 16, 1862.

"To Brig. Gen'l U.S. Grant, U.S. Army.

"Sir:

"The distribution of the forces under my command, incident to an unexpected change of commanders, and the overwhelming force under your command, compel me, notwithstanding the brilliant success of the Confederate arms yesterday, to accept the ungenerous and unchivalrous terms which you propose.

"I am sir,

"Your very obedient servant,

"S.B. Buckner, Brig. Gen. C.S.A.

The *Richmond Examiner* saw the fall of Donelson as the portent of future disasters:

The fall of Fort Donelson was the heaviest blow that had yet fallen on the Confederacy. It opened up the whole of West Tennessee to Federal occupation, and it developed the crisis which had long existed in the west. General Johnston had previously ordered the evacuation of Bowling Green, and it was executed while the battle was fought at Donelson. Nashville was utterly indefensible; on the 6th of April the surrender of Island No. 10 had been a military necessity. The Confederates had been compelled to abandon what had been entitled, "The Little Gibraltar of the Mississippi," and experienced a loss in heavy artillery, which was nigh irreparable.

No one who lived in Richmond during the war can ever forget those gloomy, miserable days.

SHILOH

While McClellan prepared to move toward Richmond in the spring of 1862, 11,000 Union troops clashed with 14,000 Confederate troops at Elkhorn Tavern in northern Arkansas on March 6-8, in a battle that would be known as Pea Ridge. In April, Confederate General Albert Sidney Johnston concentrated his forces at Corinth, Mississippi. On March 3, Union General John Pope moved on New Madrid with 20,000 men; it succumbed in ten days. On April 7, Island No. 10 was cut off and forced to surrender 7,000 Confederates.

In the meantime, Johnston gathered 40,000 troops in a line from Memphis through Corinth to Chattanooga, and sat waiting for an additional 20,000 men from the west. General Halleck ordered Grant and Buell to Savannah. Grant arrived at Pittsburg Landing with 35,000 men; Buell took his time in advancing from Nashville. Early on the morning of April 6, Johnston hit the Federal outposts. Colonel Wills De Hass analyzed Grant's position:

The country is undulating table-land, the bluffs rising to the height of one hundred and fifty feet above the alluvial. Three principal streams and numerous tributaries cut the ground occupied by the army, while many deep ravines intersect, rendering it the worst possible battle-ground. The principal streams are Lick creek, which empties into the Tennessee above the landing; Owl creek, which rises near the source of Lick creek, flows south-east, encircling the battle-field, and falls into Snake creek, which empties into the Tennessee below the landing, or about three miles below Lick creek. The country. . . was a primeval forest, except where occasional settlers had opened out into small farms. The Army of the Tennessee lay within the area indicated, extending three and a half miles from the river and nearly the same distance north and south.

When the writer reached Shiloh (April 2d) he found the impression general that a great battle was imminent. Experienced officers believed that Beauregard and Johnston would strike Grant or the Army of the Tennessee before Buell could unite the Army of the Ohio. We found the army at Shiloh listless of danger, and in the worst possible condition of defense. The divisions were scattered over an extended space, with great intervals, and at one point a most dangerous gap. Not the semblance of a fortification could be seen. The entire front was in the most exposed condition. One or two sections of batteries at remote points, no scouts, no cavalry pickets, a very light infantry picket within one mile of camp, were all that stood between us and the dark forest then filling with the very flower of the Southern army. To my inexperienced judgment, all this appeared very strange, and I communicated these views to our brigade commander, who expressed himself in the same spirit, but remarked that he was powerless. One day's work in felling trees would have placed the camp in a tolerable state of defense. The men were actually sick from inaction and over-eating. A few hours' active exercise with the axe and shovel would have benefited their health, and might have saved their camp from destruction, with thousands of valuable lives.

Confederate General P.T.G. Beauregard explained the Confederate plan of action:

By a rapid and vigorous attack on Gen. Grant, it was expected he would be beaten back into his transports and the river, or captured, in time to enable us to profit by the victory, and remove to the rear all the stores and munitions that would fall into our hands in such an event, before the arrival of Gen. Buell's army on the scene. It was never contemplated, however, to retain the position thus gained, and abandon Corinth, the strategic point of the campaign.

Want of proper officers, needful for the proper organization of divisions and brigades of an army brought thus suddenly together, and other difficulties in the way of effective organization, delayed the movement until the night of the second inst., when it was heard from a reliable quarter that the junction of the enemy's armies was near at hand. It was then, at a late hour, determined that the attack should be attempted at once, incomplete and imperfect as were our preparations for such a grave and momentous adventure. Accordingly, that night, at one o'clock a.m., the preliminary orders to the commanders of corps were issued for the movement.

On the following morning the detailed orders of movement. . . were issued, and the movement, after some delay, commenced – the troops being in admirable spirits. It was expected we should be able to reach the enemy's lines in time to attack them early on the fifth instant. The men, however, for the most part, were unused to marching – the roads narrow, and traversing a densely wooded country, became almost impassable after a severe rain-storm on the night of the fourth, which drenched the troops in bivouac; hence our forces did not reach the intersection of the roads from Pittsburg and Hamburg, in the immediate vicinity of the enemy, until late Saturday afternoon.

It was then decided that the attack should be made on the next morning, at the earliest hour practicable, in accordance with the orders of movement – that is, in three lines of battle: the first and second extending from Owl Creek on the left to Lick Creek on the right – a distance of about three miles – supported by the third and the reserve.

At eight a.m., on the sixth, a reconnoitering party of the enemy having become engaged with our advanced pickets, the commander of the forces gave the orders to begin the movement and attack as determined upon.

The battle at Shiloh raged for 12 hours and competed with Antietam for the most casualties in a single day. By mid-morning, Confederate Albert Sidney Johnston had been mortally wounded, and Union General Sherman had four horses shot from beneath him. Whitelaw Reid described the afternoon:

We have reached the last act in the tragedy of Sunday. It is half-past four o'clock. Our front line of divisions has been lost since half-past ten. Our reserve line is now gone too. The rebels occupy the camps of every division save that of W.H.L. Wallace. Our whole army is crowded in the region of Wallace's camps, and to a circuit of one half to two thirds of a mile around the Landing. We have been falling back all day. We can do it no more. The next repulse puts us into the river, and there are not transports enough to cross a single division till the enemy would be upon us.

Lew. Wallace's division might turn the tide for us – it is made of fighting men – but where is it? Why has it not been thundering on the right for three hours past? We do not know yet that it was not ordered up till noon. Buell is coming, but he has been doing it all day, and all last week. His advance-guard is across the river now, waiting ferriage; but what is an advance-guard, with sixty thousand victorious foes in front of us?

We have lost nearly all our camps and camp equippage. We have lost nearly half our field artillery. We have lost a division general and two or three regiments of our soldiers as prisoners. We have lost – how dreadfully we are afraid to think – in killed and wounded. The hospitals are full to overflowing. A long ridge bluff is set apart for surgical uses. It is covered with the maimed, the dead, the dying. And our men are discouraged by prolonged defeat. Nothing but the most energetic exertion, on the part of the officers, prevents them from becoming demoralized. Regiments have lost their favorite field-officers; companies the captains whom they have always looked to, with the implicit faith the soldier learns, to lead them to battle.

Meanwhile there is a lull in the fighting. For the first time since sunrise you fail to catch the angry rattle of musketry or the heavy booming of the field-guns. Either the enemy must be preparing for the grand, final rush that is to crown the day's success and save the Southern Confederacy, or they are puzzled by our last retreat, and are moving cautiously lest we spring some trap upon them. Let us embrace the opportunity, and look about the Landing. We pass the old-log house, lately postoffice, now full of wounded and surgeons, which constitutes the "Pittsburg" part of the Landing. General Grant and staff are in a group beside it. The General is confident. "We can hold them off till to-morrow; then they'll be exhausted, and we'll go at them with fresh troops." A great crowd is collected around the building – all in uniforms, most of them with guns. And yet we are needing troops in the front so sorely!

On the bluffs above the river is a sight that may well make our cheeks tingle. There are not less than five thousand skulkers lining the banks! Ask them why they don't go to their places in the line: "Oh! our regiment is all cut to pieces." "Why don't you go to where it is forming again?" "I can't find it," and the hulk looks as if that would be the very last thing he would want to do.

Officers are around among them, trying to hunt up their men, storming, coaxing, commanding – cursing I am afraid. One strange fellow – a Major, if I remember aright – is making a sort of elevated, superfine Fourth of July speech to everybody that will listen to him. He means well, certainly: "Men of Kentucky, of Illinois, of Ohio, of Iowa, of Indiana, I implore you, I beg of you, come up now. Help us through two hours more. By all that you hold dear, by the homes you hope to defend, by the flag you love, by the States you honor, by all your love of country, by all your hatred of treason, I conjure you, come up and do your duty now!" And so on for quantity. "That feller's a good speaker," was the only response I heard, and the fellow who gave it nestled more snugly behind his tree as he spoke.

John Rowlands was born in Wales and sailed as a cabin boy to Louisiana, where he was adopted by New Orleans merchant Henry Morton Stanley. Taking Stanley's name, Rowlands enlisted in the Dixie Grays. He fought at the Battle of Shiloh and was captured. He later enlisted in the Federal artillery, was discharged and returned to England, and still later he came back to America and enlisted in the Federal navy. In later life he achieved great fame as a journalist and explorer under his adopted name of Henry M. Stanley.

Sir Henry Stanley's, or rather John Rowland's, account of the action at Shiloh showed his early talent for writing and is among the best battle reporting of the war. Were it not known to be from Shiloh, the following narrative could well have been from almost any battlefield, so explicit is Stanley's descriptions of the horrors of war:

On April 2, 1862, we received orders to prepare three days' cooked rations. Through some misunderstanding, we did not set out until the 4th; and, on the morning of that day, the 6th Arkansas Regiment of Hindman's brigade, Hardee's corps, marched from Corinth to take part in one of the bloodiest battles of the West. We left our knapsacks and tents behind us. After two days of marching, and two nights of bivouacking and living on cold rations, our spirits were not buoyant at dawn of Sunday, the 6th April, as they ought to have been for the serious task before us.

At four o'clock in the morning, we rose from our damp bivouac, and, after a hasty refreshment, were formed into line. We stood in rank for half an hour or so, while the military dispositions were being completed along the three-mile front. Our brigade formed the centre; Cleburne's and Gladden's brigades were on our respective flanks.

Day broke with every promise of a fine day. Next to me, on my right, was a boy of seventeen, Henry Parker. I remember it because, while we stood-at-ease, he drew my attention to some violets at his feet, and said, "It would be a good idea to

At the end of August 1862, the Union and Confederate armies fought again on the same ground at Bull Run, with much the same result as a year previously. The federal army counted nearly 15,000 casualties. These men and officers of the 51st New York Infantry survived to pose for a photo after the battle. (Library of Congress)

put a few into my cap. Perhaps the Yanks won't shoot me if they see me wearing such flowers, for they are a sign of peace."

"Capital," said I, "I will do the same."

We plucked a bunch, and arranged the violets in our caps. The men in the ranks laughed at our proceedings, and had not the enemy been so near, their merry mood might have been communicated to the army.

We loaded our muskets, and arranged our cartridge-pouches ready for use. Our weapons were the obsolete flint-locks, and the ammunition was rolled in cartridge-paper, which contained powder, a round ball, and three buckshot. When we loaded we had to tear the paper with our teeth, empty the rest of the powder into the barrel, press paper and ball into the muzzle, and ram home. Then the Orderly-sergeant called the roll, and we knew that the Dixie Greys were present to a man.

Before we had gone five hundred paces, our serenity was disturbed by some desultory firing in front. It was then a quarter-past five. "They are at it already," we whispered to each other. "Stand by, gentlemen," – for we were all gentlemen volunteers at this time, – said our Captain L.G. Smith. Our steps became unconsciously brisker, and alertness was noticeable in everybody. The firing continued at intervals, deliberate and scattered, as at target practice. We drew nearer to the firing, and soon a sharper rattling of musketry was heard. "That is the enemy waking up," we said. Within a few minutes, there was another explosive burst of musketry, the air was pierced by many missiles, which hummed and pinged sharply by our ears, pattered through the tree-tops, and brought twigs and leaves down on us. "Those are bullets," Henry whispered with awe.

At two hundred yards further, a dreadful roar of musketry broke out from a regiment adjoining ours. It was followed by another further off, and the sound had scarcely died away when regiment after regiment blazed away and made a continuous roll of sound. "We are in for it now," said Henry.

"Forward, gentlemen, make ready!" urged Captain Smith. In response, we surged forward, for the first time marring the alignment. We trampled recklessly over the grass and young sprouts. Beams of sunlight stole athwart our course. . . Nothing now stood between us and the enemy.

"There they are!" was no sooner uttered, than we cracked into them with levelled muskets. "Aim low, men!" commanded Captain Smith. I tried hard to see some living thing to shoot at, for it appeared absurd to be blazing away at shadows. But, still advancing, firing as we moved, I, at last, saw a row of little globes of pearly smoke streaked with crimson, breaking-out with spurtive quickness, from a long line of blue figures in front; and simultaneously, there broke upon our ears an appalling crash of sound, the series of fusillades following one another with startling suddenness, which suggested to my somewhat moidered sense a mountain upheaved, with huge rocks tumbling and thundering down a slope, and the echoes rumbling and receding through space. Again and again, these loud and quick explosions were repeated, seemingly with increased violence, until they rose to the highest pitch of fury, and in unbroken continuity. All the world seemed involved in one tremendous ruin!

Though one's senses were preternaturally acute, and engaged with their impressions, we plied our arms, loaded and fired, with such nervous haste as though it depended on each of us how soon this fiendish uproar would be hushed. My nerves tingled, my pulses beat double-quick, my heart throbbed loudly, and almost painfully; but, amid all the excitement, my thoughts, swift as the flash of lightning, took all sound, and sight, and self, into their purview. I listened to the battle raging far away on the flanks, to the thunder in front, to the various sounds made by the leaden storm. I was angry with my rear rank, because he made my eyes smart with the powder of his musket; and I felt like cuffing him for deafening my ears! I knew how Captain Smith and Lieutenant Mason looked, how bravely the Dixie Greys' banner ruffled over Newton Story's head, and that all hands were behaving as though they knew how long all this would last. Back to myself my thoughts came, and, with the whirring bullet, they fled to the blue-bloused ranks afront. They dwelt on their movements, and read their temper, as I should read time by a clock. Through the lurid haze the contours of their pink faces could not be seen, but their gappy, hesitating, incoherent, and sensitive line revealed their mood clearly.

We continued advancing, step by step, loading and firing as we went. To every foward step, they took a backward move, loading and firing, as they slowly withdrew. Twenty thousand muskets were being fired at this stage, but, though accuracy of aim was impossible, owing to our labouring hearts, and the jarring and excitement, many bullets found their destined billets on both sides.

After a steady exchange of musketry, which lasted some time, we heard the order: "Fix Bayonets! On the double-quick!" in tones that thrilled us. There was a simultaneous bound forward, each soul doing his best for the emergency. The Federals appeared inclined to await us; but, at this juncture, our men raised a yell, thousands responded to it, and burst out into the wildest yelling it has ever been my lot to hear. It drove all sanity and order from among us. It served the double purpose of relieving pent-up feelings, and transmitting encouragement along the attacking line. I rejoiced in the shouting like the rest. It reminded me that there were about four hundred companies like the Dixie Greys, who shared our feelings. Most of us, engrossed with the musket-work, had forgotten the fact; but the wave after wave of human voices, louder than all other battle-sounds together, penetrated to every sense, and stimulated our energies to the utmost.

"They fly!" was echoed from lip to lip. It accelerated our pace, and filled us with a noble rage. Then I knew what the Berserker passion was! It deluged us with rapture, and transfigured each Southerner into an exulting victor. At such a moment, nothing could have halted us.

Those savage yells, and the sight of thousands of racing figures coming towards them, discomfited the blue-coats; and when we arrived upon the place where they had stood, they had vanished. Then we caught sight of their beautiful array of tents, before which they had made their stand, after being roused from their Sunday-morning sleep, and huddled into line, at hearing their pickets challenge our skirmishers. The half-dressed dead and wounded showed what a surprise our attack had been. We drew up in the enemy's camp, panting and breathing hard. Some precious minutes were thus lost in recovering our breaths, indulging our curiosity, and reforming our line. Signs of a hasty rouse to the battle were abundant. Military equipments, uniform-coats, half-packed knapsacks, bedding, of a new and superior quality, littered the company streets.

Meantime, a series of other camps lay behind the first array of tents. The resistance we had met, though comparatively brief, enabled the brigades in rear of the advance camp to recover from the shock of the surprise; but our delay had not been long enough to give them time to form in proper order of battle. There were wide gaps between their divisions into which the quick-flowing tide of elated Southerners entered, and compelled them to fall back lest they should be surrounded. Prentiss's brigade, despite their most desperate efforts, were thus hemmed in on all sides, and were made prisoners.

I had a momentary impression that, with the capture of the first camp, the battle was well-nigh over; but, in fact, it was only a brief prologue of the long and exhaustive series of struggles which took place that day.

Continuing our advance, we came in view of the tops of another mass of white tents, and almost at the same time, were met by a furious storm of bullets, poured on us from a long line of blue-coats, whose attitude of assurance proved to us that we should have tough work here. But we were so much heartened by our first success that it would have required a good deal to have halted our advance for long. Their opportunity for making a full impression on us came with terrific suddenness. The world seemed bursting into fragments. Cannon and musket, shell and bullet, lent their several intensities to the distracting uproar. If I had not a fraction of an ear, and an eye inclined towards my Captain and Company, I had been spell-bound by the energies now opposed to us. I likened the cannon, with their deep bass, to the roaring of a great herd of lions; the ripping, cracking musketry, to the incessant yapping of terriers; the windy whisk of shells, and zipping of minie bullets, to the swoop of eagles, and the buzz of angry wasps. All the opposing armies of Grey and Blue fiercely blazed at each other.

After being exposed for a few seconds to this fearful downpour, we heard the order to "Lie down, men, and continue your firing!" Before me was a prostrate tree, about fifteen inches in diameter, with a narrow strip of light between it and the ground. Behind this shelter a dozen of us flung ourselves. The security it appeared to offer restored me to my individuality. We could fight, and think, and observe, better than out in the open. But it was a terrible period! How the cannon bellowed, and their shells plunged and bounded, and flew with screeching hisses over us! Their sharp rending explosions and hurtling fragments made us shrink and cower, despite our utmost efforts to be cool and collected. I marvelled, as I heard the unintermitting patter, snip, thud, and hum of bullets, how anyone could live under this raining death. I could hear the balls beating a merciless tattoo on the outer surface of the log, pinging it vivaciously as they flew off at a tangent from it, and thudding into something or other, at the rate of a hundred a second. One, here and there, found its way under the log, and buried itself in a comrade's body. One man raised his chest, as if to yawn, and jostled me. I turned to him, and saw that a bullet had gored his whole face, and penetrated into his chest. Another ball struck a man a deadly rap on the head, and he turned on his back and showed his ghastly white face to the sky.

"It is getting too warm, boys!" cried a soldier, and he uttered a vehement curse upon keeping soldiers hugging the ground until every ounce of courage was chilled. He lifted his head a little too high, and a bullet skimmed over the top of the log and hit him fairly in the centre of his forehead, and he fell heavily on his face. But his thought had been instantaneously general; and the officers, with one voice, ordered the charge; and cries of "Forward, forward!" raised us, as with a spring, to our feet, and changed the complexion of our feelings. The pulse of action beat feverishly once more; and, though overhead was crowded with peril, we were unable to give it so much attention as when we lay stretched on the ground.

Our progress was not so continuously rapid as we desired for the blues were obdurate; but at this moment we were gladdened at the sight of a battery galloping to our assistance. It was time for the nerve-shaking cannon to speak. After two rounds of shell and canister, we felt the pressure on us slightly relaxed; but we were still somewhat sluggish in disposition, though the officers' voices rang out imperiously. Newton Story at this juncture strode forward rapidly with the Dixies' banner, until he was quite sixty yards ahead of the foremost. Finding himself alone, he halted; and turning to us smilingly said, "Why don't you come on, boys? You see there is no danger!" His smile and words acted on us like magic. We raised the yell, and sprang lightly and hopefully towards him. "Let's give them hell, boys!" said one. "Plug them plum-centre, every time!"

It was all very encouraging, for the yelling and shouting were taken up by thousands. "Forward, forward; don't give them breathing time!" was cried. We instinctively obeyed, and soon came in clear view of the blue-coats, who were scornfully unconcerned at first; but, seeing the leaping tide of men coming on at a tremendous pace, their front dissolved, and they fled in double-quick retreat. Again, we felt the "glorious joy of heroes." It carried us on exultantly, rejoicing in the spirit which recognizes nothing but the prey. We were no longer an army of soldiers, but so many school-boys racing, in which length of legs, wind, and condition tell.

We gained the second line of camps, continued the rush through them, and clean beyond. It was now about ten o'clock. My physical powers were quite exhausted, and, to add to my discomfiture, something struck me on my belt-clasp, and tumbled me headlong to the ground. I could not have been many minutes prostrated before I recovered from the shock of the blow and fall, to find my clasp deeply dented and cracked. My company was not in sight. I was grateful for the rest, and crawled feebly to a tree, and plunging my hand into my haversack, ate ravenously. Within half an hour, feeling renovated, I struck north in the direction which my regiment had taken, over a ground strewn with bodies and the debris of war.

The desperate character of this day's battle was now brought home to my mind in all its awful reality. While in the tumultuous advance, and occupied with a myriad of exciting incidents, it was only at brief intervals that I was conscious of wounds being given and received; but now, in the trail of pursuers and pursued, the ghastly relics appalled every sense. I felt curious as to who the fallen Greys were, and moved to one stretched straight out. It was the body of a stout English Sergeant of a neighboring company, the members of which hailed principally from the Washita Valley.

Alfred Waud drew members of the superb Virginia cavalry at a halt during the Antietam campaign. Artists or photographers seldom accompanied the Confederate forces, so on-the-spot depictions of Southern troops are relatively rare. (Library of Congress)

Close by him was a young Lieutenant, who, judging by the new gloss on his unform, must have been some father's darling. A clean bullet-hole through the centre of his forehead had instantly ended his career. A little further were some twenty bodies, lying in various postures, each by its own pool of viscous blood, which emitted a peculiar scent, which was new to me, but which I have since learned is inseparable from a battle-field. Beyond these, a still larger group lay, body overlying body, knees crooked, arms erect, or wide-stretched and rigid according as the last spasm overtook them. The company opposed to them must have shot straight.

It was the first Field of Glory I had seen in my May of life, and the first time that Glory sickened me with its repulsive aspect, and made me suspect it was all a glittering lie. . . . Under a flag of truce, I saw the bearers pick up the dead from the field, and lay them in long rows beside a wide trench; I saw them laid, one by one, close together at the bottom.

I overtook my regiment about one o'clock, and our side was preparing for another assault. The firing was alternately brisk and slack. We lay down, and availed ourselves of trees, logs, and hollows, and annoyed their upstanding ranks; battery pounded battery, and meanwhile we hugged our resting places closely. Of a sudden, we rose and raced towards the position, and took it by sheer weight and impetuosity. About three o'clock, the battle grew very hot. The enemy appeared to be more concentrated, and immovably sullen. Both sides fired better as they grew more accustomed to the din; but, with assistance from the reserves, we were continually pressing them towards the river Tennessee, without ever retreating an inch.

About this time, the enemy were assisted by the gunboats, which hurled their enormous projectiles far beyond us; but, though they made great havoc among the trees, and created terror, they did comparatively little damage to those in close touch with the enemy.

The screaming of the big shells, when they first began to sail over our heads, had the effect of reducing our fire; for they were as fascinating as they were distracting. But we became used to them.

As it drew near four o'clock . . . several of our company lagged wearily behind, and the remainder showed, by their drawn faces, the effects of their efforts. Yet, after a short rest, they were able to make splendid spurts. As for myself, I had only one wish, and that was for repose. The long-continued excitement, the successive tautening and relaxing of the nerves, the quenchless thirst, made more intense by the fumes of sulphurous powder, and the caking grime on the lips caused by tearing the paper cartridges, and a ravening hunger, all combined, had reduced me to a walking automaton, and I earnestly wished that night would come.

Finally, about five o'clock, we assaulted and captured a large camp; after driving the enemy well away from it; the front line was as thin as that of a skirmishing body, and we were ordered to retire to the tents.

An hour before dawn, I awoke and, after a hearty replenishment of my vitals with biscuit and molasses, I conceived myself to be fresher than on Sunday morning. While awaiting day-break, I gathered from other early risers their ideas in regard to the events of yesterday. They were under the impression that we had gained a great victory, though we had not, as we had anticipated, reached the Tennessee River. Van Dorn, with his expected reinforcements for us, was not likely to make his appearance for many days yet; and, if General Buell, with his 20,000 troops, had joined the enemy during the night, we had a bad day's work before us. We were short of provisions and ammunition, General Sidney Johnston, our chief Commander, had been killed; but Beauregard was safe and unhurt, and, if Buell was absent, we would win the day.

At daylight I fell in with my Company, but there were only about fifty of the Dixies present. . . . Regiments were hurried into line, but, even to my inexperienced eyes, the troops were in ill-condition for repeating the efforts of Sunday. . . . In consequence of our pickets being driven in on us, we were moved forward in skirmishing order. With my musket on the trail I found myself in active motion, more active than otherwise I would have been, perhaps, because Captain Smith had said, "Now, Mr. Stanley, if you please, step briskly forward!" This singling-out of me wounded my **amour-propre***, and sent me forward like a rocket. In a short time, we met our opponents in the same formation as ourselves, and advancing most resolutely. We threw ourselves behind such trees as were near us, fired, loaded, and darted forward to another shelter. Presently, I found myself in an open grassy space, with no convenient tree or stump near; but, seeing a shallow hollow some twenty paces ahead, I made a dash for it, and plied my musket with haste.*

I became so absorbed with some blue figures in front of me, that I did not pay sufficient heed to my companion greys . . . . Seeing my blues in about the same proportion, I assumed that the greys were keeping their position, and never once thought of retreat. However, as, despite our firing, the blues were coming uncomfortably near, I rose from my hollow; but, to my speechless amazement, I found myself a solitary grey, in a line of blue skirmishers! My companions had retreated! The next I heard was, "Down with that gun, Secesh, or I'll drill a hole through you! Drop it, quick!"

Half a dozen of the enemy were covering me at the same instant, and I dropped my weapon, incontinently. Two men sprang at my collar, and marched me, unresisting, into the ranks of the terrible Yankees. ***I was a prisoner!***

Some of the fiercest fighting in the entire war took place at the center of the Union line on April 6 – at a place called the "Hornet's Nest." Leander Stillwell accumulated diaries and letters over the years and late in the 19th century he published his recollections in *The Story of a Common Soldier of Army Life in the Civil War, 1861-1865*:

We had "turned out" about sunup, answered to roll-call, and had cooked and eaten our breakfast. We had then gone to work, preparing for the regular Sunday morning inspection, which would take place at nine o'clock. The boys were scattered around the company streets and in front of the company parade grounds, engaged in polishing and brightening their muskets, and brushing up and cleaning their shoes, jackets, trousers, and clothing generally.

It was a most beautiful morning. The sun was shining brightly through the trees, and there was not a cloud in the sky. It really seemed like Sunday in the country at home. During week days there was a continual stream of army wagons going to and from the landing, and the clucking of their wheels, the yells and oaths of the drivers, the cracking of whips, mingled with the braying of mules, the neighing of the horses, the incessant hum and buzz of the camps, the blare of bugles, and the roll of drums, – all these made up a prodigious volume of sound that lasted from the coming-up to the going-down of the sun. But this morning was strangely still. The wagons were silent, the mules were peacefully munching their hay, and the teamsters were giving us a rest. I listened with delight to the plaintive, mournful tones of a turtle-dove in the woods close by, while on a dead limb of a tall tree right in the camp a wood-pecker was sounding his "long roll" just as I had heard it beaten by his Northern brothers a thousand times on the trees in the Otter Creek bottom at home.

Suddenly, away off on the right, in the direction of Shiloh church, came a dull, heavy "Pum!" then another, and still another. Every man sprung to his feet as if struck by an electric shock, and we looked inquiringly into one another's faces. "What is that?" asked every one but no one answered. Those heavy booms then came thicker and faster, and just a few seconds after we heard that first dull, ominous growl off to the southwest, came a low, sullen, continuous roar. There was no mistakinbg that sound. That was not a squad of pickets emptying their guns on being relieved from duty; it was the continuous roll of thousands of muskets, and told us that a battle was on.

What I have been describing just now occurred during a few seconds only, and with the roar of musketry the long roll began to beat in our camp. Then ensued a scene of desperate haste, the like of which I certainly had never seen before, nor ever saw again. I remember that in the midst of this terrible uproar and confusion, while the boys were buckling on their cartridge boxes, and before even the companies had been formed, a mounted staff officer came galloping wildly down the line from the right. He checked and whirled his horse sharply around in our company street, the iron-bound hoofs of his steed crashing among the tin plates lying in a little pile where my mess had eaten its breakfast that morning. The horse was flecked with foam and its eyes and nostrils were red with blood. The officer cast one hurried glance around him, and exclaimed: "My God! this regiment not in line yet! They have been fighting on the right over an hour!" And wheeling his horse, he disappeared in the direction of the colonel's tent.

Well, the companies were formed, we marched out on the regimental parade ground, and the regiment was formed in line. The command was given: "Load at will; load!" We had anticipated this, however, as the most of us had instinctively loaded our guns before we had formed company. All this time the roar on the right was getting nearer and louder. Our old colonel rode up close to us, opposite the center of the regimental line, and called out, "Attention, battalion!" We fixed our eyes on him to hear what was coming. It turned out to be the old man's battle harangue.

"Gentlemen," said he, in a voice that every man in the regiment heard, "remember your State, and do your duty today like brave men".

That was all. . . . Immediately after the colonel had given us his brief exhortation, the regiment was marched across the little field I have before mentioned, and we took our place in line of battle, the woods in front of us, and the open field in our rear. We "dressed on" the colors, ordered arms, and stood awaiting the attack. By this time the roar on the right had become terrific. The Rebel army was unfolding its front, and the battle was steadily advancing in our direction. We could begin to see the blue rings of smoke curling upward among the trees off to the right, and the pungent smell of burning gun-powder filled the air. As the roar came travelling down the line from the right it reminded me (only it was a million times louder) of the sweep of a thunder-shower in summer-time over the hard ground of a stubble-field.

And there we stood, in the edge of the woods, so still, waiting for the storm to break on us. . . .

The time we thus stood, waiting the attack, could not have exceeded five minutes. Suddenly, obliquely to our right, there was a long, wavy flash of bright light, then another, and another! It was the sunlight shining on gun barrels and bayonets – and – there they were at last! A long brown line, with muskets at a right shoulder shift, in excellent order, right through the woods they came.

We began firing at once. From one end of the regiment to the other leaped a sheet of red flame, and the roar that went up from the edge of that old field doubtless advised General Prentiss of the fact that the Rebels had at last struck the extreme left of his line. We had fired but two or three rounds when, for some reason – I never knew what, – we were ordered to fall back across the field, and did so. The whole line, so far as I could see to the right, went back. We halted on the other side of the field, in the edge of the woods, in front of our tents, and again began firing. The Rebels, of course, had moved up and occupied the line we had just abandoned. And here we did our first hard fighting during the day. Our officers said, after the battle was over, that we held this line an hour and ten minutes. How long it was I do not know. I "took no note of time."

We retreated from this position as our officers afterward said, because the troops on our right had given way, and we were flanked. Possibly those boys on our right would give the same excuse for their leaving, and probably truly, too. Still, I think we did not fall back a minute too soon. As I rose from the comfortable log from behind which a bunch of us had been firing, I saw men in gray and brown clothes, with trailed muskets, running through the camp on our right, and I saw something else, too, that sent a chill all through me. It was a kind of flag I had never seen before. It was a gaudy sort of thing, with red bars. It flashed over me in a second that that thing was a Rebel flag. It was not more than sixty yards to the right. The smoke around it was low and dense and kept me from seeing the man who was carrying it, but I plainly saw the banner. It was going fast, with a jerky motion, which told me that the bearer was on a double-quick. About that time we left. We observed no kind of order in leaving; the main thing was to get out of there as quick as we could. I ran down our company street, and in passing the big Sibley tent of our mess I thought of my knapsack with all my traps and belongings, including that precious little packet of letters from home. I said to myself, "I will save my knapsack, anyhow;" but one quick backward glance over my left shoulder made me change my mind, and I went on. I never saw my knapsack or any of its contents afterwards.

Our broken forces halted and re-formed about half a mile to the rear of our camp on the summit of a gentle ridge, covered with thick brush. I recognized our regiment by the little gray pony the old colonel rode, and hurried to my place in the ranks. Standing there with our faces once more to the front, I saw a seemingly endless column of men in blue, marching by the flank, who were filing off to the right through the woods, and I heard our old German adjutant, Cramer, say to the colonel, "Dose are de troops of Sheneral Hurlbut. He is forming a new line dere in de bush." I exclaimed to myself from the bottom of my heart, "Bully for General Hurlbut and the new line in the bush! Maybe we'll whip 'em yet." I shall never forget my feelings about this time. I was astonished at our first retreat in the morning across the field back to our camp, but it occurred to me that maybe that was only "strategy" and all done on purpose; but when we had to give up our camp, and actually turn our backs and run half a mile, it seemed to me that we were forever disgraced, and I kept thinking to myself: "What will they say about this at home?"

I was very dry for a drink, and as we were doing nothing, just then, I slipped out of ranks and ran down to the little hollow in our rear, in search of water. Finding a little pool, I threw myself on the ground and took a copious draught. As I rose to my feet, I observed an officer about a rod above me also quenching his thirst, holding his horse meanwhile by the bridle. As he rose I saw it was our old adjutant. At no other time would I have dared accost him unless in the line of duty, but the situation made me bold.

"Adjutant," I said, "What does this mean – our having to run this way? Ain't we whipped?"

He blew the water from his mustache, and quickly answered in a careless way: "Oh, no; dat is all ride. We yoost fall back to form on the reserves. Sheneral Buell vas now crossing der river mit 50,000 men, and will be here pooty quick; and Sheneral Lew Vallace is coming up from Crump's Landing mit 15,000 more. Ve vips 'em; ve vips 'em. Go to your gompany.". . . But as the long hours wore on that day, and still Buell and Wallace did not come, my faith in the adjutant's veracity became considerably shaken.

It was at this point that my regiment was detached from Prentiss' division and served with it no more that day. We were sent some distance to the right to support a battery, the name of which I never learned. It was occupying the summit of a slope, and was actively engaged when we reached it. We were put in position of about twenty rods in the rear of the battery, and ordered to lie flat on the ground. The ground sloped gently down in our direction, so that by hugging it close, the rebel shot and shell went over us.

It was here, at about ten o'clock in the morning, that I first saw Grant that day. He was on horseback, of course, accompanied by his staff, and was evidently making a personal examination of his lines. He went by us in a gallop, riding between us and the battery, at the head of his staff. The battery was then hotly engaged; shot and shell were whizzing overhead, and cutting off the limbs of trees, but Grant paying no more attention to the missiles than if they had been paper wads.

We remained in support of this battery until about 2 o'clock in the afternoon. We were then put in motion by the right flank, filed to the left, crossed the left-hand Corinth road; then we were thrown into the line by the command: "By the left flank, march." We crossed a little ravine and up a slope, and relieved a regiment on the left of Hurlbut's line. This line was desperately engaged, and had been at this point, as we afterwards learned, for fully four hours. I remember as we went up the slope and began firing, about the first thing that met my gaze was what out West we would call a "windrow" of dead men in blue; some doubled up face downward, others with their white faces upturned to the sky, brave boys who had been shot to death in "holding the line." Here we stayed until our last cartridge was shot away. We were then relieved by another regiment. We filled our cartridge boxes again and went back to the support of our battery. The boys laid down and talked in low tones. Many of our comrades alive and well an hour ago, we had left dead on that bloody ridge. And still the battle raged. From right to left, everywhere, it was one never-ending, terrible roar, with no prospect of stopping.

Somewhere between 4 and 5 o'clock, as near as I can tell, everything became ominously quiet. Our battery ceased firing; the gunners leaned against the pieces and talked and laughed. Suddenly a staff officer rode up and said something in a low tone to the commander of the battery, then rode to our colonel and said something to him. The battery horses were at once brought up from a ravine in the rear, and the battery limbered up and moved off through the woods diagonally to the left and rear. We were put in motion by the flank and followed it. Everything kept so still, the loudest noise I heard was the clucking of the wheels of the gun-carriages and caissons as they wound through the woods. We emerged from the woods and entered a little old field. I then saw at our right and front lines of men in blue moving in the same direction we were, and it was evident that we were falling back.

All at once, on the right, the left, and from our recent front, come one tremendous roar, and the bullets fell like hail. The lines took the double-quick towards the rear. For awhile the attempt was made to fall back in order, and then everything went to pieces. A confused mass of men and guns, caissons, army wagons, ambulances, and all the debris of a beaten army surged and crowded along the narrow dirt road to the landing, while that pitiless storm of leaden hail came crashing on us from the rear. It was undoubtedly at this crisis in our affairs that the division of General Prentiss was captured.

It must have been when we were less than half a mile from the landing on our disorderly retreat before mentioned, that we saw him standing in line of battle, at ordered arms, extending from both sides of the road until lost to sight in the woods, a long well-ordered line of men in blue. What did that mean? and where had they come from?. . . I said. . . (to Enoch Wallace): "Enoch, what are those men there for?"

He answered in a low tone: "I guess they are put there to hold the Rebels in check till the army can get across the river."

And doubtless that was the thought of every intelligent soldier in our beaten column. And yet it goes to show how

The infamous "Burnside" bridge over Antietam Creek. Burnside ignored easy fords nearby and flung his troops at the well-defended span time after time. Artist Edwin Forbes depicted the taking of the bridge, but the final heroics were too little, too late. (Library of Congress)

little the common soldier knew of the actual situation. We did not know then that this line was the last line of battle of the "Fighting Fourth Division" under General Hurlbut; that on its right was the division of McClernand, the Fort Donelson boys; that on its right, at right angles to it, and, as it were, the refused wing of the army, was glorious old Sherman, hanging on with a bulldog grip to the road across Snake Creek from Crump's Landing by which Lew Wallace was coming with 5,000 men. In other words, we still had an unbroken line confronting the enemy, made up of men who were not yet ready, by any manner of means, to give up that they were whipped.

Well, we filed through Hurlbut's line, halted re-formed, and faced to the front once more. We were put in place a short distance in the rear of Hurlbut, as a support to some heavy guns. It must have been about five o'clock now. Suddenly, on the extreme left, and just a little above the landing, came a deafening explosion that fairly shook the ground beneath our feet, followed by others in quick and regular succession. The look of wonder and inquiry that the soldiers' faces wore for a moment disappeared for one of joy and exultation as it flashed across our minds that the gunboats had at last joined hands in the dance, and were pitching big twenty-pound Parrott shells up the ravine in front of Hurlbut, to the terror and discomfiture of our adversaries.

The last place my regiment assumed was close to the road coming up from the landing. As we were lying there I heard the strains of martial music and saw a body of men marching by the flank up the road. I slipped out of ranks and

The Battle of Antietam (also known as Sharpsburg) produced one of the bloodiest single days of the War. These Confederate dead near the "Cornfield" were part of the 23,500 casualties overall. Civil War battlefield photographers like Alexander Gardner, who took this grisly shot, were some of the first to capture the realities of warfare in the relatively young medium of photography. (Library of Congress)

walked out to the side of the road to see what troops they were. Their band was playing "Dixie's Land," and playing it well. The men were marching at a quick step, carrying their guns, cartridge-boxes, haversacks, canteens, and blanket-rolls. I saw that they had not been in the fight, for there was no powder-smoke on their faces. "What regiment is this?" I asked of a young sergeant marching on the flank. Back came the answer in a quick, cheery tone. "The 36th Indiana, the advance guard of Buell's army."

I did not, on hearing this, throw my cap into the air and yell. That would have given those Indiana fellows a chance to chaff and guy me, and possibly make sarcastic remarks, which I did not care to provoke. I gave one big, gasping swallow and stood still, but the blood thumped in the veins of my throat and my heart fairly pounded against my little infantry jacket in the joyous rapture of this glorious intelligence. Soldiers need not be told of the thrill of unspeakable exultation they have all felt at the sight of armed friends in danger's darkest hour. Speaking for myself alone, I can only say, in the most heart-felt sincerity, that in all my obscure military career, never to me was the sight of reinforcing legions so precious and so welcome as on that Sunday evening when the rays of the descending sun were flashed back from the bayonets of Buell's advance column as it deployed on the bluffs of Pittsburg Landing.

The casualties from Shiloh were staggering and vied for the later battle at Sharpsburg, Maryland, for the bloodiest single day of the war:

	Effectives	Killed	Wounded	Missing
Union	62,683	1,754	8,408	2,885
Confederate	40,335	1,723	8,012	959

Ulysses S. Grant assessed the whole situation:

Up to the battle of Shiloh I, as well as thousands of other citizens, believed that the rebellion against the Government would collapse suddenly and soon, if a decisive victory could be gained over any of its armies. Donelson and Henry were such victories. An army of more than 21,000 men was captured or destroyed. Bowling Green, Columbus and Hickman, Kentucky, fell in consequence, and Clarksville and Nashville, Tennessee, the last two with an immense amount of stores, also fell into our hands. The Tennessee and Cumberland rivers, from their mouths to the head of navigation, were secured. But when Confederate armies were collected which not only attempted to hold a line farther south, from Memphis to Chattanooga, Knoxville, and on to the Atlantic, but assumed the offensive and made such a gallant effort to regain what had been lost, then, indeed, I gave up all idea of saving the Union except by complete conquest. Up to that time it had been the policy of our army, certainly of that portion commanded by me, to protect the property of the citizens whose territory was invaded, without regard to their sentiments, whether Union or Secession. After this, however, I regarded it as humane to both sides to protect the persons of those found at their homes, but to consume everything that could be used to support or supply armies. Protection was still continued over such supplies as were within lines held by us and which we expected to continue to hold; but such supplies within the reach of Confederate armies I regarded as much contraband as arms or ordnance stores. Their destruction was accomplished without bloodshed and tended to the same result as the destruction of armies.

THE SECOND BATTLE OF BULL RUN

Alexander Hunter, an enlisted man in the ranks of the 17th Virginia, in *Johnny Reb and Billy Yank*, published in 1904, sets the stage for the next general to head Mr. Lincoln's army in Virginia:

About the first of August the military authorities in Washington had begun to make preparations for the campaign they knew must soon commence, to guard the national capitol against a sudden flank attack by Jackson, whose name had become synonymous with rear attacks, flank approaches and all sorts of unexpected advances. Lincoln's War Department had gathered all the tag ends of armies in northern Virginia, lately under McDowell (near Fredericksburg), Banks and Fremont (in the Shenandoah Valley), and consolidated them into the Army of Virginia.

Lincoln gave command of this new collection of armies to Maj. Gen. John Pope. It very quickly proved to be a costly and most unwise move. Pope started off on the wrong foot; his military career took a sudden slide that brought him to a quick and inglorious disappearance from the scene. Confederate Colonel E.P. Alexander and Union Colonel George H. Gordon both knew Pope and commented:

Alexander:

Pope arrived early in July and began to concentrate and organize his army. In an address to his troops, July 14, dated "Headquarters in the Saddle," he said, among other things:

"Let us understand each other. I come to you from the West. . . from an army whose business it has been to seek the adversary, and beat him when he was found; whose policy has been attack and not defense. . . . I presume I have been called here to pursue the same system."

The arrogance of this address was not calculated to impress favorably officers of greater experience, who were now overslaughed by his promotion. McDowell would have been the fittest selection, but he and Banks, both senior to Pope, submitted without a word; as did also Sumner, Franklin, Heintzelman and all the major generals of McClellan's army. Only Fremont protested, asked to be relieved and practically retired from active service.

Gordon:

Pope was a thickset man, of an unpleasant expression, about fifty years of age, average height, thick, bushy black whiskers, and wearing spectacles.

There was no reserve about General Pope; he "let out" in censure with such vigor that if words had been missiles our army would never have failed for want of ammunition. In a long talk with me at his headquarters, he attributed our want of success at Richmond to mismanagement on the part of McClellan, for whom he seemed to entertain a bitter hatred, which might have pleased the Administration but found little favor with us.

General Pope's freedom of speech infected his command. Swearing became an epidemic.

The newspapers laughed at Pope, criticized his Falstaffian pretenses and and dubbed him "five-cent Pope." Every man in his army wondered if he were not a weak and silly man – yet there were none who failed in their determination to do all that mortals could do to retrieve the losses sustained by the Army of the Potomac, be it under Pope or the Devil himself.

Alexander Hunter, a common soldier who marched with perhaps the least common of all generals in the Civil War, offers one of the best descriptions of that particular breed of man who served under the indomitable Stonewall Jackson, soldiers whose bravery and courage, and, most important, sheer endurance, made them shine above all others in the war:

Jackson, with 17,300 rank and file, set off [from

Gordonsville north to face off with General Pope].... *The drum beat the long roll for us, the 17th Virginia, and the men fell into line. The troops were all in light marching order; a blanket or oilcloth, a single shirt, a pair of drawers and a pair of socks rolled tightly therein was swung on the right shoulder while the haversack hung on the left. These, with a cartridge box suspended from the belt, and a musket carried at will, made up Johnny Reb's entire equipment. There were not two men clothed alike in the whole regiment, brigade or division; some had caps, some wore hats of every imaginable shape and in every stage of dilapidation, varied by the different shades of hair which protruded through the holes and stuck our like quills upon a porcupine; the jackets were also of different shades, ranging from light gray with gilt buttons, to black with wooden ones; the pants were for the most part of that nondescript hue which time and all wearers give to ruins; some of the men wore boots, but many were barefooted; all were dusty and dirty.*

In marching, the troops had learned how to get over the ground without raising clouds of dust. The ranks would split, one half to the right and the other to the left, and then crossing untrod ground they would proceed with infinitely less trouble than in the old way of marching in solid column.

Our rations were doled out in sparing quantities; three crackers per man and a half pound of fat pork was the daily allowance. The cravings of hunger were hardly satisfied by the dole, but soon we were to get nothing at all from the commissary.

The men were becoming veteran soldiers; they had acquired the habit of implicit obedience to superior officers; they had learned how to make a pound of meat and bread go a long way by eating at stated times; they had become adept in the art of foraging; they had learned a hundred little ways of adding to their comfort, for instance, taking off their shoes on a level stretch of sandy road, or bathing their feet in every running brook, or carrying leaves in their hats as protection against the sun or lying stretched out at full length at every halt instead of sitting down. They were little things, it is true, but in the aggregate they amounted to much and were such as marked the difference between the strong unskilled men and the trained athlete.

When a soldier had learned how to take care of himself in this manner, he rarely broke down, never grumbled, never straggled unless he had a positive cause and with enough to eat was bound to answer to his name at the evening tattoo.

On the way north in the march from Gordonsville lay Cedar Mountain, a place that would become as much a part of the Second Manassas campaign as the railroad junction itself. Late in the day on August 9, Jackson struck the isolated corps of Union General Banks. News reporter George Alfred Townsend was there. His account was published in 1866 under the title *Campaigns of a Non-Combatant:*

For a time, each party kept in the edges of the timber, firing at will, but the Confederates were moving forward in masses by detours, until some thousands of them stood in the places of the few who were at first isolated. Distinct charges were now made, and a large body of Federals attempted to capture the battery before Slaughter's house, while separate brigades charged by front and flank upon the impenetrable timber. The horrible results of the previous effort were repeated; the Confederates preserved their position, and, at nightfall, the Federals fell back a mile or more. From fifteen hundred to two thousand of the latter were slain or wounded, and though the heat of the battle had lasted no more than two hours, nearly four thousand men upon both sides were maimed or dead.

The valor of the combatants in either cause was unquestionable. But no troops in the world could have driven the Confederates out of the impregnable mazes of the wood. It was an error to expose columns of troops upon an open plain, in the face of imperceptible sharpshooters. The batteries should have shelled the thickets, and the infantry should have retained their concealment. The most disciplined troops of Europe would not have availed in a country of bog, barren, ditch, creek, forest, and mountain.

Compared to the bare plain of Waterloo, Cedar Mountain was like the antediluvian world, when the surface was broken by volcanic fire into chasms and abysses. In this battle, the Confederate batteries, along the mountainside, were arranged in the form of a crescent, and, when the solid masses charged up the hill, they were butchered by enfilading fires. On the Confederate part, a thorough knowledge of the country was manifest, and the best possible disposition of forces and means; on the side of the Federals, there was zeal without discretion, and gallantry without generalship.

During the action, Stonewall Jackson occupied a commanding position on the side of the mountain, where, glass in hand, he observed every change of position, and directed all the operations. General Banks was indefatigable and courageous; but he was left to fight the whole battle, and not a regiment of the large reserve in his rear came forward to succor or relieve him. As usual, McDowell was cursed by all sides, and some of Banks's soldiers threatened to shoot him. But the unpopular Commander had no defence to make, and said nothing to clear up the doubts relative to him. He exposed himself repeatedly, and so did Pope. The latter rode to the front at nightfall – for what purpose no one could say, as he had been in Culpeper during the whole afternoon – and he barely escaped being captured. The loss of Federal officers was very heavy. Fourteen commissioned officers were killed and captured out of one regiment. Sixteen commissioned officers only remained in four regiments. One general was taken prisoner and several were wounded. A large number of field-officers were slain.

During the progress of the fight I galloped from point to point along the rear, but could nowhere obtain a panoramic view. The common sentiment of civilians, that it is always possible to see a battle, is true of isolated contests only. Even the troops engaged know little of the occurrences around them, and I have been assured by many soldiers that they have fought a whole day without so much as a glimpse of an enemy. The smoke and dust conceal objects, and where the greatest execution is done, the antagonists have frequently fired at a line of smoke, behind which columns may or may not have been posted.

Lieutenant John Hampden Chamberlayne of the Confederate army recounted the "incredible campaign" of Second Manassas in a letter home, written after the Army of Northern Virginia had crossed the Potomac River into Maryland; his description of Jackson's deceptive march around Pope is classic:

Frederick City, Md., Saturday, Sept. 6 (1862)

My Dear Mother:

I am brimful of matter as an egg of meat. Let me try to outline our progress since my last letter – date not remembered – from Raccoon Ford – you bearing in mind that I am in A.P. Hill's division, in Jackson's corps – that corps consisting of Jackson's own division, Ewell's and Hill's. You will not think me egostistical for speaking of this corps and of the corps of Hill's division, for of them I know most, and in truth their share was, to me at least, the most memorable in the almost incredible campaign of the last fortnight.

Crossing Raccoon Ford, Jackson in front – remember, Jackson, so used, includes Hill, Ewell, and the Stonewall division – General Lee, without much opposition, reached Rappahannock River, a few miles above Rappahannock station, where a part of Longstreet's troops had a sharp fight. On Friday Evening, August twenty-second, Jackson bivouacked in Culpeper, opposite Warrenton Springs, and the same evening threw over two of Ewell's brigades. The river rose and destroyed the bridge. Saturday the bridge was rebuilt, and that night the two brigades, after some sharp fighting, were withdrawn.

On Monday morning the enemy appeared in heavy force, and the batteries of Hill's division were put in position and shelled their infantry. They retired the infantry, and bringing up a large number of batteries, threw a storm of shot and shell at us – we not replying. They must have exploded several thousand rounds, and in all, so well sheltered were we, our killed did not reach twenty. That evening Jackson's whole force moved up to Jefferson, in Culpeper County, Longstreet close to him. The enemy was completely deceived, and concluded that we had given the thing up.

Now comes the great wonder. Starting up the bank of the river on Monday, the twenty-fifth, we marched through Amosville, in Rappahannock County – still further up, crossed the Rappahannock within ten miles of the Blue Ridge, marched across open fields, by strange country paths and comfortable homesteads, by a little town in Fauquier, called Orleans, on and on, as if we would never cease – to Salem, on the Manassas Gap Railroad, reaching there after midnight. Up again by day-dawn, and still on, along the Manassas Gap road, meeting crowds – all welcoming, cheering, staring with blank amazement. So all day Tuesday, through White Plains, Haymarket, Thoroughfare Gap, in Bull Run Mountains, Gainesville, to Bristow station, on the Orange and Alexandria Railroad – making the difference from Amosville to Bristow (between forty-five and fifty miles) within the forty-eight hours. We burned up to Bristow two or three railway-trains, and moved up to Manassas Junction on Wednesday, taking our prisoners with us. Ewell's division brought up the rear, fighting all the way a force Pope had sent up from Warrenton, supposing us a cavalry party.

Upon reaching Manassas Junction, we met a brigade – the First New-Jersey – which had been sent from Alexandria on the same supposition. They were fools enough to send a flag demanding our surrender at once. Of course we scattered the brigade, killing and wounding many, and among them the Brigadier-General (Taylor), who has since died. At the Junction was a large depot of stores, five or six pieces of artillery, two trains containing probably two hundred large cars loaded down with many millions of quartermaster and commissary stores. Beside these, there were very large sutlers' depots, full of everything; in short, there was collected there, in the space of a square mile, an amount and variety of property such as I had never conceived of, (I speak soberly.) 'Twas a curious sight to see our ragged and famished men helping themselves to every imaginable article of luxury or necessity, whether of clothing, food, or what not. For my part, I got a tooth-brush, a box of candles, a quantity of lobster salad, a barrel of coffee, and other things which I forgot. But I must hurry on, for I have not time to tell the hundredth part, and the scene utterly beggars description.

A part of us hunted that New-Jersey brigade like scattered partridges over the hills just to the right of the battle-field of the eighteenth of July, 1861, while the rest were partly plundering, partly fighting the forces coming on us from Warrenton. Our men had been living on roasted corn since crossing the Rappahannock, and we had brought no wagons, so we could carry little away of the riches before us. But the men could eat for one meal at least. So they were marched up, and as much of every thing eatable served out as they could carry. To see a starving man eating lobster-salad and drinking Rhine wine, barefooted and in tatters, was curious; the whole thing was incredible.

Our situation now was very critical. We were between Alexandria and Warrenton – between the hosts of McClellan and Pope with over eighteen thousand jaded men, for the corps had not more than that. At nightfall, fire was set to the depot, storehouses, the loaded trains, several empty trains, sutlers' houses, restaurants, every thing. As the magnificent conflagration began to subside, the Stonewall or First division of Jackson's corps moved off toward the battle-field of Manassas, the other two divisions to Centreville, six miles distant.

As day broke, we came in sight of Centreville, rested a few hours, and toward evening the rear-guard of the corps crossed Bull Run at Stone Bridge – the scene of the great slaughter of last year – closely pursued by an enemy. A part of the force came up the Warrenton turnpike, and in a ridge running from Dudley Church Ford to the Warrenton turnpike. We drove them off, and on Friday morning we held the ridge, in front of which runs an incomplete railroad-cut and embankment. Now, we had made a circuit from the Gap in Bull Run Mountains around to the Junction and Centreville, breaking up the railroad and destroying their stores, and returned to within six miles of the Gap, through which Longstreet must come. The enemy disputed his passage and delayed him till late in the day, and, meanwhile, they threw against our corps, all day long, vast masses of troops – Sigel's, Banks's, and Pope's own division. We got out of ammunition and we collected more from cartridge-boxes of fallen friend and foe; that gave out, and we charged with never-failing yell and steel. All day long they threw their masses on us; all day they fell back shattered and shrieking. When the sun went down, their dead were heaped in front of the incomplete railway, and we sighed with relief, for Longstreet could be seen coming into position on our right. The crisis was over; Longstreet never failed yet; but the sun went down so slowly.

I am proud to have borne my humble part in these great operations – to have helped, even so little, to consummate the grand plan, whose history will be a text-book to all young soldiers, and whose magnificent success places Lee at the side of the greatest captains, Hannibal, Caesar, Eugene, Napoleon. I hope you have preserved my letters in which I have spoken of my faith in Lee. He and his roundtable of generals are worthy of the immortality of Napoleon and his Marshals. He moves his agencies like a god – secret, complicated, vast, resistless, complete.

An engineer with the Army of the Potomac by the name of Washington Roebling, who later was the chief engineer and builder of the Brooklyn Bridge, was with McDowell:

We encamped that night 8 miles from Warrenton, being joined by Seigel & Reynolds with their Penn. reserves. Early next morning Rickets' Div. was dispatched west to Thoroughfare Gap in Bull Run mountain to prevent Longstreet's corps from passing through & reinforcing the rebels. But the rebels, finding him there, passed through Hopewell gap 4 miles farther on and joined their main force. Rickets apparently knew nothing of Hopewell gap although laid down on every map. The main body of our army moved forward, crossing the Manassas Gap road at Gainesville where Sigel turned off following the r.r. while King & Reynolds kept on (Hatch commanded King's Div., the latter having had an epileptic fit some days previous). Suddenly a rebel battery opened on us in front with shells which came very near killing some of us, Gen. McDowell & staff as usual riding at the head of the column.

Our forces were deployed in line of battle, which took an hour, and then we proceeded to determine whether we had come up with the main body or only a portion of the enemy. By that time their battery had ceased firing and retired 2 miles. 5 men killed was the damage sustained. Well, after wasting 4 precious hours more, spent in robbing orchards & cornfields, and watching immense columns of dust in front of us, McDowell made a further division of force by leaving King there to march down the pike late in the afternoon and went himself down the R.R. towards Manassas in search of Pope, leaving Reynolds to follow him slowly.

We arrived at Manassas at dark and ascertained that Pope, with Hooker & Kearney, had gone in the direction of Centreville. We understood that Pope had been hunting McDowell & McDowell was likewise hunting Pope. While at Manassas that evening very heavy cannonading was heard about 2 miles in advance of where King had been left; it seems that King had advanced that afternoon, was attacked by the main body of the enemy, lost 500 killed & wounded in one brigade, retreated, and arrived at Manassas at 3 o'clock the next morning. McDowell, hearing that firing, wanted to get there by making a short cut across the country, but it was dark. We lost our way 3 times and finally at 1 o'clock encamped along the road side for a few hours. Getting under way again by 4 , we reached Reynolds by 6, took breakfast, found the rebels in front of Reynolds, and returned to Manassas where King & Reynolds had arrived during the night, also Porter with the regulars.

Porter was pushed out in the same direction where King was. . . only not quite so far. McDowell went out with him, put him in position, and gave him his instructions, merely as superior officer, Pope being away. But Porter obeyed none, running off as soon as the enemy opened fire with a battery. McDowell then returned towards Manassas and led his two divisions of King & Rickets towards the old battle field of Bull Run where the main body of the enemy was. It was 1 or 2 o'clock on Friday afternoon when we got there. The fight had commenced a few hours before with Hooker, Kearney & Sigel. About 30 guns were in position then and firing as fast as possible, silencing most of the enemy's guns which were poorly handled and counter-balancing the poor result of Hooker's & Kearney's infantry attack in the afternoon.

It was a very interesting scene; much valuable ammunition was, however, thrown away, for which we paid dearly the next day. Sigel arranged most of the artillery; it was massed together very well, but was placed on two high elevations. Every shot lodged where it struck, in place of glancing and bounding off to do more mischief. The day was cloudy and windstill so that the battle field was covered with a dense, livid cloud of smoke. It was late in the day before McDowell's troops were deployed in line of battle and pushed forward to the proper place on the centre & left of the centre. Before Hatch's Brigade had arrived at its place it was pitch dark. Hatch had not the remotest idea where he was going, pushed too far ahead, got into a cross fire which the rebels suddenly opened on him, had half his men killed & wounded & the other half ran off. So ended the day.

David Strother was a Virginian who stayed with the Union and served under both McClellan and Pope and later rose to the rank of brigadier general. His account of Bull Run is in

The 36th Pennsylvania Infantry parade before their tented camp, with mounted officers and the regimental band at the head. (Library of Congress)

diary form. While some have considered Strother to be inaccurate in some of his statements, his descriptions of the battle are vivid; certainly his picture of John Pope makes his narrative a valuable contribution:

August 29, Friday. – Clear and warm. At three o'clock this morning I was aroused by Colonel Ruggles in person to carry written orders to General Fitz-John Porter, supposed to be lying at Manassas Junction, or alternatively at Bristow. . . Porter's orders are to move his Corps on Centreville without delay.

. . . it was broad daylight when I reached Porter's quarters at Bristow. Entering his tent I found the handsome General lying on his cot, covered with a blanket of imitation leopard skin.

At his request I lit a candle and read the message, then handed it to him. While he cooly read it over I noted the time by his watch, which marked five o'clock and twenty minutes precisely. He then proceeded to dress himself, and continued to question me in regard to the location of the different commands and the general situation. As I was but imperfectly informed myself I could only give vague and general replies to his queries. We believed Jackson separated from the main army of Lee by a day's march at least; and General Pope desired to throw all his disposable force upon him and crush him before Lee came up. The troops were immediately ordered to cook breakfast and prepare for the march.

Meanwhile the head-quarters breakfast had been served, and I sat down with the Staff officers to partake. The General, who was busy writing dispatches on the corner of the same table, looked up and asked, How do you spell

Camp life among Confederate troops was less formal and generally less well-equipped than on the federal side. This view is from a naval yard in Florida. (Library of Congress)

"chaos?" I spelled the word letter by letter c-h-a-o-s. He thanked me, and observed, smiling, that, by a singular lapse of memory, he often forgot the spelling of the most familar words. . . .

I immediately took leave and started back to general head-quarters. The road was now lined with wagons, stragglers, and droves of cattle, all moving northward. From time to time at long intervals the cannon sounded, but no heavy firing yet. Arrived at Bull Run I found our camp broken up; that the enemy had developed in great force near Centreville, and I must seek the General in that direction. Riding rapidly forward I found the General and his Staff grouped around a house on the heights of Centreville, observing a fight which was going on some five or six miles distant in the direction of the old Bull Run battlefield. The fight was evidently thickening and extending, as could be seen by the white cumulus clouds hanging over the batteries, and the long lines of thinner smoke rising above the tree-tops.

We could furthermore see the moving dust-clouds, indicating the march of supporting columns all converging toward the centre of action. The line of the Bull Run Mountains was visible beyond and from Thoroughfare Gap, which appeared to the right of the battle-cloud. We could see the dust and reciprocal artillery-fire of our retreating and the enemy's advancing forces. Between eleven and twelve o'clock I was standing with Colonel Beckwith and commenting on these movements, when I learned that this was probably Longstreet's command forcing back Ricketts's Division from the Gap, which he had attempted to hold. I was afterward informed it was an artillery duel between the cavalry forces of Stuart and Buford.

As we approached the field the pounding of the guns was tremendous, but as we were ascending the last hill that rose between us and the magnificent drama, and just beginning to snuff the sulphurous breath of battle, a Staff officer from Sigel (I think) rode up to General Pope and reported that the ammunition was failing. Immediately the General turned to me: "Captain, ride back to Centreville and hurry up all the ammunition you can find there!" I felt for a moment disgusted and mutinous, but I could not dispute the importance of my mission, so I sullenly drew rein and galloped back over the hot and dusty road. Amidst the vast accumulation of vehicles and baggage-trains at Centreville I should have had great difficulty in finding the wagons I was in search of, had I not fortunately fallen in with Lieutenant Colonel Myers, of M'Dowell's Corps, who seemed to be always on hand in an emergency. With his assistance in a marvelously short time I got between twenty-five and thirty wagons started in the proper direction: and then, by his invitation, stopped to swallow a cup of coffee and a hasty lunch. Observing a considerable body of well-equipped troops lying here apparently idle, I expressed astonishment, and inquired the cause of it. The answer was expressed evasively, but with some bitterness: "There are officers here today who would be doing themselves far more credit by marching to the battlefield than by lying idle and exciting disaffection by doubts, sneering criticism, and open abuse of the Commander-in-Chief."

I followed my wagons until I had got them clear of Centreville and in a full trot down the turnpike; I then dug spurs into my mare's flanks, and in the shortest time possible returned to the great centre of interest. I found the General and Staff grouped around a large pine-tree which stood solitary on the crest of an open hill, overlooking our whole line of battle. The summit immediately in our front was occupied by a line of batteries, some thirty or forty pieces, blazing and fuming like furnaces. Behind these a fine brigade of Reno's command lay resting on their arms. To their right stood Heintzelman, with the divisions of Hooker and Kearney, whose musketry kept up a continuous roar. Supporting the left of this line of guns was Sigel, also sharply engaged with small-arms. On an open bluff still further to the left, and on the opposite side of the valley traversed by the Warrenton turnpike, lay Schenck's Division, which had been a good deal cut up, and was not actively engaged at this moment. The dry grass which covered the hill he occupied had taken fire, and was burning rapidly, occasionally obscuring that portion of the field with its smoke. Beyond him, on the extreme left of our line, General Reynolds, with the Pennsylvania Reserves, lay masked from the enemy by a wood. The enemy's position can only be known by the smoke of his guns, for all his troops and batteries are concealed by the wood. He occupies strong lines on a plateau and along an unfinished railroad embankment, which is equal to a regularly intrenched line. He fights stubbornly, and has thus far resisted all our efforts to dislodge him. The General relies on the advance of M'Dowell and Porter to crush him, and we are in momentary expectation of hearing their guns. The shot and shells of the enemy directed at the batteries in our front render this position rather uncomfortable, as they are continually screeching over our heads, or plowing the gravelly surface with an ugly rasping whir, that makes one's flesh creep.

Our efforts to carry the wood in front having thus far failed I was sent to General Reno with orders that he should throw forward the division lying in reserve to support the attack of Heintzelman's troops. The orders was promptly and gallanty executed, the troops moving in beautiful order and with admirable spirit. I accompanied the advance until they passed our guns beyond the summit, and remained there admiring until the troops, moving down a fine slope, reached the edge of the wood. The enemy was pelting away industriously from his wooded strong-hold, and the air was lively with singing bullets. For half an hour or more the roar of musketry was unceasing. At length Reno in person reported to the General, and stated that he had failed to carry the wood. Simultaneously with his return our position was so sharply raked with shot and shell that the General withdrew a short distance to the right, establishing himself on the verge of a wood.

It was now about four o'clock when General Phil Kearney came in and received orders to attack and carry the disputed position at all hazards. He rode off promising to do so. While he was forming his troops for the advance it was thought necessary to pound the position with artillery. Reno, who was riding beside the Commanding General, remarked, "The wood is filled with the wounded of both armies." The Commander replied, "And yet the safety of this army and the nation demands their sacrifice, and the lives of thousands yet unwounded." After a moment's hesitation the necessity of the order was acquiesced in, and forty guns were opened upon the fatal wood. The artillerymen worked with a fiendish activity, and the sulphurous clouds which hung over the field were tinged with a coppery hue by the rays of the declining sun. Meanwhile Kearney had gone in, and the incessant roar of musketry resembled the noise of a cataract.

An hour later Kearney again appeared, and informed the General that the coveted position was carried. I stood beside him as he gave in his report, and while elated with the tidings he communicated, admired the man as the finest specimen of the fighting soldier I had ever seen. With his small head surmounted by the regulation forage-cap, his thin face with its energetic neck, his colorless eyes, glaring as it were with a white heat, his erect figure with the empty coatsleeve pinned across his breast, down to the very point of his sabre, he looked the game-cock all over. His very voice had the resolute gutteral cluck which characterizes that gallant fowl.

Meanwhile M'Dowell in person arrived on the field, and reported the approach of his command. It is a relief to see him here, although it is too late for him to accomplish any thing decisive. While exchanging greetings with me M'Dowell looked toward the west, where the radiance of a rich golden sunset was breaking through the grim battle-clouds, illuminating the mingled glories and horrors of the hard-fought field. "Look," said he, "what a dramatic and magnificent picture! How tame are all Vernet's boasted battle-pieces in comparison with such a scene as this! Indeed, if an artist could successfully represent that effect it would be criticised as unreal and extravagant."

I warmed toward a man who amidst the dangers and responsibilities of the occasion would mark its passing beauties and sublimities. At this point the two Generals, with their aids and escort, rode to the front to inspect the situation. . . . The battery was still working rapidly, and the enemy fighting back with equal spirit, when one of the guns burst, throwing off a heavy fragment of the muzzle, which described an arc immediately over the heads of the line of officers and fell with a thud, just clearing the last man and horse; two feet lower and it would have swept off the whole party. I had remarked since we came over that the ammunition used seemed miserably and dangerously defective; nearly all the shells bursting prematurely, and several so close to the muzzles of the pieces as to endanger the artillerymen.

We remained on this hill until after sunset, when the firing gradually ceased. When it became quite dark there was a beautiful pyrotechnical display about a mile distant on our left, and near the Warrenton turnpike, occasioned by a collision of King's Division of M'Dowell's Corps with the enemy's right. The sparkling lines of musketry shone in the darkness like fire-flies in a meadow, while the more brilliant flashes of artillery might have been mistaken for swamp meteors. This show continued for an hour, the advancing and receding fires indicating distinctly the surging of the battle tide; and this time not the slightest sound either of small-arms or artillery was perceptible. It seemed at length that the fire of the enemy's line began to extend and thicken, while ours wavered and fell back, but still continued the contest. Between eight and nine o'clock it ceased entirely, and we returned to our head-quarters station, where we picketed our horses and prepared to pass the night beside a camp-fire.

By this time the 17th Virginia was a part of Hood's Division. Hood led the attack on August 30th. Alexander Hunter wrote of the final phase of the battle:

The rapid pounding of the artillery caused us to hurry through the morning meal, almost before the sun rose above the hill, and we pushed for Thoroughfare Gap to rejoin the regiment. We knew by instinct that there would be a battle that day; for there was blood upon the moon. . . . Never had life seemed more worth living than on a morning such as this; never existence sweeter; never Death so loath the dying.

Long streams of soldiers were wending their way to the front. The troops seemed everywhere; they filled the railroad track as far as the eye could reach; they emerged from the narrow gap in the mountain and spread out over the fields and meadows; they wound along the base of the hills, and marched in a steady tramp over the dusty highways; following a dozen different routes, but each face turned directly or obliquely northward. Ordnance wagons were being pushed rapidly ahead; batteries were taking position, staff officers were riding at a gallop, as if seconds and minutes were golden. In short, all fighting material was pushing to the van and all the peacefully inclined were valiantly seeking the rear. By a law as fixed as that which bound the Stoics, as unalterable as those which govern the affinities of the chemical world, this separation of the two types ever occurred on the eve of battle. An instant sifting of wheat from the tares took place quietly but surely in every company, and the mass of men so lately mingled became as incapable of mixture as oil and water.

The great receding tide at full ebb sank back toward the Gap; the mighty army of the backsliders whom naught could hinder, non-combatants, camp darkies, shirking soldiers playing possum, and camp followers. Warm work was expected and all this genus, like war-horses, "sniffed danger from afar."

Reaching the Gap we found that the brigade had passed through. Following hard upon the track, our little squad after an hour's march caught up and took its place in rank.

The men were in a fearful humor, grumbling at their luck and cursing the commissary. They had ample cause; not a single ration has been issued to the troops for several days and the soldiers were savage from hunger.

The forenoon had passed and the sound of hostile cannon was breaking the silence in our front while a battle was being fought on our left.

"Fall in!" the officers shouted, and the men sprang to their feet, the line was dressed, and the brigade headed to the front to take position. On the way we were halted, and every soldier was compelled to strip for the fight by discarding his blanket, – if he had one, which was not often – oilcloth or overcoat. All these were deposited in a large pile, and guards set over them, looking very much as if we did not intend to retreat. Cartridge-boxes were filled with forty rounds, and in our haversacks we carried twenty more, making sixty rounds per man.

Soon the crack of the skirmisher's rifles were heard, then the artillery opened, and the purple-colored smoke drifted like mist from lowland marshes, across the valley.

"Forward! Guide to the colors! March!"

Across that level plateau the First Brigade moved, the flower of Virginia in its ranks, the warm blood rushing in its veins as it did in warrior ancestors centuries ago. It was a glorious and magnificent display, the line keeping perfect time, the colors showing red against the azure sky. There was no cheering, only the rattling of the equipments and the steady footfalls of the men who trod the earth with regular beat. As the brigade swept across the plain it was stopped by a high Virginia snake fence; hundreds of willing hands caught the rails, tossed them aside, and then instinctively touching each other's elbows, the ranks were dressed as if by magic.

The first shell now shrieked over us. Another burst not ten feet from the ground directly over the heads of our forces. The long chain kept intact, though close to the spot where the explosion occurred; the links vibrated and oscillated for a moment, then grew firm again and pressed onward.

How the shells rained upon us now; a Yankee six-gun

battery, on a hill about half a mile off, turned its undivided attention upon us and essayed to shatter the advancing line. It did knock a gap here and there, but the break was mended almost as soon as broken, and the living wall kept on. Shells were bursting everywhere, until it seemed as if we were walking on torpedoes. They frackled, split and exploded all around, throwing dirt and ejecting little spirits of smoke that for a moment dimmed the sky.

Colonel Marye dismounted, drew his sword from the scabbard, and looking the beau ideal of a splendid soldier, placed himself at the head of his men. He stopped for a moment and pointed his sword with an eloquent and vivid gesture toward the battery on the hill. A cheer answered him, and the line instinctively quickened its pace. Though the shells were tearing through the ranks, the men did not falter. One man's resonant voice was sounding above the din, exercising a magical influence; one man's figure strode on in front and where he led, his men kept close behind. We followed unwaveringly our colonel over the hill, down the declivity, up the slope, straight across the plain toward the battery, with even ranks, though the balls were tearing a way through flesh and blood. The brigade stretched out for several hundred yards, forming, as they marched, a bow with concave toward the enemy. The Seventeenth was on the right of the line, and the other regiments dressed by our colors as we bore right oblique toward the battery, which was now hidden by a volleying fume that settled upon the crest.

Still the advance was not stayed nor the ranks broken. We neared the Chinn House, when suddenly a long line of the enemy rose from behind an old stone wall and poured straight in our breasts a withering volley at pointblank distance. It was so unexpected, this attack, that it struck the long line of men like an electric shock. Many were falling killed or wounded, and but for the intrepid coolness of its colonel, the Seventeenth would have retired from the field in disorder. His clear, ringing voice was heard, and the wavering line reformed. A rattling volley answered the foe, and for a minute or two the contest was fiercely waged. Then the colonel fell with his knee frightfully shattered by a Minie-ball. Once down, the calm, reassuring tones heard no longer, the line broke. Now individual bravery made up for the disaster. The officers surged ahead with their swords waving in the air, cheering on the men, who kept close to their heels, loading and firing as they ran. The line of blue was not fifty yards distant and every man took a sure, close aim before his finger pressed the trigger. It was a decisive fight of about ten minutes, and both sides stood off gamely to their work. Our foes were a Western regiment from Ohio, who gave and received and asked no odds. The left of our brigade having struck the enemy's right and doubled it up, now sent one volley into their flank.

In a moment the blue line quivered and then went to pieces. Officers and men broke for the rear, one regimental colors captured by Jim Coleman, of the Seventeenth. In a few moments there were none left except the dead and wounded.

There was hardly a breathing spell, only time indeed to take a full draught from the canteen, transfer the cartridges from the haversacks to the cartridge-box, and the enemy was upon us with a fresh line.

We were now loading and firing at the swiftly approaching enemy, who were about two hundred yards distant, advancing straight towards us and shouting with their steady hurrah, so different from the Rebel yell. It was a trying moment and proved the metal of the individual man. Some ran, or white with fear cowered behind the Chinn House, while others hid in a long gulley near by; others yet stood in an irregular form and loaded and fired, unmindful of the dust and noise of the hurtling shell and screaming shot.

The brigade was scattered everywhere now. For an hour they had fired as fast as the cartridges could be rammed home. When the Union troops came up to retake the Chinn House, our men began to give ground. On came the Yankees in splendid style, with the Stars and Stripes waving and their line capitally dressed. It was a perfect advance, and some of us forgot to fire our muskets while watching them. In their front line was a little drummer beating a **pas de charge**, *the only time we ever heard the inspiriting sound on the battlefield. The dauntless little fellow was handling his sticks lustily, too, for the roll of the drum was heard above the noise of the guns.*

It was high time to be leaving, we thought, and now our men were turning to fire one good shot before heeling it to the rear, when right behind us there came with a rush and a vim a fresh Rebel brigade aiming straight for the Yankees. They ran over us and we joined their lines. Not a shot was fired by them in response to the fusilade of musketry that was raining lead all around. Every man with his head bent sideways and down, like people breasting a hailstorm, for soldiers always charge so, and the Gray and the Blue met with a mighty shock. A tremendous sheet of flame burst from our line; the weaker side went to the ground in a flash, and with a wild yell the Gray swept on toward the six-gun battery that had been sending forth a stream of death for the past hour. We could only see the flashes of light through the dense smoke.

The line stopped a moment at the foot of the hill to allow itself to catch up. It was late in the evening and the battle was raging in all its deadliest fury. On our right, on our left, in the front, in the rear, from all directions came the warring sound of cannon and musketry. We could see nothing but smoke, breathe nothing except the fumes of burning powder, feel nothing save the earth jarred by the concussion of the guns, hear nothing but the dire, tremendous clamor and blare of sound swelling up into a vast volume of fire. How hot it was! The clothes damp with perspiration, the canteens empty, throats parched with thirst, faces blackened by powder, the men mad with excitement.

The left of the line came up and then some one asked:

"Whose brigade is this?"

"Hood's" was the answer. Then burst a ringing cry, "Forward, Texans!"

The line sprang like a tightly-bent bow suddenly loosened, and rushed up the hill in a wild, eager dash – a frenzied, maddening onset up the hill through the smoke, nearer and nearer to the guns.

When about a hundred yards from them the dense veil lifted, floated upward and softly aside, and discovered to us that the battery had ceased firing. We could see the muzzles of the guns, their sullen black mouths pointing at us, and behind them the gunners, while from the center of the battery was a flag that lay drooping upon its staff. It was for a second only, like the rising of the curtain for a moment on a hideous tableau, only to be dropped as the eye took in the scene in all its horrors, yet it impressed itself, that vivid picture, brief as it was, upon mind, heart and brain.

At once came a noise like a thunder shock, that seemed as if an earthquake had riven the place. The ground trembled with the concussion. The appalling sound was heard of iron grapeshot tearing its way through space and through bodies of bone, flesh and blood.

Mercifully for us, but not intended by our foes, the guns were elevated too high, or it would have been simply annihilation; for when those six guns poured their volley into the charging lines they were loaded to the muzzle with grape, and the distance was only about pistol shot. Of course the execution was fearful, and for a second the line was stupefied and nearly senseless from the blow. The ground was covered with victims and the screams of the wounded rose high above the din and were awful to hear.

The advance was not stayed long.

"Forward, boys! Don't stop now! Forward, Texans!" and with a cry from every throat the Southerners kept on, officers and men together without form or order, the swiftest runners ahead, the slowest behind, 'tis true, but struggling desperately to better their time. Up! Still up! until we reached the crest! As the Yankees pulled the lanyards of the loaded pieces our men were among them. A terrific shock. A lane of dead in front. Those standing before the muzzles were blown to pieces like captured Sepoy rebels. I had my hand on the wheel of one cannon just as it fired, and I fell like one dead, from the concussion. There was a frenzied struggle in the semi-darkness around the guns, so violent and tempestuous, so mad and brain-reeling that to recall it is like fixing the memory of a horrible, blood-curdling dream. Every one was wild with uncontrollable delirium.

Then the mists dissolved and the panting, gasping soldiers could see the picture as it was. The battery had been captured by the Texans and every man at the pieces taken prisoner. Many were killed by a volley that we had poured into them when only a few paces distant, and a large proportion wounded. The few who escaped unhurt stood in a group, so blackened with powder that they ceased to look like white men. These soldiers had nobly worked their guns and had nothing to be ashamed of. All that men could do they had done.

Just as the day was drawing to a close a mighty yell arose, a cry from twice ten thousand throats, as the Rebel reserves, fresh from the rear, rushed resistlessly to the front. Never did mortal eyes behold a grander sight; not even when MacDonald put his columns in motion at Wagram or Ney charged the Russian center at Borodino.

It was an extended line, reaching as far as the eye could see, crescent in form, and composed of many thousand men. It was, in fact, a greater part of Longstreet's corps. The onset was thrilling in the extreme, as the men swept grandly forward, the little battle-flags with the Southern cross in the center fluttering saucily and jauntily aloft, while the setting sun made of each bayonet and musket-barrel a literal gleam of fire that ran along the chain of steel in a scintillating flame. As they swept over the plain they took up all the scattered fighting material, and nothing was left but the wounded which had sifted through, and the dead.

Then ensued the death struggle, a last fearful grappling in mortal combat. The enemy threw forward all their reserves to meet the shock, and for the space of fifteen minutes the commotion was terrible. Bursts of sound surpassed everything that was ever heard or could be conceived. The baleful flashes of the cannon, darting out against the dusky horizon, played on the surface of the evening clouds like sharp, vivid lightning. Long lines of musketry vomited through the plain their furious volleys of pestilential lead, sweeping scores of brave soldiers into the valley of the Shadow of Death.

At last the enemy staggered, wavered, broke and fled in utter rout. Where Longstreet was dealing his heavy blows, they were throwing away their knapsacks and rushing madly for the rear. Only one final stand was made by a brigade in the woods close by; but as the long gray line closed in on each flank they threw down their arms and surrendered with but few exceptions; those few, as they ran, turned and fired.

On the hill, which had been occupied by the Washington Artillery of eighteen guns in the earlier part of the day, the eye took in a dim and fast-fading yet extended view of the whole surrounding country. A vast panorama stretched out on an open plain with patches of wood here and there on its surface, and with but two or three hills in the whole range of sight to break the expanded level. It was unutterably grand. Jackson could be seen swinging his left on his right as a pivot, and Longstreet with his entire corps in the reverse method. The whole Yankee army was in retreat, and certainly nothing but darkness prevented it from becoming ***une affaire flambée****.*

LEE'S INVASION OF MARYLAND AND THE BATTLE OF ANTIETAM

Pope was defeated. His army was in total disarray and the Federal capital was once more open to attack from the aggressive Confederates. Both armies had taken a severe pounding at Second Manassas, but, as the President saw it, he had to move with speed to reorganize his defenses. Over opposition from his cabinet, Mr. Lincoln restored George McClellan to

With Burnside in command after McClellan lost his post for the second time, the Union suffered another disastrous defeat at Fredericksburg. Alfred Waud sketched this charge by Humphrey's Division. (Library of Congress)

command. As with the appointment of John Pope, in the long run it proved to be a bad move, although the President had little choice.

That McClellan was a marvelous organizer was undeniable, but the general had been a disappointment on the battlefield in the Peninsular Campaign earlier in the year, and he would change little in the Maryland Campaign. Secretary of the Navy Gideon Welles expressed grave concerns:

September 3, 1862

McClellan is an intelligent engineer and officer, but not a commander to lead a great army in the field. To attack or advance with energy and power is not in him; to fight is not his forte. I sometimes fear his heart is not earnest in the cause; yet I do not entertain the thought that he is unfaithful. The study of military operations interests and amuses him. It flatters him to have on his staff French princes and men of wealth and position; he likes show, parade, and power. Wishes to outgeneral the Rebels, but not to kill and destroy them. In a conversation which I had with him in May last at Cumberland on the Pamunkey, he said he desired of all things to capture Charleston; he would demolish and annihilate the city. He detested, he said, both South Carolina and Massachusetts, and should rejoice to see both States extinguished. Both were and always had been ultra and mischievous, and he could not tell which he hated most. These were the remarks of the General-in-Chief at the head of our armies then in the field, and when as large a portion of his troops were from Massachusetts as from any State in the Union.

I cannot relieve my mind from the belief that to him, in a great degree, and to his example, influence, and conduct, are to be attributed some portion of our late reverses, more than to any other person on either side. His reluctance to move or to have others move, his inactivity. . . his omission to send forward supplies unless Pope would send a cavalry escort from the battle-field, and the tone of his conversation and dispatches, all show a moody state of feeling. The slight upon him and the generals associated with him, in the selection of Pope, was injudicious, impolitic, wrong perhaps, but is no justification for their withholding one tithe of strength in a great emergency, where the lives of their countrymen and the welfare of the country were in danger. The soldiers whom McClellan has commanded are doubtless attached to him. They have been trained to it, and he has kindly cared for them while under him. With partiality for him they have imbibed his prejudices, and some of the officers have, I fear, a spirit more factious and personal than patriotic.

McClellan, with his typical sense of self esteem, wrote of the transfer of power:

On the morning of September 2, while I sat at breakfast, the President and General Halleck came to my house.

Without one moment's hesitation, and without making any conditions whatever, I at once said that I would accept the command and stake my life that I would save the city. Both the President and Halleck again asserted that it was impossible, and I repeated my firm conviction that I could and would save it. The President verbally placed me in entire command of the city and of the troops.

He then left with many thanks and showing much feeling. I immediately went to work.

General James Longstreet on the opening conflict of the campaign, South Mountain:

A little after dark on September 13, General Lee received information of the advance of the Union forces to the foot of South Mountain. General Lee still held to the thought that he had ample time. He sent for me, and I found him over his map. He asked my views. I thought it too late to man the passes properly at South Mountain, and expressed preference for concentrating behind the Antietam at Sharpsburg. Lee, however, preferred to make the stand at the passes of South Mountain and ordered the troops to march next morning. The hallucination that McClellan was not capable of serious work seemed to pervade our army, even at this moment of dreadful threatening. . . .

Before sunrise of September 14, General D.H. Hill had ridden to the top of the mountain to view the front. He found Garland's brigade there, and withdrew all advanced troops to the summit.

The battle was opened by Union batteries, which were posted near the foot of the mountain, in fine position to open upon the Confederate at the summit.

General Hill rode off to his right, and as he passed near Fox's Gap, two or three miles to the south, he heard the noise of troops working their way towards him, and soon artillery opened fire across the gap over his head. He hurried back and sent General Samuel Garland's brigade to meet the approaching enemy. After a severe contest, in which Garland fell, the enemy advanced in a gallant charge, part of our brigade breaking in confusion down our side of the mountain. Fortunately, General Hill had posted two batteries on the summit and they threw a destructive cross fire on the enemy.

In the afternoon the head of my column reached the top of South Mountain, filed to the right to meet the battle, and soon after General Hood arrived with two brigades. The last reinforcement braced the Confederate front to a successful stand, and we held it till after night in hot contest.

Major General Jesse L. Reno, on the Union side, an officer of high character and attainments, was killed about 7:00 p.m. Among the Union wounded was Colonel Rutherford B. Hayes, afterward President of the United States.

After nightfall General Lee inquired of the prospects for continuing the fight. General Hill explained that the enemy was in great force with commanding positions on both flanks, making the cramped position of the Confederates untenable. General Lee ordered withdrawal of the commands, making Sharpsburg the point of assembly.

Knowing that following his defeat at South Mountain his plans to go on to Pennsylvania were as well defeated, Lee elected to make a stand in Maryland along the banks of the Antietam Creek at Sharpsburg. Owens continues his narration:

We reached the vicinity of Sharpsburg early in the morning of September 15, and formed line of battle along the range of hills between the town and the stream, with our backs to the Potomac.

On the opposite shore of the Antietam the banks are quite steep and afford good position for artillery. All the batteries present were placed in position along the ridge. Longstreet said, "Put them all in, every gun you have, long range and short range."

A courier arrived in hot haste, with news that Jackson had captured Harpers Ferry, with its garrison of 12,000 men, 70 pieces of artillery, and 13,000 small arms.

"This is indeed good news," said General Lee; "let it be announced to the troops"; and staff officers rode at full gallop down the line, and the announcement was answered by great cheering.

Our lines were scarcely formed when the enemy appeared upon the opposite bank of the Antietam, and our artillery opened upon him with a few guns, just to let him know that we were going no further and were at bay.

Couriers were sent to Jackson and A.P. Hill to come to us as soon as possible. Our numbers in their absence were fearfully small, hardly 15,000 men, and McClellan had almost 100,000. Where did all of these men come from? Pope had but 50,000 after the battle at Groveton [Second Manassas] last month.

All this day our thin line faced the whole of McClellan's army, and it closed with a little artillery practice on each side.

At daylight, on the morning of the sixteenth, the enemy was in plain view on the high ground upon the opposite bank of the Antietam. His batteries were in position. They opened fire, and we replied, but the distance was too great to make a duel effective, and the firing was stopped by order of General Lee.

Riding through the town, I met General Lee on foot, leading his horse by the bridle. It was during the artillery firing and the shells of the enemy were falling in close proximity to him, but he seemed perfectly unconscious of danger.

Daylight was slow in coming on the morning of September 17. The rain had stopped but it had left a heavy overcast, a foggy mist that covered the fields. Incidental firing, which had started at about 3:00 a.m., began to pick up. The actual time that the battle began is not known, but it is estimated between 5:30 and 6 o'clock. Though it was an overcast morning, most accounts give the time of initial movements at first "faint streaks of daylight;" "at the peep of day 'ere the sun had cast a ray over the towering Blue Ridge." Official recorded sunrise that morning was 5:43 a.m. The temperature at daybreak was 65 degrees. It would rise to about 75 degrees by afternoon and the relative humidity would measure 71 percent. The winds would run at two miles per hour from the west and the clouds would be scattered. All in all, it would be a typical September day.

George McClellan's own account of the fighting:

On September 16, I rode along the whole front and observed that the ground at the left, near what was to become known as "Burnside's Bridge," was favorable for defense on our side, and that an attack across it would lead to favorable results. I therefore at once ordered Burnside to move his corps nearer the bridge, as he would probably be ordered to attack there next morning.

My plan for the impending engagement was to attack on our right with the corps of Hooker and Mansfield, supported by Sumner's and, as soon as matters looked favorable there, to move the corps of Burnside on our extreme left and, having carried the enemy's position, to press along the crest toward our right and, whenever either of these flank movements should be successful, to advance our center with all the forces then disposable.

About 2: p.m. on September 16, General Hooker was ordered to cross the Antietam to attack and, if possible, turn the enemy's left. It was perhaps half past three to four o'clock before Hooker got fairly in motion. I accompanied the movement until the top of the ridge was gained and then returned to headquarters.

During the night General Mansfield's corps crossed the Antietam at the same ford and bridge and bivouacked about a mile in rear of General Hooker's position.

On reaching the vicinity of the enemy's left, a sharp contest commenced by General Hooker's advance. The firing lasted until after dark, when Hooker's corps rested on their ground won from the enemy.

At daylight on the seventeenth the action continued. The whole of General Hooker's corps was soon engaged and drove the enemy into a second line. This contest was obstinate, and as the troops advanced, the opposition became more determined, and the number of the enemy greater. General Hooker then ordered up the corps of General Mansfield, which moved promptly toward the scene of action.

During the deployment that gallant veteran, General Mansfield, fell mortally wounded.

For about two hours the battle raged with varied success, the enemy endeavoring to drive our troops, and ours in turn to get possession of the line in front. Our troops ultimately succeeded in forcing the enemy back. At about 9:00 a.m. the first division of General Sumner's corps arrived. At about that time General Hooker was severely wounded in the foot and taken from the field, and General George G. Meade was placed in command of his corps.

While the conflict was so obstinately raging on the right, another division was pushing against the enemy further to the left. This division was assailed by a fire of artillery, but steadily advanced, and encountered the enemy infantry in some force at the group of houses known as the Roulette's farm.

The enemy was pressed back to near the crest of the hill, where he was encountered in great strength posted in a sunken road forming a natural rifle pit running in a northwesterly direction. In a cornfield in rear of this road were also strong bodies of the enemy. As our line reached the crest of the hill, a galling fire opened on it from the sunken road and cornfield. Here a terrific fire of musketry burst from both lines, and the battle raged along the whole line with great slaughter.

The enemy attempted to turn the left of our line, but were repulsed. Foiled in this, they made a determined assault on the front, but were met by a charge from our lines which drove them back with severe loss, leaving in our hands some 300 prisoners and several stands of colors.

On the left of the center we were also hotly engaged in front of Roulette's house and continued to advance under a heavy fire nearly to the crest of the hill overlooking Piper's house, the enemy being posted in a continuation of the sunken road and cornfield. Here the brave Irish brigade opened upon the enemy a terrific musketry fire and sustained its well-earned reputation. After suffering terribly in officers and men, and strewing the ground with their enemies as they drove them back, their ammunition nearly expended, and their commander, General Meagher, disabled by the fall of his horse shot under him, this brigade was ordered to the rear.

The ground over which our center divisions were fighting was very irregular, intersected by numerous ravines, hills covered with growing corn, enclosed by stone walls, behind which the enemy could advance unobserved upon any exposed point of our lines.

Our troops on the left of this part of the line drove the enemy through a cornfield into an orchard beyond. This advance gave us possession of Piper's house, the strong point contended for by the enemy at this part of the line, it being a defensible building several hundred yards in advance of the sunken road.

One corps, General Porter's held in reserve. It occupied a

A Union division storms across a ford at a key moment in the odd Battle of Stones River in Tennessee, as depicted in a field sketch by Henry Lovie. This indecisive battle cost both sides dearly in men but gave no advantage to either in the campaign for the West. (Library of Congress)

position on the east side of the Antietam Creek, upon the main turnpike leading to Sharpsburg and directly opposite the center of the enemy's line. This corps filled the interval between the right wing and General Burnside's command, and guarded the main approach from the enemy's position to our trains of supplies.

It was necessary to watch this part of our line with the utmost vigilance, lest the enemy should take advantage of the first exhibition of weakness here to push upon us a vigorous assault for the purpose of piercing our center and turning our rear, as well as to capture or destroy our supply trains. Once having penetrated this line, the enemy's passage to our rear could have met with but feeble resistance, as there were no other reserves to reinforce or close up the gap.

Toward the middle of the afternoon, proceeding to the right, I found that all three corps so far engaged, Sumner's, Hooker's and Mansfield's, had met with serious losses. Several general officers had been carried from the field severely wounded, and the aspect of affairs was anything but promising. At the risk of greatly exposing our center, I ordered two brigades from Porter's reserve corps, the only available troops, to reinforce the right.

General Sumner expressed the most decided opinion against another attempt during that day to assault the enemy's position in front, as portions of our troops were so much scattered and demoralized. In view of these circumstances, I directed the different commanders to hold their positions and, being satisfied that this could be done without the assistance of the two brigades from the center, I countermanded the order which was in course of execution.

This ended the battle on the right and center of the field.

The fighting in and around the Sunken Road, later to be called "Bloody Lane," was some of the most critical of the day. Confederate Gen. John B. Gordon narrates:

From the position assigned me near the center of Lee's lines, both armies and the entire field were in view. Hooker's compact columns of infantry had fallen in the morning upon our left with the crushing weight of a landslide. The Confederate line was too weak to withstand the momentum of such a charge. Pressed back, the Southern troops reformed their lines and rushed in countercharge upon the exulting Federals, hurled them back in confusion, and recovered all the ground that had been lost. Again and again, hour after hour, by charges and countercharges, this portion of the field was lost and recovered, until the corn that grew upon it looked as if it had been struck by a storm of bloody hail.

Up to this hour not a shot had been fired in my front near the center. There was an ominous lull in the left. From sheer exhaustion, both sides seemed willing to rest. General Lee took advantage of the respite and rode along his lines on the right and center. With that wonderful power which he possessed of divining the plans and purposes of his antagonist, General Lee had decided that the Union commander's next heavy blow would fall upon our center, and we were urged to hold on at any sacrifice. My troops held the most advanced position on this part of the field, and there was no supporting line behind us. To comfort General Lee I called aloud to him as he rode away: "These men are going to stay here, General." Alas! Many of the brave fellows are there now.

The predicted assault came. The men in blue formed in my front, four lines deep. The brave Union commander, superbly mounted, placed himself in front, while his band in the rear cheered them with martial music. It was a thrilling spectacle. To oppose man against man was impossible, for there were four lines of blue to my one line of gray. The only plan was to hold my fire until the advancing Federals were almost upon my lines. No troops with empty guns could withstand the shock. My men were at once directed to lie down upon the grass. Not a shot would be fired until my voice should be heard commanding "Fire!"

There was no artillery at this point upon either side, and not a rifle was discharged. The stillness was literally oppressive, as this column of Union infantry moved majestically toward us. Now the front rank was within a few rods of where I stood. With all my lung power I shouted "Fire!"

Our rifles flamed and roared in the Federals' faces like a blinding blaze of lightning. The effect was appalling. The entire front line, with few exceptions, went down. Before the rear lines could recover, my exultant men were on their feet, devouring them with successive volleys. Even then these stubborn blue lines retreated in fairly good order.

The fire now became furious and deadly. The list of the slain was lengthened with each passing moment. Near nightfall, the awful carnage ceased; Lee's center had been saved.

T.F. DeBurgh Galwey was with the Eighth Ohio at Bloody Lane:

As we came up, the Confederates disappeared down into an old rain-worn lane that ran along through a depression in the ridge. We halted upon a slight crest from which we had a plunging fire into the lane, which looked to us then like a mere ditch and was distant about fifty or sixty yards.

We thought the Confederates in taking refuge there had put themselves into a trap, for the ground behind them, on which the corn grew, was a steep rise and, though we could see that they had reinforcements in that corn, there appeared to be hesitation among them. There were Confederate battle flags at intervals in the Sunken Lane, six or seven, I think, along our front, and more in the cornfield behind, indicating, I suppose, just so many regiments.

It is almost certain that for a very short while after our arrival we could have carried the lane and the slope beyond by a dash, though on the several occasions within the first hour when our men, by their own impulse, rose and fixed bayonets to charge, the Confederates met us with a murderous fire. It was about this time that I noticed that the Confederates in the cornfield were no longer visible; perhaps they had withdrawn. But the minutes slipped by, and the opportunity was gone.

At one time a lull occurred in the Confederate fire from the lane, and then we saw perhaps a dozen little white squares rise above the fence rails; whether they were white handkerchiefs (a luxury hardly to be expected then and there) or the white cotton haversacks used by the Confederates, we could not distinguished. It was quickly plain, however, that though there might be some in the lane who wished to surrender, these were in the minority, for we met a musketry fire so rapid and well aimed that we all unfixed bayonets and backed up step by step until we were on the old ground, where we dropped down again and resumed our fire as before.

For what seemed like an hour after our arrival on the ground, we were all alone. We could look far to the rear, but no Union troops were in sight, and we were now sadly in need of some relief. Our numbers were reduced; our ammunition was running low. Our men had all begun with sixty rounds, and now they endeavored to economize their cartridges and to gather more from the cartridge boxes of the dead or wounded.

At length the Irish Brigade came into close touch with us, an orderly sergeant kneeling down, I remember, just at my left shoulder and banging away at the enemy. He was a redheaded, red-bearded man, and the whole circumstance is impressed on my mind from the fact that he put his hand into the haversack of a dead Confederate and took therefrom a bag of coffee, which he kept for himself, handing to me a bag of sugar.

The Confederate artillery off toward the Dunker Church had now found our line and were enfilading us from right to left.

Noon came and went, and we had not yet made headway, though many times we had fixed bayonets and rushed toward the lane, but at each of these efforts the Confederates rose and drove us back. Our line of battle had now become a mere line of skirmishers; the rest lay about us wounded or dead or had gone disabled to the rear. It seemed as if we could not endure it much longer. We ***must*** *go forward, or else altogether abandon the ground. To our rear was nothing.*

The Irish Brigade had moved on and left nothing on our left.

It was about this time that the captain of my company appeared, passing the order along the line as he approached, "Fix bayonets! Battalion, forward, right wheel, double quick," and the word of execution, "March!" he spoke as soon as he reached us on the knoll.

It was a good thing for us to have a voice of command, and the order was obeyed at once. It seemed like merely a hop, skip, and jump till we were at the lane, and into it, the Confederates breaking away in haste and fleeing up the slope. What a sight was that lane! I shall not dwell on the horror of it; I saw many a ghastly array of dead afterward, but none, I think, that so affected me as did the sight of the poor brave fellows in butternut homespun that had there died for what they believed to be honor and a righteous cause.

Henry Kyd Douglas, aide to Stonewall Jackson and whose home was near the Antietam battlefield, wrote, "Why Burnside's bridge?" Indeed, it is a dubious honor for the bridge, for Burnside presented the most troublesome spot for the Army of the Potomac that day. As demonstrated in McClellan's account of the afternoon phase of the battle, written some twenty years later, Burnside hesitated and faltered in all of his attempts to take this bridge that crossed Antietam Creek, a stream that, at this point, was easily fordable by simply wading across.

The troops of General Ambrose Burnside held the left of the line opposite the lowest bridge. The attack on our right was to have been supported by an attack on the left.

At eight o'clock on the morning of September 17, an order was sent to Burnside to carry the bridge, then to gain possession of the heights beyond and to advance along their crest upon Sharpsburg and its rear.

After some time had elapsed, I dispatched an aide to ascertain what had been done. The aide returned with the information that but little progress had been made. I then sent him back with an order to General Burnside to assault the bridge at once and carry it at all hazards. The aide returned to me a second time with the report that the bridge was still in the possession of the enemy. Whereupon I directed Colonel Sackett, inspector general, to deliver to General Burnside my positive order to push forward his troops without a moment's delay and, if necessary, to carry the bridge at the point of the bayonet; and I ordered Colonel Sackett to remain with General Burnside and see that the order was executed promptly.

After these three hours' delay the bridge was carried at one o'clock by a brilliant charge of the 51st New York and 51st Pennsylvania Volunteers. Other troops were then thrown over and the opposite bank occupied, the enemy retreating to the heights beyond.

A halt was then made by General Burnside's advance until 3:00 P.M.; upon hearing which I directed one of my aids to inform General Burnside that I desired him to push forward his troops with the utmost vigor and carry the enemy's position on the heights; that the movement was vital to our success; that this was a time when we must not stop for loss of life, if a great object could thereby be accomplished. He replied that he would soon advance, and would go up the hill as far as a battery of the enemy on the left would permit. Upon this report I again immediately sent Colonel Key to General Burnside with orders to advance at once, if possible to flank the battery, or storm it and carry the heights; repeating that if he considered the movement impracticable, to inform me, so that his troops might be recalled. The advance was then gallantly resumed, the enemy driven from the guns, the heights handsomely carried, and a portion of the troops even reached the outskirts of Sharpsburg. By this time it was nearly dark, and strong reinforcements just then reaching the enemy from Harpers Ferry attacked General Burnside's troops on their left flank and forced them to retire to a lower line of hills nearer the bridge.

If this important movement had been consummated two hours earlier, a position would have been secured upon the heights from which our batteries might have enfiladed the greater part of the enemy's line, and turned their right and rear. Our victory might thus have been much more decisive.

General James Longstreet:

General Robert Toombs was defending the crossing at the Burnside Bridge against the 9th Corps, commanded by General Burnside. Toombs's orders were, when dislodged, to retire so as to open the field to fire to all the troops on the heights behind him, the fire of his batteries to be concentrated upon the bridge, and his infantry arranged for a like converging fire.

In the afternoon the Union 2nd Maryland and 6th New Hampshire Regiments were ordered forward in double time with bayonets fixed to carry the bridge. They made a gallant, dashing charge, crowding the bridge almost to its western **debouche**, *but the fire concentrated a storm that stunned their ranks and cut them down until they were forced to retire. General Burnside repeated the order to force the way at all hazards. Arrangements were made, and when concluded the 51st New York and 51st Pennsylvania Regiments found a route better covered from the Confederate fire than that of the first column.*

By a dashing charge in double time they passed it, under exulting hurrahs and most gallant work, and gained the west bank. The crossing by other troops at a lower ford made our position at the bridge untenable, and General Toombs was forced to retire.

About four o'clock a strong force was over and advanced under severe fire of artillery and infantry, increasing in force as they ascended the heights, the troops engaging in steady, brave fight as they marched. Overreaching my right, they forced it back.

When General Lee found that General Jackson had left six of his brigades under General A. P. Hill to receive the property and garrison surrendered at Harpers Ferry, he sent orders for them to join him and by magic spell had them on the field to

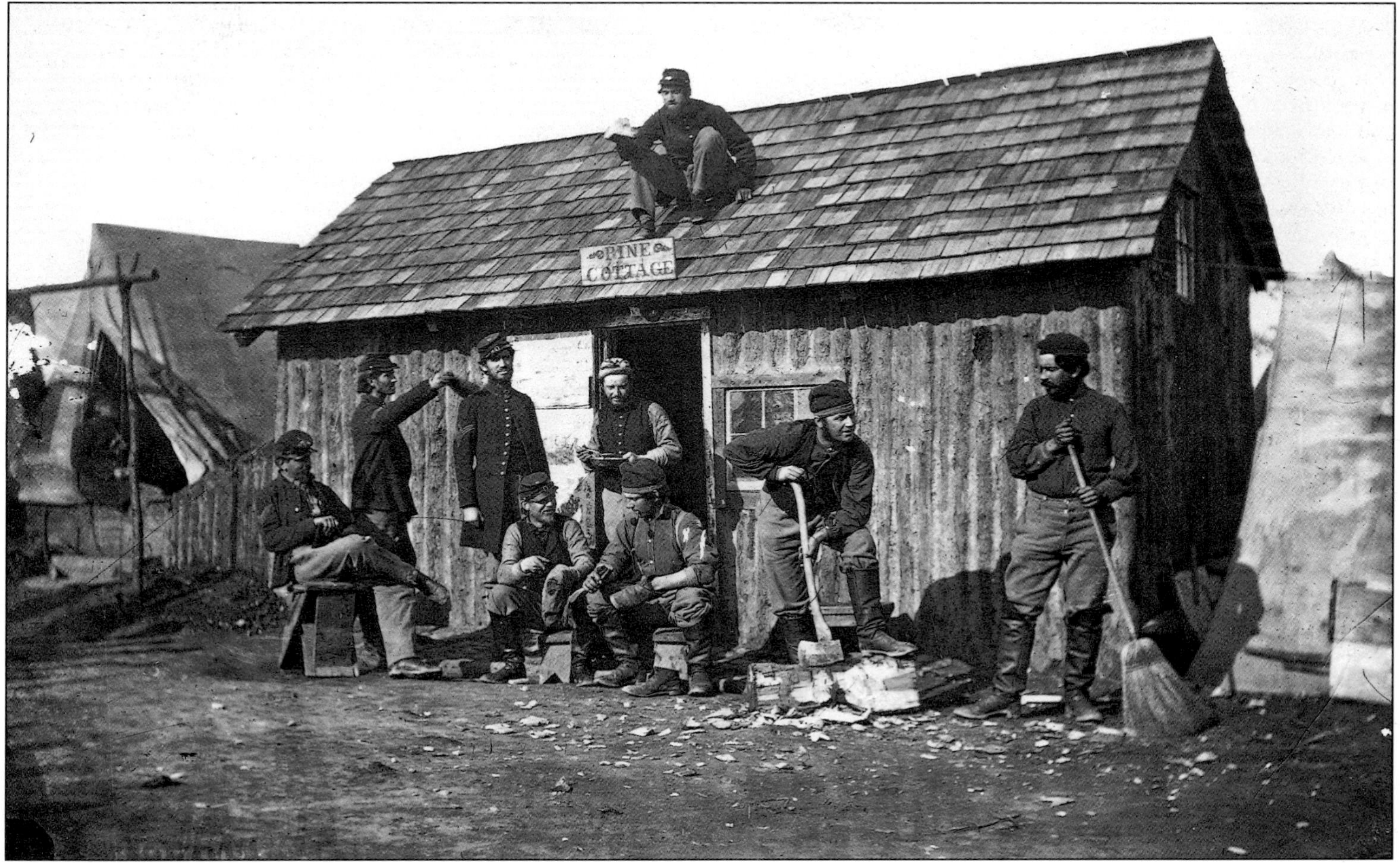

After two years of war, men of the Army of the Potomac knew how to settle in comfortably for the winter. (Library of Congress)

meet the final crisis. He ordered two of them to guard against approach of other forces that might come against him by another bridge, and threw the remainder against the forefront of the battle. The strong forces concentrating against General Burnside seemed to spring from the earth as his march bore him farther from the river.

The Union troops, assailed in front and on their flank by concentrating fires that were crushing, found it necessary to withdraw. A.P. Hill's brigades followed. They recovered the ground that had been lost on the right before the night dropped her mantle upon the field of seldom-equalled strife.

When the 9th Corps dropped back under the crest they had so bravely won, the Battle of Sharpsburg virtually ended.

That night George Smalley of the *New York Tribune* called all associates together to work out the dispatch that must be transmitted immediately in order to scoop the other New York newspapers. By candlelight they composed until the late hours. At midnight Smalley rode off towards Frederick where he wired his column to New York via Baltimore: "Fierce and desperate battle between two hundred thousand men has raged since daylight, yet night closes on an uncertain field, It is the greatest fight since Waterloo. . .".

Mr. Smalley's dispatch took a circuitous route. At Baltimore, the American Telegraph Company agent, acting on an intelligent hunch that the report might be of some value to Washington, wired the Frederick message to the War Department. By noon on the 18th, Smalley's account of Antietam was on Mr. Lincoln's desk at the White House, replacing McClellan's reports which were, typically, delayed.

Late that night the star *Tribune* reporter changed trains in Baltimore, switching from the box car he had taken out of Frederick to one on the New York express, continuing without a wink of sleep to compose what would be hailed by the world's press as the outstanding battle account of all time. At 6:00 a.m. on the 19th, he stumbled into the composing room at the *Tribune* building and within two hours heard his headlines being shouted from every street corner in New York. Antietam and Sharpsburg had become household words.

Confederate John G. Walker:

We had fought an indecisive battle, and General Lee determined to withdraw from Maryland. At dark on the night of September 18 the rearward movement began; and a little after sunrise next morning the entire Confederate army had safely recrossed the Potomac.

Detained in superintending the removal of the wounded, I was among the last to cross. As I rode into the river, I passed General Lee, sitting on his horse in the stream, watching the crossing of the wagons and artillery. Returning my greeting, he inquired as to what was still behind. There was nothing but the wagons containing my wounded and a battery, all of which were near at hand, and I told him so.

"Thank God!" I heard him say as I rode on.

THE BATTLE AT FREDERICKSBURG, VIRGINIA

Lincoln came to Sharpsburg to see why McClellan did not pursue Lee across the Potomac. While McClellan wrote that the President was satisfied with the course of events, in fact he was not. The battle presented only an empty Union victory, far short of what Mr. Lincoln wanted and had assumed McClellan would give him. The general's excuses were remarkably like those he gave for not advancing into Richmond in the Spring. His horses were too tired, he said. In God's name, the President wanted to know, what had the horses done to make them tired? McClellan had sat still with the entire Fifth Corps, under Fitz-John Porter, unused. It made no sense to Lincoln. The Army of the Potomac could have and should have taken care of Lee on the 18th, and, if not, certainly followed him across the river and brought the war to a conclusion. It had been possible.

On his way back to Washington from Antietam, Mr. Lincoln pondered to one of his associates, "General Meigs, did you ever try to fertilize a field with a fart?"

The President determined that if McClellan let Lee get away, he would remove him from command. On November 5, McClellan received the following telegram from Washington:

"General: On receipt of the order of the President, sent herewith, you will immediately turn over your command to Maj.-Gen. Burnside, and repair to Trenton, N.J., reporting on your arrival at that place, by telegraph, for further orders."

The reaction to McClellan's departure from the military was immediate and passionate, and filled pages of diaries and memoirs and thousands of letters home. One soldier was angry and loyal:

A War Department order relieved Major General McClellan from duty in command of the Army of the Potomac. The publication of this announcement had a startling effect. With armies actively in the field the emotional is unheard of. But for McClellan there had grown such an affection that a total severance of his authority savored of disruption. No other commander ever so captured his soldiers, ever so entranced his followers. Sweeping denunciation, violent invective, were heaped without stint on the government. Subdued threats of vengeance, mutterings of insurrection slumbered in their incipiency but, restrained by good sense, patriotism and discipline, they never reached consummation in overt act. The mails teemed with correspondence to friends and relatives at home denouncing the action of the War Department, raging at the authorities.

A sadder gathering of men could not well have been assembled than that of the army drawn up to bid farewell to its beloved commander. Our corps was reviewed in the morning and, as General McClellan passed along its front, whole regiments broke and flocked around him, and with tears and entreaties besought him not to leave them, but to say the word and they would soon settle matters in Washington. Indeed, it was thought at one time there would be a mutiny, but by a word he calmed the tumult and ordered the men back to their colors and their duty. He was obliged to halt in front of us, as Meagher's Irish brigade were pressing on him so that further progress was impossible. They cast their colors in the dust for him to ride over, of course, he made them take them up again. Another general who was riding near McClellan was forced by the crowd toward our line, and I heard him say that he wished to God that McClellan would put himself at the head of the army and throw the infernal scoundrels at Washington into the Potomac. At twelve noon McClellan met the officers and bade them goodby, and as he grasped each officer by the hand there was not a dry eye in the assemblage. Before parting he made a short address, in which he urged on us all to return to our respective commands and do our duty to our new commander as loyally and as faithfully as we had served him.

These and other accounts paint the picture of a "savior" being wronged by his government and hordes of followers protesting. Perhaps this was the case immediately after McClellan was dismissed from command. But two years later, when the general ran against Mr. Lincoln on the Democrat ticket for the Presidency, the soldiers had come to things in a different light. The military did not support McClellan in the election.

Meanwhile, Burnside took command of the Army of the Potomac, and, three months after Antietam, faced Lee on the Rappahannock at Fredericksburg. A Confederate officer described the scene:

December 11, 1862. *The little valley in which Fredericksburg is situated is enclosed on the south side of the Rappahannock by a range of hills, directly opposite the town, which are known as Marye's Heights and approach within half a mile of the river. Most of these hills are covered with a thick copse of oak, and only in front of the town are they quite bare of trees. The ground toward the Rappahannock is open and flat, is intersected only by some small streams and is broken immediately upon the river by several large and deep ravines, which afford shelter to troops.*

On this semicircle of hills our army, numbering in all about 80,000 men, rested in order of battle behind a continuous line of entrenchments, concealed from the enemy's view by the thick underwood. Longstreet's corps formed the left, Jackson's the right of our lines. The bulk of the artillery, numbering about 250 pieces, was well distributed. On its northern bank the Rappahannock is closely lined by a range of commanding hills, on which the hostile artillery, more than 300 pieces, some of them of heavier caliber than had ever before been employed in the field, were advantageously posted. The greater part of them, especially those on the Stafford Heights, bore immediately on the town, but nearly all were in a position to sweep the plains on our side of the river.

We found General Lee on an eminence which afforded a view over nearly the whole plain before him. Longstreet and several other generals were also assembled here, looking anxiously toward Fredericksburg, as yet concealed from their sight by a dense fog which hung heavily over the little valley.

So several hours passed wearily away. Already the road leading up to the heights from Fredericksburg was thronged with a confused mass of fugitives, bearing with them such of their effects as they could bring away. Ten o'clock came, and the hammers of the church clocks were just sounding the last peaceful stroke of the hour, when suddenly, at the signal of a single cannon shot, more than 150 pieces of artillery, including some of the enemy's most ponderous guns, opened their iron mouths with a terrific roar and hurled a tempest of destruction upon the devoted town. The air shook, and the very earth beneath our feet trembled at this deafening cannonade, the heaviest that had ever yet assailed my ears. The thick fog still prevented us from obtaining a satisfactory view of the bombardment; but the howling of the solid shot, the bursting of the shells, the crashing of the missiles through the thick walls and the dull sound of falling houses united in a dismal concert of doom. Very soon the site of the unhappy town was indicated, even through the fog, by a column of smoke and dust and the flames of burning buildings. Our batteries did not respond to the guns of the enemy. It was evident that nothing could be done to save the place. The horrible din lasted two hours and was succeeded by perfect silence – the silence of solitude. About noon the sun, breaking through the clouds, seemed to mock the smoking ruins it revealed. Every heart of the thousands of brave Confederate soldiers who witnessed this spectacle burned for revenge.

General Lee knew very well that he would not be able to prevent the passage of the river by the Federal army and, having entertained from the beginning no idea of seriously contesting this, he now gave orders for Barksdale's brigade, which had furnished the sharpshooters on the shore, to withdraw gradually and to keep up only a feigned resistance. During the rest of the afternoon and evening the Federal army commenced to move over to our side of the river.

We exchanged felicitations on the great blunder of the Federal commander in preparing to attack us in a position of our own choice. Even the face of our great commander Lee, which rarely underwent any change of expression at the news of either victory or disaster, seemed to be lighted up with pleasure at every fresh report that a greater number of the enemy had crossed the river.

The *Cincinnati Commercial* reporter speculated on the opening of battle:

On Friday morning those of us not fully posted, and not conversant with all the mysteries of "strategy," expected a battle. But the morning passed quietly, the smoke veiling all distant objects from observation. Our troops were crossing into Fredericksburgh. Some adventurers were straggling back bearing boxes of tobacco, which was as eagerly sought by our men as if it had been gold, or something more precious even than fine gold. I suppose it does rank in the army as one of the chief necessaries of life. The Town, in the afternoon, literally swarmed with troops. The enemy's batteries were ominously silent. If the rebel general had any particular objections to the presence of our troops in the town, why did he not open upon them from his batteries? What was to prevent the enemy from shelling the town, as we had done? I asked several military gentlemen the question, for the situation appeared to present to me to be one of the deepest peril. One said: "The enemy have not ammunition to spare." Another: "Oh! a bombardment don't amount to any thing any how." Another: "They don't care about bombing us, it is an inconsequential sort of business. We threw four thousand shells yesterday, and it amounted to nothing." Another: "They're afraid of our siege-guns this side." Another: "General Lee thinks he will have a big thing on us about the bombardment of this town. He proposes to rouse the indignation of the civilized world, as they call it. You'll see he won't throw a shell into it. He is playing for the sympathies of Europe." Another thought the enemy were skedaddling, and spoke of the laugh that would be raised at Burnside's expense in that case. He said, with the usual expletives: "They want us to get in. Getting out won't be quite so smart and easy. You'll see if it will."

A Union officer describes crossing the Rappahannock:

General Burnside's first plan, to force a passage several miles below Fredericksburg, having failed, he resolved to meet in front the obstacle which he could not turn.

On the evening of December 10 the order arrived to hold ourselves ready to march the next morning. "This time," it was said, "the dance is going to begin."

The night was full of suppressed agitation and of those distant rumors which denote preparations for battle. The fires remained burning longer than usual. In different directions was heard the rolling of wagons going to the rear and of cannon going to the front. Confused noises indicated the march of regiments changing position. Their bayonets flashed through the obscurity, lighted up by the bivouac fires.

We were awakened at daybreak by the sound of the cannon. Every one was quickly on foot. The men hastened to swallow their hot coffee.

At half past seven our division drew near the river and was held in reserve behind the Stafford Heights, which were crowned by artillery. Under their protection, and favored by a thick fog, the head of our columns began to occupy the city.

On the twelfth the different corps continued to cross the Rappahannock, Sumner on the right, Franklin on the left. The two corps commanded by Hooker, forming the center, were the last to cross. On both sides the sharpshooters were exchanging fire, and the artillery duel continued; no serious action occurred.

December 13, 1862, was a day as radiant as a fete day. Our brigade was already massed on the summit of the hill, arms stacked, awaiting its turn to cross the river. Some of the men, careless and with loud cries, were chasing frightened rabbits through the bushes.

From this point the view was splendid. At our feet the river was spanned by two bridges of boats, across one of which defiled the infantry, and across the other the cavalry and the artillery. We looked at the regiments as they marched out on the plain to take their place in order of battle in front of the enemy's positions, which arose by steps at the back of the picture. On the left the view extended to the horizon, which was spotted with little clouds, the nature of which we well knew. It was Franklin, who was throwing some shells at Stuart's cavalry. We could easily distinguish in that direction the crackling of the skirmishers' shots, emphasized by the firing of the cannon. And on the right a projecting hill concealed Fredericksburg from our view and we were able to see only the steeples. But farther on clearly appeared above the fog a line of heights, covered with entrenchments and bristling with cannon.

When our turn came to descend into the arena, I thought involuntarily of the gladiators of old, entering into the amphitheater in the presence of Caesar. **Morituri te salutamus!** *"We who are about to die salute thee!"*

A Confederate diary narrates:

December 12, 1862. *The enemy seemed busy as bees. Interminable columns of infantry, blue in color and blurred by distance, flowed toward us like the waves of a steadily advancing sea. On and on they came, with flash of bayonets and flutter of flags, to the measure of military music, and we could distinctly observe them deploy into line of battle. About eleven o'clock I was asked by General Stuart to accompany him on a ride along our line of battle. It was a pleasure and an encouragement to pass the extended lines of our soldiers, who were lying carelessly behind their earthworks or actively engaged in throwing up new ones – some cooking, others gaily discussing the designs of the enemy, and greeting with loud cheers of derision the enormous shells, which they called "Yankee flour barrels," as these came tumbling into the woods around them. The fog was rolling up again from the low swampy grounds.*

December 13. *Jackson had chosen his position on an eminence, within a few hundred yards of Hamilton's Crossing, which rose above the general elevation of the ridge in a similar manner to Lee's Hill on the left, and which has ever since borne the name of "Jackson's Hill." Jackson and Stuart concurred on the opinion that it would be the best plan to make a sudden general attack upon the enemy under cover of the fog, but General Lee had decided in council of war against any offensive movement.*

Nine o'clock came, and still the vaporous curtain overhung the plateau, still the brooding silence prevailed, when suddenly it seemed as though a tremendous hurricane had burst upon us, and we became sensible upon the instant of a howling tempest of shot and shell hurled against our position from not fewer than 300 pieces of artillery. Hundreds of missiles of every size and description crashed through the woods, breaking down trees and scattering branches and splinters in all directions.

And now the thick veil of mist that had concealed the plain rolled away, like the drawing up of a drop scene at the opera, and revealed to us the countless regiments of the Federal army forming their lines of attack. At this moment I was sent by Stuart to General Jackson with the message that the Yankees were about to commence their advance. I found old Stonewall standing at ease on his hill, unmoved in the midst of the terrible fire, narrowly observing the movements of the enemy through his field glass. The atmosphere was not perfectly clear, and from this eminence was afforded a distant view of more than two-thirds of the battlefield, a military panorama the grandeur of which I had never seen equaled. On they came, in a beautiful order, as if on parade, a moving forest of steel; on they came, waving their hundreds of regimental flags, which relieved with warm bits of coloring the dull blue of the columns and the russet tinge of the wintry landscape, while their artillery beyond the river continued the cannonade with unabated fury over their heads and gave a background of white fleecy smoke, like midsummer clouds, to the animated picture.

I could not rid myself of a feeling of depression and anxiety as I saw this innumerable host steadily moving towards our lines, which were hidden by the woods, where our artillery maintained as yet a perfect silence, General Lee having given orders that our guns should not open fire until the Yankees had come within easy canister range. Upon my mentioning this feeling to Jackson, the old chief answered me in his characteristic way, "Major, my men had sometimes failed **to take** *a position, but* **to defend** *one, never!"*

In a few minutes solid shot were plowing at short range with fearful effect through the dense columns of the Federals. The boldness of the enterprise and the fatal accuracy of the firing seemed to paralyze for a time and then to stampede the whole of the extreme left of the Yankee army, and terror and confusion reigned there during some minutes; soon,

In a damaged studio portrait, Sgt. Stephen Clinton Adams of the Sixth Virginia Cavalry and friend. (Library of Congress)

Union casualties after Fredericksburg. These men were luckier than most – medical facilities and knowledge were crude at the time. To be wounded was usually to be consigned to ghastly treatment and conditions. (Library of Congress)

however, several batteries moved into position and, uniting with several of those on the Stafford Heights, concentrated a tremendous fire upon our guns.

The thunder soon rolled all along our lines, while from the continuous roar the ear caught distinctly the sharp, rapid rattling volleys of the musketry, especially in the immediate form of General A.P. Hill, where the infantry were very hotly engaged. At intervals above the tumult of the conflict we could hear the wild hurrah of the attacking hosts of the Federals and the defiant yell of the Confederates as the assault was repulsed.

Along Jackson's lines the fury and tumult of the battle lasted all the forenoon and until two o'clock in the afternoon. A comparative quietude then succeeded, the infantry firing died away, and only an intermittent cannonade was kept up in our immediate front; but from the left opposite Fredericksburg there came to us the heavy boom of artillery and the distant rattle of small arms, and we knew the fight still raged there with undiminished vehemence.

About three o'clock there seemed to be a new movement preparing on the enemy's left, and General Stuart, suspecting it might be a movement on our right mark flank, ordered me to proceed with twenty couriers to our extreme right and send him a report every five minutes. The view which presented itself to our eyes far exceeded our expectations. The Yankees, not more than a thousand yards distant from us, were evidently preparing for a new advance; reinforcements were moving up at a double-quick and forming into line of battle as they arrived; we saw the Federal lines moving forward to their new attack, which was introduced and supported by a cannonade of several hundred pieces equal in fury to that of the morning.

Two hours of anxiety and doubt passed away, until at five o'clock we saw scattered fugitives straggling to the rear, their numbers augmenting every moment. Finally whole regiments, brigades and divisions, in utter confusion and bewildered flight, covered the plain before us. All discipline was lost for the moment, and those thousands of troops, whom an hour before we had seen advancing in beautiful military order, now presented the spectacle of a stampeded and demoralized mob. Off we now hastened to Jackson, who at once sent to General Lee the request that he might fall upon the enemy and render the victory complete. Our commander in chief, however, adhering to his earlier idea, still objected to a forward movement, for which, in my judgement, the golden moment had now passed, had he inclined to favor it.

About seven o'clock the battles ceased.

A *London Times* reporter traveling with the Army of Northern Virginia was convinced that this was "a memorable day" in American history; he was probably the only newspaper reporter of the entire war who failed to capitalize the word "Confederate:"

At half-past eight a.m. Gen. Lee, accompanied by his full staff, rode slowly along the front of the confederate lines from left to right, and took up his station for a time beyond Hamilton's crossing, and in rear of the batteries on the extreme confederate right. It would be presumptuous in me to say one word in commendation of the serenity, or, if I may so express it, the unconscious dignity of Gen. Lee's courage, when he is under fire. No one who sees and knows his demeanor in ordinary life would expect any thing else from one so calm, so undemonstrative and unassuming. But the description applied after the battle of Alma to Lord Raglan, by Marshal St. Arnaud, and in which, noticing Lord Raglan's unconsciousness under fire, he speaks of his "antique heroism," seems to me so applicable to Gen. Lee, that I cannot forbear his station on the hill which takes its name from him, and thence, in company with Gen. Longstreet, calmly watched the repulse of the repeated Federal efforts against the heights on which he stood. Occasionally Gen. Jackson rode up to the spot and mingled in conversation with the other two leading generals. Once General Longstreet exclaimed to him, "Are you not scared by that file of Yankees you have before you down there?" to which Gen. Jackson replied: "Wait till they come a little nearer, and they shall either scare me or I'll scare them."

The battle opened when the sun had let in enough light through the mist to disclose the near proximity of the Federal lines and field-batteries. The first shot was fired before ten a.m. from the batteries in the Federal centre, and was directed against Gen. Hood's division. The Pennsylvania reserves advanced boldly under a heavy fire against the confederates who occupied one of the copsewood spurs, and were for a time permitted to hold it; but presently the confederate batteries opened on them, and a determined charge of the Texans drove the Yankees out of the wood in a confusion from which nothing could subsequently rally them.

Simultaneously a heavy fire issued from the batteries of General A.P. Hill's and General Early's divisions, which was vigorously replied to by the Federal field-batteries. The only advantage momentarily gained by the Federals in this quarter, and which is noticed in Gen. Lee's report, was on the occasion of the collapse of a regiment of North Carolina conscripts, who broke and ran, but whose place was rapidly taken by more intrepid successors. The cannonading now became general along the entire line. Such a scene, at once terrific and sublime, mortal eye never rested on before, unless the bombardment of Sebastopol by the combined batteries of France and England revealed a more fearful manifestation of the hate and fury of man.

The thundering, bellowing roar of hundreds of pieces of artillery, the bright jets of issuing flame, the screaming, hissing, whistling, shrieking projectiles, the wreaths of smoke as shell after shell burst into the still air, the savage crash of round-shot among the trees of the shattered forest, formed a scene likely to sink forever into the memory of all who witnessed it, but utterly defying verbal delineation. A direct and enfilading fire swept each battery upon either side as it was unmasked; volley crash succeeded crash, until the eye lost all power of distinguishing the lines of combatants, and the plain seemed a lake of fire, a seething lake of molten lava, coursed over by incarnate fiends drunk with fury and revenge.

The confederates drove them with horrid carnage across the plain, and only desisted from their work when they came under fire of the Federal batteries across the river. Upon the extreme confederate right General Stuart's horse-artillery drove hotly upon the fugitives, and kept up the pursuit, subsequently understood to have been effective, until after dark. Upon the confederate right, where the antagonists fought upon more equal terms, the loss sustained by the confederates was greater than on the confederate left; the Federal loss in officers and men far outbalanced that of their opponents.

Meanwhile the battle, which had dashed furiously against the lines of Gens. Hood, A.P. Hill, and Early, was little more than child's play as compared with the onslaught directed by the Federals in the immediate neighborhood of Fredericksburgh. The impression that the confederate batteries would not fire heavily upon the Federals advancing in this quarter, for fear of injuring the town of Fredericksburgh, is believed to have prevailed among the Northern generals. How bitterly they deceived themselves subsequent events served to show.

To the Irish division, commanded by Gen. Meagher, was principally committed the desperate task of bursting out of the town of Fredericksburgh, and forming, under the withering fire of the confederate batteries, to attack Marye's Heights, towering immediately in their front. Never at Fontenoy, Albuera, or at Waterloo was more undoubted courage displayed by the sons of Erin than during those six frantic dashes which they directed against the almost impregnable position of their foe. There are stories that General Meagher harangued his troops in impassioned language on the morning of the thirteenth, and plied them extensively with the whiskey found in the cellars of Fredericksburgh. After witnessing the gallantry and devotion exhibited by his troops, and viewing the hill-sides for acres strewn with their corpses thick as autumnal leaves, the spectator can remember nothing but their desperate courage, and regret that it was not exhibited in a holier cause.

That any mortal men could have carried the position before which they were wantonly sacrificed, defended as it was, it seems to me idle for a moment to believe. But the bodies which lie in dense masses within forty yards of the muzzles of Col. Walton's guns are the best evidence what manner of men they were who pressed on to death with the dauntlessness of a race which has gained glory on a thousand battlefields, and never more richly deserved it than at the foot of Marye's Heights on the thirteenth day of December, 1862.

A member of the 4th New York:

Our line was now formed at the foot of Marye's hill, which was crowned by earth-works, rifle-pits, and a stone wall, defended by both infantry and artillery, and completely commanded in the rear by an elevated plateau, red with the flashes of guns. Now the order came to advance, and up the hill moved French's division to one of the most desperate charges of the whole four years of war. Ranks torn by shot and shell; men falling from terrible grape and canister wounds; the very air lurid, and alive with the flashes of guns, and rent with the long shriek of solid shot and shell, and the wicked whistle of grape; with compressed lips and shortened breath, closing up shoulder to shoulder, at length we gained the brow; then while within a few yards of the rifle-pits and stone wall, up rose rank after rank of infantry, adding to the avalanche of artillery fire a perfect rain of the less noisy, but more destructive rifle ball. Here, almost blown off our feet, staggering as though against a mighty wind, the line for a few minutes held its ground; then (but not until orders to that effect had been given, more by the motions of the officers than by their voices), slowly and sullenly it gave way, and retiring a few paces below the brow of the hill, there lay down, panting for breath, and clinging to the ground so desperately attained. The division, (as later reports showed), had lost nearly one-half its numbers inside of fifteen or twenty minutes.

After a slight lull in the roar of battle, the ball against opened, and looking back, we saw the advance of Hancock's division, over the same ground that we had passed. The same tragedy re-occurred, and this splendid division, or what was left of it, lay immediately in our rear. Again was the charge repeated by another division, which we afterwards learned was Humphrey's, of the Fifth corps, but the result was the same. . . .

General James Longstreet's account appeared in Vol. III of the immensely popular *Battles and Leaders of the Civil War:*

From the moment of their appearance began the most fearful carnage. With our artillery from the front, right and left tearing through their ranks, the Federals pressed forward with almost invincible determination, maintaining their steady step and closing up their broken ranks. Thus resolutely they marched upon the stone fence behind which quietly waited the Confederate brigade of General Cobb. As they came within reach . . . a storm of lead was poured into their advancing ranks and they were swept from the field like chaff before the wind. A cloud of smoke shut out the scene for a moment, and, rising, revealed the shattered fragments recoiling from their gallant but hopeless charge. The artillery still plowed through their retreating ranks and searched the places of concealment into which the troops had plunged. A vast number went pell-mell into an old railroad cut to escape fire from the right and front. A battery on Lee's Hill saw this and turned its fire into the entire length of the cut, and the shells began to pour down upon the Federals with the most frightful destruction.

The casualties were appalling, as reported by Captain Conyngham of the Irish Brigade:

A cold, bitter, bleak December night closed upon the field of blood and carnage. Thousands lay along that hill-side, and in the valleys, whose oozing wounds were frozen, and whose cold limbs were stiffened, for they had no blankets; they had flung them away going into the fight. Masses of dead and dying were huddled together; some convulsed in the last throes of death; others gasping for water – delirious, writhing in agony, and stiffened with the cold frost. The living tried to shelter themselves behind the bodies of the dead.

Cries, moans, groans, and shrieks of agony rang over that sad battlefield. There was no one to tend them; no one to bring them a drop of cold water to moisten their swollen tongues; for that field was still swept with shot and shell, and in the hands of the enemy.

And this was war – "glorious war" - with all its pomp and parade – all its glittering attractions. If we could see it in its true colors, it is the most horrible curse that God could inflict upon mankind.

As 1862 approached an end with still no substantial Union victory to present to the North, President Lincoln sent the following telegram to the men of his army in Virginia:

EXECUTIVE MANSION

WASHINGTON, December 23, 1862

TO THE ARMY OF THE POTOMAC:

I have just read your Commanding General's preliminary report of the battle of Fredericksburgh. Although you were not successful, the attempt was not an error, nor the

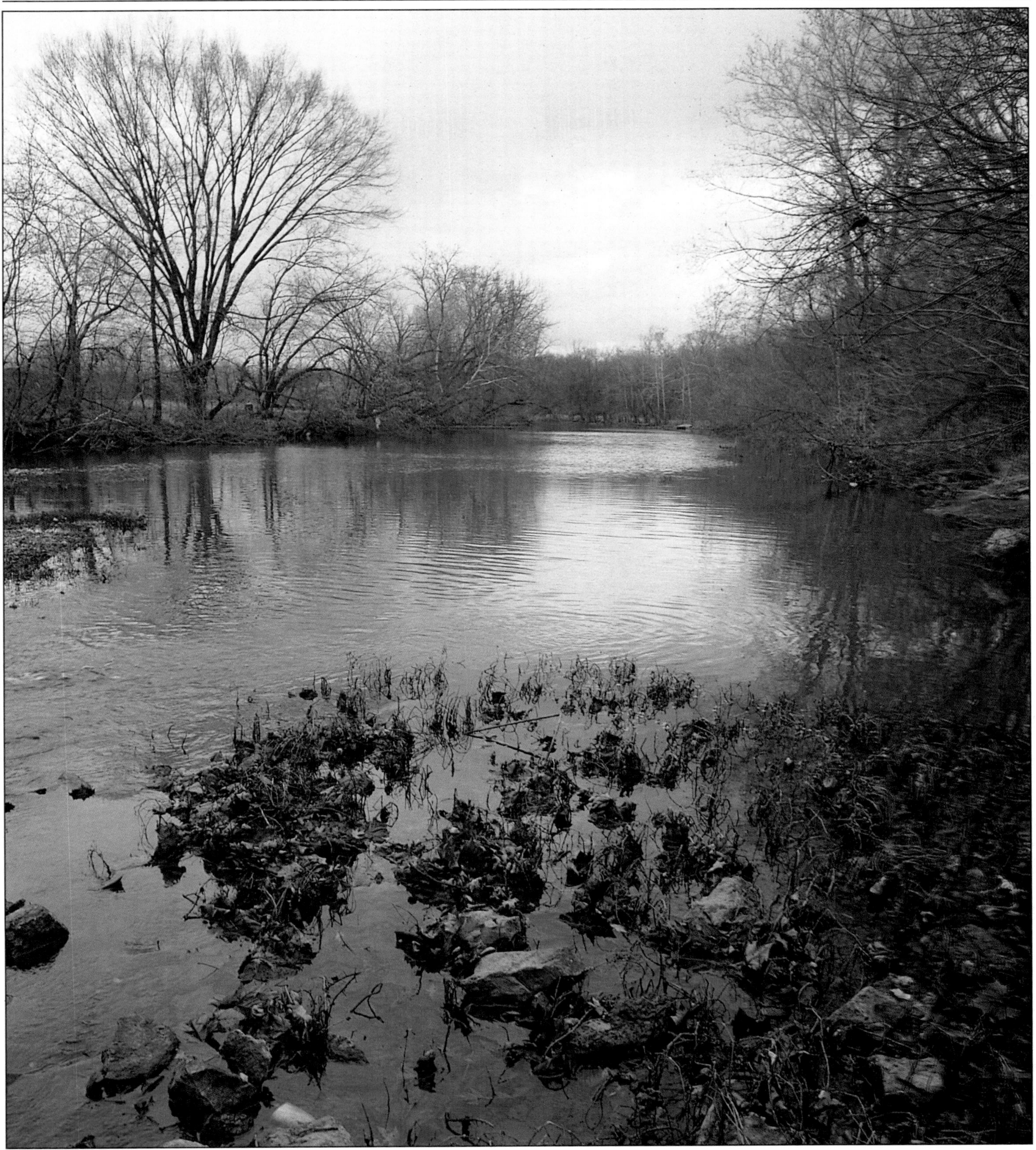

Two large armies met along the meandering Stones River near Murfreesboro, Tennessee, in an odd but costly two-day battle on December 31, 1862 and January 2, 1863 (the armies rested on New Year's Day). Parts of the battlefield, now Stones River National Military Park (these pages), were wooded (below) and cut by the river. Confederate Gen. Braxton Bragg struck first and nearly drove Union Gen. William Rosecrans' troops into full retreat. Only a last-ditch stand with artillery saved the Northern army. Reinforced, Rosecrans pushed the Confederates back on the second day, leaving both sides exhausted from a bloody but inconclusive fight.

IN MEMORIAM
RICHARD ROWLAND KIRKLAND
CO. G, 2ND SOUTH CAROLINA VOLUNTEERS
C. S. A.
AT THE RISK OF HIS LIFE, THIS AMERICAN
SOLDIER OF SUBLIME COMPASSION BROUGHT
WATER TO HIS WOUNDED FOES AT
FREDERICKSBURG. THE FIGHTING MEN ON
BOTH SIDES OF THE LINE CALLED HIM
"THE ANGEL OF MARYE'S HEIGHTS."
FELIX DE WELDON
SC. 1965

A relatively small region of Virginia that embraces the towns of Fredericksburg, Chancellorsville and Spotsylvania was contested in four major battles between late 1862 and mid-1864. The first was the Battle of Fredericksburg (overleaf), in which Burnside attacked Lee's strongly held positions on the heights overlooking the town. Huge numbers of futile casualties resulted, especially at Marye's Heights, where a commemorative statue (above) now stands. The disaster halted the Union march on Richmond. The same ground was fought over again in May 1863 as an adjunct to a major battle at Chancellorsville, a few miles away, where Confederates at Salem Church (facing page top) held off Union reinforcements and saved Lee's flank. Facing page bottom: the 18th-century mansion of Chatham in Fredericksburg and Spotsylvania National Military Park.

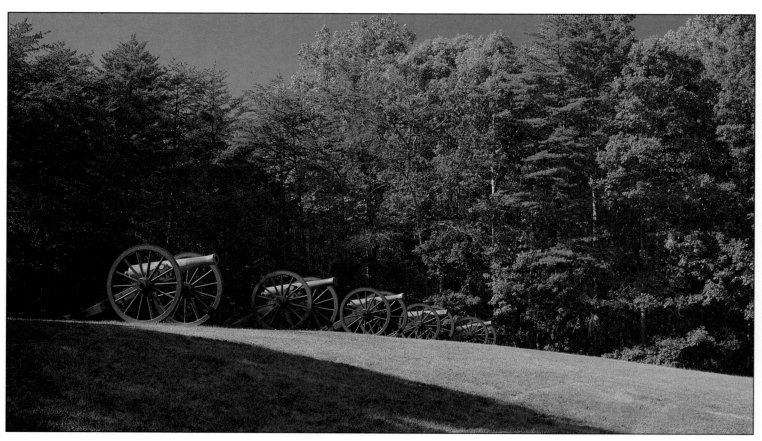

Confederate daring and Union confusion gave the South a great victory at Chancellorsville. After an attempt to cut off Confederate troop movements near Catherine Furnace (facing page top right), Union forces mistakenly pulled back and abandoned the commanding artillery positions at Hazel Grove (above), allowing the Southern guns to destroy much of the Federal force during the rest of the day. Despite a triumph on the field, the Confederacy took a mighty blow when Stonewall Jackson was mistakenly shot by his own men, at a point marked (top left) on the battlefield today, and died a few days later at the Chandler Plantation (facing page bottom). The Wilderness (facing page top left), a tangled thicket of trees and underbrush near Chancellorsville, was the scene of a terrible battle in May 1864. A few days later, near Spotsylvania, the Bloody Angle (top right) was the focus of hideous hand-to-hand fighting.

CATHARINE FURNACE

Grant's long campaign to capture Vicksburg on the Mississippi was one of the most important series of connected battles during the Civil War. So long as the Confederacy controlled the great river, it could prevent the Union from bringing its full weight to bear against Lee in Virginia. Vicksburg's situation on a bend of the river made it extraordinarily hard to attack. Naval assaults were fruitless, as shown by the fate of the U.S.S. *Cairo*, which was sunk in a few moments. Above: U.S.S. *Cairo's* guns raised from the river. Facing page: monuments to Minnesota troops (bottom left), Alabamians (bottom center) and the U.S. Navy (bottom right) marking the battlefield today, together with a Union cemetery (left). Facing page top: sunset over the Mississippi River, seen from Fort Hill.

Grant tried four unsuccessful schemes to by-pass or cut off Vicksburg, which could only be approached by an army from the east. Finally, in spring 1863, Grant and his army crossed the Mississippi south of the city, seized Jackson, thus cutting the rail line to the east, and, in the battle of Champion's Hill, drove the Confederate army under John Pemberton back behind its fortifications in Vicksburg. Following two unsuccessful direct assaults, Grant laid seige to the city. After a month and a half, a starving Vicksburg surrendered. The Illinois Monument (above) shares the Vicksburg battle site (these pages) with the Mississippi Memorial (facing page).

MISSISSIPPI
MISSISSIPPI.

Gettysburg was the largest battle of the Civil War, causing a total of 50,000 casualties, lasting three days and covering almost 25 square miles. Gettysburg National Military Park (these pages) is the most impressive of all the preserved battle sites. Lee had invaded the North again, scattering his armies across Maryland and the Pennsylvania border. Some of his troops met Union cavalry on a road outside the village on July 1, 1864. For once, the Union side held the defensive position and Lee was forced to attack. From his headquarters (facing page bottom) Union commander George Meade handled his forces well. Little Round Top (facing page top left) was the anchor of the Union left, and Cemetery Ridge (facing page top right) held the center. More forces from each side gathered at the point of conflict over the ensuing two days. The National Cemetery (above) and monuments throughout the park mark the battle.

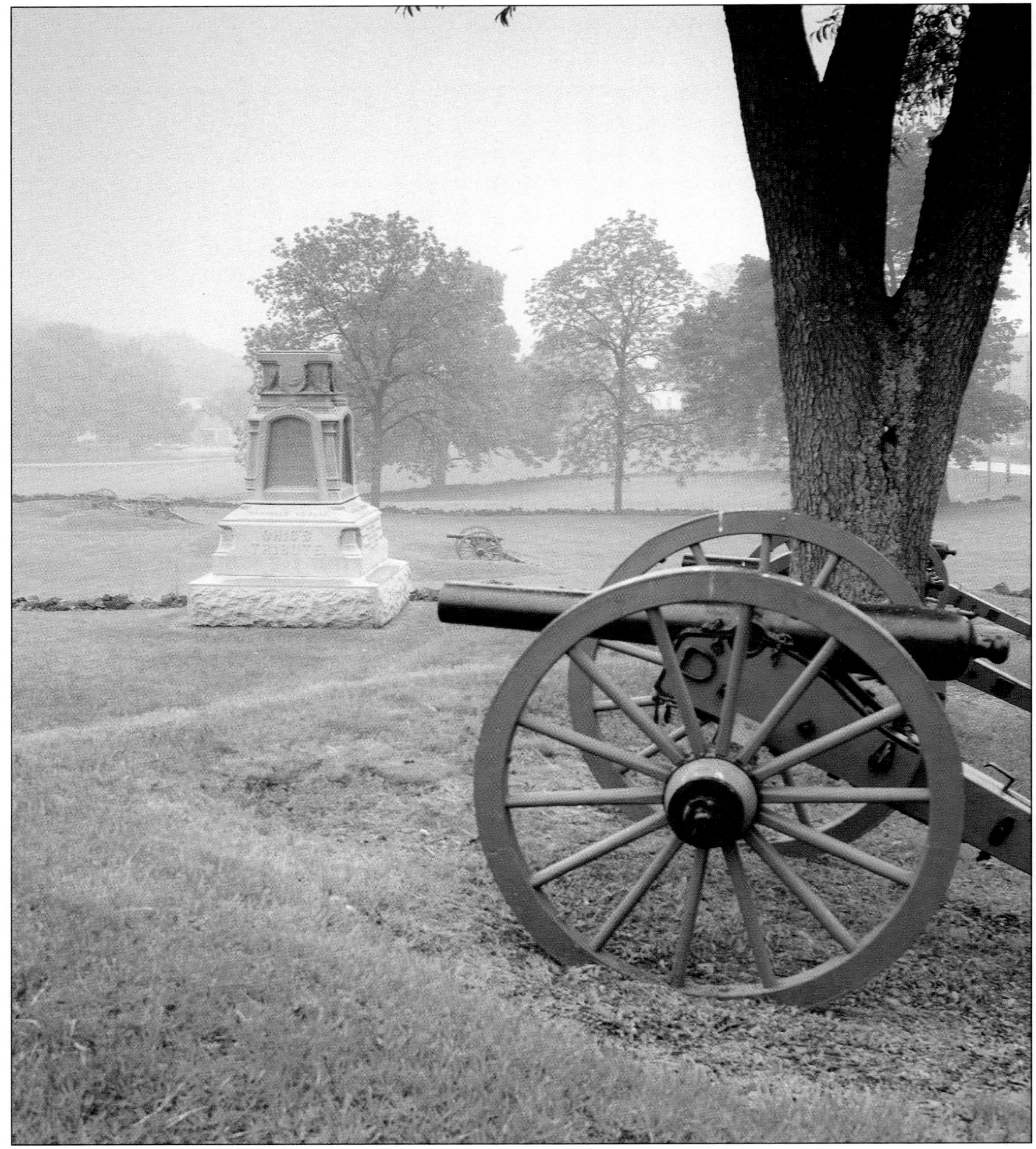
OHIO'S
TRIBUTE

failure other than accident. The courage with which you on an open field maintained the contest against an intrenched foe, and the consummate skill and success with which you crossed and re-crossed the river in the face of the enemy, show that you possess all the qualities of a great army, which will yet give victory to the cause of the country and of popular government.

Condoling with the mourners of the dead, and sympathizing with the wounded, I congratulate you that the number of both is comparatively small.

I tender to you, officers and soldiers, the thanks of the nation.

A. LINCOLN

A week later, in the war's western theatre, two armies met in a weird, costly, and inconclusive battle near the small Tennessee town of Murfreesboro. The Union Army of the Cumberland under newly-appointed commander Major General William S. Rosecrans fought to a standstill with Confederate General Braxton Bragg's Army of Tennessee.

During the last days of December 1862, the two forces faced each other from positions astraddle the meandering Stones River. Rosecrans had about 44,000 troops and Bragg commanded 38,000. Both generals reached the same tactical conclusion: they intended to mount massive attacks against the right side of the enemy's line. Had they both been successful, the entire engagement would have resembled a rotating wheel – as it was, Bragg's orders were to strike at dawn on December 31; Rosecrans told his commanders to let their men eat breakfast first.

Moving forward at first light, Confederate troops on Bragg's left wing under General William J. Hardee surprised the Union soldiers over their early morning campfires and folded the right side of the Federal line back on itself, inflicted heavy damage. The Union forces fought well, especially Phil Sheridan's men who held their positions until the last moment, allowing an orderly withdrawal of other Federals to new positions, but the Confederate cavalry had captured the Union ammunition wagons during the morning, leaving many embattled Federal infantrymen with empty weapons.

Rosecrans was slow to realize Bragg had beaten him to the punch, but once alerted to the danger of a complete roll-up of his right, Rosecrans moved energetically to hold on. He dashed about the field, stiffening new defensive positions. Before seeing to dispositions on his back-bent right wing, he visited the key river ford on the left, still held by Union soldiers and crucial to preventing more Rebels joining the battle.

Rosecrans found a brigade under Unionist Kentuckian Colonel Samuel W. Price holding the crossing:

"Will you hold this ford?" Rosecrans inquired of Price.

"I will try, sir," was the reply.

"Will you hold this ford?" Rosecrans repeated.

"I will die right here," Price answered.

"Will you hold this ford?" Rosecrans said for the third time of asking, more interested in the position than Price's statements of valor.

"Yes sir," Price replied, finally getting Rosecrans' drift.

"That will do," said Rosecrans, and galloped off.

As he rode toward the center of the battle, a cannonball squarely decapitated his chief of staff, who was riding beside the Union commander. Rosecrans fought the rest of the day in a uniform drenched in the gore of his aide.

The key to the day's battle focused on a salient on the Union right where the folded back lines joined. At the center was General George Thomas, perhaps the least excitable and most resolute of all Union commanders in the war. Rosecrans added all the artillery he could muster at the elevated salient and awaited the Rebel assaults. They were not slow in coming. Bragg was intent on crushing the Federals and sent in two massive attacks, but both failed under the slaughter of Union cannon. Near the end of the day, about 4 p.m., a third attack went in. With terrible losses on both sides, the assault was repulsed as the sun went down.

Still, by the usual standards Bragg should have been the victor, and so he believed himself during the following day's lull. His cavalry reported wagons moving behind Union lines, and Bragg assumed this meant a Federal withdrawal toward Nashville.

Rosecrans, however, was determined to hold the field, and the movements were merely his efforts to strengthen his new positions and re-enforce the vital river crossings, held – as Price had promised – throughout the first day's battle by the Federals. A day of respite, New Year's 1863, allowed the Union commander to make good his lost supplies.

On January 2, Bragg realized he still faced a Union army. Delaying until late afternoon, he finally ordered General John C. Breckinridge (a Kentuckian and former Vice-President of the United States) who held a position on the north side of the river, separated from the rest of the Confederate army, to assault the Union lines to his front across a open, flat field. Breckinridge protested furiously, but Bragg insisted.

Charging into the mouth of massed Federal artillery, Breckinridge's Kentuckians lost 1,800 men. When Ohio and Illinois regiments splashed across the river on foot and struck the Rebel forces on the flank, the battle was over.

The two days of fighting, separated by a one-day lull, produced casualties to match the great battles of the East. The South lost nearly 12,000 men; the North 13,000. Yet, neither side could claim a clear-cut victory, nor did either obtain any strategic advantage from all the carnage. Bragg withdrew into winter quarters, and Rosecrans quietly occupied Murfreesboro with no attempt to pursue.

The blood of the soldiers at Stones River, however, baptised prophetically the coming of the new year.

CHAPTER 4
1863

The year in the East began with failure once again for the Union. Burnside had been defeated at Fredericksburg. "The boys all knew that a blunder had been committed," wrote a young Union soldier, "that the attack against the frightful heights ought never to have been made; and although General Burnside gallantly took all the responsibility on himself yet there sprang up a brooding spirit of discontent, which soon spread throughout the entire army from the privates in the rear rank to the generals in command of corps and grand divisions."

Burnside's military career was on the line, and he knew it. In an attempt to save it, he ordered a futile movement that ultimately became known as the "Mud March." General Regis de Trobriand and a Union private described it thusly:

De Trobriand:

Burnside's first thought after Fredericksburg was to try to obtain revenge. Keeping to himself his secret designs, he got ready for a new advance movement and set to work immediately. He himself carefully reconnoitered the banks of the Rappahannock above Falmouth and completed his preparations to cross all his forces at Banks' and United States fords – fords which were not passable at that season of the year; but he had pontoons with him.

We received the order to march on January 20. We had not expected it. What likelihood was there of commencing active operations in the middle of the winter?

In the evening of January 20 we arrived in rear of Banks' Ford. It was a dismal night, one of those sleepless nights when everything has a funereal aspect in which enthusiasm is extinguished, courage worn out, the will enfeebled and the mind stupefied.

The rain had been falling for twelve hours, and there were no indications of any cessation. A few fires were tolerated at first, then authorized. The soldier, benumbed with frost, soaked from head to foot, could at least prepare his coffee and warm his stomach, if not his limbs. Everyone understood that the passage of the river was out of the question.

The rain lasted thirty hours without cessation. To understand the effect one must have lived in Virginia through a winter. In vain had efforts been made to fill up the mudholes or open new side roads; in vain had whole companies dragged at the cannons, the caissons, the wagons carrying ammunition – all was useless. The powers of heaven and earth were against us.

A private in the 118th Pennsylvania:

On January 20 a flaming general order indicating prospective success was published to every regiment. But stirring appeals had lost their effectiveness; what was to be done, we considered, had better be done – and talked of afterward.

During the night a pouring, pelting rain set in, an undoubted indication of the commencement of the usual January thaw. The wind blew a gale; rest was out of the question. All the solid ground disappeared, and in its place, on the roads and in the fields, there was mud of a depth and consistency that held tight whatever penetrated it, so that release without assistance was almost impossible. It seemed scarcely conceivable that less than twenty-four hours should produce such a surprising change. The feet of men and animals, the wheels of gun, caisson, limber and wagon had so stirred and agitated the pasty substance that, as the nature of the soil varied, in one place it was a deep, sticky loam, and in another a thick fluid extract. Twelve horses could not move a gun. The wheels of vehicles disappeared entirely. Pontoons on their carriages stood fixed and helpless in the roadway. Human skill, strength and ingenuity were exhausted in the attempt to get forward the indispensable artillery, ammunition and bridges. The woods were resonant with "Heave! Ho, heave!" as if sailors were working away at the capstan. When night came on, the regiment, which had started in the early morning, had heaved itself along a distance of about three miles.

There was no improvement on the twenty-second; further progress was impracticable, and the command remained fastened to its uncomfortable bivouac. On the other side of the river the enemy had erected large boards, on which were displayed taunting phrases. On one: "Burnside stuck in the mud"; on another: "Yanks, if you can't place your pontoons yourself, we will send you help." They had impressed all the plows in the neighborhood and could be seen turning the sod in every direction, intending to assist the elements in their purpose to stop the progress of our army. They needed no such aid: their purpose had been fully accomplished unassisted.

On the twenty-third it was officially announced that the campaign was abandoned and the troops were ordered to return to their former camping grounds. Such directions were easy to publish, but their execution was not so easy. The army was fairly fast where it was – literally stuck in the mud. It was some twelve miles back to the nearest camp. Pontoons, artillery trains could not be moved. Subsistence was exhausted and the Army of the Potomac felt the pinch of hunger. To relieve this pressure the whole army was set to road-making, and by night a very creditable corduroy road had been completed all the way to the rear. Over it during the night all wheels were successfully moved. The troops followed on the twenty-fourth, the rain for the first time subsiding. Before evening the brigade was back to its old quarters, not to be disturbed until bud, blossom and flower indicated that the elements had ceased to war with man, and that, freed from their interference, man might again make war against himself.

When Burnside abandoned the campaign, he in effect abandoned his military career. Lincoln relieved him of command of the Army of the Potomac and replaced him with "Fighting Joe" Hooker. Lincoln's letter to Hooker was anything but complimentary, but in his own way, the President offered what support he could. It had been noted, the President rather firmly pointed out, that during the past campaign, Hooker had been most vocal in his criticisms of Burnside. This kind of abrasive public slander was not befitting the kind of commander needed for the Army of the Potomac, and Lincoln cautioned against it in the future. It was essential, he said, that such differences be put aside and that for the common good a Northern victory should be quickly brought to the battlefield. One senses the urgency, the near desperation with which the Federal government had now to set a new course for the war. First there was McDowell, then McClellan, Pope, McClellan again, and then Burnside. Hooker faced an incredible responsibility. Lincoln told him so:

EXECUTIVE MANSION,

WASHINGTON, January 26, 1863

MAJOR GENERAL HOOKER:

GENERAL.

I have placed you at the head of the army of the Potomac. Of course I have done this upon what appear to me to be sufficient reasons. And yet I think it best for you to know that there are some things in regard to which, I am not quite satisfied with you. I believe you to be a brave and a skilful soldier, which, of course, I like. I also believe you do not mix politics with your profession, in which you are right. You have confidence in yourself, which is a valuable, if not an indispensable quality. You are ambitious, which, within reasonable bounds, does rather good than harm. But I think that during Gen. Burnside's command of the Army, you have taken counsel of your ambition, and thwarted him as much as you could, in which you did a great wrong to the country, and to a most meritorious and honorable brother officer. I have heard, in such a way as to believe it, of your recently saying that both the Army and the Government needed a Dictator. Of course it was not **for** *this, but in spite of it that I have given you the command. Only those generals who gain successes, can set up dictators. What I now ask of you is military success, and I will risk the dictatorship. The government will support you to the utmost of its ability, which is neither more nor less than it has done and will do for all commanders. I much fear that the spirit which you have aided to infuse into the Army, of criticizing their Commander, and withholding confidence from him, will now turn upon you. I shall assist you as far as I can, to put it down. Neither you, nor Napoleon, if he were alive again, could get any good out of an army, while such a spirit prevails in it.*

And now, beware of rashness. Beware of rashness, but with energy, and sleepless vigilance, go forward, and give us victories.

Yours very truly

A. LINCOLN

Hooker was a graduate of West Point and a veteran of the conflict with Mexico, who had distingushed himself thus far in the Civil War. Again, Lincoln looked for the most logical choice. In Hooker he felt he had found the man who might stand and fight. The army sensed this also and almost immediately spirits improved.

CHANCELLORSVILLE

Within three months Hooker had devised a plan, and it was a good one. He had 120,000 men. Detaching 40,000 to face Lee, who was still entrenched around Fredericksburg with about 60,000, Hooker took the other half of the army and set out for the upper fords of the Rappahannock in a flanking movement that, if successful, would engage Lee on two fronts, capturing him in a pincer movement or force a withdrawal to Richmond. De Trobriand explains:

On April 27 Hooker began his movement on Chancellorsville. Chancellorsville was not a city, a village or even a hamlet. It was a solitary house in the midst of a cultivated clearing, surrounded on all sides by woods, which gave the region the name of the **Wilderness**. *A veritable solitude, impenetrable for the deploying or quick maneuvering of an army. It was not there that Hooker had planned to give battle, but it was a well-chosen point for concentrating his forces. From that point he could strike the enemy, or at least force him to come out of his position, which was as weak from the rear as it was strong from the front. If the Confederate army fell back on Richmond, it presented its flank to our attack, and if Lee were stopped or delayed by some obstacle and pursued at the same time by a force strong enough to press his rear guard vigorously, his retreat might be changed to a rout. If, on the contrary, he marched toward Chancellorsville to meet us, he was forced to accept battle in the open field, in unforeseen conditions, exposed to attack by a pursuing army as much as on the Richmond road. Attacked at the same time both in front and rear, Lee ran the chance of being cut to pieces and would be very fortunate if he saved the remnant of his forces.*

Such was Hooker's well-conceived plan, the secret of which was confided to no one, not even to his most intimate friends among the officers.

In 1898, in a privately published book, Charles Fessendon Morse, a colonel in the 2nd Massachusetts, narrated the battle:

On Monday, April 17th, our corps broke camp early in the morning and marched to Hartwood Church, ten miles; there it went into camp for the night. The Eleventh and Fifth Corps also came up there and camped that night near Kelly's Ford. A pontoon bridge was thrown across and the corps followed rapidly and the advance began towards the Rapidan. The Eleventh and Twelfth marched on the road to Germana Ford, the Fifth on the road to Ely's Ford; all three of the corps were under command of General Slocum. I was detailed, the morning of the advance, as Aide to General Slocum, and another officer was made Acting Provost Marshal. All the companies of the Second Massachusetts were sent to the Regiment. We skirmished all the way to Germana Ford; there we met quite a determined resistance; our cavalry was drawn in and the Second Massachusetts and the Third Wisconsin sent forward to clear the way, they drove everything before them and, by their heavy fire, forced the rebels at the Ford to surrender (about one hundred officers and men). We lost in this skirmish about a dozen killed and wounded.

General Slocum now determined to cross the Rapidan though there was no bridge and the ford was almost impassable. . . . At about noon [on April 30], we arrived at Chancellorsville, and found the Fifth Corps already there. We had a small cavalry skirmish, . . . but besides that, nothing of importance occurred during that day; the troops were formed in line of battle, but were not attacked. Up to this time you see everything had gone well and success seemed certain.

Towards night, General Hooker arrived with his staff, and we heard of the crossing at the U.S. Ford of the Second, Third and First Corps. All the headquarters were in the vicinity of the Chancellor House, a large, fine brick mansion. General Hooker took supper with General Slocum; he didn't seem to be able to express his gratification at the success of General Slocum in bringing the three corps up so rapidly. Then in the most extravagant, vehement terms, he went on to say how he had got the rebels, how he was going to crush them, annihilate them, etc.

The next morning at ten, the Fifth and Twelfth Corps advanced in order of battle on two parallel roads; we soon met the enemy and skirmished for about two miles, when they appeared in considerable force and the battle began. We were in a splendid position and were driving the enemy when an order came to General Slocum to retire his command to its former position. No one could believe that the order was genuine, but almost immediately, another of General Hooker's staff brought the same order again. Now, perhaps, you don't know that to retire an army in the face of an enemy when you are engaged is one of the most difficult operations in war; this we had to do. I carried the order to General Geary to retire his division in echelon by brigades, and stayed with him till the movement was nearly completed. It was a delicate job; each brigade would successively bear the brunt of the enemy's attack. Before the last brigades of the Fifth and Twelfth Corps were in position, the enemy made a furious attack on the Chancellor House; luckily we had considerable artillery concentrated there and they were driven back. The next attack was on our corps, but the enemy was severely repulsed. This about ended the fighting on Friday; we lost, I suppose, about five hundred men.

During the night, the men were kept at work digging trenches and throwing up breastworks of logs. Our headquarters were at Fairview, an open piece of ground rising into quite a crest in the centre. Skirmishing began at daylight next morning and continued without much result to either side, till afternoon, when the enemy began to move, in large force, towards our right, opposite General Howard, Eleventh Corps. This corps was in a fine position in intrenchments, with almost open country in front of them, the right resting on Hunting Creek. At about four P.M. the Third Corps, General Sickles, was removed out to the right of the Twelfth and advanced towards Fredericksburg. The order then came to General Slocum that the enemy were in full retreat, and to advance his whole line to capture all he could of prisoners, wagons, etc. Our right, General Williams' Division, advanced without much trouble, driving the enemy before it, but the Second Division had hardly got out of the trenches before it was attacked with great determination, yet it steadily retained its position.

At about five P.M. a tremendous and unceasing musketry fire began in the direction of the Eleventh Corps. As it was necessary to know what was going on there in order to regulate the movements of the Twelfth Corps, General Slocum and the rest of us rode for our lives towards this new scene of action. What was our surprise when we found that instead of a fight, it was a complete Bull Run rout. Men, horses, mules, rebel prisoners, wagons, guns, etc. etc. were coming down the road in terrible confusion, behind them an unceasing roar of musketry. We rode until we got into a mighty hot fire, and found that no one was attempting to make a stand, but every one running for his life. Then General Slocum dispatched me to General Hooker to explain the state of affairs, and three other staff officers to find General Williams and order him back to his trenches with all haste.

I found General Hooker sitting alone on his horse in front of the Chancellor House, and delivered my message; he merely said, "Very good, sir." I rode back and found the Eleventh Corps still surging up the road and still this terrible roar behind them. Up to this time, the rebels had received no check, but now troops began to march out on the plank road and form across it, and Captain Best, Chief of Artillery of our corps, had on his own responsibility gathered together all the batteries he could get hold of, and put them in position (forty-six guns in all) on Fairview, and had begun firing at the rate of about one hundred guns a minute, into the rebels.

This, in my opinion, saved our army from destruction.

The artillery men were hard at work all night, throwing up traverse to project their guns, and about two in the morning we all lay down on the ground and slept until about four, when daylight began to appear. Our right was now formed by the Third, Fifth and First Corps, about five hundred yards in the rear of our first position. The rebels began to attack as soon as there was light enough, from the left of our First Division to about the right of the Third Corps. General Birney's Division of the Third Corps was out in front of General Williams; his men behaved badly, and after a slight resistance, fell back into our lines, losing a battery.

The rebels now charged down our First Division, but were met with such a deadly fire that they were almost annihilated. Their second line was then sent in, but met the same fate, and their third and last line advanced. Our men now had fired more than forty rounds of cartridges and were getting exhausted. General Slocum sent almost every one of his staff officers to General Hooker, stating his position and begging for support; Hooker's answer was, "I can't make men or ammunition for General Slocum."

Meantime, Sickle's Corps was holding its own on the right of ours, but it was rapidly getting into the same condition as the Twelfth. The rebels were driven back every time they advanced, and we were taking large numbers of prisoners and colors. All this time while our infantry was fighting so gallantly in front, our battery of forty-six guns was firing incessantly. The rebels had used no artillery until they captured the battery from Birney, when they turned that on us, making terrible destruction in General Geary's line. General Meade, Fifth Corps, now went to Hooker and entreated that he might be allowed to throw his corps on the rebel flank, but General Hooker said, "No, he was wanted in his own position." On his own responsibility General Meade sent out one brigade, which passed out in the rear of the enemy's right, recaptured a battery, three hundred of our men who were prisoners, and four hundred of the rebels, and took them safely back to their corps.

It was now after seven o'clock. Our men had fired their sixty rounds of cartridges and were still holding their position; everything that brave men could do, these men had done, but now nothing was left but to order them to fall back and give up their position to the enemy. This was done in good order and they marched off under a heavy fire to the rear of our batteries. The rebels, seeing us retreating, rushed forward their artillery and began a fearful fire. I found I could be useful to Captain Best, commanding our artillery, so I stayed with him. I never before saw anything so fine as the attack on that battery; the air was full of missiles, solid shot, shells, and musket balls. I saw one solid shot kill three horses and a man, another took a leg off one of the captains of the batteries. Lieutenant Crosby of the Fourth Artillery was shot through the heart with a musket ball; he was a particular friend of Bob Shaw and myself; he lived just long enough to say to Captain Best, "Tell father I die happy."

The rebels came up to the attack in solid masses and got within three hundred yards, but they were slaughtered by the hundreds by the case-shot and canister, and were driven back to the woods. Still not an infantry man was sent to the support of the guns. More than half the horses were killed or wounded; one caisson had blown up, another had been knocked to pieces; in ten minutes more the guns would have been isolated. They, too, therefore, were ordered to retire, which they did without losing a gun. You see, now our centre was broken, everything was being retired to our second line, the rebel artillery was in position, their line of battle steadily advancing across our old ground. This fire of the batteries was concentrated on the Chancellor House, Hooker's original headquarters, and it was torn almost to pieces by solid shot and was finally set on fire by a shell.

The army was now put in position in the second line; the centre was on a rising piece of ground and protected by a battery of forty or fifty guns. . . . You can easily see that, if the enemy once forced our right or left, our communications would at once be cut and all possibility of retreat prevented. Late that night we lay down close beside the Rappahannock. By three o'clock next morning we were awakened by a heavy artillery fire and shells bursting over us. Our guns replied and kept at it for about an hour, when the enemy's batteries were silenced. We now mounted our horses and rode along the lines to look at our position; we found that it was a very strong one and capable of being made very much more so.

I doubt if ever in the history of this war, another chance will be given us to fight the enemy with such odds in our favor as we had last Sunday, and that chance has been worse than lost to us. I don't believe any men ever fought better than our Twelfth Corps, especially the First Division; for two hours they held their ground without any support, against the repeated assaults of the enemy; they fired their sixty rounds of cartridges and held their line with empty muskets until ordered to fall back. The old Second, of course, did splendidly, and lost heavily.

On May 2, Stonewall Jackson was sent in a sweeping move around Hooker and to his rear. Although Hooker had been warned, he totally disregarded the Confederate march, insisting that it was a retreat. General Alfred Pleasanton, commanding Federal cavalry, wrote *The Successes and Failures of Chancellorsville* for the Century Company:

On arriving at Hazel Grove, about one mile from Chancellorsville, I found that General Sickles was moving two of the divisions of the Third Corps in the direction of Catherine Furnace, and shortly after he became engaged there with a strong rear-guard. Hazel Grove was the highest ground in the neighborhood and was the key of our position, and I saw that if Lee's forces gained it the Army of the Potomac would be worsted.

General Sickles wanted some cavalry to protect his flanks, and I gave him the 6th New York. This left me with only the 8th and 17th Pennsylvania regiments and Martin's New York battery of horse artillery. I posted this command at the extreme west of the clearing, about two hundred yards from the woods in which the Eleventh Corps was encamped. This position at Hazel Grove was about a quarter of a mile in extent, running nearly north-east and south-west, but was in no place farther than two hundred yards from the woods, and on the south and east it sloped off into a marsh and a creek. It commanded the position of the army at Fairview and Chancellorsville and enfiladed our line. The moving out to the Furnace of the two divisions of the Third Corps left a gap of about a mile from Hazel Grove to the right of the Twelfth Corps. Shortly after General Sickles had been engaged at the Furnace, he sent me word that the enemy were giving way and cavalry couldbe used to advantage in pursuit. Before moving my command I rode out to the Furnace to comprehend the situation. It was no place for cavalry to operate, and as I could hear spattering shots going more and more toward the north-west, I was satisfied that the enemy were not retreating.

I hastened back to my command at Hazel Grove; when I reached it, the Eleventh Corps to our rear and our right was in full flight, panic-stricken beyond description. We faced about, having then the marsh behind us. It was an ugly marsh, about fifty yards wide, and in the stampede of the Eleventh Corps, beef cattle, ambulances, mules, artillery, wagons, and horses became stuck in the mud, and others coming on crushed them down, so that when the fight was over the pile of debris in the marsh was many feet high. I saw that something had to be done, and that very quickly, or the Army of the Potomac would receive a crushing defeat. The two cavalry regiments were in the saddle, and as I rode forward Major Keenan of the 8th Pennsylvania came out to meet me, when I ordered him to take the regiment, charge into the woods, which, as we had previously stood, were to our rear, and hold the enemy in check until I could get some guns into position. He replied, with a smile at the size of the task, that he would do it, and started off immediately. Thirty men, including Major Keenan, Captain Arrowsmith, and Adjutant Haddock, never came back.

I then directed Captain Martin to bring his guns into battery, load with double charges of canister, and aim them so that the shot would hit the ground half-way between the guns and the woods. I also stated that I would give the order to fire. Just then a handsome young lieutenant of the 4th U.S. Artillery, Frank B. Crosby (son of a distinguished lawyer of New York City), who was killed the next day, galloped up and said, "General, I have a battery of six guns; where shall I go? what shall I do?" I told him to place his battery in line on the right of Martin's battery, and gave him the same instructions I had given Martin as to how I wanted him to serve his guns. These 2 batteries gave me 12 guns, and to obtain more I then charged 2 squadrons of the 17th Pennsylvania Cavalry on the stragglers of the Eleventh Corps to clear the ground, and with the assistance of the rest of the regiment succeeded in placing 10 more pieces of artillery in line. The line was then ready for Stonewall Jackson's onset. It was dusk when his men swarmed out of the woods for a quarter of a mile in our front (our rear ten minutes before). They came on in line five and six deep, with but one flag – a Union flag dropped by the Eleventh Corps.

I suspected deception and was ready for it. They called out not to shoot, they were friends; at the same time they gave us a volley from at least five thousand muskets. As soon as I saw the flash I gave the command to fire, and the whole line of artillery was discharged at once. It fairly swept them from the earth; before they could recover themselves the line of artillery had been loaded and was ready for a second attack. After the second discharge, suspecting that they might play the trick of having their men lie down, draw the fire of the artillery, then jump up and charge before the pieces could be reloaded, I poured in the canister for about twenty minutes, and the affair was over.

For half an hour General Jackson had the Army of the Potomac at his mercy. That he halted to re-form his troops in the woods, instead of forging ahead into the clearing, where he could reform his troops more rapidly, and where he could have seen that he was master of the situation, turned out to be one of those fatalities by which the most brilliant prospects are sacrificed. When he advanced upon the artillery at Hazel Grove Jackson had another opportunity to win, if his infantry had been properly handled. The fire of his infantry was so high it did no harm; they should have been ordered to fire so low as to disable the cannoneers at the guns. Had his infantry fire been as effective as that of our artillery, Jackson would have carried the position. The artillery fire was effective because I applied it to that principle of dynamics in which the angle of incidence is equal to the angle of reflection, – that is to say, if the muzzle of a gun is three feet from the ground and it is discharged so that the shot will strike the ground at a distance of one hundred yards, it will glance from the earth at the same angle at which it struck it, and in another one hundred yards will be three feet from the ground. I knew my first volley must be a crushing one, or Jackson, with his superior numbers, would charge across the short distance which separated us and capture the artillery before the guns could be reloaded.

Heros von Borcke, a Prussian officer serving in the Confederate army, reported the battle on the third day at Chancellorsville:

The enemy, fully three times our number, occupied a piece of wood extending about two miles from our immediate front towards the plateau and open fields around Chancellorsville, a village consisting of only a few houses. The Federals had made good use of their time, having thrown up in the wood during the night three successive lines of breastworks, constructed of strong timber, and on the plateau itself, occupied by their reserves, had erected a regular line of redoubts, mounted by their numerous artillery, forty pieces of which were playing on the narrow plank-road.

All our divisions now moving forward, the battle soon became general, and the musketry sounded in one continued roll along the lines. Nearly a hundred hostile guns opening fire at the same time, the forest seemed alive with shot, shell, and bullets, and the plank-road, upon which, as was before mentioned, the fire of forty pieces was concentrated, was soon enveloped in a cloud of smoke from the bursting of shells and the explosion of caissons. This road being our principal line of communication, and crowded therefore with ambulances, ammunition-trains, and artillery, the loss of life soon became fearful, and dead and dying men and animals were strewing every part of it. How General Stuart, and those few staff-officers with him who had to gallop to and fro so frequently through this **feu infernal**, *escaped unhurt, seems to me quite miraculous.*

Stuart was all activity, and wherever the danger was greatest there was he to be found, urging the men forward, and animating them by the force of his example. The shower of missiles that hissed through the air passed round him unheeded; and in the midst of the hottest fire I heard him, to an old melody, hum the words, "Old Joe Hooker get out of the Wilderness."

After a raging conflict, protracted for several hours, during which the tide of battle ebbed and flowed on either side, we succeeded in taking the advanced works, and driving the enemy upon their third line of intrenchments, of a still stronger character than those before it. This partial success was only gained with a sad sacrifice of life, with countless numbers seen limping and crawling to the rear. The woods had caught fire in several places from the explosion of shells – the flames spreading principally, however, over a space of several acres in extent where the ground was thickly covered with dry leaves; and here the conflagration progressed with the rapidity of a prairie-fire, and a large number of Confederate and Federal wounded thickly scattered in the vicinity, and too badly hurt to crawl out of the way, met a terrible death. The heartrending cries of the poor victims, as the flames advanced, entreating to be rescued from their impending fate – entreaties which it was impossible to heed in the crisis of the battle, and amidst duties on which the lives of many others depended – seem still in my ears.

Among the heart-sickening scenes of this terrible conflict which are still vivid in my memory, is one no lapse of time can ever efface, and in contemplating which I scarcely could check the tears from starting to my eyes. Riding to the front, I was hailed by a young soldier, whose boyish looks aand merry songs on the march had frequently attracted my attention and excited my interest, and who was now leaning against a tree, and life-blood streaming down his side from a mortal wound, and his face white with the pallor of approaching death. "Major," said the poor lad, "I am dying, and I shall never see my regiment again; but I ask you to tell my comrades that the Yankees have killed but not conquered me." When I passed the place again half an hour afterwards I found him a corpse. Such was the universal spirit of our men, and in this lay the secret of many of our wonderful achievements.

The enemy had in the meanwhile been strongly reinforced, and now poured forth from their third line of intrenchments a fire so terrible upon our advancing troops that the first two divisions staggered, and, after several unsuccessful efforts to press onward, fell back in considerable confusion. In vain was it that our officers used every effort to bring them forward once more; in vain even was it that Stuart, snatching the battle-flag of one of our brigades from the hands of the colour-bearer and waving it over his head, called on them as he rode forward to follow him. Nothing could induce them again to face that tempest of bullets, and that devastating hurricane of grape and canister vomited at close range from more than sixty pieces of artillery, and the advantages so dearly gained seemed about to be lost. At this critical moment, we suddenly heard the yell of Rodes's division behind us, and saw these gallant troops, led by their heroic general, charge over the front lines, and fall upon the enemy with such impetus that in a few minutes their works were taken, and they were driven in rapid flight from the woods to their redoubts on the hills of Chancellorsville.

A slight pause now intervened in the conflict, both sides, after the terrible work of the last few hours, being equally willing to draw breath awhile; and this gave us an opportunity to re-form our lines and close up our decimated ranks. The contest, meanwhile, was sustained by the artillery alone, which kept up a heavy cannonade; and the nature of the ground being now more favorable, most of our batteries had been brought into action, while from a hill on our extreme right, which had only been abandoned by the enemy after the charge of Rodes's division, twenty 12-pounder Napoleons played with a well-directed flank-fire upon the enemy's works, producing a terrible effect upon their dense masses.

About half-past ten we had news from General Lee, informing us that, having been pressing steadily forward the entire morning, he had now, with Anderson's and M'Laws's divisions, reached our right wing. I was at once dispatched by Stuart to the Commander-in-Chief to report the state of affairs, and obtain his orders for further proceedings. I found him with our twenty-gun battery, looking as calm and dignified as ever, and perfectly regardless of the shells bursting round him, and the solid shot ploughing up the ground in all directions. General Lee expressed himself much satisfied with our operations, and intrusted me with orders for Stuart, directing a general attack with his whole force, which was to be supported by a charge of Anderson's division on the left flank of the enemy.

With renewed courage and confidence our three divisions now moved forward upon the enemy's strong position on the hills, encountering, as we emerged from the forest into the open opposite the plateau of Chancellorsville, such a storm of canister and bullets, that for a while it seemed an impossibility to take the heights in the face of it. Suddenly we heard to our right, piercing the roar of tumult of the battle, the yell of Anderson's men, whom we presently beheld hurled for-

ward in a brilliant charge, sweeping everything before them. Short work was now made of the Federals, who, in a few minutes, were driven from their redoubts, which they abandoned in disorderly flight, leaving behind them cannons, small-arms, tents, and baggage in large quantities, besides a host of prisoners, of whom we took 360 in one redoubt.

A more magnificent spectacle can hardly be imagined than that which greeted me when I reached the crest of the plateau, and beheld on this side the long lines of our swiftly advancing troops stretching as far as the eye could reach, their red flags fluttering in the breeze, and their arms glittering in the morning sun; and farther on, dense and huddled masses of the Federals flying in utter rout towards the United States Ford, whilst high over our heads flew the shells which our artillery were dropping amidst the crowd of the retreating foe. The Chancellorsville House had caught fire, and was now enveloped in flames, so that it was with difficulty that we could save some portion of the Federal wounded lying there, to the number of several hundreds, the majority of whom perished. . . . The flight and pursuit took the direction of United States Ford, as far as about a mile beyond Chancellorsville, where another strong line of intrenchments offered their protection to the fugitives, and heavy reserves of fresh troops opposed our further advance.

The Army of Northern Virginia suffered heavy casualties, nearly 11,000, but the most severe was the mortal wounding of Stonewall Jackson. It would prove to be an irreparable loss. Jackson's aide-de-camp describes what happened:

When Jackson had reached the point where his line now crossed the turnpike, scarcely a mile west of Chancellorsville, and not half a mile from a line of Federal troops, he had found his front line unfit for the further and vigorous advance he desired, by reason of the irregular character of the fighting now right, now left, and because of the dense thickets, through which it was impossible to preserve alignment. Division commanders found it more and more difficult as the twilight deepened to hold their broken brigades in hand. Regretting the necessity of relieving the troops in front, General Jackson had ordered A.P. Hill's division, his third and reserve line, to be placed in front.

While this change was being effected, impatient and anxious, the general rode forward on the turnpike, followed by two or three of his staff and a number of couriers and signal sergeants. He passed the swampy depression and began the ascent of the hill toward Chancellorsville, when he came upon a line of the Federal infantry lying on their arms. Fired at by one or two muskets (two musket-balls from the enemy whistled over my head as I came to the front), he turned and came back toward his line, upon the side of the road to his left.

As he rode near to the Confederate troops, just placed in position and ignorant that he was in the front, the left company began firing to the front, and two of his party fell from their saddles dead – Captain Boswell, of the Engineers, and Sergeant Cunliffe, of the Signal Corps. Spurring his horse across the road to his right, he was met by a second volley from the right company of Pender's North Carolina brigade. Under this volley, when not two rods from the troops, the general received three balls at the same instant. One penetrated the palm of his right hand. A second passed around the wrist of the left arm and out through the left hand. A third ball passed through the left arm half-way from shoulder to elbow. The large bone of the upper arm was splintered to the elbow-joint, and the wound bled freely. His horse turned quickly from the fire, through the thick bushes which swept the cap from the general's head, and scratched his forehead, leaving drops of blood to stain his face.

As he lost his hold upon the bridle-rein, he reeled from the saddle, and was caught by the arms of Captain Wilbourn, of the Signal Corps. Laid upon the ground, there came at once to his succor General A.P. Hill and members of his staff. [I] . . . reached his side a minute after, to find General Hill holding the head and shoulders of the wounded chief. Cutting open the coat-sleeve from wrist to shoulder. I found the wound in the upper-arm, and with my handkerchief I bound the arm above the wound to stem the flow of blood. Couriers were sent for Dr. Hunter McGuire, the surgeon of the corps and the general's trusted friend, and for an ambulance. Being outide of our lines, it was urgent that he should be moved at once. With difficulty litter-bearers were brought from the line nearby, and the general was placed upon the litter and carefully raised to the shoulder, I myself bearing one corner.

A moment after, artillery from the Federal side was opened upon us; great broadsides thundered over the woods; hissing shells searched the dark thickets through, and shrapnels swept the road along which we moved. Two or three steps farther, and the litter-bearer at my side was struck and fell, but, as the litter turned, Major Watkins Leigh, of Hill's staff, happily caught it. But the fright of the men was so great that we were obliged to lay the litter and its burden down upon the road. As the litter-bearers ran to the cover of the trees, I threw myself by the general's side and held him firmly to the ground as he attempted to rise. Over us swept the rapid fire of shot and shell – grape-shot striking fire upon the flinty rock of the road all around us, and sweeping from their feet horses and men of the artillery just moved to the front.

Soon the firing veered to the other side of the road, and I sprang to my feet, assisted the general to rise, passed my arm around him, and with the wounded man's weight thrown heavily upon me, we forsook the road. Entering the woods, he sank to the ground from exhaustion, but the litter was soon brought, and again rallying a few men, we essayed to carry him farther, when a second bearer fell at my side. This time, with none to assist, the litter careened and the general fell to the ground, with a groan of deep pain. Greatly alarmed, I sprang to his head, and, lifting his head as a stray beam of moonlight came through clouds and leaves, he opened his eyes and wearily said: "Never mind me, Captain, never mind me." Raising him again to his feet, he was accosted by Brigadier-General Pender: "Oh, General, I hope you are not too seriously wounded, I will have to retire my troops to re-form them, they are so much broken by this fire." But Jackson, rallying his strength, with firm voice said: "You must hold your ground, General Pender; you must hold your ground, sir!" and so uttered his last command on the field.

Again we resorted to the litter, and with difficulty bore it through the bush, and then under a hot fire along the road. Soon an ambulance was reached, and stopping to seek some stimulant at Chancellor's (Dowdall's Tavern), we were found by Dr. McGuire, who at once took charge of the wounded man. Passing back over the battle-field of the afternoon, we reached the Wilderness store, and then, in a field on the north, the field-hospital of our corps under Dr. Harvey Black. Here we found a tent prepared, and after midnight the left arm was amputated near the shoulder, and a ball taken from the right hand.

All night long it was mine to watch by the sufferer, and keep him warmly wrapped and undisturbed in his sleep. At 9 A.M., on the next day, when he aroused, cannon firing again filled the air, and all the Sunday through the fierce battle raged, General J.E.B. Stuart commanding the Confederates in Jackson's place. A dispatch was sent to the commanding general to announce formally his disability, – tidings General Lee had received during the night with profound grief. There came back the following note:

"GENERAL: I have just received your note, informing me that you were wounded. I cannot express my regret at the occurrence. Could I have directed events, I should have chosen, for the good of the country, to have been disabled in your stead. I congratulate you upon the victory which is due to your skill and energy. Most truly yours, R.E. LEE, GENERAL."

When this dispatch was handed to me at the tent, and I read it aloud, General Jackson turned his face away and said, "General Lee is very kind, but he should give the praise to God."

The long day was passed with bright hopes for the wounded general, with tidings of success on the battlefield, with sad news of losses, and messages to and from other wounded officers brought to the same infirmary.

On Monday the general was carried in an ambulance by way of Spotsylvania Court House, to most comfortable lodging at Chandler's, near Guinea's Station, on the Richmond, Fredericksburg and Potomac Railroad. And here, against our hopes. notwithstanding the skill and care of wise and watchful surgeons, attended day and night by wife and friends, amid the prayers and tears of all the Southern land, thinking not of himself, but of the cause he loved, and for the troops who had followed him so well and given him so great a name, our chief sank, day by day, with symptoms of pneumonia and some pains of pleurisy, until, at 3:15 P.M. on the quiet of the Sabbath afternoon, May 10th, 1863, he raised himself from his bed, saying, "No, no, let us pass over the river, and rest under the shade of the tree"; and, falling again to his pillow, he passed away, "over the river, where, in a land where warfare is not known or feared, he rests forever 'under the trees.'"

No other man lost in the Civil War was mourned more than Stonewall Jackson, with the exception of Abraham Lincoln, and, until Robert E. Lee died, no other Southern figure was so remembered as a giant of a hero. George F.R. Henderson, in his 1898 biography of Jackson, concluded with these words:

It is possible that the conflicts of the South are not yet ended. In America men pray for peace, but dark and mysterious forces, threatening the very foundations of civic liberty, are stirring even now beneath their feet. The War of Secession may be the precursor of a fiercer and a mightier struggle, and the volunteers of the Confederacy, enduring all things and sacrificing all things, the prototype and model of a new army, in which North and South shall march to battle side by side. Absit omen! But in whatever fashion his own countrymen may deal with the problems of the future, the story of Stonewall Jackson will tell them in what spirit they should be faced. Nor has that story a message for America alone. The hero who lies buried at Lexington, in the Valley of Virginia, belongs to a race that is not confined to a single continent; and to those who speak the same tongue, and in whose veins the same blood flows, his words come home like an echo of all that is noblest in their history: "What is life without honor? Degradation is worse than death. We must think of the living and of those who are to come after us, and see that with God's blessing we transmit to them the freedom we have ourselves inherited."

GETTYSBURG

Lee's invasion of Pennsylvania in June 1863 has frequently been called the "High Tide of the Confederacy" or the "turning point of the Civil War," justifying such comments with the theories that the Army of Northern Virginia could well have gone on to Harrisburg, Philadelphia, or Washington if it had been successful at Gettysburg, or that the Confederacy could have been recognized by foreign nations. Indeed, these theories have some validity, but they were also true of Lee's invasion of Maryland the year before. Antietam was a far more decisive battle than Gettysburg; *it* was the turning point of the Civil War, without question, for it was on the fields surrounding the village of Sharpsburg that Lee came very close to losing the war. His army was never quite the same after Antietam; the balance of the war, which had up to September of 1862 been so heavily tipped in favor of the Confederacy, at least in the East, began to swing in the other direction.

Yet Gettysburg is probably the best known of all the Civil War battles. It was the greatest battle fought on the North American continent, and to students around the world, the name is synonymous with America and the Civil War.

Reorganizing his army following Chancellorsville in June, Lee left A.P. Hill at Fredericksburg to keep Hooker engaged and marched off toward the Shenandoah Valley. His target was clear. "I considered the problem in every possible phase," he wrote, "and to my mind, it resolved . . . into a choice of one of two things – either to retire to Richmond and stand a siege, which must ultimately have ended in surrender, or to invade Pennsylvania."

On June 8, he wrote to the Secretary of War, James Seddon:

As far as I can judge, there is nothing to be gained by this army remaining quietly on the defensive, which it must do unless it can be re-enforced. I am aware that there is difficulty and hazard in taking the aggressive with so large an army in its front, intrenched behind a river, where it cannot be advantageously attacked. Unless it can be drawn out in a position to be assailed, it will take its own time to prepare and strengthen itself to renew its advance upon Richmond and force this army back within the intrenchments of that city. This may be the result in any event; still, I think it is worth a trial to prevent such a catastrophe. Still, if the Department thinks it better to remain on the defensive, and guard as far as possible all the avenues of approach, and await the time of the enemy, I am ready to adopt this course. You have, therefore, only to inform me.

Jefferson Davis explained it further:

In the spring of 1863 the enemy occupied his former position before Fredericksburg. He was in great strength and was preparing on the grandest scale for another advance against Richmond, which in political if not military circles was regarded as the objective point of the war.

The defense of our country's cause had already brought nearly all of the population fit for military service into the various armies then in the field, so that but little increase could be hoped for by the Army of Northern Virginia. To wait until the enemy should advance was to take the desperate hazard of his great superiority of numbers, as well as his ability to reinforce.

It was decided by a bold movement to transfer hostilities to the north by marching into Maryland and Pennsylvania, simultaneously driving the foe out of the Shenandoah Valley. Thus, it was hoped, General Hooker would be called from Virginia to meet our advance.

If, beyond the Potomac, some opportunity should be offered to enable us to defeat the enemy, the measure of our success would be full; but if the movement only resulted in freeing Virginia from the hostile army, it was more than could fairly be expected.

William Christian wrote to his wife as the Army of Northern Virginia crossed the Mason Dixon Line:

Burnside's decision to move his army in January 1863, after the Battle of Fredericksburg, produced the ill-fated "Mud March." Alfred Waud's sketch gives a good idea of the difficulties encountered. (Library of Congress)

Camp near Greenwood, Pa., June 28, 1863

My own darling wife: You can see by the date of this that we are now in Pennsylvania. We crossed the line day before yesterday and are resting today near a little one-horse town on the road to Gettysburg, which we will reach tomorrow. We are paying back these people for some of the damage they have done us, though we are not doing them half as bad as they done us. We are getting up all the horses, etc., and feeding our army with their beef and flour, etc., but there are strict orders about the interruption of any private property by individual soldiers.

Though with these orders, fowls and pigs and eatables don't stand much chance. I felt when I first came here that I would like to revenge myself upon these people for the desolation they have brought upon our own beautiful home, that home where we could have lived so happy, and that we loved so much, from which their vandalism has driven you and my helpless little ones. But though I have such severe wrongs and grievances to redress and such great cause for revenge, yet when I got among these people I could not find it in my heart to molest them. They looked so dreadfully scared and talked so humble that I have invariably endeavored to protect their property and have prevented soldiers from taking chickens, even in the main road; yet there is a good deal of plundering going on, confined principally to the taking of provisions. No houses were searched and robbed, like our houses were done by the Yankees. Pigs, chickens, geese, etc., are finding their way into our camp; it can't be prevented, and I can't think it ought to be. We must show them something of war. I have sent out today to get a good horse; I have no scruples about that, as they have taken mine. We took a lot of Negroes yesterday. I was offered my choice, but as I could not get them back home I would not take them. In fact my humanity revolted at taking the poor devils away from their homes. They were so scared that I turned them all loose.

I dined yesterday with two old maids. They treated me very well and seemed greatly in favor of peace. I have had a great deal of fun since I have been here, The country that we have passed through is beautiful, and everything in the greatest abundance. You never saw such a land of plenty. We could live here mighty well for the next twelve months, but I suppose old Hooker will try to put a stop to us pretty soon. Of course we will have to fight here, and when it comes it will be the biggest on record. Our men feel that there is to be no back-out. A defeat here would be ruinous. This army has never done such fighting as it will do now, and if we can whip the armies that are now gathering to oppose us, we will have everything in our own hands. We must conquer a peace. If we can come out of this country triumphant and victorious, having established a peace, we will bring back to our own land the greatest joy that ever crowned a people. We will show the Yankees this time how we can fight.

The astute Christian was right about the forthcoming battle, but he was wrong about Hooker. Lincoln made another switch in command. Reporter Charles Carleton Coffin:

General Hooker had waited in front of Washington till he was certain of Lee's intention, and then by a rapid march pushed on to Frederick [Maryland]. He asked that the troops at Harpers Ferry might be placed under his command. This was refused, whereupon he informed the War Department that, unless this condition were complied with, he wished to be relieved of his command. The matter was laid before the President, and Hooker's request was granted. General [George Gordon] Meade was placed in command; and what was denied to Hooker was conceded to Meade.

It was a dismal day at Frederick when the news was promulgated that General Hooker was relieved of the command. Notwithstanding the result at Chancellorsville, the soldiers had a good degree of confidence in him. General Meade was unknown except to his own corps. He had entered the war as brigadier in the Pennsylvania Reserves and commanded a division at Antietam and at Fredericksburg, and the 5th Corps at Chancellorsville.

General Meade cared but little for the pomp and parade of war. His own soldiers respected him because he was always prepared to endure hardships. They saw a tall, slim, gray-bearded man, wearing a slouch hat, a plain blue blouse, with his pantaloons tucked into his boots. He was plain of speech and familiar in conversation.

I saw him soon after he was informed that the army was under his command. There was no elation, but on the contrary he seemed weighed down with a sense of responsibility. It was in the hotel at Frederick. He stood silent and thoughtful by himself. Few of all the noisy crowd around knew what had taken place. No change was made in the machinery of the army, and there was but a few hours' delay in its movement.

Lee sent Jeb Stuart and his cavalry to look for Hooker, not knowing that Meade was now in command. Typically, Stuart took the liberty to "ride around" the Union army and was far afield when Lee moved into Pennsylvania. General Henry J. Hunt, chief of artillery for the Army of the Potomac recorded the events that brought the two armies together around the village of Gettysburg:

Hearing nothing from Stuart, and therefore believing that Hooker was still south of the Potomac, Lee, on the afternoon of . . . [June] 28th, ordered Longstreet and A.P. Hill to join Ewell at Harrisburg; but late that night one of Longstreet's scouts came in and reported that the Federal army had crossed the river, that Meade had relieved Hooker and was at Frederick. Lee thereupon changed the rendezvous of his army to Cashtown, which place Heth reached on the 29th. Next day Heth sent Pettigrew's brigade on to Gettysburg, nine miles, to procure a supply of shoes. Nearing this place, Pettigrew discovered the advance of a large Federal force and returned to Cashtown. Hill immediately notified Generals Lee and Ewell, informing the latter that he would advance next morning on Gettysburg. Buford, sending Merritt's brigade to Mechanicstown as guard to his trains, had early on the morning of the 29th crossed into and moved up the Cumberland valley via Boonsboro and Fairfield with those of Gamble and Devin, and on the afternoon of Tuesday, June 30th, under instructions from Pleasonton, entered Gettysburg, Pettigrew's brigade withdrawing on his approach.

From Gettysburg, near the eastern base of the Green Ridge, and covering all the upper passes into the Cumberland valley, good roads lead to all important points between the Susquehannah and the Potomac. It is therefore an important strategic position. On the west of the town, distant nearly half a mile, there is a somewhat elevated ridge running north and south, on which stands the "Luthern Seminary." The ridge is covered with open woods through its whole length, and is terminated nearly a mile and a half north of the seminary by a commanding knoll, bare on its southern side, called Oak Hill. From this ridge the ground slopes gradually to the west, and again rising forms another ridge about 500 yards from the first upon which, nearly opposite the seminary, stand McPherson's farm buildings.

The second ridge is wider, smoother, and lower than the first, and Oak Hill, their intersection, has a clear view of the slopes of north ridges and of the valley between them. West of McPherson's ridge Willoughby Run flows south into Marsh Creek. South of the farm buildings and directly opposite the seminary, a wood borders the run for about 300 yards, and stretches back to the summit of McPherson's ridge. From the town two roads run: one south-west to Hagerstown via Fairfield, the other north-westerly to Chambersburg via Cashtown. The seminary is midway between them, about 300 yards from each. Parallel to and 150 yards north of the Chambersburg pike, is the bed of an unfinished railroad, with deep cuttings through the two ridges. Directly north of the town the country is comparatively flat and open; on the east of it, Rock Creek flows south. On the south, and overlooking it, is a ridge of bold, high ground, terminated on the west by Cemetery Hill and on the east by Culp's Hill, which, bending to the south, extends half a mile or more and terminates in low grounds near Spangler's Spring. Culp's Hill is steep toward the east, is well wooded, and its eastern base is washed by Rock Creek.

Impressed by the importance of the position, Buford, expecting the early return of the enemy in force, assigned to Devin's brigade the country north, and to Gamble's that west of the town; sent out scouting parties on all the roads to collect information, and reported the condition of affairs to Reynolds. His pickets extended from below the Fairfield road, along the eastern bank of Willoughby Run, to the railroad cut, then easterly some 1500 yards north of the town, to a wooded hillock near Rock Creek.

On the night of June 30th Meade's headquarters and the Artillery Reserve were at Taneytown; the First Corps at Marsh Run, the Eleventh at Emmitsburg, Third at Bridgeport, Twelfth at Littlestown, Second at Uniontown, Fifth at Union Mills, Sixth and Gregg's cavalry at Manchester, Kilpatrick's at Hanover. A glance at. . . [a] map will show at what disadvantage Meade's army was now placed. Lee's whole army was nearing Gettysburg, while Meade's was scattered over a wide region to the east and south of that town.

Meade was now convinced that all designs on the Susquehannah had been abandoned; but as Lee's corps were reported as occupying the country from Chambersburg to Carlisle, he ordered, for the next day's moves, the First and Eleventh corps to Gettysburg, under Reynolds, the Third to Emmitsburg, the Second to Taneytown, the Fifth to Hanover, and the Twelfth to Two Taverns, directing Slocum to take command of the Fifth in addition to his own. The Sixth Corps was left at Manchester, thirty-four miles from Gettysburg, to await orders. But Meade, while conforming to the current of Lee's movement, was not merely drifting. The same afternoon he directed the chiefs of engineering and artillery to select a field of battle on which his army might be concentrated, whatever Lee's lines of approach, whether by Harrisburg or Gettysburg, – indicating the general line of Pipe Creek as a suitable locality. Carefully drawn instructions were sent to the corps commanders as to the occupation of this line, should it be ordered; but it was added that developments might cause the offensive to be assumed from present positions. These orders were afterward cited as indicating General Meade's intention not to fight at Gettysburg. They were, under any circumstances, wise and proper orders, and it would probably have been better had he concentrated his army behind Pipe Creek rather than at Gettysburg; but events finally controlled the actions of both leaders.

At 8 A.M., July 1st, Buford's scouts reported Heth's advance on the Cashtown road, when Gamble's brigade formed on McPherson's Ridge, from the Fairfield road to the railroad cut; one section of Calef's battery A, 2d United States, near the left of his line, the other two across the Chambersburg or Cashtown pike. Devin formed his disposable squadrons from Gamble's right toward Oak Hill, from which he had afterward to transfer them to the north of the town to meet Ewell. As Heth advanced, he threw Archer's brigade to the right, Davis's to the left of the Cashtown pike, with Pettigrew's and Brockenbrough's brigades in support. The Confederates advanced skirmishing heavily with Buford's dismounted troopers. Calef's battery, engaging double the number of its own guns, was served with an efficiency worthy of its former reputation as "Duncan's battery" in the Mexican war, and so enabled the cavalry to hold their long line for two hours. When Buford's report of the enemy's advance reached Reynolds, the latter, ordering Doubleday and Howard to follow, hastened toward Gettysburg with Wadsworth's small division (two brigades, Meredith's and Cutler's) and Hall's 2d Maine battery. As he approached he heard the sound of battle, and directing the troops to cross the fields toward the firing, galloped himself to the seminary, met Buford there, and both rode to the front, where the cavalry, dismounted, were gallantly holding their ground against heavy odds. After viewing the field, he sent back to hasten up Howard, and as the enemy's main line was now advancing to the attack, directed Doubleday, who had arrived in advance of his division, to look to the Fairfield road, sent Cutler with three of his five regiments north of the railroad cut, posted the other two under Colonel Fowler, of the 14th New York, south of the pike, and replaced Calef's battery by Hall's, thus relieving the cavalry. Cutler's line was hardly formed when it was struck by Davis's Confederate brigade on its front and right flank.... This order not reaching the 147th New York, its gallant major, Harvey, held that regiment to its position until, having lost half its numbers, the order to retire was repeated. Hall's battery was now imperiled, and it withdrew by sections, fighting at close canister range and suffering severely. Fowler thereupon changed his front to face Davis's brigade, which held the cut, and with Dawes's 6th Wisconsin – sent by Doubleday to aid the 147th New York – charged and drove Davis from the field. The Confederate brigade suffered severely, losing all its field-officers but two, and a large proportion of its men killed and captured, being disabled for further effective service that day.

General Longstreet:

On the morning of July 1, General Lee and I left his headquarters together and had ridden three or four miles when we heard heavy firing along Hill's front. The firing became so heavy that General Lee hurried forward to see what it meant, and I followed. The firing proceeded from the engagement between our advance and Reynolds' corps, which was totally unexpected on both sides. As an evidence of the doubt in which General Lee was enveloped, I quote from General R.H. Anderson the report of a conversation I had with him during the engagement.

About ten o'clock in the morning he received a message notifying him that General Lee desired to see him. He found General Lee intently listening to the fire of the guns, and very much disturbed and depressed. At length he said, more to himself than to General Anderson, "I cannot think what has become of Stuart. In his absence I am in ignorance as to what we have in front of us. It may be the whole Federal army, or it may be only a detachment. If it is the whole Federal force, we must fight a battle here; if we do not gain a victory, those defiles and gorges through which we passed this morning will shelter us from disaster."

When I overtook General Lee at five o'clock that afternoon, he said, to my surprise, that he tought of attacking General Meade on the heights the next day. I suggested that this course seemed to be at variance with his plan of the campaign. He said, "If the enemy is there tomorrow, we must attack him."

I replied, "If he is there, it will be because he is anxious that we should attack him – a good reason, in my judgement, for not doing so." I urged that we should move around by our right to the left of Meade and put our army between him and Washington, threatening his left and rear, and thus force him to attack us in such position as we might select. I called Lee's attention to the fact that the country was admirably adapted for a defensive battle, and that we should surely repulse Meade with crushing loss if we would take position so as to force him to attack us, and suggested that, even if we carried the heights in front of us, we should be so badly crippled that we could not reap the fruits of victory.

But General Lee was impressed with the idea that, by attacking the Federals, he could whip them in detail. I reminded him that if the Federals were there in the morning, it would be proof that they had their forces well in hand, and that, with Pickett in Chambersburg and Stuart out of reach, it was we who should be somewhat in detail. However, the sharp battle fought by Hill and Ewell on that day had given him a taste of victory.

When I left General Lee on the night of the first, I believed that he had made up his mind to attack.

Augustus Bell was a young cannoneer in the 1st Division, 1st Corps, Army of the Potomac. His account of the first day at Gettysburg is considered by many as the finest:

We were turned out... about daybreak [July 1], harnessed up, and, after crossing the creek, halted to let the infantry of Wadsworth's Division file by. There was no mistake now. While we stood there watching these splendid soldiers file by with their long, swinging "route-step," and their muskets glittering in the rays of the rising sun, there came out of the northwest a sullen "boom! boom! boom!" of three guns, followed almost immediately by a prolonged crackling sound, which, at that distance, reminded one very much of the snapping of a dry brush-heap when you first set it on fire. We soon reasoned out the state of affairs up in front. Buford, we calculated, had engaged the leading infantry of Lee's army, and was probably trying to hold them with his cavalry in heavy skirmish line, dismounted, until our infantry could come up. They said that the enemy had not yet developed more than a skirmish line, because if he had shown a heavy formation Buford would be using his artillery, of which he had two or three batteries, whereas we had thus far heard only the three cannon shots mentioned. These apparently trifling incidents show how the men in our Army were in the habit of observing things, and how unerring their judgment was, as a rule, even in matters of military knowledge far beyond their sphere or control.

But my eyes were riveted on the infantry marching by. No one now living will every again see those two brigades of Wadsworth's Division – Cutler's and the Iron Brigade – file by as they did that morning. The little creek made a depres-

Thomas "Stonewall" Jackson was second only to Lee among Southern commanders. Jackson's drive, daring, and tactical brilliance gave the Army of Northern Virginia a weapon the Union could not match. Jackson's death at the Battle of Chancellorsville in May 1863 (shot mistakenly by his own troops) robbed the Confederacy of one of its most important assets. (Library of Congress)

Union dead before a stone wall at the foot of Marye's Heights near Fredericksburg, Va., May 3, 1863. (Library of Congress)

sion in the road, with a gentle ascent on either side, so that from our point of view the column, as it came down one slope and up the other, had the effect of huge blue billows of men topped with a spray of shining steel, and the whole spectacle was calculated to give nerve to a man who had none before. Partly because they had served together a long time, and, no doubt, because so many of their men were in our ranks, there was a great affinity between the Battery and the Iron Brigade, which expressed itself in cheers and good-natured chaffing between us as they went by. "Find a good place to camp; be sure and get near a good dry rail fence; tell the Johnnies we will be right along," were the salutations that passed on our part, while the infantry made such responses as "All right; better stay here till we send for you; the climate up there may be unhealthy just now for such delicate creatures as you," and all that sort of thing. It was probably 8 o'clock when the last brigade had passed, and then we got the order to march, moving with Doubleday's Division. As we moved up the road we could see the troops of the next division coming close behind. By this time the leading regiments of Wadsworth's infantry had got on the ground, and the sounds of battle were increasing rapidly.

The sounds of the cavalry fight had been distinct ever since we left Marsh Creek – a fitful crackle – but now we heard fierce, angry crash on crash, rapidly growing in volume and intensity, signifying that our leading infantry – Cutler's and the Iron Brigade – had encountered the "doughboys" of Lee's advance. It is well known that the men of the Iron Brigade always preferred slouch hats (Western fashion), and seldom or never wore caps. At the time this heavy crashing began we were probably half way up from Marsh Creek, and, as the Battery was marching at a walk, most of us were walking along with the guns instead of riding on the limbers. Among the Cannoneers was a man from the 2d Wisconsin (John Holland) who took great pride in the Iron Brigade. So, when that sudden crash! crash! crash! floated over the hills to our ears, John said, with visible enthusiasm, "Hear that, my son! That's the talk! The old slouch hats have got there, you bet!!"

Now the artillery began to play in earnest, and it was evident that the three batteries which had preceded us were closely engaged, while the musketry had grown from the cracking sound of the skirmishing we had heard early in the morning to an almost incessant crash, which betokened the file firing of a main line of battle. Just before reaching the brow of the hill, south of the town, where we could get our first sight of the battle itself, there was a provoking halt of nearly half an hour. We could hear every sound, even the yells of the troops fighting on the ridge beyond Gettysburg, and we could see the smoke mount up and float away lazily to the northeastward; but we could not see the combatants. While halted here Doubleday's Division passed up the road, each regiment breaking into double quick as it reached the top of the hill. The Eleventh Corps also began by this time to arrive from Emmitsburg. Finally, when the last of the Second Brigade of Doubleday's (Stone's) had passed, we got the order to advance again, and in two minutes the whole scene burst upon us like the lifting of the curtain in a grand play. The spectacle was simply stupendous. It is doubtful if there was ever a battle fought elsewhere of which such a complete view was possible from one point as we got of that battle when we reached the top of the hill abreast of Round Top. . . .

Our guns pointed about due west, taking the Cashtown Pike **en echarpe**. *The right half-battery was in line with us on the north side of the cut. Its right gun rested on the edge of a little grove, which extended some distance farther to the right, and was full of infantry (the 11th Pennsylvania) supporting us. There was also infantry in our rear, behind the crest and in the Railroad Cut (the 6th Wisconin). One of our squad volunteered the facetious remark that these infantry "were put there to shoot the recruits if they flinched," for which he was rebuked by Corp'l Packard, who told him to "see that he himself behaved as well as the recruits." As Stewart commanded the right half-battery in person, he did not have much to do with us, directly, during the action that followed.*

At this time, which was probably about noon, all the infantry of the First Corps, except that massed immediately about our position, together with Hall's, Reynolds's and one of the cavalry horse-batteries – Calef's – had been struggling desperately in the fields in our front, and for a few moments we had nothing to do but witness the magnificent scene. The enemy had some batteries firing down the pike, but their shot – probably canister – did not reach us. In a few minutes they opened with shell from a battery on a high knoll to the north of us (Oak Hill), and, though at long range, directly enfilading our line. But they sent their shells at the troops who were out in advance. We stood to the guns and watched the infantry combat in our front. Over across the creek (Willoughby's) we could see the gray masses of the Rebel infantry coming along all the roads and deploying in the fields, and it seemed that they were innumerable. At this time some 200 or 300 Rebel prisoners passed by our position on their way to our rear. They were a tough-looking set. Some had bloody rags tied round their limb or heads, where they had received slight wounds.

In the meantime our infantry out in the field toward the creek was being slowly but surely overpowered, and our lines were being forced in toward the Seminary. It was now considerably past noon. In addition to the struggle going on in our immediate front, the sounds of a heavy attack from the north side were heard, and away out beyond the creek, to the south, a strong force could be seen advancing and overlapping our left. The enemy was coming nearer, both in front and on the north, and stray balls began to zip and whistle around our ears with unpleasant frequency. Then we saw the batteries that had been holding the position in advance of us limber up and fall back toward the Seminary, and the enemy simultaneously advance his batteries down the road. All our infantry out toward the creek on both sides of the pike began to fall back.

The enemy did not press them very closely, but halted for nearly an hour to reform his lines, which had been very much shattered by the battle of the forenoon. At last, having reformed his lines behind the low ridges in front, he made his appearance in grand shape. His line stretched from the railroad grading across the Cashtown Pike, and through the fields south of it half way to the Fairfield Road – nearly a mile in length. First we could see the tips of the color-staffs coming up over the little ridge, then the points of their bayonets, and the Johnnies themselves, coming on with a steady tramp, tramp, and with loud yells. It was now apparent that the old Battery's turn had come again, and the embattled boys who stood so grimly at their posts felt that another page must be added to the record of Buena Vista and Antietam. The term "boys" is literally true, because of our gun detachment alone, consisting of a Sergeant, two Corporals, seven Cannoneers and six Drivers, only four had hair on their faces, while the other 12 were beardless boys whose ages would not average 19 years, and who, at any other period of our history, would have been at school! The same was more or less true of all the other gun detachments. But if boys in years they were, with one or two exceptions not necessary to name, veterans in battle, and braver or steadier soldiers than they were never faced a foe! A glance along our line at that moment would have been a rare study for an artist. As the day was very hot many of the boys had their jackets off, some with sleeves rolled up, and they exchanged little words of cheer with each other as the gray line came on. In quick, sharp tones, like successive reports of a repeating rifle, came Davison's orders:

"Load – Canister – Double!" There was a husting of Cannoneers, a few thumps of the rammer-heads, and then "Ready! – By piece! – At will! – Fire!!". . .

Directly in our front – that is to say, on both sides of the pike – the Rebel infantry, whose left lapped the north side of the pike quite up to the line of the railroad grading, had been forced to halt and lie down by the tornado of canister that we had given them from the moment they came in sight over the bank of the creek. But the regiments in the field to their right (south side) of the pike kept on, and kept swinging their right flanks forward as if to take us in reverse to cut us off from the rest of our troops near the Seminary. At this moment Davison, bleeding from two desperate wounds, and so weak that one of the men had to hold him up on his feet (one ankle being totally shattered by a bullet), ordered us to form the half-battery, action left, by wheeling on the left gun as a pivot, so as to bring the half-battery on a line with the Cashtown Pike, muzzles facing south, his object being to take the front of the Rebel line closing in on us from that side.

Of the four men left at our gun when this order was given two had bloody heads, but they were still "standing by," and Ord. Serg't Mitchell jumped on our off wheels to help us. "This is tough work, boys" he shouted, as we wheeled the gun around, "but we are good for it."

And Pat Wallace, tugging at the near wheel, shouted back: "If we ain't, where'll you find them that is!"

Well, this change of front gave us a clean rake along the Rebel line for a whole brigade length, but it exposed our right flank to the raking volleys of their infantry near the pike, who at that moment began to get up again and come on. Then for seven or eight minutes ensued probably the most desperate fight ever waged between artillery and infantry at close range without a particle of cover on either side. They gave us volley after volley in front and flank, and we gave them double canister as fast as we could load. The 6th Wisconsin and 11th Pennsylvania men crawled up over the bank of the cut or behind the rail fence in rear of Stewart's caissons and joined their musketry to our canister, while from the north side of the cut flashed the chainlightning of the Old Man's half-battery in one solid streak!

At this time our left half-battery, taking their first line ***en echarpe****, swept it so clean with double canister that the Rebels sagged away from the road to get cover from the fences and trees that lined it. From our second round on a gray squirrel could not have crossed the road alive.*

How those peerless Cannoneers sprang to their work! Twenty-six years have but softened in memory the picture of "Old Griff" (Wallace), his tough Irish face set in hard lines with the unflinching resolution that filled his soul, while he sponged and loaded under that murderous musketry with the precision of barrack drill; of the burly Corporal, bareheaded, his hair matted with blood from a scalp wound, and wiping the crimson fluid out of his eyes to sight the gun; of the steady Orderly Sergeant, John Mitchell, moving calmly from gun to gun, now and then changing men about as one after another was hit and fell, stooping over a wounded man to help him up, or aiding another to stagger to the rear; of the dauntless Davison on foot among the guns, cheering the men, praising this one and that one, and ever and anon profanely exhorting us to "Feed it to 'em, G– D– em, feed it to 'em!" the very guns became things of life – not implements, but comrades. Every man was doing the work of two or three. At our gun at the finish there were only the Corporal, No. 1 and No. 3, with two drivers fetching ammunition. The water in Pat's bucket was like ink. His face and hands were smeared all over with burnt powder. The thumbstall of No. 3 was burned to a crisp by the hot vent-field. Between the black of the burnt-powder and the crimson streaks from his bloody head, Packard looked like a demon from below! Up and down the line men reeling and falling; splinters flying from wheels and axles where bullets hit; in rear, horses tearing and plunging, mad with wounds or terror; drivers yelling, shells bursting, shot shrieking overhead, howling about our ears or throwing up great clouds of dust where they struck; the musketry crashing on three sides of us; bullets hissing, humming and whistling everywhere; cannon roaring; all crash on crash and peal on peal, smoke, dust, splinters, blood, wreck and carnage indescribable; but the brass guns of Old B still bellowed and not a man or boy flinched or faltered! Every man's shirt soaked with sweat and many of them sopped with blood from wounds not severe enough to make such bulldogs "let go" – bareheaded, sleeves rolled up, faces blackened – oh! if such a picture could be spread on canvas to the life! Out in front of us an undulating field, filled almost as far as the eye could see with a long, low, gray line creeping toward us, fairly fringed with flame!

For a few moments the whole Rebel line, clear down to the Fairfield Road, seemed to waver, and we thought that maybe we could repulse them, singled-handed as we were. At any rate, about our fifth or sixth round after changing front made their first line south of the pike halt, and many of them sought cover behind trees in the field or ran back to the rail fence parallel to the pike at that point, from which they resumed their musketry. But their second line came steadily on, and as Davison had now succumbed to his wounds Ord. Serg't Mitchell took command and gave the order to limber to the rear, the 6th Wisconsin and the 11th Pennsylvania having begun to fall back down the railroad track toward the town, turning about and firing at will as they retreated.

On the second day, July 2, the Army of the Potomac occupied Cemetery Ridge and Culp's Hill. To the right of General Meade's line stood two prominent hills known as Big Round Top, about 300 feet, and Little Round Top, about 200 feet. Control of these two features meant control of the battlefield. Neither side realized this until late in the day, however, and thus the second day of battle got off to a slow start. It was James Longstreet to whom Lee had assigned the attack, planned for the morning on the right. It was well into the afternoon before it was launched. Longstreet, who would be blamed for the delays, defended his plan:

On the morning of July 2 I was confident that Lee had not yet decided when and where the attack should be made. He finally determined that I should make the main attack on the extreme right. It was fully eleven o'clock when General Lee arrived at this conclusion and ordered the movement. In the meantime, by General Lee's authority, E. McIver Law's brigade was ordered to rejoin my command and, on my sugeston that it would be better to await its arrival, General Lee assented. We waited about forty minutes for these troops and then moved forward. A delay of several hours occurred because we had been ordered by General Lee to proceed cautiously so as to avoid being seen by the enemy. At length the column halted. Looking up toward Little Round Top, I saw a signal station in full view. It was apparent that our columns had been seen, and that further efforts to conceal ourselves would be a waste of time.

The troops were rapidly thrown into position, and preparations were made for the attack. Our army was stretched in an elliptical curve from the front of the Round Tops around Seminary Ridge, and enveloping Cemetery Heights on the left, thus covering a space of four or five miles. The enemy occupied the high ground in front of us, being massed within a curve of about two miles, nearly concentric with the curve described by our forces. His line was about 1,400 yards from ours. The proposition for our inferior forces to assault and drive out the masses of troops on the heights was a very problematical one. My orders from General Lee were to "envelop the enemy's left, and begin the attack there."

My corps, with Pickett's division still absent, numbered hardly 13,000 men. At half past three o'clock the order was given General Hood to advance and, hurrying to the head of McLaws' division, I moved with his line.

Colonel James Feemantle of Britain's Coldstream Guards was serving as an observer with the Confederate army:

General Longstreet advised me if I wished to have a good view of the battle to return to my tree of yesterday. I did so, and remained there. . . during the rest of the afternoon. But until four forty-five p.m. all was profoundly still and we began to doubt whether a fight was coming off today at all. At that time, however, Longstreet suddenly commenced a heavy cannonade on the right. Ewell immediately took it up on the left. The enemy replied with at least equal fury . . . A dense smoke rose for six miles . . . so soon as the firing began, General Lee joined Hill just below our tree, and he remained there nearly all the time looking through his field glasses – sometimes talking to Hill and sometimes to Colonel Long of his staff. But generally he sat quite alone on the stump of a tree. . . When the cannonade was at its height, a Confederate band of music, between the cemetery and ourelves, began to play polkas and waltzes, which sounded very curious accompanied by the hissing and bursting of shells.

Then an amazing thing happened. Union General Daniel Sickles, impetuous politician, who had already become a household name four years before when he shot his wife's lover, the grandson of Francis Scott Key, and had gotten off with an insanity plea (the first of its kind), decided to take the battle into his own hands. Lieutenant F.A. Haskell:

Somewhat after 1:00 p.m. a movement of the 3rd Corps occurred. I could not conjecture the reason for it. General Sickles commenced to advance his whole corps straight to the front. This movement had not been ordered by General Meade, as I heard him say, and he disapproved of it as soon as it was made known to him. Generals Hancock and John Gibbon criticized its propriety sharply, as I know, and foretold quite accurately what would be the result. This move of the 3rd Corps was an important one – it developed the battle. Oh, if this corps had kept its strong position on the crest [of Cemetery Ridge] and, supported by the rest of the army, had waited for the attack of the enemy!

It was magnificent to see these 10,000 or 12,000 men with their batteries, and some squadrons of cavalry on the left flank, all in battle order, sweep steadily down the slope, across the valley and up the next ascent toward their destined position. The 3rd Corps now became the absorbing object of interest of all eyes. The 2nd Corps took arms; and the 1st Division of this corps was ordered to be in readiness to support the 3rd Corps, should circumstances render support necessary. The 3rd Corps, as it advanced, became the extreme left of our line, and if the enemy was assembling to the west of Round Top with a view to turn our left, as we had heard, there would be nothing between the left flank of the corps and the enemy; and the enemy would be square upon its flank by the time it had attained the Emmitsburg Road. So when this advance line came near the road, and we saw the smoke of some guns, away to Sickles' left, anxiety became an element in our interest. The enemy opened slowly at first, and from long range, but he was square upon Sickles' left flank.

General John C. Caldwell was ordered at once to put his division – the first of the 2nd Corps. . . in motion and to take post in the woods at the west slope of Round Top in such a manner as to resist the enemy, should he attempt to come around Sickles' left and gain his rear. The division moved as ordered, toward the point indicated, between two and three o'clock in the afternoon. About the same time Sykes's 5th Corps of regulars, which had been held in reserve, could be seen marching by the flank from its position on the Baltimore Pike, heading to where the 1st Division of the 2nd Corps had gone. The 6th Corps had now come up and was halted on the Baltimore Pike. So the plot thickened.

It was now about five o'clock. The enemy batteries were opening and, as we watched, they pressed those of Sickles and pounded them until they began to retire to positions nearer the infantry. The enemy seemed fearfully in earnest. And, what was more ominous than the thunder of his advancing guns, far to Sickles' left appeared the long lines and the columns of the Rebel infantry, now unmistakably moving out to the attack. The position of the 3rd Corps became one of great peril, and it is probable that Sickles by this time began to realize his true situation. All was astir now on our crest. Generals and their staffs were galloping hither and thither;

the men were all in their places, and you might have heard the rattle of 10,000 ramrods as they drove home the little globes and cones of lead. As the Confederates were advancing upon Sickles' flank, he commenced a change of front, or at least a partial one, by swinging back his left and throwing forward his right, in order that his lines might be parallel to those of his adversary, his batteries meantime doing what they could to check the enemy's advance. But this movement was not completely executed before new Rebel batteries opened upon Sickles' right flank – his former front – and in the same quarter appeared the Rebel infantry also.

Now can the dreadful battle picture, of which we for a time could be but spectators. Upon the front and right flank of Sickles came sweeping the infantry of Longstreet and Hill. Hitherto there had been skirmishing and artillery practice – now the battle started; for amid the heavier smokes and longer tongues of flame of the batteries began to appear the countless flashes and the long, fiery sheets of musket fire. We saw the long gray lines come sweeping down upon Sickles' front and mix with the battle smoke. Now the same colors emerged from the bushes and orchards on his right and enveloped his flank in the confusion of the conflict. Oh, the din and the roar, and these Rebel wolf cries! What a hell was there down in that valley! These 10,000 or 12,000 men of the 3rd Corps fought well, but it soon became apparent that they must be swept from the field or perish there. To move down and support them was out of the question, for this would be to do as Sickles did – relinquish a good position and advance to a bad one. There was no other alternative – the 3rd Corps must fight itself out of its position of destruction!

In the meantime some dispositions had to be made to meet the enemy in the event that Sickles was overpowered. With his corps out of the way, the enemy would have been in a position to advance upon our 2nd Corps, not in front, but obliquely from the left. To meet this contingency, the left of the 2nd Division of the 2nd Corps was thrown back slightly, and two regiments were advanced down to the Emmitsburg Road. This was all General Gibbon could do.

The enemy was still giving the 3rd Corps fierce battle. Sickles had been borne from the field minus one of his legs, and General D.B. Birney now commanded. We of the 2nd Corps, a thousand yards away with our guns, were, and had to remain, idle spectators. The Rebels, as anticipated, tried to gain the left of the 3rd Corps and were now moving into the woods at the west of Round Top. We knew what they would find there.

No sooner had the enemy got a considerable force into these woods than the roar of the conflict was heard there also. The 5th Corps and the 1st Division of the 2nd were there at the right time and promptly engaged him; and the battle soon became general and obstinate. Now its roar became twice the volume that it was before, and its rage extended over more than twice the space. The 3rd Corps had been pressed back considerably, and the wounded were streaming to the rear by hundreds, but still the battle there went on.

When the 1st Division of the 2nd Corps first engaged the enemy, for a time it was pressed back somewhat. After the 5th Corps became well engaged, fresh bodies of the Rebels continued to swell the numbers of the assailants. Our men there began to show signs of exhaustion; their ammunition was nearly expended; they had now been fighting more than an hour against greatly superior numbers. From the sound of the fighting and the place where the smoke rose above the troops, we knew that the 5th Corps was still steady and holding its own there, and as we saw the 6th Corps marching and near at hand to that point, we had no longer fears for the left; we had more apparent reason to fear for ourselves.

The 3rd Corps was being overpowered. Here and there its lines started to break. The men began to pour back to the rear in confusion. The enemy were close upon them and among them. Guns and caissons were abandoned and in the hands of the enemy. The 3rd Corps, after a heroic but unfortunate fight, was being literally swept from the field. That corps gone, what was there between the 2nd Corps and those yelling masses of the enemy!

The time was at hand when we must be actors in this drama. Five or six hundred yards away the enemy was hotly pressing his advantage and throwing in fresh troops, whose line extended still more along our front, when Generals Hancock and Gibbon rode up.

Just at this time we saw another thing that made us glad: we looked to our rear, and there, and all up the hillside which had been the rear of the 3rd Corps before it went forward, were rapidly advancing large bodies of men from the extreme right on our line, coming to the support of the part now so hotly pressed. They formed lines of battle at the foot of the hill by the Taneytown Road, and when the broken fragments of the 3rd Corps were swarming by them toward the rear, they came swiftly up and with glorious cheers, under fire, took their places on the crest in line of battle to the left of the 2nd Corps. Now Sickles' blunder was repaired. Now we said to ourselves, "Rebel chief, hurl forward your howling lines and columns! Yell out your loudest and your last, for many of your host will never yell again!"

The 3rd Corps was out of the way. Now we were in for it. The battery men were ready by their loaded pieces. All along the crest everything was ready. Gun after gun, along the batteries, in rapid succession leaped where it stood and bellowed its canister upon the enemy. They still advanced. The infantry opened fire, and soon the whole crest, artillery and infantry, was one continuous sheet of fire. From Round Top to near the Cemetery stretched an uninterrupted field of conflict.

It was late in the day when the two armies, almost at the same instant, realized that both Big and Little Round Top had been virtually ignored, and that immediate possession might save the day. That part of the battlefield would forever be remembered by three men – William Oates, Fifteenth Alabama; W.F. Perry, Forty-eighth Alabama; and Howard L. Prince, Twentieth Maine:

Oates:

I now ordered my regiment to drive the Federals from the ledge of rocks and from the hill. My men advanced about halfway to the enemy's position, but the fire was so destructive that my line wavered like a man trying to walk against a strong wind, and then slowly, doggedly, gave back a little; then, with no one on the left or right of me, to stand there and die was sheer folly; either to advance or retreat became a necessity.

I again ordered the advance. . . I passed through the line waving my sword, shouting, "Forward, men, to the ledge!" and was promptly followed by the command in splendid style. . . . Five times they rallied and charged us, twice coming so near that some of my men had to use the bayonet. . . . It was our time now to deal death. . . .

Perry:

A sheet of flame burst from the rocks less than fifty yards away. A few scattering shots in the beginning gave warning in time for my men to fall down, and this largely to escape the effect of the main volley. They doubtless seemed to the enemy to be all dead, but the volley of the fire which they immediately returned proved that they were very much alive. . . . Before the enemy had time to load their guns a decision was made. Leaping over the prostrate line before me, I shouted the order, "Forward!" and started for the rocks. The response was a bound, a yell, and a rush, and in ten seconds my men were pouring into the Den, and the enemy were escaping from the opposite side. . . . In the charge the left wing of the regiment struck the hill on which the artillery were stationed, and the center and right swept into the rocks east of it. Major George W. Carey led the left wing up the hill, and bounding over the rocks on its crest, landed among the artillerymen ahead of the line, and received their surrender. . . . The Major a few moments later found me near the foot of the hill, completely prostrated by heat and excessive exertion.

Prince:

The front surged backward and forward like a wave. At times our dead and wounded were in front of our line, and then by a superhuman effort our gallant lads would carry the combat forward beyond their prostrate forms. Continually the gray lines crept up by squads under protecting trees and boulders, and the firing became at closer and closer range. And even the enemy's line essayed to reach around the thin front of blue that stretched out in places in single rank and could not go much farther without breaking. So far had they extended, that their bullets passed beyond and into the ranks farther up the hill, and Captain Woodward, commanding the Eighty-third, sent his adjutant to ask if the Twentieth had been turned. . . . Meanwhile the brigade in front of the hill was hard pushed to hold its own, and the heavy roar of musketry in the fitful lulls of our guns came to the anxious ears of our commander and told too plainly what would be the result if our line gave way. Not a man in that devoted band but knew that the safety of the brigade, and perhaps of the army, depended on the steadfastness with which that point was held, and so fought on and on, with no hope of assistance, but not a thought of giving up. Already nearly half of the little force is prostrate. The dead and the wounded clog the footsteps of the living.

Haskell ended his tale of horror:

All senses for the time were dead but the one of sight. The roar of the discharges and the yells of the enemy all passed unheeded, but the impassioned soul was all eyes and saw all things that the smoke did not hide. How madly the battery men were driving the double charge of canister into those broad-mouthed Napoleons! How rapidly those long blue-coated lines of infantry delivered their fire down the slope! There was no faltering – the men stood nobly to their work. Men were dropping, dead, or wounded, on all sides, by scores and by hundreds. Poor mutilated creatures, some with an arm dangling, some with a leg broken by a bullet, were limping and crawling toward the rear. They made no sound of pain but were as silent as if dumb and mute. A sublime heroism seemed to pervade all, and the intuition that to lose that crest was to lose everything.

Such fighting as this could not last long. It was now near sundown, and the battle had gone on wonderfully long already. But a change had occurred. The Rebel cry had ceased, and the men of the Union began to shout, and their lines to advance. The wave had rolled upon the rock, and the rock had smashed it.

Back down the slope, over the valley, across the Emmitsburg Road, shattered, without organization, in utter confusion the men in gray poured into the woods, and victory was with the arms of the Republic.

That night, General Meade called a meeting of his top officers. General John Gibbon was the junior member:

I had never been a member of a council of war before. . . and did not feel very confident that I was properly a member of this one; but I was engaged in the discussion. . . . By the customs of war the junior member votes first, as on courts-martial; and when Butterfield read off his question, the substance of which was: "Should the army remain in its present position or take up some other?" he addressed himelf first to me. To say "Stay and fight" would be to ignore the objections made by [engineer] General Newton [who had said that this was not a fit place to fight a battle], and I therefore answered somewhere in this way: "Remain here, and make such correction in our position as may be deemed necessary, but take no step which even looks like retreat." The question was put to each member and his answer taken down, and when it came to Newton who was first in rank, he sided pretty much the same way I did, and he had some playful sparring as to whether he agrees with me or I with him; the rest voted to remain.

The next question put by Butterfield was: "Should the army attack or await the attack of the enemy?" I voted not to attack, and all the others voted substantially the same way; and on the third question, "How long shall we wait?" I voted "Until Lee moves." The answer to this last question showed

the only material variation on the opinion of the members. When the meeting was over, General Meade said, quietly but decidedly, "Such then is the decision" and certainly he said nothing which produced a doubt in my mind as to his being in accord with the members of the council.

Battle would go to a third day, so indecisive was the action thus far. This time, Lee planned to use the entire army in an all out effort to take the field from Meade. He informed Longstreet that Pickett would lead the charge. Before the day was over, Pickett's name would forever be linked with Gettysburg.

I had not seen General Lee on the night of July second [wrote Longstreet]. On the next morning he came to see me and, fearing that he was still in the disposition to attack, I tried to anticipate him by saying, "General, I find that you still have an excellent opportunity to move around to the right of Meade's army and maneuver him into attacking us."

He replied, pointing with his fist at Cemetery Hill, "The enemy is there, and I am going to strike him."

I said, "General, I have been a soldier all my life. It is my opinion that no 15,000 men ever arrayed for battle can take that position."

General Lee in reply to this ordered me to prepare Pickett's men to get into position. The plan of assault was as follows: our artillery was to be massed in a wood from which Pickett was to charge, and it was to pour a continuous fire upon the cemetery. Under cover of this fire and supported by it, Pickett was to charge.

Our artillery was in command of Colonel E.P. Alexander, a brave and gifted officer. The arrangements were completed about one o'clock. Alexander had ordered a battery of seven 11-pound howitzers, with fresh horses and full caissons, to charge with Pickett, but General W.N. Pendleton, from whom the guns had been borrowed, recalled them and thus deranged this wise plan. Never was I so depressed as that day. Unwilling to trust myself with the entire responsibility, I had instructed Colonel Alexander to observe carefully the effect of the fire upon the enemy and, when it began to tell, to notify Pickett to begin the assault. I was so impressed with the hopelessness of the charge that I wrote the following note to Alexander:

If the artillery fire does not have the effect to drive off the enemy or greatly demoralize him, I would prefer that you should not advise General Pickett to make the charge. I shall

A federal battery prepares for action on the south bank of the Rappahannock River in June 1863. This was probably a posed shot (close inspection shows artillerymen grinning toward the camera). Smoke and dust usually obscured the battlefields and photographic techniques were too slow and cumbersome to capture movement, so there are almost no authentic action photos from the Civil War. (Library of Congress) *rely a great deal on your judgment to determine the matter, and shall expect you to let Pickett know when the moment offers.*

To my note the Colonel replied as follows:

I will only be able to judge the effect of our fire upon the enemy by his return fire, for his infantry is but little exposed to view, and the smoke will obscure the whole field. If there is an alternative to this attack, it should be carefully considered before opening our fire, for it will take all the artillery ammunition we have left.

Pickett met with Lee and Longstreet that afternoon and, moments before his famous charge, he penned the following letter to his fiancee:

A summons came from Peter [*or Old Pete, the affectionate name given to Longstreet by his comrades*], *and I immediately rode where he and Marse Robert* [*Lee*] *were making a reconnaissance of Meade's position.*

"Great God!" said Old Peter as I came up. "Look, General Lee, at the surmountable difficulties between our line and that of the Yankees – the steep hills, the tiers of artillery, the fences, the heavy skirmish line – and we'll have to fight our infantry against their batteries."

"The enemy is there, General Longstreet, and I am going to strike him," said Marse Robert in his firm, quiet, determined voice.

I rode with them along our line of prostrate infantry. The men had been forbidden to cheer, but they arose and lifted in reverential adoration their caps to our beloved commander. Oh, the responsibility for the lives of such men as these! Well, my darling, their fate and that of our beloved Southland will be settled ere your glorious brown eyes rest on these scraps of penciled paper.

Our line of battle faces Cemetery Ridge. The men are lying in the rear, and the hot July sun pours its scorching rays almost vertically down on them. The suffering is almost unbearable.

I have never seen Old Peter so grave and troubled. For several minutes after I had saluted him he looked at me without speaking. Then in an agonized voice, the reserve all gone, he said, "Pickett, I am being crucified. I have instructed Alexander to give you your orders, for I can't."

While he was yet speaking, a note was brought to me from Alexander. After reading it I handed it to Pete, asking if I should obey and go forward. He looked at me for a moment, then held out his hand. Presently, clasping his other hand over mine without speaking, he bowed his head on his breast. I shall never forget the look in his face nor the clasp of his hand, and I saw tears glistening on his cheeks and beard. The stern old war horse, God bless him, was weeping for his men and, I know, praying too that this cup might pass from them. It is almost three o'clock.

Haskell watched from the Union line:

A hundred and twenty-five rebel guns, we estimate, are now active, firing twenty-four pound, twenty, twelve, and ten pound projectiles, solid shot and shells, spherical, conical, spiral. The enemy's fire is chiefly concentrated upon the position of the Second Corps. From the Cemetery to Round Top, with over a hundred gun, and to all parts of the enemy's line, our batteries reply. . . .

Who can describe such a conflict as is raging around us? To say that it was like a summer storm, with the crash of thunder, the glare of lightning, the shrieking of the wind, and the clatter of hailstones, would be weak. The thunder and lightning of these two hundred and fifty guns and their shell, whose smoke darkens the sky, are incessant, all pervading, in the air above our heads, on the ground at our feet, remote, near, deafening, ear-piercing, astounding; and these hailstones are massy iron, charged with exploding fire. And there is little of human interest in a storm; it is an absorbing element of this. . . . These guns are great infuriate demons, not of the earth, whose mouths blaze with smoky tongues of living fire, and whose murky breath, sulphur-laden, rolls around them and along the ground, the smoke of Hades. These grimy men, rushing, shouting, their souls in frenzy, plying the dusky globes and the igniting spark, are in their league, and but their willing ministers.

The projectiles shriek long and sharp. They hiss, they scream, they growl, they sputter; all sounds of life and rage; and each had its different note, and all are discordant. . . . We see the solid shot strike axle, or pole, or wheel, and the tough iron and heart of oak snap and fly like straws. The great oaks there by Woodruff's guns heave down their massy branches with a crash, as if the lightning smote them. The shells swoop down among the battery horses standing there apart. A half a dozen horses start, they tumble, their legs stiffen, their vitals and blood smear the ground. And these shot and shells have no repect for men either. We see the poor fellows hobbling back from the crest, or unable to do so, pale and weak, lying on the ground with the mangled stump of an arm or leg, dripping their life-blood away; or with a cheek torn open, or a shoulder mashed. And many, alas! hear not the roar as they stretch upon the ground with upturned faces and open eyes, though a shell should burst at their very ears. Their ears and their bodies this instant are only mud. We saw them but a moment since there among the flame, with brawny arms and muscles of iron wielding the rammer and pushing home the cannon's plethoric load.

Then Pickett's men began to march. "Thank God," One Union soldier said, "there comes the infantry!" Almost anything was better than the "horrors of that cannonade," and the inability to defend oneself against it. Confederate reporters for the *Richmond Enquirer*, who had followed their soldiers into Pennsylvania, prepared their notes for telegraphing:

Where is that division which is to play so conspicuous a part in this day's tragedy? Just fronting that frowning hill from which heavy batteries are belching forth shell and shrapnel with fatal accuracy, the men are lying close to the ground, sweltering, almost suffocating in the murderous heat, only partially protected, powerless to fight back. Hours have passed and the deadly missiles have come thick and fast. See that shattered arm; that leg shot off; that headless body; and here the mangled form of a young and gallant lieutenant who had braved the perils of many battles.

That hill over there must be carried to rout the enemy. That is his stronghold. With that hill captured, his rout is inevitable; but the hill is exceedingly strong by nature, and rendered more so by the works thrown up the night before. It is a moment of the greatest emergency, but if unshrinking valor or human courage can carry those heights, it will be done.

Now the storming party is moved up, Pickett's division in advance, supported on the right by Wilcox's brigade and on the left by Henry Heth's division, commanded by James J. Pettigrew, I have seen brave men pass over that fated valley the day before. I have observed them return a bleeding mass, but with unstained banners. Now I see their valiant comrades prepare for the same bloody trail. They move forward; with steady, measured tread they advance before the foe. Their banners float defiantly, as onward in beautiful order they press across the plain. I have never seen, since the war began, troops enter a fight in such splendid order as does this division of Pickett's.

Now Pettigrew's command emerges from the woods on Pickett's left and sweeps down the slope of the hill to the valley beneath, some 200 or 300 yards in rear of Pickett. But – wait – I notice by the wavering of his line as they enter the conflict that they want the firmness of nerve and steadiness of tread which so characterized Pickett's men! I fear that these men cannot, will not, stand the tremendous ordeal to which they will be soon subjected. They are mostly raw troops, have perhaps never been under fire – certainly never been in any severe fight – and I tremble for their conduct.

General Pickett receives the order to charge those batteries at the opportune moment. James L. Kemper, with as gallant men as ever trod beneath that flag, leads the right, Tobert Garnett brings up the left, and the veteran Lewis A. Armistead, with his braver troops, moves forward in support. The distance is more than half a mile.

Our batteries have ceased firing. Why do not our guns reopen? is the inquiry that rises on every lip. Still our batteries are silent as death. But on press Pickett's brave Virginians.

And now the enemy opens upon them a terrible fire. Yet on, on they move in unbroken line, delivering a deadly fire as they advance. Now they have reached the Emmitsburg Road, and here they meet a severe fire from the enemy's infantry, posted behind a stone fence, while their artillery turn their whole fire upon this devoted band. Still they remain firm. That flag goes down. See how quickly it again mounts upward, borne by some gallant man who feels keenly the honor of his old Commonwealth in this hour which is to test her manhood.

The line moves onward, straight onward – cannon roaring, grape and canister plunging and plowing through the ranks – bullets whizzing as thick as hailstones in winter, and men falling as leaves fall when shaken by the blasts of autumn. In a double-quick, and with a shout which rises above the roar of battle, they charge. Now they pour in volleys of musketry – they reach the works – the contest rages with intense fury – men fight almost hand to hand – the red cross and gridiron wave defiantly in close proximity – the enemy are slowly yielding – a Federal officer dashes forward in front of his shrinking columns and, with flashing sword, urges them to stand.

General Pickett, seeing the splendid valor of his troops, moves among them as if courting death by his own daring intrepidity. The brave Kemper, with hat in hand, still cheering on his men, falls from his horse into the ranks of the enemy. His men rush forward, rescue their general, and he is borne mortally wounded from the field.

Again they advance. They storm the stone fence. The Yankees flee. The enemy's batteries are, one by one, silenced in quick succession as Pickett's men deliver their fire at the gunners and drive them from their pieces. I see them plant their banner in the enemy's works. I hear their glad shout of victory!

But it was not to be a Confederate victory, as Haskell later wrote:

General H.J. Hunt, chief of artillery of the army, began swiftly moving about on horseback, giving some orders about the guns. Thought we, What could this mean? In a moment afterward we met a captain, pale and excited. "General, they say the enemy's infantry is advancing." We sprang into our saddles. A score of bounds brought us upon the all-seeing crest. To say that none grew pale at what we saw would not be true. Might not 6,000 men be brave and yet turn ashy when seeing a hostile horde of 18,000 less than five minutes away?

General Gibbon rode down the lines, cool and calm, and in an unimpassioned voice he said, "Do not hurry, men. Let them come up close before you fire, and then aim low." We could not be supported or reinforced until support would be too late. On the ability of two divisions of the 2nd Corps to hold the crest depended defeat or victory at Gettysburg.

The general said I had better go and tell General Meade of this advance. Great Heaven! Were my senses mad? The larger portion of A.S. Webb's brigade – my God, it was true! – there by the group of trees and the angles of the wall – was breaking from the cover of the works and, without order or reason, with no hand uplifted to check it, was falling back, a fear-stricken flock of confusion. The fate of Gettysburg hung on a spider's single thread.

A great, magnificent passion came to me at the instant. My sword that had always hung idle by my side, I drew, bright and gleaming, the symbol of command. As I met the flock of those rabbits, the red flags of the Rebels began to thicken and flaunt along the wall they had just deserted, and one was already waving over the guns. I ordered "Halt!" and "Face about!" and "Fire!" and they heard my voice, and gathered my meaning, and obeyed my commands. On some unpatriotic backs, or those not quick of comprehension, the flat of my saber fell, not lightly. And at its touch their love of country returned, and with a look at me as if I were the destroying angel they again faced the enemy.

This portion of the wall was lost to us, and the enemy gained the cover of the reverse side, where he now stormed with fire. But our men sent back as fierce a storm. Those red flags were accumulating at the wall every moment, and they maddened us as the same color does the bull. Webb's men were falling fast, and in not many minutes they would be overpowered.

Oh! where was Gibbon? Where was Hancock? Some general, anybody, with the power and the will to support this wasting, melting line? I thought of Alexander Hays on the right, but from the smoke and roar along his front it was evident he had enough on his hands. Doubleday on the left was too far off, and too slow.

Not a moment was to be lost. I found Colonel Norman J. Hall just in rear of his line, sword in hand, cool, vigilant, directing the battle of his brigade. The fire was constantly diminishing in his front.

"Webb is hotly pressed, and must have support."

"I will move my brigade at once."

In the briefest time I saw five friendly colors hurrying to the aid of the imperiled spot.

Before us the enemy was massed, his front at the stone wall. Between his front and us extended the very apex of the crest. Formation of companies and regiments was lost: companies, regiments and brigades were blended and intermixed. Although no abatement of the general conflict had at any time been appreciable now it was as if a new battle, deadlier, stormier than before, had sprung from the body of the old. The jostling, swaying lines on either side boiled and roared, two hostile billows of a fiery ocean. Thick flashes streamed from the wall; thick volleys answered from the crest.

No threats or expostulations now. Individuality was drowned in a sea of clamor, and timid men, breathing the breath of the multitude, were brave. The dead and wounded lay where they had fallen; there was no humanity for them. The men did not cheer or shout – they growled.

Now the loyal wave rolled up as if to overleap its barrier, the crest. Pistols flashed with the muskets. My "Forward to the wall!" was answered by the Rebel countercommand, "Steady, men!" and the wave swung back. Again it surged, and again it sank.

These men of Pennsylvania, on the soil of their own homesteads, the first and only ones to flee the wall, must be the first to storm it. The line sprang. The crest of the solid ground, with a great roar, heaved forward its maddened load – men, arms, smoke, fire, a fighting mass. It rolled to the wall. Flash met flash. The wall was crossed. A moment of thrusts, yells, blows, shots, an indistinguishable conflict, followed by a shout, universal, that made the welkin ring again. The enemy had been repulsed, and the bloodiest fight of the great Battle of Gettysburg was ended.

The *Richmond Enquirer:*

While the victorious shout of the gallant Virginians was still ringing in my ears, I turned my eyes to the left, and there, all over the plain, in utmost confusion, was scattered Pettigrew's strong division. Their line was broken; they were flying, panic-stricken, to the rear. The gallant Pettigrew was wounded, but he still was vainly striving to rally his men. The moving mass rushed pell-mell to the rear, and Pickett was left alone to contend with the hordes of the enemy now pouring in upon him on every side. General Garnett fell, killed by a Minie ball, and Kemper, the brave and chivalrous, was mortally wounded. Now the enemy moved strong flanking bodies of infantry around and rapidly gained Pickett's rear.

The order was given to fall back, and our men commenced the movement, doggedly contending for every inch of ground. The enemy pressed heavily our retreating line, and many noble spirits who had passed safely through the fiery ordeal of the advance and charge fell on the right and on the left. Armistead was wounded and left in the enemy's hands. At this critical moment the shattered remnant of Ambrose R. Wright's Georgia brigade was moved forward to cover their retreat, and the fight closed here.

That night Pickett wrote again to his beloved:

My brave boys were so full of hope and confident of victory as I led them forth! Over on Cemetery Ridge the Federals beheld a scene which has never previously been enacted – an army forming in line of battle in full view, under their very eyes – charging across a space nearly a mile in length, pride and glory soon to be crushed by an overwhelming heartbreak.

Well, it is all over now. The awful rain of shot and shell was a sob – a gasp.

I can still hear them cheering as I gave the order, "Forward!" the thrill of their joyous voices as they called out, "We'll follow you, Marse George, we'll follow you!" On, how faithfully they followed me on – on – to their death, and I led them on – on – on – Oh God!

I can't write you a love letter today, my Sally. But for you, my darling, I would rather, a million times rather, sleep in an unknown grave.

Your sorrowing
Soldier

The battle at Gettysburg lasted three days. Lee lost 3,903 killed, 18,735 wounded (including mortally wounded and captured), and 5,425 missing, of a total 75,000 engaged; Meade's losses were 3,155 killed, 14,529 wounded, and 5,365 missing, of a total of 88,289 engaged. Almost immediately arguments started over who should have done what, and why Lee failed. One man summed it up:

The plain truth is this: Lee blundered, Stuart blundered, Longstreet, Ewell and Pickett blundered. The whole campaign was a blunder, but Lee was the only man magnanimous enough to bear the burden. Here we find the defensive general selecting his own battleground. General

Lee should have declined battle, and drawn the Federal commander into the open where the ground was equal and victory more certain.

Lacerated and bleeding, the devoted army recrossed the Potomac; but Gettysburg was its Waterloo.

VICKSBURG - THE GREAT BATTLE OF THE WEST

Between Cairo, Illinois, and the Gulf of Mexico, the Mississippi River meanders over a course nearly 1,000 miles long. During the Civil War, control of this stretch of the river was of vital importance to the Federal government. Command of the Mississippi would allow uninterrupted passage of Union troops and supplies into the South. It would also isolate the States of Texas and Arkansas and most of Louisiana, comprising nearly half the land area of the Confederacy and a region upon which the South depended heavily for supplies and soldiers.

From the beginning of the war in 1861, the Confederacy, to protect this vital lifeline, erected fortifications at strategic points along the river. Federal forces, however, fighting their way southward from Illinois and northward from the Gulf of Mexico, steadily captured post after post, until by late summer of 1862 only Vicksburg and Port Hudson posed any major constraints to the Union domination of the Mississippi.

Of the two posts, Vicksburg was the strongest and most important. It sat on a high bluff overlooking a bend in the river, protected by artillery batteries along the riverfront and by a maze of swamps and bayous to the north and south. President Lincoln called Vicksburg "the key" and believed that "the war can never be brought to a close until that key is in our pocket." So far the city had defied Union efforts to force it into submission.

In October 1862, Ulysses S. Grant was appointed commander of the Department of the Tennessee and charged with clearing the Mississippi of Confederate resistance. That same month, Lt. Gen. John C. Pemberton, a West Point graduate and a Pennsylvanian by birth, assumed command of the approximately 50,000 widely scattered Confederate troops defending the Mississippi. His orders were to keep the river open. Vicksburg became the focus of military operations for both men.

During the winter of 1862-63, Grant conducted a series of amphibious operations (called the Bayou Expeditions) aimed at reducing Vicksburg. All of them failed. By spring Grant had decided to march his army of approximately 45,000 men down the west (Louisiana) bank of the Mississippi, cross the river well below Vicksburg, and then swing into position to attack the city from the south.

On March 31, 1863, Grant moved his army south from its encampments at Milliken's Bend, 20 miles northwest of Vicksburg. By April 28, it was camped at Hard Times on the Mississippi above Grand Gulf. On the 29th, Adm. David D. Porter's gunboats bombarded the Confederate forts at Grand Gulf to prepare the way for a crossing, but the attack was repulsed. Undaunted, Grant marched his troops a little further south and, on April 30, stormed across unopposed at Bruinsburg. Striking rapidly eastward to secure the bridgehead, the Northerners met elements of Pemberton's Confederate forces near Port Gibson on May 1. The Rebels fought a gallant holding action, but they were overwhelmed and fell back toward Vicksburg. After meeting and defeating a small Confederate force near Raymond on May 12, Grant's troops attacked and captured Jackson, the State capital, on May 14, scattering the Southern defenders.

Turning his army westward, Grant moved toward Vicksburg along the line of the Southern Railroad of Mississippi. At Champion Hill on May 16 and at Big Black River Bridge on May 17, his soldiers attacked and overwhelmed Pemberton's disorganized troops, driving them back into the Vicksburg fortifications. By May 18, advanced units of the Federal army were approaching the bristling Confederate defenses.

A Union corporal by the name of Byers recorded the battle at Champion Hill:

It was a very hot day, and we had marched hard, slept little and rested none. Among the magnolias on Champion's Hill the enemy turned on us. We were in that most trying position of soldiers, being fired on without permission to return the shots. A good many men were falling, and the wounded were being borne to the rear, close to an old well whose wooden curb seemed to offer the only protection.

"Colonel, move your men a little by the left flank," said a quiet though commanding voice.

On looking around, I saw immediately behind us Grant, the commander in chief, mounted on a beautiful bay mare and followed by perhaps half a dozen of his staff. For some reason he dismounted, and most of his officers were sent off, bearing orders, to other quarters of the field. It was Grant under fire.

The rattling musketry increased on our front and grew louder, too, on the left flank. Grant had led his horse to the left and thus kept near the company to which I belonged. He now stood leaning complacently against his favorite steed, smoking the stump of a cigar. His was the only horse near the line and must, naturally, have attracted some of the enemy's fire. I am sure everyone who recognized him wished him away; but there he stood – clear, calm and immovable. I was close enough to see his features. Earnest they were, but sign of inward movement there was none. It was the same cool, calculating face I had seen before; the same careful, half-cynical face I afterward saw busied with affairs of state.

Whatever there may have been in his feelings there was no effort to conceal; there was no pretense, no trick; whatever the face was, it was natural. A man close by me had the bones of his leg shattered by a ball and was being helped to the rear. His cries of pain attracted Grant's attention, and I noticed the curious though sympathizing shades that crossed his quiet face as the bleeding soldier seemed to look toward him for help.

We had not waited many minutes when an orderly dashed up to Grant and handed him a communication. Then followed an order to move rapidly to the left and into the road. The fire grew heavier, and the air seemed too hot to be borne. I had been selected by the colonel to act as sergeant major, and I now ran behind and along the line, shouting at the top of my voice, "Fix bayonets!" The orders were not heard, and we were charging the enemy's position with bare muskets. A moment more and we were at the top of the ascent and among thinner wood and larger trees. The enemy had fallen back a few rods, forming a solid line parallel with our own, and now commenced in good earnest the fighting of the day. We had forty rounds each in our cartridge boxes, and probably nine-tenths of them were fired in that half-hour.

"Stop! Halt! Surrender!" cried a hundred Rebels, whose voices seem to ring in my ears to this very day. But there was no stopping and no surrender. We ran and ran manfully. It was terribly hot, a hot afternoon under a Mississippi sun, and an enemy on flank and rear shouting and firing. The grass, the stones, the bushes, seemed melting under the shower of bullets that was following us to the rear. We tried to halt and tried to form. It was no use. Again we ran, and harder, and farther, and faster. We passed over the very spot where, half an hour before, we had left Grant leaning on his bay mare and smoking his cigar. Like ten thousand starving and howling wolves the enemy pursued, closer and closer, and we scarcely dared look back to face the fate that seemed certain.

Grant had seen it all, and in less time than I can tell it a line of cannon had been thrown across our path, which, as soon a we had passed, belched grapeshot and canister into the faces of our pursuers. They stopped, they turned, and they too ran and left their dead side by side with our own. Our lines protected by the batteries, rallied and followed, and Champion's Hill was won, and with it was won the door to Vicksburg.

Grant passed along the lines after the fight as we stood in the narrow roads. Every hat was in the air, and the men cheered till they were hoarse. But speechless and almost without a bow he pushed on past, like an embarrassed man hurrying to get away from some defeat. Once he stopped near the colors and without addressing himself to anyone in particular, said, "Well done!"

The Confederates retreated and occupied entrenchments in front of the Big Black River. A man by the name of Bevier narrates:

The Big Black River formed an elbow in the rear of the army; the fortifications constituted a crescent in its front.

Lee invaded Maryland and Pennsylvania in the summer of 1863. The climactic battle was the three-day conflict at Gettysburg, in which the Union army held good defensive ground and eventually beat off the valiant but futile Confederate assaults. This engraving shows a Union countercharge at Cemetery Hill. (Library of Congress)

The only means of crossing the stream was over a railroad bridge.

The 1st Missouri Brigade occupied the space to the right of the railroad, General Martin E. Green's brigade on the extreme left, General J.C. Vaughn's brigade of Tennesseeans and Mississippians in the center, while Stevenson's division on the opposite side of the river was held in reserve. Captain Landis' battery was placed on the western bluffs.

At daylight the enemy opened their Parrott guns, which were briskly replied to. At 9:00 a.m. they made a determined assault, which was easily repulsed. Shortly after this General Sherman's whole corps in solid columns, six lines deep, advanced against our left wing. The veteran troops of Green's brigade received them with a withering fire and deadly aim, producing great gaps in their array and for a time staggering the assault. At this moment Vaughn's brigade became panic-stricken, broke, and fled in confusion, without firing a gun or striking a blow. On perceiving this, the Federals rallied and at double-quick darted past Green's men and occupied the place made vacant by the flying Mississippians.

The Yankees now occupied our center. Bowen's division was cut entirely in two, and Green's brigade was nearly surrounded and more than half of it captured. The rest threw their arms into the river and swam across – the only means of escape left to them.

Although the enemy immediately opened an enfilading fire on the 1st Brigade, it did not move from its rifle pits until ordered, and then they started with reluctance. But when they found a whole corps of the enemy making a race with them for the bridge, they "let out" and showed that they were as fleet-footed as they were courageous. A few of the artillerists remained at their pieces, loading and firing until they were captured.

By nightfall the fugitive and disordered troops were pouring into the streets of Vicksburg, and the citizens beheld with dismay the army that had gone out to fight for their safety returning to them in the character of a wild, tumultuous and mutinous mob.

Believing that the battles of Champion Hill and Big Black River Bridge had broken Confederate morale, Grant immediately scheduled an assault on the Vicksburg lines. The first attack took place against the Stockade Redan on May 19. It failed. A second attack, launched on the morning of May 22, was also repulsed.

Realizing that it was useless to expend further lives in attempts to take the city by storm, Grant reluctantly began formal siege operations. Batteries of artillery were established to hammer the Confederate fortifications from the land side, while Admiral Porter's gunboats cut off communications and blasted the city from the river. By the end of June, with little hope of relief and no chance to break out of the Federal cordon, Pemberton knew that it was only a matter of time before he must "capitulate upon the best attainable terms." On the afternoon of July 3, Pemberton met with Grant to discuss terms for the surrender of Vicksburg.

Grant wrote about his siege plans:

I . . . determined on a regular siege. With the navy holding the river, the investment of Vicksburg was complete. The enemy was limited in supplies of food, men and munitions of war. These could not last always. The work to be done was to make our position as strong against the enemy as his was against us. The problem was complicated by our wanting our line as near to that of the enemy as possible. We had but four engineer officers with us. We had no siege guns except six 32-pounders, and there were none in the West to draw from. Admiral Porter, however, supplied us with a battery of navy guns of large calibre and, with these and the field artillery used in the campaign, the siege began.

In no place were our lines more than 600 yards from the enemy. It was necessary, therefore, to cover our men by something more than the ordinary parapet. Sandbags were placed along the tops of the parapets far enough apart to make loopholes for musketry. On top of these logs were put. By these means the men were enabled to walk about erect when off duty.

From the twenty-third of May the work of fortifying and pushing forward had been steadily progressing. At three points a sap was run up to the enemy's parapet, and by the twenty-fifth of June we had it undermined and the mine charged. The enemy had countermined but did not succeed in reaching our mine. At times the enemy threw over hand grenades, and often our men, catching them in their hands, returned them.

On the twenty-fifth of June at three o'clock, all being ready, our mine was exploded. A heavy artillery fire all along the line had been ordered to open with the explosion. The effect was to blow the top of the hill off and make a crater where it had stood. The breach, however, was not sufficient to enable us to pass a column through. In fact, the enemy had thrown up a line farther back. A few men were thrown into the air, some of them coming down on our side still alive. I remember one colored man, at work underground when the explosion took place, who was thrown to our side. He was not much hurt but terribly frightened. Someone asked him how high he had gone up. "Dunno, massa, but t'ink 'bout t'ree mile."

Another mine was exploded on the first of July, but no attempt to charge was made, the experience of the twenty-fifth admonishing us.

From this time forward the work of mining and pushing our position nearer to the enemy was prosecuted with vigor, but I determined to explode no more mines until we were ready to explode a number at different points and assault immediately after.

By the first of July our approaches had reached the enemy's ditch at a number of places. Orders were given to make all preparations for an assault on the sixth of July.

Mrs. James Loughborough, the wife of a Confederate soldier, who had come to Vicksburg to be with her husband, wrote of life during the siege:

Very few houses are without evidence of the bombardment, and yet the inhabitants live in their homes happy and contented, not knowing what moment the houses may be rent over their heads by the explosion of a shell.

"Ah!" said I to a friend, "How is it possible you live here?"

"After one is accustomed to the change," she answered, "we do not mind it. But becoming accustomed – that is the trial."

I was reminded of the poor man in an infected district who was met by a traveler and asked, "How do you live here?" "Sir, we die," was the laconic reply.

One night I was sleeping profoundly when the deep boom of the signal cannon awoke me. I sprang from my bed and went out on the veranda. The river was illuminated by large fires on the bank, and we plainly could discern huge black masses floating down with the current, now and then belching forth fire from their sides. We could hear the gallop of couriers on the paved streets. The rapid firing from the boats, the roar of the Confederate batteries, made a new and fearful scene to me. The boats were rapidly nearing the lower batteries, and the shells were beginning to fly unpleasantly near. The gentlemen urged the ladies to go down into a cave at the back of the house. While I hesitated, a shell exploded near by. Fear instantly decided me, and I ran. Breathless and terrified, I found the entrance and ran in, having left one of my slippers on the hillside.

The cave was an excavation in the earth the size of a large room, high enough for the tallest person to stand perfectly erect, provided with comfortable seats and altogether quite a large and habitable abode.

When the danger was over, we returned to the house and from the veranda looked on a burning boat, the only one, so far as we could ascertain, that had been injured. It was found that very few of the Confederate guns had been discharged at all. The fuses recently sent from Richmond had been found this night, of all others, to be defective.

Sunday, May 17, as we were dressing for church, we heard the loud booming of cannon. We passed groups of anxious men with troubled faces, but very few soldiers. Gloom seemed to hang over the men: a sorrowful waiting for tidings that all knew would tell of disaster. Soon wagons came rattling down the streets; now and then a worn and dusty soldier would be seen passing; then straggler after straggler came by; finally groups of soldiers, worn and dusty with a long march.

"What can be the matter?" we all cried.

"We are whipped, and the Federals are after us."

"It's all Pem's fault," said an awkward, long-limbed, weary-looking man. "We would ha' fit well, but General Pemberton came up and said, 'Stand your ground, boys! Your General Pemberton is with you.' And then, bless you, lady, the next we seed of him, he was sitting on his horse behind a house! And when we seed that, we thought 'tain't no use."

The caves were plainly becoming a necessity, as some persons had been killed by fragments of shells. The room that I had so lately slept in had been struck and a large hole made in the ceiling. Terror-stricken, we remained crouched in the cave while shell after shell followed one another in quick succession. My heart stood still as we would hear reports from the guns and the rushing and fearful sound of the shell as it came toward us. As it neared, the noise became more deafening; the air was full of the rushing sound; pains darted through my temples; my ears were bursting. And as it exploded, the report flashed through my head like an electric shock, leaving me in a quiet state of terror.

Even the dogs seemed to share the general fear. They would be seen in the midst of the noise to gallop up the street, and then to return, as if fear had maddened them. On hearing the descent of a shell, they would dart aside – then as it exploded, sit down and howl in the most pitiful manner.

One evening I heard the most heart-rending screams and moans. I was told that a mother had taken a child into a cave about a hundred yards from us and laid it on its bed. A mortar shell entered the earth about it, crushing in the upper part of the little sleeping head.

A servant brought me one day a present from an officer that was acceptable indeed: two large, yellow, ripe June apples, sealed in a large envelope. Another gentleman sent me four large slices of ham. While we were conversing, my little two-year-old daughter quietly secured them. When she had finished eating, she turned around to me, saying, "Mamma, it's so dood!" – the first intimation I had that my portion had disappeared. Fruits and vegetables were not to be procured at any price.

Already the men in the rifle pits were on half rations. Many of them ate it all at one and the next day fasted, preferring, as they said, to have one good meal. I often remarked how cheerfully the soldiers bore the hardships of the siege. I would see them pass, whistling and chatting pleasantly, as around them the balls and shells flew thick.

About this time the town was aroused by the arrival of a courier from General Johnson, who brought private dispatches to General Pemberton and letters to the inhabitants from friends without. His manner of entering the city was singular: he took a skiff in the Yazoo and proceeded to its confluence with the Mississippi, where he tied it up. At dark he took off his clothing, placed his dispatches securely within them, bound the package firmly to a plank and, going into the river, sustained his head above water by holding to the plank. In this manner he floated through the fleet to Vicksburg.

One evening I noticed one of the horses tied in the ravine writhing and struggling as if in pain. He had been very badly wounded in the flank by a Minie ball. The poor creature's agony was dreadful: he would reach his head up as far as possible into the tree to which he was tied, and cling with his mouth, while his neck and body quivered with pain. Every motion, instead of being violent as most horses' would have been when wounded, had a stately grace of eloquent suffering that is indescribable. How I wanted to go to him and pat and sooth him! His halter was taken off and he was turned free. He went to a tree, leaned his body against it and moaned, with half-closed eyes, shivering frequently throughout his huge body as if the pain were too great to bear.

Then he would turn his head entirely around and gaze at the group of soldiers that stood pitying near, as if he were looking for human sympathy. The master refused to have him shot, hoping he would recover, but the noble black was doomed. Becoming restless with the pain, the poor brute staggered blindly on. My eyes filled with tears, for he fell with a weary moan, the bright intelligent eyes turned still on the men who had been his comrades in many a battle.

Poor fellow, you were far beyond human sympathy! In the midst of all the falling shells could not one reach him, giving him peace and death? I saw an ax handed to one of the bystanders and suddenly turned away from the scene. The glossy black body was being taken out from our sight, to be replaced by new sufferings and to be forgotten in new incidents.

Ulysses S. Grant:

On the third day of July about ten o'clock white flags appeared on a portion of the Rebel works. Hostilities ceased at once. Soon two persons were seen coming toward our lines bearing a white flag. They proved to be General Bowen and Colonel L.M. Montgomery, aide-de-camp to Pemberton, bearing a letter to me proposing an armistice.

The news soon spread to all parts of the command. The troops felt that their weary marches and hard fighting were at last at an end.

I sent back an oral message saying that, if Pemberton desired it, I would meet him in front of McPherson's corps at three o'clock that afternoon. At the appointed time Pemberton appeared at the point suggested, accompanied by the same officers who had borne his letter of the morning. Several officers of my staff accompanied me. Our place of meeting was on a hillside within a few hundred feet of the Rebel line. Near by stood a stunted oak tree, which was made historical by the event. It was but a short time before the last vestige of its body, root and limb, had disappeared, the fragments having been taken as trophies.

Pemberton proposed that the Confederate army should be allowed to march out with the honors of war, carrying their small arms and field artillery. This was promptly and unceremoniously rejected. The interview here ended, I agreeing, however, to send a letter giving final terms by ten o'clock that night.

When I returned to my headquarters I sent for all my corps and division commanders. I informed them that I was ready to hear any suggestions but would hold the power of deciding entirely in my own hands. Against the general and almost unanimous judgment of the council I sent the following letter to Pemberton:

"You will be allowed to march out, the officers taking with them their side arms and clothing, and the field and cavalry officers one horse each. The rank and file will be allowed all their clothing, but no other property."

Had I insisted on an unconditional surrender, there would have been over 30,000 men to transport to Cairo, very much to the inconvenience of the Army of the Mississippi. Thence the prisoners would have had to be transported by rail to Washington or Baltimore. Pemberton's army was largely composed of men whose homes were in the Southwest; I knew many of them were tired of the war and would go home.

Pemberton promptly accepted these terms.

Vicksburg officially surrendered at 10 a.m. on July 4, 1863. When Port Hudson surrendered five days later, the great Northern objective of the war in the West – the opening of the Mississippi River and the severing of the Confederacy – was at last realized. For the first time since the war began, the Mississippi was free of Confederate troops and fortifications. As President Lincoln put it, "The Father of Waters again goes unvexed to the sea."

THE BATTLE OF CHICKAMAUGA

On Tennessee fields and hills, Union and Confederate armies clashed during the fall of 1863 in some of the hardest fighting of the Civil War. The prize was Chattanooga, key rail center and gateway to the heart of the Confederacy. The campaign that brought the armies here began late in June 1863, when Gen. William S. Rosecrans' Army of the Cumberland, almost 60,000 strong, moved from Murfreesboro, Tennessee, against Gen. Braxton Bragg's 43,000 Confederates dug in 20 miles to the southwest defending the road to Chattanooga. Six months earlier, these same armies had clashed at Stones River where, after a three-day struggle, the Confederates had retreated. Now, once more, through a series of skillful marches, Rosecrans forced the Southerners to withdraw into Chattanooga. There Bragg dug in again, guarding the Tennessee River crossing northeast of the city, where he expected Rosecrans to attack. But early in September the Federals crossed the Tennessee well below Chattanooga and again Bragg had to withdraw southward.

Eluding his Federal pursuers, Bragg concentrated his forces at LaFayette, Georgia, 26 miles south of Chattanooga. Here reinforcements from East Tennessee, Virginia, and Mississippi swelled his ranks to more than 66,000 men. Twice he tried unsuccessfully to destroy isolated segments of Rosecrans' army. Then, on September 18, hoping to wedge his troops between the Federals and Chattanooga, Bragg posted his army on the west bank of Chickamauga Creek along a line from Reed's Bridge to just opposite Lee and Gordon's Mill.

Charles Dana described the situation with the Army of the Cumberland the day before the battle:

By noon of September 18th the concentration was practically complete. Our army then lay up and down the valley, with West Chickamauga Creek in front of the greater part of the line. The left was held by Crittenden, the center by [*General George H.*] *Thomas, and the right by McCook, whose troops were now all in the valley except one brigade. The army had not concentrated any too soon, for that very afternoon the enemy appeared on our left, and a considerable engagement occurred. It was said at headquarters that a battle was certain the next day. The only point Rosecrans had not determined at five o'clock on the afternoon of the 17th was whether to make a night march and fall on Bragg at daylight or to await his onset.*

But that night it became pretty clear to all that Bragg's plan was to push by our left into Chattanooga. This compelled another rapid movement by the left down the Chickamauga. By a tiresome night march Thomas moved down behind Crittenden and below Lee and Gordon's Mills, taking position on our extreme left. Crittenden followed, connecting with Thomas's right, and thus taking position in the center. McCook's corps also extended downstream to the left. . . . These movements were hurriedly made, and the troops, especially those of Thomas, were very much exhausted by their efforts to get into position.

Fighting began shortly after dawn on September 19, when Union infantry encountered Confederate cavalry at Jay's Mill. This brought on a general battle that spread south for nearly four miles. Dana narrates:

About nine o'clock . . . at Crawfish Spring, where the general headquarters were, we heard firing on our left, and reports at once came in that the battle had begun there. Bragg being in command of the enemy. Thomas had barely headed the Confederates off from Chattanooga. We remained at Crawfish Springs on this day until after one o'clock, waiting for the full proportions of the conflict to develop. When it became evident that the battle was being fought entirely on our left, Rosecrans removed his headquarters nearer to the scene, taking a little house near Lee and Gordon's Mills, known as the Widow Glenn's. Although closer to the battle, we could see no more of it here than at Crawfish Springs, the conflict being fought altogether in a thick forest, and being invisible to outsiders.

. . . It was not until after dark that firing ceased and final reports began to come in. From these we found that the enemy had been defeated in his attempt to turn and crush our left flank and secure possession of the Chattanooga roads, but that he was not wholly defeated, for he still held his ground in several places, and was preparing, it was believed, to renew the battle the next day.

That evening Rosecrans decided that if Bragg did not retreat he would renew the fight at daylight, and a council of war was held at our headquarters at the Widow Glenn's, to which all the corps and division commanders were summoned. . . . Rosecrans began by asking each of the corps commanders for a report on the condition of his troops and of the position they occupied; also for his opinion of what was to be done. Each proposition was discussed by the entire council as it was made. General Thomas was so tired – he had not slept at all the night before, and he had been in battle all day – that he went to sleep every minute. Every time Rosecrans spoke to him he would straighten up and answer, but he always said the same thing, "I would strengthen the left," and then he would be asleep, sitting up in his chair. General Rosecrans, to the proposition to strengthen the left, made always the same reply, "Where are we going to take it from?"

After the discussion was ended, Rosecrans gave his orders for the disposition of the troops on the following day. Thomas's corps was to remain on the left with his line somewhat drawn in, but substantially as he was at the close of the day. McCook was to close on Thomas and cover the position at Widow Glenn's, and Crittenden was to have two divisions in reserve near the junction of McCook's and Thomas's line, to be able to succor either. These orders were written for each corps commander. They were also read in the presence of all, and the plans fully explained. Finally, after everything had been said, hot coffee was brought in, and then McCook was called upon to sing the Hebrew Maiden. McCook sang the song, and the council broke up and the generals went away.

This was about midnight, and, as I was very tired, I lay down on the floor to sleep, beside Captain Horace Porter, who was at that time Rosecrans' chief of ordnance. There were cracks in the floor of the Widow Glenn's house, and the wind blew up under us. We would go to sleep, and then the wind would come up so cold through the cracks that it would wake us up, and we would turn over together to keep warm.

Federal General J.S. Fullerton:

The morning of Sunday, the 20th, opened with a cloudless sky, but a fog had come up from the warm water of the Chickamauga and hung over the battle-field until 9 o'clock. A silence of desertion was in the front. This quiet continued till nearly 10 o'clock; then, as the peaceful tones of the churchbells, rolling over the land from the east, reached the meridian of Chickamauga, they were made dissonant by the murderous roar of the artillery of Bishop Polk, who was opening the battle on Thomas's front [the Federal left]. Granger, who had been ordered at all hazards to hold fast where he was, listened and grew impatient. Shortly before 10 o'clock, calling my attention to a great column of dust moving from our front toward the point from which came the sound of battle, he said, "They are concentrating over there. That is where we ought to be." The corps flag marked his headquarters in an open field near the Ringgold road. He walked up and down in front of his flag, nervously pulling his beard. Once stopping, he said, "Why the hell does Rosecrans keep me here? There is nothing in front of us now. There is the battle" – pointing in the direction of Thomas. Every moment the sounds of battle grew louder, while the many columns of dust rolling together here mingled with the smoke that hung over the scene.

At 11 o'clock, with Granger, I climbed a high hayrick nearby. We sat there for ten minutes listening and watching. Then Granger jumped up, thrust his glass into its case, and exclaimed with an oath:

"I am going to Thomas, orders or no orders!"

"And if you go," I replied, "it may bring disaster to the army and you to a court-martial."

"There's nothing in our front now but ragtag, bobtail cavalry," he replied. "Don't you see Bragg is piling his whole army on Thomas? I am going to his assistance."

. . . Thomas was nearly four miles away. The day had now grown very warm, yet the troops marched rapidly over the narrow road, which was covered ankle-deep with dust that rose in suffocating clouds. Completely enveloped in it, the moving column swept along like a desert sandstorm. Two miles from the point of starting, and three-quarters of a mile from the left of the road, the enemy's skirmishers and a section of artillery opened fire on us from an open wood. This force had worked round Thomas's left, and was then partly in his rear. Granger halted to feel them. Soon becoming convinced that it was only a large party of observation, he again started his column and pushed rapidly forward.

A little farther on we were met by a staff-officer sent by General Thomas to discover whether we were friends or enemies; he did not know whence friends could be coming, and the enemy appeared to be approaching from all directions. All of this shattered Army of the Cumberland left on the field was with Thomas; but not more than one-forth of the men of the army who went into battle at the opening were there. Thomas's loss in killed and wounded during the two days had been dreadful. As his men dropped out his line was contracted to half its length. Now its flanks were bent back, conforming to ridges shaped like a horse-shoe.

On the part of Thomas and his men there was no thought but that of fighting. He was a soldier who had never retreated, who had never been defeated. He stood immovable, the "Rock of Chickamauga." Never had soldiers greater love for a commander. He imbued them with his spirit, and their confidence in him was sublime.

To the right of Thomas's line was a gorge, then a high ridge, nearly at right angles thereto, running east and west. . . . Confederates . . . were passing through the gorge. . . ; divisions were forming on this ridge for an assault; to their left the guns of a battery were being unlimbered for an enfilading fire. There was not a man to send against the force on the ridge, none to oppose this impending assault. The enemy saw the approaching colors of the Reserve Corps and hesitated.

At 1 o'clock Granger shook hands with Thomas. Something was said about forming to fight to the right and rear.

"Those men must be driven back," said Granger, pointing to the gorge and ridge. "Can you do it?" asked Thomas.

"Yes. My men are fresh, and they are just the fellows for that work. They are raw troops, and they don't know any better than to charge up there."

Granger quickly sent Aleshire's battery of 3-inch rifle guns which he brought up to Thomas's left to assist in repelling another assault about to be made on the Kelly farm front. Whitaker's and Mitchell's brigades under Steedman were wheeled into position and projected against the enemy in the gorge and on the ridge. With ringing cheers they advanced in two lines by double-quick – over open fields, through weeds waist-high, through a little valley, then up the ridge. The enemy opened on them first with artillery, then with a murderous musketry fire. When well up the ridge the men, almost exhausted, were halted for breath. They lay on the ground two or three minutes, then came the command, "Forward!" Brave, bluff old Steedman, with a regimental flag in his hand, led the way. On went the lines, firing as they ran and bravely receiving a deadly and continuous fire from the enemy on the summit. The Confederates began to break and in another minute were flying down the southern slope of the ridge. In twenty minutes from the beginning of the charge the ridge had been carried. . . .

The enemy massed a force to retake the ridge. They came before our men had rested; twice they assaulted and were driven back. During one assault, as the first line came within range of our muskets, it halted, apparently hesitating, when we saw a colonel seize a flag, wave it over his head, and rush forward. The whole line instantly caught his enthusiasm, and with a wild cheer followed, only to be hurled back again. Our men ran down the ridge in pursuit. In the midst of a group of Confederate dead and wounded they found the brave colonel dead, the flag he carried spread over him where he fell.

Soon after 5 o'clock Thomas rode to the left of his line, leaving Granger the ranking officer at the center. The ammunition of both Thomas's and Granger's commands was now about exhausted. . . . The cartridge-boxes of both our own and the enemy's dead within reach had been emptied by our men. When it was not yet 6 o'clock, and Thomas was still on the left of his line, Brannan rushed up to Granger, saying, "The enemy are forming for another assault; we have not another round of ammunition – what shall we do?" "Fix bayonets and go for them," was the reply. Along the whole line ran the order, "Fix bayonets." On came the enemy – our men were lying down. "Forward," was sounded. In one instant they were on their feet. Forward they went to meet the charge. The enemy fled. So impetuous was this countercharge that one regiment, with empty muskets and empty cartridge-boxes, broke through the enemy's line, which, closing in their rear, carried them off as in the undertow.

One more feeble assault was made by the enemy; then the day closed and the battle for Chickamauga was over.

After dark, Thomas withdrew his men from the field. The defeat forced the Union troops to retreat into Chattanooga. The Confederates pursued, occupying Missionary Ridge, Lookout Mountain, and Chattanooga Valley. By placing artillery on the heights overlooking the river and blocking the roads and rail lines, the Southerners prevented Federal supplies from entering the city. Unless something was done to break the Confederate stranglehold, Rosecrans' army must surrender or starve.

Pickett's Charge at Gettysburg (shown in this field sketch by Alfred Waud) was the high-mark of the Confederate advance on the North and has remained a symbol of inspiring but unsuccessful gallantry. (Library of Congress)

Aware of Rosecrans' plight, Federal authorities in Washington ordered reinforcement to his relief. Gen. Joseph Hooker, who had made his name at Antietam and then disgraced it at Chancellorsville, came in late October with 20,000 men, and Gen. William T. Sherman brought in 16,000 more from Mississippi in mid-November. Thomas replaced Rosecrans as head of the Army of the Cumberland, and Gen. Ulysses S. Grant assumed overall command.

Within days of Grant's arrival at Chattanooga in October, the situation began to change dramatically. On October 28, Federal troops opened a short supply route from Bridgeport, Alabama. On November 23, Thomas' men attacked and routed the Confederates from Orchard Knob. On the 24th, aided by a heavy fog that enshrouded the slopes of Lookout Mountain during most of the day, Hooker's soldiers pushed the Confederates out of their defenses around the Cravens House. On November 25, with most of Bragg's army now concentrated on Missionary Ridge, Grant launched Sherman's troops against the Confederate right flank and sent Hooker's men from Lookout Mountain to attack the Confederate left. Thomas' soldiers, in the center at Orchard Knob, were held in reserve.

Hooker was delayed crossing Chattanooga Creek and the Confederates halted Sherman's attack. To relieve the pressure on Sherman, Grant ordered Thomas' Army of the Cumberland to assault the rifle pits at the base of Missionary Ridge. This was quickly accomplished. Then, without orders, Thomas' men scaled the heights in one of the great charges of the war. The Confederate line collapsed, and Bragg's troops fled to the rear. During the night they retreated into Georgia. The siege and battle of Chattanooga were over, and Union armies now controlled the city and nearly all of Tennessee. The next spring, Sherman used Chattanooga for his base as he started his march to Atlanta and the sea.

Back in the East, on November 19, President Abraham Lincoln addressed a crowd of people gathered to dedicate the Gettysburg National Cemetery. Mr. Lincoln was not the main speaker. He followed the great orator Edward Everett, whose words were recorded but not remembered. The President's speech, barely a few moments in length, is probably the finest ever written:

Four score and seven years ago our fathers brought forth on this continent, a new nation, conceived in Liberty, and dedicated to the proposition that all men are created equal.

Now we are engaged in a great civil war, testing whether that nation, or any nation so conceived and so dedicated, can long endure. We are met on a great battle-field of that war. We have come to dedicate a portion of that field, as a final resting place for those who here gave their lives that that nation might live. It is altogether fitting and proper that we should do this.

But, in a larger sense, we can not dedicate – we can not consecrate – we can not hallow – this ground. The brave men, living and dead, who struggled here, have consecrated it, far above our poor power to add or detract. The world will little note, nor long remember what we say here, but it can never forget what they did here. It is for us the living, rather, to be dedicated here to the unfinished work which they who fought here have thus far so nobly advanced. It is rather for us to be here dedicated to the great task remaining before us – that from these honored dead we take increased devotion to that cause for which they gave the last full measure of devotion – that we here highly resolve that these dead shall not have died in vain – that this nation, under God, shall have a new birth of freedom – and that government of the people, by the people, for the people, shall not perish from the earth.

CHAPTER 5
1864

1864 THE WILDERNESS

On March 8, 1864, Ulysses S. Grant was appointed Lieutenant General and given command of all the Union forces. It was the first such commission in the United States Army. Grant wasted no time in drafting a plan to end the war. He wrote:

When I assumed command of all the armies, the situation was about this: the Mississippi River was ours from St. Louis to New Orleans. East of the Mississippi we held substantially all of the state of Tennessee. Virginia north of the Rapidan and east of the Blue Ridge was also held. On the seacoast we had Fort Monroe and Norfolk in Virginia, and other ports or islands all the way to Key West. The balance of the Southern territory, an empire in extent, was still in the hands of the enemy.

In the East the opposing forces stood in substantially the same relations toward each other as when the war began: both were between the Federal and Confederate capitals.

That portion of the Army of the Potomac not engaged in guarding lines of communications was on the northern bank of the Rapidan. The Army of Northern Virginia confronted it on the opposite bank.

My plan now was to concentrate all the forces possible against the Confederate armies. There were but two – the army of Northern Virginia, General Robert E. Lee commanding; the second, under General Joseph E. Johnston (who had succeeded Bragg) at Dalton, Georgia, opposed to Sherman, who was still at Chattanooga. Besides, the Confederates had to guard the Shenandoah Valley, a great storehouse to feed their armies from. Forrest, a brave and intrepid cavalry general, was in the West with a large force, making a larger command necessary to hold Middle and West Tennessee.

Since our forces could guard their special trusts as well when advancing from them as when remaining at them, I arranged for a simultaneous movement all along the line. Sherman was to move from Chattanooga, Johnston's army and Atlanta being his objective points. George Crook, commanding in West Virginia, had the Virginia and Tennessee Railroad as his objective. Sigel in the Shenandoah Valley was to advance up the valley, covering the North from an invasion through that channel. Butler was to advance by the James River, having Richmond and Petersburg as his objective. Banks in the Department of the Gulf had Mobile as his objective.

By April 27, 1864, spring had so far advanced as to justify me in fixing May 4 for the great move. Meade was notified to bring his troops forward. On the following day Butler was directed to move the same day and get as far up the James River as possible. Sherman was directed to get his forces ready to advance on the 5th. Sigel was notified to move in conjunction with the others.

This was the plan, and I will now endeavor to give the method of its execution, outlining first the operations of the detached columns.

Banks failed to accomplish what he has been sent to do on the Red River, and eliminated the use of 40,000 veteran troops. Sigel's record is almost equally brief. He moved out according to program but just when I was hoping to hear of good work being done in the valley I received instead the following announcement from Halleck: "Sigel is in full retreat on Strasburg. He will do nothing but run; never did anything else." The enemy had intercepted him at New Market and handled him roughly.

Butler embarked at Fort Monroe with all his command and seized City Point and Bermuda Hundred early in the day, very much to the surprise of the enemy. By the sixth of May he had begun entrenching and on the seventh he sent out his cavalry to cut the Weldon Railroad and to destroy the railroad between Petersburg and Richmond but no great success attended these efforts. He neglected to attack Petersburg, which was almost defenseless. About the eleventh he advanced slowly until he reached the works at Drewry's Bluff. About halfway between Bermuda Hundred and Richmond. In the meantime. Beauregard had been gathering reinforcements, and on the sixteenth he attacked Butler with such success as to limit very materially the further usefulness of the Army of the James as a factor in the campaign.

Soon after midnight, May 3-4, the Army of the Potomac started on the memorable Wilderness Campaign.

The country over which the army had to operate was cut by numerous streams, which formed a considerable obstacle. The roads were narrow and poor. Most of the country was covered with a dense forest, almost impenetrable even for infantry.

All conditions were favorable for defensive operations.

The major portion of the Army of the Potomac, now under Grant's direct command, crossed the Rapidan River at Germanna Ford on May 3 and 4. Confederate General G. Moxley Sorrel wrote of how he viewed the move:

We were at no loss to understand Grant's intention. The Northern papers, as well as himself, had boldly and brutally announced the purpose of "attrition" – that is, the Federals could stand the loss of four or five men to the Confederates' one, and throw nice strategy into the background. It was known that we were almost past recruiting our thin ranks, and the small figures of the army as it now stood; while the double numbers of the Federals could be reproduced from the immense resources in population, not to speak of their foreign field of supplies under inducement of liberal bounties.

Grant started his march the night of May 3d, via Germanna and Ely's Fords, Wilson's and Gregg's cavalry leading. Burnside also was ordered to him.

The wilderness was a wild, tangled forest of stunted trees, with in places impassable undergrowth, lying between Fredericksburg and Orange Court House, probably sixteen or seventeen miles square. Some farm clearing and a shanty or two for a few poor inhabitants might occasionally be seen. Two principal roads penetrated this repulsive district, the Orange Plank Road and the turnpike. The ground generally lay flat and level.

And now was to begin the last and greatest of the campaigns of the Army of Northern Virginia. The campaign of **attrition** *on one side met and foiled by the fine flower of the ablest strategy of the other. It was Grant's stubborn perseverance, indifferent to the loss of life, against Lee's clear insight and incessant watchfulness. . . .*

An unidentified Union eyewitness relates the terrible battle that began on the morning of May 5:

"Forward! by the right flank; forward!" *rings along the lines. Yonder in front are the gleaming bayonets of our first line of battle; back, just in rear, is the second line, the anxious eyes of the soldiers peering through the trees.*

Was it a sadder wind than usual that swept down from the front that moment, bearing the first earnest clangor of the combat? Else why, as that wind touched the faces of the men, did such a mournful fervor blend with, but not blight the resolve curves of lips that pride forbade to tremble?

"Forward! by the right flank; forward!" again and again repeated far to right and left, until it becomes an echo.

And through a thicket, blind and interminable; over abattis of fallen trees; through swamps, and ditches, and brush-heaps; and once – a glorious breathing-space – across a half acre of open field, the obedient troops move on. . . . Sometimes the eyes of the men sink to note a bypath in the forest, like that which many a one has travelled in old days to some old spring of home-like memory. And here is the "birr" of a bullet, like that which startled one who heard it one summer afternoon, when a brother hunter was careless, and fired at a partridge as he stood in range. The bee-like sounds are thicker on this ridge; in the forest, a little way ahead, there is a crackling, roaring tumult, seasoned with wild cheers.

The Fifth corps had begun the fight in earnest – Griffin is pressing on. Wadsworth, and Robinson, and Crawford are going in; the latter on the left, supported by Getty, is advancing toward the enemy at Parker's store. Behind Crawford and Getty, who are on the Orange Court-house road, is the junction of that and the Brock road, up which, from the direction of Chancellorsville, Hancock is advancing to make connection. **That** *is the vital point – that junction; to be held against all odds unto the death, else the army is severed. . . .*

Here, marching through the forest with General John Sedgwick and his officers, between the first and second lines of battle of that great old corps, which has left its mark in blood on every great battle-field in Virginia, we can hear but not see the progress of the contest in front and on the left. We hear that Griffin and Wadsworth, after gallantly charging the enemy, advancing over two lines of works, have met with superior numbers, have fought courageously, but have been pushed back. The cannon that spake a moment ago are silent. They were two guns of Captain Winslow's (Second Massachusetts) battery, the horses of which have been killed, the men of which have been sorely pressed, and which have been spiked and abandoned. We hear that Crawford's division of Pennsylvania Reserves, sent forward to Parker's store to check the surging tide of Hill's troops, pouring on to attack that junction of two roads on which so much depends, have been hurled back by the same overwhelming pressure that forces Wadsworth, and that the Seventh Pennsylvania regiment has been captured. We hear that everywhere the enemy is strongly posted, everywhere; on height, in the dense forest, using occasional open fields in the rear for artillery, but forcing us to attack in positions where the use of our own artillery is impossible. A cunning and a deceitful foe, knowing of old the splendid aim and discipline of our batteries, now compelled to silence.

The air is stifling, the sun sends its rays down through the jagged limbs of the chapparal around like red hot spears. This march is long, these bullets from an unseen foe are staining some sleeves and jackets too soon. . . .

They are there at last; the bushwhackers, thick as the sprigs and leaves that partly hide their treacherous faces. As the ponderous battle-line of the Sixth corps swings into level in their front, it sends a volley in greeting that thins those faces even as a wind of autumn rushing through an oak. General Ricketts is on the left. General Wright next, General Neill, of the Second division, whose iron brigade is made up of men who never flinched a desperate strait, holds the right of the line in support.

His victories in the western theatre – some of them close-run – singled out Ulysses S. Grant from among the motley Union high command. Lincoln elevated the scruffy, iron-willed general to head the federal armies after Grant's triumphs at Vicksburg and in Tennessee. In the Spring of 1864, Grant began a long, bloody but implacable campaign against Lee and Richmond. (Library of Congress)

The fighting – who shall describe it? Not a thousand men can be seen at once, yet for miles in the front thousands are engaged. The volleyed thunders of the combat roll among the glens and ravines hoarser and higher than the voices of an Eastern jungle. The woods are alive with cries and explosions, and the shrill anvil-clatter of musketry. One cannon, pitched afar, times the wild tumult like a tolling bell. The smoke is a shroud about our heroes; there is not wind enough to lift it into a canopy.

And now, out of the concealed and awful scenery where the fight goes on, there comes the ruins it has wrought, in shapes borne in blankets and on litters – maimed, tortured, writhing; with eyes dull with the stupor of coming death, or bright with delirious fire. Listen to the hell raging beyond and below; behold this silent, piteous procession, that emerges ceaselessly, and passes on. . . .

Two o'clock. In the momentary calm that sinks upon the forest in front we can hear a louder conflict gathering and growing on the left. There Crawford has been driven back; there the enemy are passing in hordes down the turnpike, to gain the junction of the Brock road. Getty has advanced and met them. Hancock has come up at last, and Birney is going in on Getty's right. Mott and Barlow are forming on the left of the line, and Gibbon's division is coming up as a reserve. The enemy are checked, but their concentration continues. Troops are sent to the left from the Fifth corps, and by four o'clock General Hancock is in command of half the army in action.

And now, from left to right the sound of the shock of battle arises anew. Hancock is advancing, Sedgwick is advancing, Warren is in partial wait. Along the left a guttural, oceanic roar prevails, without an interval of rest. Like a great engine, dealing death in return. Companies fall, regiments are thinned, brigades melt away. Stricken in the head by a bullet, General Alexander Hays, commanding the Second brigade of Birney's division, has rolled from his horse, dead. General Getty is wounded; Colonel Carroll, commanding the Third brigade of the Second division, is wounded; a host of line officers are stricken low; the enemy fights like a demon, but the fight moves on.

Sedgwick moves on, breaking the enemy's line for a moment, and taking four or five hundred prisoners. There are ripples of disaster on all the line, but they are quickly repaired.

Slowly, for the enemy is stubborn; slower yet on the extreme right, toward the river, for the enemy there has massed another force, and strives to break our flank. He

The terrible Battle of the Wilderness was fought in a nearly impenetrable forest, which caught fire and roasted the wounded where they fell. Alfred Waud (who seemed to be everywhere during the War) drew this dramatic scene of wounded men escaping the flames. (Library of Congress)

finds a rock, and though he checks our advance, though hundreds of soldiers make the obeisance of death before him, he does not come on.

And as the day dies, and the darkness creeps up from the west, although no cheer of victory swells through the Wilderness from either side, we have accomplished this much at least, with much sore loss: the concentration of our army, the holding of the junction of the Orange Court-house and Brock roads; the turning back of the enemy's right flank from our path toward Richmond, and the average gain of a half mile of ground.

The battle the next day, May 6, as recorded by Theodore Lyman:

. . .General Grant ordered the attack all along the line, the next morning at 4:30; but put it off to 5 o'clock on the representation that Burnside could not get up in time. He was ordered to get in position by day-light and to go in on Hill's left flank . . . nearly parallel to the Parker's Store road. We were all up right early on that Friday the 6th of May, you may depend. "Lyman," said . . . General [Meade], "I want you to take some orderlies and go to General Hancock and report how things go there during the day."

It was after five when I mounted, and already the spattering fire showed that the skirmishers were pushing out; as I rode down the crossroad, two or three crashing volleys rang through the woods, and then the whole front was alive with musketry. I found General Hancock at the crossing of the plank: he was wreathed with smiles. "We are driving them, sir; tell General Meade we are driving them most beautifully. Birney has gone in and he is just cleaning them out be-au-ti-fully!" This was quite apparent from the distance of the receding firing and the absence of those infernal minie balls. "I am ordered to tell you, sir, that only one division of General Burnside is up, but that he will go in as soon as he can be put in position." Hancock's face changed. "I knew it!" he said vehemently. "Just what I expected. If he could attack **now**, *we would smash A.P. Hill all to pieces!" And very true were his words.*

Meantime, some hundreds of prisoners were brought in; all from Hill's troops. Presently, however, the firing seemed to wake again with renewed fury; and in a little while a soldier came up to me and said: "I was ordered to report that this prisoner here belongs to Longstreet's Corps." "Do you belong to Longstreet?" I hastened to ask. "Ya-as, sir," said grey-back, and was marched to the rear. It was too true! Longstreet, coming in all haste from Orange Court House, had fallen desperately on our advance; but he had uphill work. Birney's and Getty's men held fast and fought with fury, a couple of guns were put in the plank road and began to fire solid shot over the heads of our men, adding their roar to the other din. The streams of wounded came faster and faster back; here a field officer, reeling in the saddle; and there another, hastily carried past on a stretcher. I stood at the crossing and assisted in turning back stragglers or those who sought to go back, under pretext of helping the wounded. To some who were in great pain I gave some opium, as they were carried past me.

In his published recollections entitled *A Soldier's Letters to Charming Nellie*, J.B. Polley gave the Confederate side of that morning:

Our position was on an open hill immediately in rear of a battery. Within 300 yards were the Yankees. Here General Lee, mounted on the same horse (a beautiful dapple-gray) that had carried him at Fredericksburg in 1862, rode up near us and gave his orders. "The Texas Brigade always has driven the enemy, and I expect them to do it today. Tell them, General, that I shall witness their conduct."

Galloping in front, General John Gregg delivered the message and shouted, "Forward, Texas Brigade!"

Just then Lee rode in front, as if intending to lead the charge, but a shout went up, "Lee to the rear!" A soldier sprang from the ranks and, seizing the dapple-gray by the reins, led him and his rider to the rear.

The Yankee sharpshooters soon discovered our approach, and some of our best men were killed and wounded before a chance was given them to fire a shot. Three hundred yards, and the leaden hail began to thin our ranks perceptibly; four hundred yards, and we were confronted by a line of blue which, however, fled before us without firing a single volley. Across the Plank Road stood another line, and against this we moved rapidly. The storm of battle became terrific. The Texas Brigade was alone: no support on our right, and not only none on the left, but a terrible enfilading fire poured on us from that direction. We crossed the road and pressed forward 200 yards farther when, learning that a column of Federals was double-quicking from the left and would soon have us surrounded, General Gregg gave the order to fall back. General Lee's object was gained, his trust in the Texans justified. Two divisions had been driven by one small brigade, of whose men more than one-half were killed and wounded.

Gen. G. Moxley Sorrel:

Longstreet had moved at 1 a.m., the march being difficult and slow in the dense forest by side tracks and deep furrowed roadways. At daylight he was on the Plank Road and in close touch with Lee when Hancock struck the two unprepared divisions [Heth's and Wilcox's]. The situation when we came on the scene, that of May 6th, was appalling. Fugitives from the broken lines of the Third Corps were pouring back in disorder and it looked as if things were past mending.

But not so to James Longstreet; never did his great qualities as a tenacious, fighting soldier shine forth in better light. He instantly took charge of the battle, and threw his two divisions across the Plank Road, Kershaw on the right, Field on the left. None but seasoned soldiers like the First Corps could have done even that much. . . . Hill's men were prompt to collect and reform in our rear and soon were ready for better work.

General Lee was under great excitement immediately on the left. He wanted to lead some of our troops into action, but the Texas Brigade was about him and swore they would do nothing unless he retired. A confident message from Longstreet through Colonel Venable that his line would be restored within an hour also helped him regain his calm; and then at it we went in earnest, on both sides of the road.

Hancock's success had lessened his ranks somewhat, which helped us when we fell on him. It was a hard shock of battle by six of our brigades, three on each side of the road. No artillery came into play, the ground not being fit for it. . . .

Theodore Lyman:

. . . Longstreet knew full well (they know everything, those Rebels) that Burnside was coming up with two divisions, on his flank; and knew too that he was late, very late. If Hancock could first be paralyzed, the day was safe from defeat, which now impended. Gathering all his forces, of both corps, he charged furiously. At a little after eleven Mott's left gave way. On the right the brigade of Stevenson, consisting of three raw Massachusetts regiments miscalled "Veterans," broke, on being brought under a tremendous fire. . . .

The musketry now drew nearer to us, stragglers began to come back, and, in a little while, a crowd of men emerged from the thicket in full retreat. They were not running, nor pale, nor scared, nor had they thrown away their guns; but were just in the condition described by the Prince de Joinville, after Gaines's Mill. They had fought all they meant to fight for the present, and there was an end of it! If there is anything that will make your heart sink and take all of the backbone out of you, it is to see men in this condition! I drew my sword and rode in among them, trying to stop them at a little rifle-pit that ran along the road. I would get one squad to stop, but, as I turned to another, the first would quietly walk off.

There was a German color-bearer, a stupid, scared man (who gave him the colors, the Lord only knows!), who said, "Jeneral Stavenzon, he telled me for to carry ze colors up ze road." To which I replied I would run him through the body if he didn't plant them on the riflepit. And so he did, but I guess he didn't stick. Meanwhile there was no danger at all; the enemy did not follow up – not he. He was busy swinging round to oppose Burnside, and was getting his men once more in order. At half-past one I rode to General Meade and reported the state of affairs. The Provost-General went out at once and stopped and organized the stragglers. At two o'clock Burnside, who had been marching and counter-marching, **did** *attack. He made some impression, but it was too late, and he had not enough force to follow on. About this time I returned to General Hancock. His men were rallied along the road; but regiments and brigades were all mixed up; and we were obliged to listen to Burnside's fighting without any advance on our part.*

Colonel William C. Oates of Longstreet's corps:

Lee's object manifestly was to have Longstreet turn Grant's left flank and attack him in the rear, but Longstreet was too slow. He had put his two divisions in bivouac on the night of the fifth more than six miles away from Hill. General Lee foresaw that Hill's troops could not withstand the assaults of the next morning from Hancock's veteran corps of 30,000, and that before Longstreet could reach Hancock's rear, the latter would beat Hill and drive him deep into the Wilderness, destroy the alignment and render a junction of our two corps difficult and hazardous. Longstreet had not moved down that parallel road with the celerity which Lee had expected, and hence could not turn Grant's left before the afternoon, although we had started our march at night to support Hill on time.

At about 2:00 a.m. on the sixth we had begun to move, but we progressed so slowly along the devious neighborhood road that it was daylight when the head of the column reached the Plank Road, about two miles in the rear of where the fighting had ceased the previous evening and where, just at this moment, it recommenced with great fury. In anticipation that his troops would be relieved early the next morning, Hill had not prepared to receive the attack which was made on him.

Longstreet's column reached the scene of action none too soon. Hancock was just turning Hill's right and driving his men from their positions, although they were manfully contesting every inch of ground. To reach our position we had to pass within a few feet of General Lee. He sat his fine gray horse Traveler, with the cape of his black cloak around his shoulders, his face flushed and full of animation. The balls were flying around him from two directions. His eyes were on the fight then going on south of the Plank Road between Kershaw's division and the flanking columns of the enemy. He had just returned from attempting to lead the Texas brigade in a charge. He turned in his saddle and called to his chief of staff while pointing with his finger across the road, "Send an active young officer down there."

I thought him at that moment the grandest specimen of manhood I ever beheld. He looked as though he ought to have been, and was, the monarch of the world. He glanced his eye down on the ragged Rebels as they filed to their place in line, and inquired, "What troops are these?" and was answered "Law's Alabama brigade." He exclaimed in a strong voice, "God bless the Alabamians!" The men cheered and went into line with a whoop. The advance began.

It was now nearly nine o'clock in the morning. The Federal lines were some distance in front of the Brock Road, the most direct route to Spotsylvania Court House and to Richmond. They had constructed on it a triple line of fortifications. Situated as the armies were, it was the obvious policy of each commander to double back the wing of the opposing force. The success of General Grant would have opened an unobstructed road to Richmond and might have been decisive of the campaign. That of General Lee might have ended as did the Battle of Chancellorsville a year before. It would at least have interposed his army between General Grant and his objective point. The arrival of Longstreet's corps defeated the plan of Grant and threw him on the defensive.

Grant (at left of photo, bending over pew) and his commanders hold a council of war at Bethesda Church, Va., before the Battle of Cold Harbor, in June 1864. The Union staff had pulled pews into the open for the conference, and photographer Timothy O'Sullivan captured the moment from the church steeple. (Library of Congress)

The effort of General Lee was still to come. The plan of attack was to throw a force upon the flank and rear of Hancock and at the same time assail his front, so as to roll up and press back his entire left wing toward Fredericksburg. The left brigades were to conform their movements to those on their right, holding back, however, so as to constitute a moveable pivot on which the whole line might wheel. The successful execution of such a movement would not only have disposed of Hancock for the day, but would have thrown a powerful force perpendicular to General Grant's center and right wing, already confronted by General Ewell.

There was a lull all along the line. It was the ominous stillness that precedes the tornado. Three brigades under Mahone – a dangerous man – were already in position for the flank attack, whose specter seemed to have been haunting Hancock from the beginning. A yell and a volley announced the opening of the tragedy. The din of battle rolled eastward; the enemy was giving way. It was a moment pregnant with momentous results and one of intense anxiety. The left brigades began to move forward. Already they had made considerable progress, and still eastward rolled the fiery billows of war. Could it be that we were on the eve of a great victory? But the fire began to slacken; the advance movement ceased. What could be the cause? Had that single line of attack expended its strength? Oh! for a fresh division to be hurled upon that shattered, reeling flank! But no, there were no reserves. The firing ceased, and the victory, almost won, slipped from our grasp.

Longstreet with five brigades had been making the circuit around the enemy's left and had pretty well succeeded in reaching his rear. But the unseen intervened. He and General Micah Jenkins, whose brigade was the largest in the army, were riding together in front of their advancing lines when suddenly they came in view of the enemy. They turned and, while they were riding back through the dense forest, some of their own men mistook them for enemies, fired on them, killed Jenkins and severely wounded Longstreet. This put an end to that movement. What a striking similarity to the fatality which had taken Stonewall Jackson from us!

Sorrel:

The shot which had laid Longstreet low had entered near the throat, and he was almost choked with blood, but he directed me to hasten to General Lee, report what had been accomplished and urge him to continue the movement. The troops were ready, and Grant, he firmly believed, would be driven back across the Rapidan. I rode immediately to General Lee. He was minute in his inquiries, and praised the handling of the flank attack. Longstreet's message was given, but the general was not in sufficient touch with the position of the troops to proceed with it; at least I received that impression, because activity came to a stop for the moment. A new attack with stronger forces was to be made directly on the enemy's works, lower down the Plank Road, in the hope of dislodging him.

But, meantime, the foe had not been idle. He had used the intervening hours in strengthing his position and making really formidable works across the road. When the Confederate troops assaulted them late in the afternoon, they met with a costly repulse, and with this the principal operations on our part of the field ceased for the day. It was coming on dark.

The Wilderness casualties were staggering: Union – 2,246 killed, 12,037 wounded, 3,383 missing: Confederate – 7,750 killed and wounded.

Lyman:

The result of this great Battle of the Wilderness was a drawn fight, but strategically it was a success, because Lee marched out **to stop our advance on Richmond**, *which, at this point, he did not succeed in doing. We lost a couple of guns and took some colors. On the right we made no impression; but, on the left, Hancock punished the enemy so fearfully that they, that night, fell back entirely from his front and shortened their own line, as we shortened ours, leaving their dead unburied and many of their wounded on the ground. The Rebels had a very superior knowledge of the country and had marched shorter distances. Also I consider them more daring and sudden in their movements; and I fancy their discipline on* **essential** *points is more severe than our own – that is, I fancy they shoot a man when he ought to be shot, and we do not. As to* **fighting**, *when two people fight without cessation for the best part of two days, and then come out about even, it is hard to determine.*

Horace Porter, author of *Campaigning With Grant*, tells of the general's reception on the battlefield:

Soon after dark, Generals Grant and Meade, accompanied by their staffs, after having given personal supervision to the starting of the march, rode along the Brock road toward Hancock's headquarters, with the intention of waiting there till Warren's troops should reach that point. While moving close to Hancock's line, there occurred an unexpected demonstration on the part of the troops, which created one of the most memorable scenes of the campaign. Notwithstanding the darkness of the night, the form of the commander was recognized, and word was passed rapidly along that the chief who had led them through the mazes of the Wilderness was again moving forward with his horse's head turned toward Richmond.

Troops know but little about what is going on in a large army, except the occurrences which take place in their immediate vicinity; but this night ride of the general-in-chief told plainly the story of success, and gave each man to understand that the cry was to be "On to Richmond!" Soldiers weary and sleepy after their long battle, with stiffened limbs and smarting wounds, now sprang to their feet, forgetful of their pain, and rushed forward to the roadside. Wild cheers echoed through the forest, and glad shouts of triumph rent the air. Men swung their hats, tossed up their arms, and pressed forward to within touch of their chief, clapping their hands, and speaking to him with the familiarity of comrades. Pine-knots and leaves were set on fire, and lighted the scene with their weird, flickering glare.

The night march had become a triumphal procession for the new commander. The demonstration was the emphatic verdict pronounced by the troops upon his first battle in the East. The excitement had been imparted to the horses, which soon became restive, and even the general's large bay, over which he possessed ordinarily such perfect control, became difficult to manage. Instead of being elated by this significant ovation, the general, thoughtful only of the practical question of the success of the movement, said: "This is most unfortunate. The sound will reach the ears of the enemy, and I fear it may reveal our movement." By his direction, staff-officers rode forward and urged the men to keep quiet so as not to attract the enemy's attention; but the demonstration did not really cease until the general was out of sight.

The war in Virginia now became a chess game between Grant and Lee, the two generals matching move for move. After the Wilderness, Grant became the aggressor. Lee recognized this and prepared for his countermove. Confederate Gen. John B. Gordon:

On the morning of May 7, I was invited by the commanding general to ride with him. I endeavored to learn what movements he had in contemplation. It was then that I learned for the first time of his intention to move at once to Spotsylvania. Reports had it that General Grant's army was retreating or preparing to retreat, but these had not made the slightest impression on his mind. He said in so many words, "General Grant is not going to retreat. He will move his army to Spotsylvania."

I asked him if he had information of such a comtemplated change. "Not at all," said Lee, "not at all; but Spotsylvania is now General Grant's best strategic point. I am so sure of his next move that I have already made arrangements to march by the shortest practicable route, so that we may meet him there."

The climax of the battle at Spotsylvania cost the Confederates dearly. Another of Lee's lieutenants fell. The terrible clash is narrated by Union General Sheridan and Confederate H.B. McClellan.

Sheridan:

By forced marches General [J.E.B.] Stuart succeeded in reaching Yellow Tavern ahead of me on May 11; and the presence of his troops on the Ashland and Richmond road becoming known to Merritt as he was approaching the Brock turnpike, this general pressed forward at once to the attack. Pushing his division to the front, he soon got possession of the turnpike and drove the enemy back several hundred yards to the east of it. This success had the effect of throwing the head of my column to the east of the pike, and I quickly brought up Wilson and one of Gregg's brigades to take advantage of the situation by forming a line of battle on that side of the road. Meanwhile the enemy, desperate but still confident, poured in a heavy fire from his line and from a battery which enfiladed the Brock road, and made Yellow Tavern an uncomfortably hot place. Gibb's and Devin's brigades, however, held fast there, while Custer, supported by Chapman's brigade, attacked the enemy's left and battery in a mounted charge.

Custer's charge, with Chapman on his flank and the rest of Wilson's division sustaining him, was brilliantly executed. Beginning at a walk, he increased his gait to a trot, and then at full speed rushed at the enemy. At the same moment the dismounted troops along my whole front moved forward, and as Custer went through the battery, capturing two of the guns with their cannoneers and breaking up the enemy's left, Gibbs and Devin drove his centre and right from the field. Gregg meanwhile, with equal success, charged the force in his rear – Gordon's brigade – and the engagement ended by giving us complete control of the road to Richmond.

McClellan:

We reached the vicinity of the Yellow Tavern that morning about ten o'clock, and found that we were in advance of the enemy's column, and in time to interpose between it and Richmond. Not knowing what force we had there, the General was uncertain whether to place himelf at once between the enemy and the city, or to take a position on his flank, near the Yellow Tavern – the latter he preferred if he could be satisfied that we had a sufficient force in the trenches to defend Richmond. To ascertain this he sent me to see General Bragg. When I returned to him about two o'clock, I found that a heavy engagement had taken place, and, that after driving in a portion of our line, the enemy had been heavily repulsed. When I found the General there was a lull in the fight, and we sat quietly near one of our batteries for more than an hour, resting and talking. About four o'clock the enemy suddenly threw a brigade of cavalry, mounted, upon our extreme left, attacking our whole line at the same time. As he always did, the General hastened to the point where the greatest danger threatened – the point against which the enemy directed the mounted charge. My horse was so much exhausted by my severe ride of the morning that I could not follow him, but Captain Dorsey gave the particulars that follow.

The enemy's charge captured our battery on the left of our line, and drove back almost the entire left. Where Captain Dorsey was stationed – immediately on the Telegraph road – about eighty men had collected together, and among these the General threw himself, and by his personal example held them steady while the enemy charged entirely past their position. With these men he fired into their flank and rear, as they passed him, in advancing and retreating, for they were met by a mounted charge of the First Virginia cavalry and driven back some distance. As they retired, one man, who had been dismounted in the charge and was running out on foot, turned, as he passed the General, and, discharging his pistol, inflicted the fatal wound. When Captain Dorsey discovered that he was wounded, he came at once to his assistance and endeavored to lead him to the rear; the General's horse became so restive and unmanageable that he insisted upon being taken down and allowed to rest against a tree. When this was done Captain Dorsey sent for another horse. While waiting for this horse, the General ordered him to leave him alone and return to his men and drive back the enemy; said that he feared he was mortally wounded and could be of no more service. Captain Dorsey told him that he could not obey that order – that he would sacrifice his life rather than leave him until he had placed him out of all danger. The situation was a dangerous one. Our men were sadly scattered, and there was hardly a handful of men between that little group and the advancing enemy. But the horse arrived in time; the General was lifted onto him and led by Captain Dorsey to a safer place. There, by the General's order, he gave him into charge of Private Wheatly, of his company, and returned to rally our scattered men. Wheatly procured an ambulance, placed the General in it with the greatest care, and supporting him in his arms, he was driven from the field. As he was being brought off, he spoke to our men, whom he saw retreating, and said: "Go back! go back! and do your duty as I have done mine, and our country will be safe. Go back! go back! I had rather die than be whipped."

Heros von Borcke, Stuart's aide:

Stuart's brother-in-law, Dr. Brewer, informed me that my general had been wounded severely and was anxious to see me. I found him in a small room, surrounded by most of the members of his staff. He received me with a smile, saying, "I'm glad you've come, Von. I don't think I'm badly wounded, and hope I shall get over it."

He then recounted to me the manner in which he had been wounded. For more than six hours he had fought with 1,100 men against 8,000. At about four o'clock, the Federals succeeded by a general charge in driving back one of our regiments which General Stuart was rallying in an open field. Seeing near him some of the dismounted Federal cavalry, Stuart rode up to them calling them to surrender and firing at them as they countinued to fight. He had just discharged the last barrel of his revolver when the hindmost of the fugitives fired his revolver at him, the ball taking effect in the lower part of the stomach and traversing the whole body. Stuart turned his charger round and galloped half a mile to the rear, where he was taken from his horse nearly insensible from loss of blood and sent in an ambulance to Richmond. During the early part of the morning the general felt comparatively easy, and the physician entertained great hope that the wound might not prove fatal. Toward noon, however, a change took place for the worse.

About this time President Davis visited the prostrate hero. Taking his hand, he said, "General, how do you feel?"

He replied, "Easy, but willing to die."

As evening approached, mortification set in. He became delirious, and his mind wandered over battlefields, then to his wife and children, and again to the front. About five o'clock the general asked Dr. Brewer how long he could live and, being told that death was rapidly approaching, he nodded and said, "I am resigned, if it be God's will."

At about seven o'clock death relieved the suffering hero from his agonies.

The Richmond *Examiner* reported his last minutes:

At half-past seven o'clock it was evident to the physicians that death was setting its clammy seal upon the brave, open brow of the General, and told him so; asked if he had any last messages to give. The General, with a mind perfectly clear and possessed, then made dispositions of his staff and personal effects. To Mrs. General R.E. Lee he directed that his golden spurs be given as a dying momento of his love and esteem of her husband. To his staff officers he gave his horses. So particular was he in small things, even in the dying hour, that he emphatically exhibited and illustrated the ruling passion strong in death. To one of his staff, who was a heavy built man, he said "You had better take the larger horse; he will carry you better." Other momentoes he disposed of in a similar manner. To his young son he left his glorious sword.

His wordly matters closed, the eternal interest of his soul engaged his mind. Turning to the Rev. Mr. Peterkin, of the Episcopal Church, and of which he was an exemplary member, he asked him to sing the hymn commencing –

Rock of ages cleft for me,
Let me hide myself in thee –

he joined in with all the voice his strength would permit. He then joined in prayer with the ministers. To the Doctor he again said, "I am going fast now; I am resigned; God's will be done." Thus died General J.E.B. Stuart.

On the day Stuart died, the battle around Spotylvania Court House reached its climax at a point in the Confederate ever after known as the "Bloody Angle." One Federal narrative:

The battle near the "angle" was probably the most desperate engagement in the history of modern warfare, and presented features which were absolutely appalling. It was chiefly a savage hand-to-hand fight across the breastworks. Rank after rank was riddled by shot and shell and bayonet-thrusts, and finally sank, a mass of torn and mutilated corpses; then fresh troops rushed madly forward to replace the dead, and so the murderous work went on. Guns were run up close to the parapet, and double charges of canister played their part in the bloody work. The fence-rails and logs in the breastworks were shattered into splinters, and trees over a foot and a half in diameter were cut completely in two by the incessant musketry fire. . . .

We had not only shot down an army, but also a forest. The opposing flags were in places thrust against each other, and muskets were fired with muzzle against muzzle. Skulls were crushed with clubbed musket, and men stabbed to death with swords and bayonets thrust between the logs in the parapet which separated the combatants. Wild cheers, savage yells, and frantic shrieks rose above the sighing of the wind and the pattering of the rain, and formed a demoniacal accompaniment to the booming of the guns as they hurled their missiles of death into the contending ranks. Even the darkness of night and pitiless storm failed to stop the fierce contest, and the deadly strife did not cease till after midnight. Our troops had been under fire for twenty hours, but they still held the position which they had so dearly purchased.

Federal casualties were 17,000; Confederate, 12,000. But the campaign was not yet over. Frontal assault not working for Grant, he attempted to move around Lee's flank, stepping cautiously to the east. Lee followed. Theodore Lyman:

The great feature of this campaign is the extraordinary use made of earthworks. Bayonets with a few picks and shovels, in the hands of men who work for their lives, soon suffice to make a cover, and within one hour there is a shelter against bullets, extending often for a mile or two. When our line advances, there is the line of the enemy, nothing showing but the bayonets and the battle flags stuck on the top of the work. It is a rule that, when the Rebels halt, the first day gives them a good rifle pit; the second, a regular infantry parapet with artillery in position; and the third a parapet with an abatis in front and entrenched batteries behind. Sometimes they put this three-days' work into the first twenty-four hours. Our men can do, and do the same. But remember, our object is offense – to advance.

Lee is **not** *retreating. He is a brave and skillful soldier and will fight while he has a division or a day's rations left. These Rebels are not half-starved – a more sinewy, tawny, formidable-looking set of men could not be. In education they are certainly inferior to our native-born people, but they are usually very quick-witted, and they know enough to handle weapons with terrible effect. Their great characteristic is their stoical manliness: they never beg or whimper or complain but look you straight in the face, with as little animosity as if they had never heard a gun fired.*

Grant arrived at Cold Harbor on June 1. Horace Porter:

A serious problem now presented itself to General Grant – whether to attempt to crush Lee's army on the north side of the James, with the prospect of driving him into Richmond, capturing the city perhaps without siege, or to move the Union army south of the James without giving battle and transfer the field operations to the vicinity of Petersburg. It was a nice question of judgment. After discussing the matter thoroughly with his principal officers and weighing all the chances, he decided to attack Lee's army in its present position. He had succeeded in breaking the enemy's line at other places in circumstances which were not more favorable, and the results to be obtained now would be so great that it seemed wise to make the attempt. . . .

In passing along on foot among the troops the previous evening (June 2), I noticed that many of the soldiers had taken off their coats and seemed to be engaged in sewing up rents in them. On closer examination it was found that the men were calmly writing their names and home addresses on slips of paper and pinning them on the backs of their coats, so that their dead bodies might be recognized and their fate made known to their families at home.

At 4:30 a.m., June 3, three columns under Hancock, Wright and W.F. Smith, respectively, moved forward to the attack. Hancock's troops struck a salient of the enemy's works and after a desperate struggle captured it, taking a couple of hundred prisoners, three guns and a stand of colors. Then turning the captured guns upon the enemy, they drove him from that part of the line into his main works, a short distance in the rear. Our second line, however, did not move up in time to support the first, which was finally driven back and forced out. Another division had rushed forward, but an impassable swamp divided the troops, who were now subjected to a galling fire of artillery and musketry and, although a portion of them gained the enemy's entrenchments, their ranks had become too much weakened and scattered to hold their position, and they were compelled to fall back.

Wright's corps had moved forward and carried the rifle pits in its front, and then assaulted the main line. This was too strong, however, to be captured, and our troops were compelled to retire. Nevertheless, they held a line and protected it as best they could, at a distance of only thirty or forty yards from the enemy.

Smith made his assault by taking advantage of a ravine, but the same cross fire from which Wright had suffered made further advances extremely hazardous. His troops were so cut up that there was no prospect of carrying the works in his front, unless the enfilading fire on his flank could be silenced.

At eleven o'clock General Grant rode out along the lines. Hancock reported that the position in his front could not be taken. Wright stated that a lodgment might be made in his front, but that nothing would be gained by it unless Hancock and Smith were to advance at the same time. Smith thought that he might be able to carry the works before him, but was not sanguine.

The general in chief at half past twelve wrote the following order to General Meade: "You may direct a suspension of farther advance for the present."

That evening the general said, "I regret this assault more than any one I have ever ordered. I regarded it as a stern necessity; but, as it has proved, no advantages have been gained sufficient to justify the heavy losses suffered." Subsequently the matter was seldom referred to in conversation.

A member of the 48th New York Volunteers saw what Grant would later admit was a mistake:

Arrived at Cold Harbor, we received the order to attack the enemy's works. The 47th New York Regiment, which was on our left, had already moved away, and still no word of command was given. What should we do? The greatest excitement prevailed. "Charge bayonets!" sounded across the field, and the first line of the enemy's rifle pits was occupied. In little more time than it takes to write it he had captured and occupied a section of the main line of Confederate works and had more prisoners marching to the rear than the whole number present in the regiment.

How much was crowded into the short time that we occupied that line of entrenchment! It was a dreadful place to hold, with the Rebels pouring in upon us a deadly flanking fire. Repeated messages were sent to the commanding general explaining our situation, but no help, and no word of any kind, was received. Efforts were made to induce the 47th New York, which was separated from us by a little ravine, to unite with us in a charge, but without avail. And so we were compelled to wait and suffer.

As the shadows deepened about us, there came a rush. The enemy was fairly upon us and, before we could gather ourselves, someone without authority had called out to retreat. Back through the woods we went, broken and dispirited. There we found the commander of a division reclining under a tree in a state of helplessness and demoralization. Completely beside himself because of the defeat and disperion of his command, he insisted that our

ANNIE
MAE
BB 410

In the months after Gettysburg, the War shifted west again to the region around Chattanooga. Following a long rest after Stones River, Rosecrans and Bragg met again at Chickamauga Creek, a few miles over the Georgia line. Reinforced with troops from the East, Bragg's army smashed the Union forces, driving at the Federal center past the Brotherton House (right). Only a stand by Gen. George Thomas, the "Rock of Chickamauga", prevented total disaster. Memorials (above and inset) now mark this part of the combined Chickamauga and Chattanooga National Military Park.

15TH U.S. INF

The Union forces withdrew to Chattanooga after their defeat, and Bragg took possession of the commanding heights surrounding the river city, cutting off Federal supply lines and threatening to starve the Union army. The Confederate left was atop Lookout Mountain (these pages), a towering point commanding a bend in the Tennessee River. Commercial developments, memorials and relics dot Lookout Mountain today. The view from the crest of Lookout Mountain (facing page top) gives an idea of the Confederate position, but Grant was now in charge, and he moved with his usual determination to gather a large force to dislodge Bragg and free the Union armies to move into Georgia. A makeshift supply route, called the "cracker line" was devised across the river peninsula and Grant prepared to assault both Lookout Mountain and the center of the Southern line at Missionary Ridge. Lookout Mountain fell when Bragg neglected signs of Union movement below the crest around the Cravens House (below), now restored and open to visitors. At Missionary Ridge, frustrated Union foot soldiers launched a seemingly insane charge, without orders, straight up the mountain and overran the Confederates. Bragg had to withdraw.

Artillery duels were the daily norm during the seige of Petersburg. The Union brought into play mammoth guns, such as the 2000-pound "Dictator" mortar, on display (facing page bottom right) in replica today in Petersburg National Battlefield Park (these pages), along with demonstrations of artillery fire power (facing page bottom left and facing page top). The Confederate gunners replied effectively, and neither side could gain a decisive advantage. Behind the lines, Union troops built log huts (above) for the winter.

While Grant pushed in the East, Sherman tried to bring Joe Johnston to battle in Georgia, succeeding only once, at Kennesaw Mountain (facing page), where stout Confederate defensive positions once again triumphed. Johnston was replaced by the impetuous John Hood, whom Sherman defeated. In Virginia, Grant's path of advance passed by earlier battle sites, such as Beaver Creek Dam (above) and the Watt House (below) near Gaines' Mill. Right: a cannon at Ft. Darling, which held a Confederate strongpoint on the James River near Richmond.

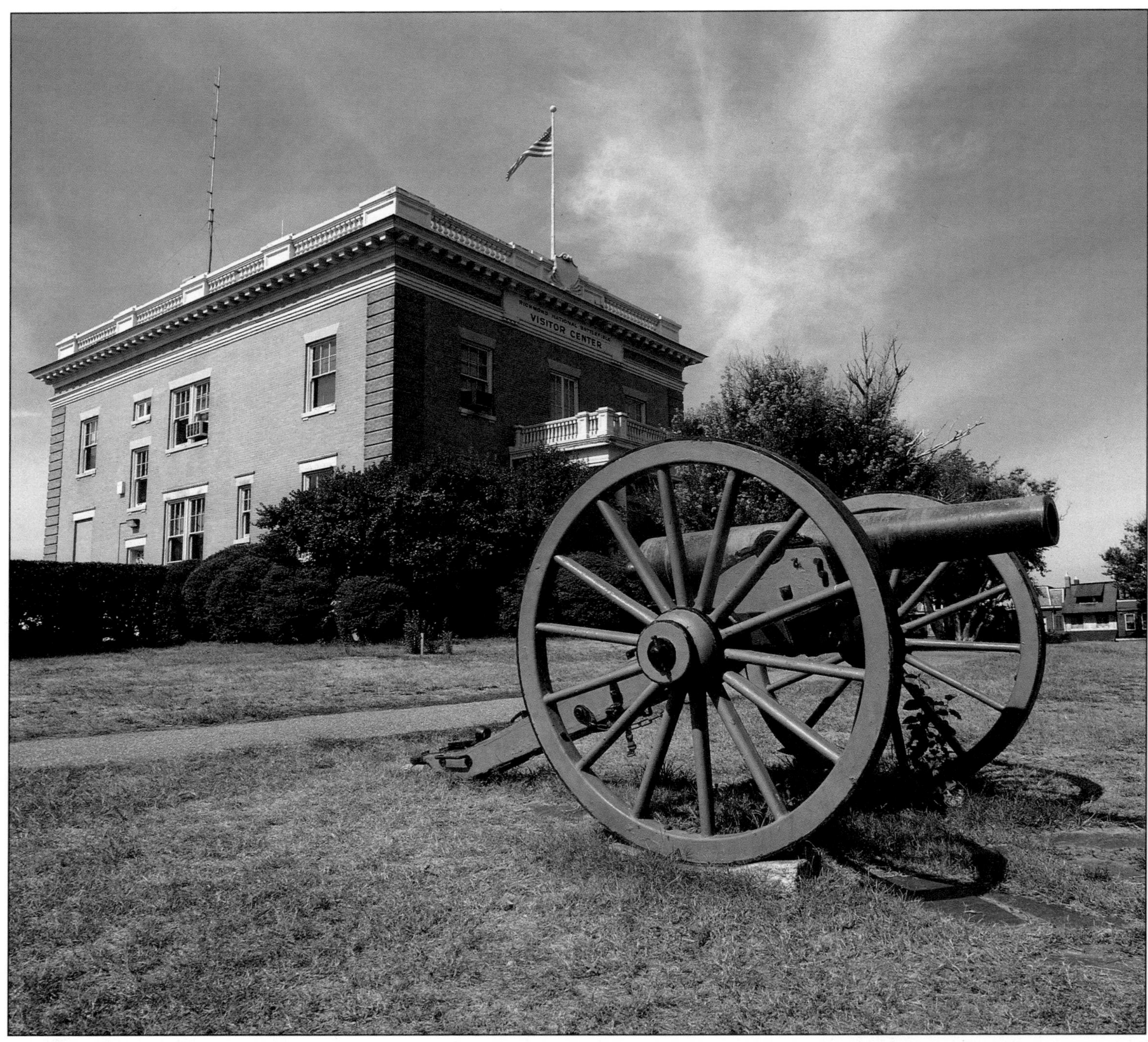

Fiercely defended Confederate trenches at Cold Harbor (facing page bottom) inflicted severe casualties on Grant's forces, but he pressed on to cross the James River, defended by Ft. Harrison and Ft. Hoke (facing page top) to invest Petersburg and threaten Richmond. The visitors' center (above) at Richmond National Battlefield (these pages) affords tourists an interpretive view of the complex of battles that took place nearby.

Lee held his lines at Petersburg for nearly a year but, when Sherman took Atlanta, marched to the sea and destroyed Richmond's source of supply, the end was inevitable. During the first days of April 1865, Lee's army slipped out of its defensive position and tried for a breakout that might allow it to unite with Joe Johnston's remaining forces in Carolina and yet again snatch victory. The plan failed when Lee's supply train was captured. Facing no hope, Lee asked Grant to meet and discuss surrender terms. On April 9, Grant and Lee rode in separately to the small town of Appomattox. They met in the McLean House (facing page top), now restored and, together with the Court House (above), part of Appomattox Court House National Historical Park (these pages). In the parlour (facing page bottom) of the McLean House Lee signed the surrender terms. The War was over.

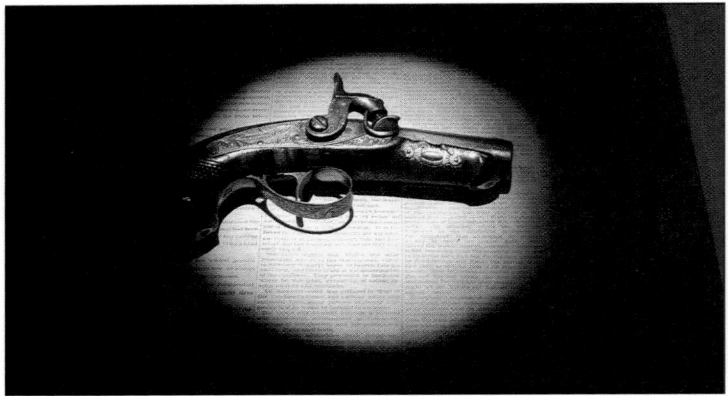

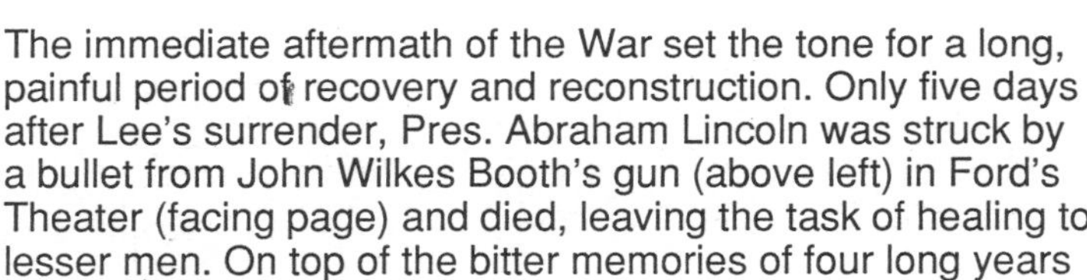

The immediate aftermath of the War set the tone for a long, painful period of recovery and reconstruction. Only five days after Lee's surrender, Pres. Abraham Lincoln was struck by a bullet from John Wilkes Booth's gun (above left) in Ford's Theater (facing page) and died, leaving the task of healing to lesser men. On top of the bitter memories of four long years of war and death, the North had to absorb news such as that of the suffering and cruelty of Andersonville prison camp in Georgia, where thousands of Union prisoners died from disease caused by contaminated waterholes (above right) and lack of food, and are movingly commemorated in Andersonville National Cemetery (top).

7534
S.B. CAMPBELL
MICH.
7535
BENJ. BRADLEY
MICH.
J. B. HENRY
PA.
MASS.
7539
JNO. CRASTY
7540
OHIO
7541
PA.

At mid-year of 1864, Grant began a prolonged siege at Petersburg, Va., just outside the Confederate capital of Richmond. As the campaign wore on, the armies settled into full-scale trench warfare. This Alexander Gardner photo shows a "bombproof" shelter behind the Union lines. (Library of Congress)

feeble line of officers and men should renew the attack, when a whole division had been defeated and scattered. We left him to his own reflections.

Already darkness had settled on us, and we lay down for a little rest in the field over which the regiment had so gallantly charged that afternoon.

Colonel William Oates of the Fifteenth Alabama:

Just before I could see the sun, I heard a volley in the woods, saw the Major running up the ravine in the direction of Anderson's brigade, which lay to the right of Law's, and the skirmishers running in, pursued by a column of the enemy ten lines deep, with arms at a trail, and yelling "Huzzah! huzzah!" I ordered my men to take arms and fix bayonets. Just then I remembered that not a gun in the regiment was loaded. I ordered the men to load and the officers each to take an ax and stand to the works. I was apprehensive that the enemy would soon be on our works before the men could load.

As Capt. Noah B. Feagin and his skirmishers crawled over the works I thought of my piece of artillery, I called out: "Sergeant, give them double charges of canister; fire, men, fire!" The order was obeyed with alacrity. The enemy were within thirty steps. They halted and began to dodge, lie down, and recoil. The fire was terrific from my regiment, the Fourth Alabama on my immediate right, and the Thirteenth Mississippi on my left, while the piece of artillery was fired more rapidly and better handled than I ever saw one before or since. The blaze of fire from it at each shot went right into the ranks of our assailants and made frightful gaps through the dense mass of men. They endured it but for one or two minutes, when they retreated, leaving the ground covered with their dead and dying. There were 3 men in my regiment killed, 5 wounded. My piece of artillery kept up a lively fire on the enemy where they halted in the woods, with shrapnel shell.

After the lapse of about forty minutes another charge was made by the Twenty-third and Twenty-fifth Massachusetts regiments, in a column by divisions, thus presenting a front of two companies only. Bryan's Georgia brigade came up from the rear and lay down behind Law's. The charging column, which aimed to strike the Fourth Alabama, received the most destructive fire I ever saw. They were subjected to a front and flank fire from the infantry, at short range, while my piece of artillery poured double charges of canister into them. The Georgians loaded for the Alabamians to fire. I could see the dust fog out of a man's clothing in two or three places at once where as many balls would strike him at the same moment. In two minutes not a man of them was standing. All who were not shot down had lain down for protection. One little fellow raised his head to look, and I ordered him to come in. He came on a run, the Yankees over in the woods firing at him every step of the way, and as he climbed over our works one shot took effect in one of his legs. They evidently took him to be a deserter. I learned from him that there were many more out there who were not wounded. This I communicated to Colonel Perry, who was again in command, General Law having been wounded in the head during the first assault; and thereupon Perry sent a company down a ravine on our right to capture them; they soon brought the colonel who led the charge, and about one hundred other prisoners. The colonel was a brave man. He said he had been in many places, but that was the worst.

Ulysses S. Grant:

I have always regretted that the last assault at Cold Harbor was ever made. . . . No advantage whatever was gained to compensate for the heavy loss we sustained. Indeed, the advantages other than those of relative losses, were on the Confederate side. Before that, the Army of Northern Virginia seemed to have acquired a wholesome regard for the courage, endurance, and soldierly qualities generally of the Army of the Potomac. They no longer wanted to fight them "one Confederate to five Yanks." Indeed, they seemed to have given up any idea of gaining any advantage of their antagonist in the open field. They had come to much prefer breastworks in their front to the Army of the Potomac.

Grant and his staff, summer 1864. (Library of Congress)

This charge seemed to revive their hopes temporarily, but it was of short duration. . . . When we reached the James River . . . all effects of the battle of Cold Harbor seemed to have disappeared.

THE BATTLES FOR ATLANTA

When Ulysses S. Grant was called to the East, he turned over command of the Army of the Cumberland, the Army of the Tennessee, and the Army of the Ohio to William Tecumseh Sherman. The Federal offensive was now narrowed to two objectives, according to Sherman, "Lee's army behind the Rapidan in Virginia, and Joseph E. Johnston's army at Dalton, Georgia." Sherman's objective was to push deep into the heart of the Confederacy, through Georgia, dividing it from the rest of the South. He outlined his plan of approach toward Johnston – not directly, but a feint at Johnston's front while actually moving on the town of Resaca, 18 miles to the rear:

On the eighteenth of March, 1864, I relieved Lieutenant General Grant in command of the Military Division of the Mississippi and addressed myself to the task of organizing a large army to move into Georgia.

The great question of the campaign was one of supplies. Nashville, our chief depot, was itself partially in a hostile country, and even the routes from Louisville to Nashville had to be guarded. Chattanooga, our starting point, was 136 miles in front of Nashville, and every foot of the way had to be strongly guarded against a hostile population and the enemy's cavalry.

About the early part of April, I was much disturbed by a bold raid made by the Rebel General Nathan B. Forrest between the Mississippi and Tennessee rivers. He reached the Ohio River at Paducah, then swung down toward Memphis and successfully assaulted Fort Pillow.

I also had another serious cause of disturbance about that time. I wanted badly the two divisions of troops which had been loaned to General Banks for his Red River Campaign, with the express understanding that their absence was to endure only one month. But rumors were reaching us of defeat and disaster in that quarter, and General Banks could or would not spare those two divisions. This was a serious loss.

My three armies, by the first of May, 1864, totaled 100,000 men. In Generals Thomas, McPherson and Schofield I had three generals of education and experience, admirably qualified for the work before us.

General Grant had indicated May 5 as the day for our simultaneous advance. The sixth of May was given to Schofield and McPherson to get into position, and on the seventh General Thomas moved in force against Tunnel Hill, from where I could look into the gorge called the Buzzard Roost through which the railroad passed.

Mill Creek, which formed the gorge, had been dammed up, filling the road, and the enemy's batteries crowned the cliffs on either side. The position was very strong, and I knew that such a general as Joe Johnston had fortified it to a maximum. Therefore I had no intention to attack the position seriously in front but depended on McPherson to capture the railroad to its rear, which would force Johnston to evacuate his position at Dalton [Georgia]. My orders to Generals Thomas and Schofield were merely to press strongly at all points, ready to rush in on the first appearance of "Let go."

On the ninth McPherson's head of column entered and passed through a narrow pass named Snake Creek Gap, which was undefended, and accomplished a complete surprise to the enemy. A Confederate cavalry brigade, retreating hastily north toward Dalton, doubtless carried to Johnston the first intimation that a heavy force was to his rear near Resaca and within a few miles of his railroad. I renewed orders to Thomas and Schofield to be ready for the pursuit of what I expected to be a broken and disordered army.

But that night I received notice from McPherson that he had found Resaca too strong for a surprise; that in consequence he had fallen back three miles to the mouth of Snake Creek Gap and was there fortified.

McPherson had not done the full measure of his work. He could have walked into Resaca, then held only by a small brigade, or he could have placed his whole force astride the railroad above Resaca and there have easily withstood an attack of Johnston's army, with the knowledge that Thomas and Schofield were on his heels. Had he done so, I am certain that Johnston would have retreated eastward, and we should have captured half his army and all his artillery and wagons. Such an opportunity does not occur twice in a life time.

I now determined to pass the whole army through Snake Creek Gap and to move with it on Resaca.

Major James Austin Connolly of the 123rd Illinois:

Just as I had written the date above [May 15, 1864], I said: "Hello, the enemy are shelling us." . . . It is now about nine o'clock at night, the moon is shining with a misty light through the battle smoke that is slowly settling down like a curtain, over these hills and valleys; the mournful notes of a whippoorwill, near by, mingle in strange contrast with the exultant shouts of our soldiers – the answering yells of the rebels – the rattling fire of the skirmish line, and the occasional bursting of a shell. Today we have done nothing but shift positions and keep up a heavy skirmish fire. Yesterday our Division and Judah's Division of Schofield's Corps, had some hard fighting. We drove the enemy about a mile and entirely within his fortifications, several of our regiments planting their colors on his fortifications, but were compelled to withdraw under a terrible fire. We, however, fell back but a short distance to the cover of the woods, where we still are, and the enemy have not ventured outside their works since. A report has just reached us that Hooker drove the enemy about a mile today. . . . We have men enough here to whip Johnston, and if he don't escape pretty soon he never will.

The Confederate side by Lt. L.D. Young:

At Resaca was fought the first battle of magnitude in the celebrated Georgia Campaign. From then on there was not a day or night, yes, scarcely an hour, that we did not hear the crack of a rifle or roar of a cannon. To their music we slept, by their thunderings we were awakened and to the accompanying call of the bugle we responded on the morning of May 14 to engage in the death grapple with Sherman's well-clothed, well-fed and thoroughly rested veterans who moved against us in perfect step, with banners flying and bands playing, as though expecting to charm us.

When they had come within seventy-five or eighty yards, our lines opened a murderous fire from both infantry and double-shotted artillery. Having retired in disorder to their original position in the woods, they rallied and again moved to the attack to be met in the same manner and with similar results. Three times during the morning and early afternoon were these attacks made upon our lines. It was a veritable picnic for the Confederates, protected as we were by earthworks with clear and open ground in front. Had Sherman continued this business during the entire day (as we hoped he would) the campaign would have ended right there.

This day's work, however, was a clever ruse of Sherman's for, while he was entertaining us with the main part of his army, he was planning our undoing by sending down the river to our rear Dodge's corps to cut our communications and intercept our retreat. But Johnston had foreseen this move, and we were the first to cross the Oostanaula [River].

Johnston retreated on the night of May 15, and Sherman quickly followed. "About noon I got a message that the enemy had drawn up in line of battle about halfway between Kingston and Cassville," wrote Sherman, "and that appearances indicated his willingness and preparation for battle. But when day broke the next morning, May 20, the enemy was gone, and our cavalry reported him beyond the Etowah River."

Sherman attempted to carry battle into the open; Johnston stayed behind breastworks. Sherman tried to flank Johnston. There was New Hope Church, Pickett's Mill, Pumpkin Vine Creek, and Dallas, until Johnston came to Kennesaw Mountain.

Sherman:

On June 15 we advanced our lines, intending to attack at any weak point discovered between Kennesaw and Pine Mountain; but Pine Mountain was found to be abandoned, and Johnston had contracted his front somewhat on a direct line connecting Kennesaw with Lost Mountain. On the sixteenth Lost Mountain was abandoned by the enemy.

I had consulted Generals Thomas, McPherson and Schofield, and we all agreed that we could not with prudence stretch any more, and therefore there was no alternative but to attack "fortified lines," a thing carefully avoided up to that time. The twenty-seventh of June was fixed as the day for the attempt.

At 9 a.m. on June 27, Sherman launched his attack against Kennesaw. Confederate Gen. Samuel G. French:

June 27. – This morning there appeared great activity among staff officers and Generals all along my front and up and down the line. The better to observe what it portended, myself and staff seated ourselves on the brow of the mountain, sheltered by a large rock that rested between our guns and those of the enemy, the infantry being still lower down the side of the mountain.

Artillery firing was common on the line at all times, but now it swelled in column and extended down to the extreme left, and then from fifty guns burst out in my front, and thence, battery after battery following on the right, disclosed a general attack on our entire line. Presently, and as if by magic, there spring from the earth a host of men, and in one long waving line of blue the infantry advanced and the battle of Kennesaw Mountain began.

I could see no infantry on my immediate front, owing to the woods at the base of the mountain, and therefore directed the guns from their elevated position to enfilade Walker's front. In a short time the flank fire down the line drove them back, and Walker was relieved from the attack.

We sat there, perhaps an hour, enjoying a bird's-eye view of one of the most magnificent sights ever allotted to man – to look down upon an hundred and fifty thousand men arrayed in the strife of battle on the plain below.

As the infantry closed in, the blue smoke of the musket marked out our line for miles, while over it rose in cumuli-like clouds the white smoke of the artillery. Through the rifts of smoke, or, as it was wafted aside the struggle was hard, and there it lasted longest. So many guns were trained on those by our side, and so incessant was the roar of cannon and sharp the explosion of shells, that naught else could be heard. From the fact that I had seen no infantry in my front, and had heard no musketry near, and the elevation of my line on the mountain, I thought I was exempted from the general infantry attack; I was therefore surprised and awakened from my dreams when a courier came to me about 9 o'clock and said General Cockrell wanted assistance, that his line had been attacked in force. General Ector was at once directed to send two regiments to report to him. Soon again a second courier came and reported the assault on the left of my line. I went immediately with the remainder of Ector's brigade to Cockrell, but on joining him found the Federal forces had been repulsed. The assaulting column had struck Cockrell's works near the centre, recoiled under the fire, swung around into a steep valley where – exposed to the fire of the Missourians in front and right flank and of Sear's men on the left – it seemed to melt away or sink to the earth to rise no more.
The assault on my line repulsed, I returned to the mountain top. The intensity of the fire had slackened and no movement of troops was visible; and although the din of arms yet resounded far and near, the battle was virtually ended.

From prisoners and from papers on their persons shown us, I learned my line had, from its position, been selected for assault by General McPherson, as that of Cheatham's had been by General Thomas. . . .

The battle, in its entirety, became a pageantry on a grand scale, and barren of results, because the attacking columns were too small in numbers, considering the character of the troops they knew they would encounter.

General Cheatham's loss was one hundred and ninety-five (195); mine (French's) one hundred and eighty-six (186); all other Confederate losses were one hundred and forty-one (141), being a total of five hundred and twenty-two. What the Federal loss was I do not know. It has been variously estimated from three to eight thousand.

As nothing decisive was obtained by Sherman's attack, the firing slackened except on the skirmish line. After dark the enemy withdrew to their main trenches, the roar of guns died gradually away, and the morning of the 28th dawned on both armies in their former positions. The battle of Kennesaw, then, was a display of force and advance of troops by the enemy on the entire length of our line, that opened a furious fire of artillery and musketry, under cover of which two grand attacks were made by assaulting columns – the one on my line and the other on Cheatham's.

The *New York Tribune*:

Sherman did not choose to rest on his bloody repulse; but having waited only to bury the dead and care for the wounded, he again threw forward his right. McPherson was ordered to move rapidly down to the Chattahoochee and to threaten a crossing at or near Turner's Ferry. The success of this maneuver was instantaneous. Though its execution began at nighfall, Kennesaw was forthwith evacuated by Johnston; our skirmishers stood on the summit at dawn; and – our whole army pressing forward – General Sherman rode into Marietta on the heels of the Rebel rearguard.

Sherman expected to catch Johnston crossing the Chattahoochee and destroy half his army, but the wary Confederate had, ere this, strongly entrenched a position on the west side, covering the passage of the river, and stood here awaiting – in fact, inviting – an assault. Sherman paused and cautiously approached. He sent forward at length a strong skirmish line, which carried the enemy's outer line of rifle pits, taking some prisoners. Next morning, July 5, Johnston was partly over the river, and our army advanced in triumph to its bank at several points, with Atlanta just at hand.

But the Chattahoochee is here a large stream, rapid as well as deep, and barely fordable at one or two points. The railroad and other bridges, or course, were covered by the enemy's strong work on our side which they still held.

General Sherman:

I knew that Johnston would not remain on our bank of the Chattahoochee, for I could entrench a goodly force in his front and with the rest of our army cross the river and threaten either his rear or the city of Atlanta itself.

Schofield effected a crossing at Soap Creek very handsomely on July 9. By night he was on the high ground beyond, strongly entrenched, with two good pontoon bridges finished, and was prepared, if necessary, for an assault by the whole Confederate army.

That night Johnston evacuated his trenches, crossed over the Chattahoochee, burned the railroad bridge and his pontoon and trestle bridges and left us in full possession of the north bank.

On July 18, Sherman and his generals were shocked with news from the Confederacy. It would change everyone's perspective of the campaign. Confederate Capt. Thomas Key's diary:

July 18th. This morning the whole army was surprised by the announcement that the Secretary of War had removed General Johnston from command of this army and placed it in the hands of General [John Bell] *Hood. Every man looked sad and disheartened at this information, and felt that evil would result from the removal of Johnston, whom they esteem and love above any previous commander. His address touched every heart, and every man thought that his favorite General had been grievously wronged. The cause for this procedure on the part of the President at this eventful moment when the enemy is pressing us we have been unable to conjecture. General Hood is a gallant man, but Johnston had been tried and won the confidence of the soldiery.*

July 19th. The rumor prevailed that General Johnston was still in command of this army. The report cheered the despondent hearts, but I was of the impression that it was done to prevent desertions and to cause the troops to fight with their former bravery in the now approaching conflict. So soon as I dispatched a hasty breakfast, I mounted my horse, which I call General Longstreet, and rode with the other officers of the battalion along the line of battle to select the commanding points for artillery. . . . Most of Sherman's thieves are across the Chattahoochee River and are now skirmishing about two miles from the lines of rifle pits that we are now constructing. They are making some bold maneuvers for Atlanta, but at the same time will not come up fearlessly and fight us on the ground of our choice.

Sherman:

On July 19 our three armies were converging toward Atlanta, meeting such feeble resistance that I really thought the enemy intended to evacuate the place. On the twentieth soon after noon I heard heavy firing which lasted an hour or so and then ceased. I soon learned that the enemy had made a furious sally, the blow falling mainly on Hooker's corps (the 20th).

Our troops had crossed Peach Tree Creek, were deployed but at the time were resting for noon when, without notice, the enemy came down upon them. They became commingled and fought in many places hand-to-hand. General Thomas happened to be near and got some field batteries in a good

A dramatic explosion at a rail yard in City Point during August 1864. The engraving is based on an Alfred Waud drawing. (Library of Congress).

position from which he directed a furious fire. After a couple of hours of hard and close conflict the enemy retired slowly within his trenches. We had met successfully a bold sally and were also put on our guard.

During the night of July 21-22, finding that McPherson was stretching out too much on his left flank, I wrote him a note early in the morning not to extend so much by his left, for we had not troops enough to invest Atlanta completely.

McPherson came over to see me. While we sat there we could hear lively skirmishing going on near us and could hear similar sounds all along down the lines to our right. The firing was too far to our left rear to be explained by known facts, and he hastily called for his horse, saying he would send me back word. I was walking up and down listening, when an aide dashed up and reported that McPherson's horse had come back, bleeding and riderless.

McPherson was dead. How this happened on the eve of the battle at Atlanta was told by Capt. Richard Beard of the Confederate army:

I had been in command of a brigade line of skirmishers, and early on the morning of July 22 we were furnished with sixty additional rounds of ammunition and were told that there was a hard day's work before us.

We were placed in line of battle about twelve or one o'clock in the day. Shortly afterward a heavy and rapid cannonading commenced which announced that the ball was about to open in good earnest. We commenced a double-quick through a forest covered with dense underbush. Suddenly we came up to the edge of a little wagon road running parallel with our line of march and down which General McPherson came thundering at the head of his staff and, according to the best of my recollection, followed by his bodyguard. He had evidently just left the last conference he ever had with General Sherman and was on his way to see what the sudden and rapid firing on his left meant. I estimated his rank not only by his personal appearance but by the size of his retinue, and in that estimate I fixed his rank as nothing less than a corps commander.

While Grant besieged Richmond, pinning down Lee's Army of Northern Virginia, Gen. William Sherman was directed to crush the Confederate strength in Georgia and the Carolinas. In September 1864 he took Atlanta, and two months later burned much of the evacuated city. (Library of Congress)

He was certainly surprised to find himself suddenly within a few feet of where we stood. I threw up my sword to him as a signal to surrender. Not a word was spoken. He checked his horse slightly, raised his hat as politely as if he were saluting a lady, wheeled his horse's head directly to the right and dashed off to the rear in a full gallop. Young Corporal Coleman who was standing near me was ordered to fire on him. He did so and brought General McPherson down. He was shot as he was bending over his horse's neck in order to pass under the thick branches of a tree. He was shot in the back and the ball ranged upward across the body and passed through his heart.

I ran immediately up to where the general lay just as he had fallen upon his knees and face. There was not a quiver of his body to be seen, not a sign of life. Even as he lay there in his major general's uniform with his face in the dust, he was as magnificent a specimen of manhood as I ever saw.

Right by his side lay a man who was but slightly wounded. I took him to be the adjutant or inspector general of staff. Pointing to the dead man I asked him, "Who is this lying here?"

He answered with tears in his eyes, "Sir, it is General McPherson. You have killed the best man in our army."

Sherman:

. . . the sounds of the battle had become more and more furious on our extreme left.

The reports that came to me revealed clearly the game of my antagonist. Hood, during the night of July 21, had withdrawn from his Peach Tree line, had marched out to the road leading to Decatur and had turned so as to strike the left and rear of McPherson's line "in air." At the same time he had

sent Wheeler's division of cavalry against the trains parked in Decatur.

The enemy had been enabled, under cover of the forest, to approach quite near before he was discovered. The right of his line struck Dodge's troops in motion; but, fortunately, this corps (the 16th) had only to halt, face to the left and was in line of battle. It not only held the enemy in check but drove him back. One or two brigades of the 15th Corps came rapidly across the open field to the rear and filled up the gap, thus forming a strong left flank, at right angles to the original line of battle. The enemy attacked, boldly and repeatedly, the whole of this flank but met an equally fierce resistance, and a bloody battle raged from little after noon till into the night.

A part of Hood's plan of action had been to sally from Atlanta at the same moment, but this sally was not made simultaneously. I urged Generals Thomas and Schofield to take advantage of the absence of so considerable a body and to make a lodgment in Atlanta itself, but they reported that the lines to their front were strong and fully manned. About 4:00 p.m. the expected sally came from Atlanta, directed mainly against Leggett's Hill and along the Decatur Road. At Leggett's Hill they were met and bloodily repulsed. Along the railroad they were more successful. Sweeping over a small force with two guns, they reached our main line and broke through it. General Charles R. Woods reported to me in person that the line on his left had been swept back and that his connection with General Logan on Leggett's Hill was broken. I ordered him to wheel his brigades to the left, to advance in echelon and to catch the enemy in flank. General Schofield brought forward all his available batteries, to the number of twenty guns, and directed a heavy fire over the heads of General Woods's men against the enemy; and we saw Woods's troops advance and encounter the enemy, who had secured possession of the parapets which had been held by our men. These forces drove the enemy back into Atlanta.

This battle of July 22 is usually called the Battle of Atlanta.

Hood put up an impressive fight to hold Atlanta, and Sherman attempted to cut off the supply lines, continuing his tactic of flanking movements against the Confederates. Determining that Hood would not be defeated in this manner, Sherman settled down to a state of siege, encircling the city. When Hood evacuated Atlanta. Sherman telegraphed Washington, "Atlanta is ours, and fairly won."

On September 3, the President responded:

EXECUTIVE MANSION
WASHINGTON, D.C., September 3, 1864

The national thanks are rendered by the President to Major-General W.T. Sherman and the gallant officers and soldiers of his command before Atlanta, for the distinguished ability and perseverance displayed in the campaign in Georgia, which, under Divine favor, has resulted in the capture of Atlanta. The marches, battles, sieges, and other military operations that have signalized the campaign, must render it famous in the annals of war, and have entitled those who participated therein to the applause and thanks of the nation.

ABRAHAM LINCOLN,

President of the United States

William Tecumseh Sherman, second among Union commanders at war's end, brought the destructive power of total war to Georgia with his "March to the Sea." (Library of Congress)

It had been a costly campaign. Sherman estimated 4,423 killed, 22,822 wounded, and 4,442 missing; Confederate figures were approximately 3,044 killed, 18,952 wounded, and 12,983 missing.

Atlanta was already in flames when Sherman, determining to move his army on toward the coast, ordered the city destroyed. In one of the most significant documents of the Civil War, Sherman directed that Atlanta be evacuated of all citizens. The following letter to the "City Council" reveals much of Sherman's understanding of the South and of his basic philosophy of war:

Gentlemen: I have your letter . . . in the nature of a petition to revoke my orders removing all the inhabitants from Atlanta. I have read it carefully, and give full credit to your statements of the distress that will be occasioned, and yet shall not revoke my orders, because they were not designed to meet the humanities of the case, but to prepare for the future struggles in which millions of good people outside of Atlanta have a deep interest. We must have peace, not only at Atlanta, but in all America. To secure this, we must stop the war that now desolates our once happy and favored country. To stop war, we must defeat the rebel armies which are arrayed against the laws and Constitution that all must respect and obey. To defeat those armies, we must prepare the way to reach them in their recesses, provided with the arms and instruments which enable us to accomplish our purpose. Now, I know the vindictive nature of our enemy, that we may have many years of military operations from this quarter; and, therefore, deem it wise and prudent to prepare in time. The use of Atlanta for warlike purposes is inconsistent with its character as a home for families. There will be no manufactures, commerce, or agriculture here, for the maintenance of families, and sooner or later want will compel the inhabitants to go. Why not go now, when all the arrangements are completed for the transfer, instead of waiting till the plunging shot of contending armies will renew the scenes of the past month? Of course, I do not apprehend any such thing at this moment, but you do not suppose this will be here until the war is over. I cannot discuss this subject with you fairly, because I cannot impart to you what we propose to do, but I assert that our military plans make it necessary for the inhabitants to go away, and I can only renew my offer of services to make their exodus in any direction as easy and comfortable as possible.

You cannot qualify war in harsher terms than I will. War is cruelty, and you cannot refine it; and those who brought war into our country deserve all the curses and maledictions a people can pour out. I know I had no hands in making this war, and I know I will make more sacrifices to-day than any of you to secure peace. But you cannot have peace and a division of our country. If the United States submits to a division now, it will not stop, but will go on until we reap the fate of Mexico, which is eternal war. The United States does and must assert its authority, wherever it once had power; for, if it relaxes one bit to pressure, it is gone, and I believe that such is the national feeling. This feeling assumes various shapes, but always comes back to that of Union. Once admit the Union, once more acknowledge the authority of the national Government, and, instead of devoting your houses and streets and roads to the dread uses of war, I and this army become at once your protectors and supporters, shielding you from danger, let it come from what quarter it may. I know that a few individuals cannot resist a torrent of error and passion, such as swept the South into rebellion, but you can point out, so that we may know those who desire a government, and those who insist on war and its desolation.

You might as well appeal against the thunder-storm as against these terrible hardships of war. They are inevitable, and the only way the people of Atlanta can hope once more to live in peace and quiet at home, is to stop war, which can only be done by admitting that it began in error and is perpetuated in pride.

We don't want your Negroes, or your horses, or your houses, or your lands, or any thing you have, but we do want and will have a just obedience to the laws of the United States. That we will have, and if it involves the destruction of your improvements, we cannot help it.

You have heretofore read public sentiment in your newspapers, that live by falsehood and excitement; and the quicker you seek for truth in other quarters, the better. I repeat then that, by the original compact of government, the United States has certain rights in Georgia, which have never been relinquished and never will be; that the South began war by seizing forts, arsenals, mints, custom-houses, etc., etc., long before Mr. Lincoln was installed, and before the South had one jot or title of provocation. I myself have seen in Missouri, Kentucky, Tennessee, and Mississippi, hundreds and thousands of women and children fleeing from your armies and desperadoes, hungry and with bleeding feet. In Memphis, Vicksburg, and Mississippi, we fed thousands upon thousands of the families of rebel soldiers left on our hands, and whom we could not see starve. Now that war comes home to you, you feel very different. You deprecate its horrors, but did not feel them when you sent car-loads of soldiers and ammunition, and moulded shells and shot, to carry war into Kentucky and Tennessee, to desolate the homes of hundreds and thousands of good people who only asked to live in peace at their old homes, and under the Government of their inheritance. But these comparisons are idle. I want peace, and believe it can only be reached through union and war, and I will ever conduct war with a view to perfect an early success.

But, my dear sirs, when peace does come, you may call on me for any thing. Then will I share with you the last cracker, and watch with you to shield your homes and families against danger from every quarter.

Now you must go, and take with you the old and feeble, feed and nurse them, and build for them, in more quiet places, proper habitations to shield them against the weather until the mad passions of men cool down, and allow the Union and peace once more to settle over your old homes at Atlanta.

Sherman's own narration of his "march to the sea" is the best account of the campaign that sliced the Confederacy in halves and sealed its fate:

About 7 a.m. of November 16th we rode out of Atlanta by the Decatur road, filled by the marching troops and wagons of the Fourteenth Corps; and reaching the hill, just outside of the old rebel works, we naturally paused to look back upon the scenes of our past battles. We stood upon the very ground whereon was fought the bloody battle of July 22d and could see the copse of wood where McPherson fell. Behind us lay Atlanta, smoldering and in ruins, the black smoke rising high in air and hanging like a pall over the ruined city. Away off in the distance, on the McDonough road, was the rear of Howard's column, the gun barrels glistening in the sun, the white-topped wagons stretching away to the south, and right before us the Fourteenth Corps, marching steadily and rapidly with a cheery look and swinging pace that made light of the thousand miles that lay between us and Richmond. Some band by accident struck up the anthem of "John Brown's soul goes marching on"; the men caught up the strain, and never before or since have I heard the chorus of "Glory, glory, hallelujah!" done with more spirit or in better harmony of time and place.

Then we turned our horses' heads to the east; Atlanta was soon lost behind the screen of trees and became a thing of the past. Around it clings many a thought of desperate battle, of hope and fear, that now seem like a memory of a dream; and I have never seen the place since. [**The Memoirs of General William T. Sherman** *were published in 1875.*] *The day was extremely beautiful, clear sunlight, with bracing air, and an unusual feeling of exhilaration seemed to pervade all minds – a feeling of something to come, vague and undefined, still full of venture and intense interest. Even the common soldiers caught the inspiration, and many a group called out to me as I worked my way past them, "Uncle Billy, I guess Grant is waiting for us at Richmond!" Indeed, the general sentiment was that we were marching for Richmond and that there we could end the war, but how and when they seemed to care not; nor did they measure the distance or count the cost in life or bother their brains about the great rivers to be crossed and the food, required for man and beast, that had to be gathered by the way. There was a devil-may-*

care feeling pervading officers and men that made me feel the full load of responsibility, for success would be accepted as a matter of course, whereas should we fail, this march would be adjudged with wild adventure of a crazy fool. I had no purpose to march direct for Richmond by way of Augusta and Charlotte but always designed to reach the seacoast first at Savannah or Port Royal, South Carolina, and even kept in mind the alternative of Pensacola.

The first night out we camped by the roadside near Lithonia. Stone Mountain, a mass of granite, was in plain view, cut out in clear outline against the blue sky; the whole horizon was lurid with the bonfires of rail ties, and groups of men all night were carrying the heated rails to the nearest trees and bending them around the trunks. Colonel Poe had provided tools for ripping up the rails and twisting them when hot, but the best and easiest way is . . . heating the middle of the iron rails on bonfires made of the crossties and then winding them around a telegraph pole or the trunk of some convenient sapling. I attached much importance to this destruction of the railroad, gave it my personal attention, and made reiterated orders to others on the subject.

The next day we passed through the handsome town of Covington, the soldiers closing up their ranks, the color-bearers unfurling their flags, and the band striking up patriotic airs. The white people came out of their houses to behold the sight, spite of their deep hatred of the invaders, and the Negroes were simply frantic with joy. Whenever they heard my name, they clustered about my horse, shouted and prayed in their peculiar style, which had a natural eloquence that would have moved a stone. I have witnessed hundreds, if not thousands, of such scenes and can now see a poor girl, in the very ecstasy of the Methodist "shout," hugging the banner of one of the regiments and jumping up to the "feet of Jesus."

I remember, when riding around by a bystreet in Covington to avoid the crowd that followed the marching column, that some one brought me an invitation to dine with a sister of Samuel Anderson, who was a cadet at West Point with me; but the messenger reached me after we had passed the main part of the town. I asked to be excused and rode on to a place designated for camp, at the crossing of the Ulcofauhachee River, about four miles to the east of the town. Here we made our bivouac, and I walked up to a plantation house close by, where were assembled many Negroes, among them an old gray-haired man, of as fine a head as I ever saw. I asked him if he understood about the war and its progress. He said he did; that he had been looking for the "angel of the Lord" ever since he was knee-high, and though we professed to be fighting for the Union, he supposed that slavery was the cause and that our success was to be his freedom. I asked him if all Negro slaves comprehended this fact, and he said they surely did. I then explained to him that we wanted the slaves to remain where they were and not to load us down with useless mouths, which would eat up the food needed for our fighting men, that our success was their assured freedom, that we could receive a few of their young, hearty men as pioneers, but that if they followed us in swarms of old and young, feeble and helpless, it would simply load us down aand cripple us in our great task. I think Major Henry Hitchcock was with me on that occasion and made a note of the conversation, and I believe that old man spread this message to the slaves, which was carried from mouth to mouth to the very end of our journey, and that it in part saved us from the great danger we incurred of swelling our numbers so that famine would have attended our progress.

It was at this very plantation that a soldier passed me with a ham on his musket, a jug of sorghum molasses under his arm, and a big piece of honey in his hand, from which he was eating, and catching my eye, he remarked **sotto voce** *and carelessly to a comrade, "Forage liberally on the country," quoting from my general orders. On this occasion, as on many others that fell under my personal observation, I reproved the man, explained that foraging must be limited to the regular parties properly detailed, and that all provisions thus obtained must be delivered to the regular commissaries to be fairly distributed to the men who kept their ranks.*

From Covington the Fourteenth Corps, with which I was traveling, turned to the right for Milledgeville via Shady Dale. General Slocum was ahead at Madison with the Twentieth Corps, having torn up the railroad as far as that place, and thence had sent Geary's division on to the Oconee to burn the bridges across that stream when this corps turned south by Eatonton for Milledgeville, the common objective for the first stage of the march. We found abundance of corn, molasses, meal, bacon, and sweet potatoes. We also took a good many cows and oxen and a large number of mules. In all these the country was quite rich, never before having been visited by a hostile army; the recent crop had been excellent, had been just gathered and laid by for the winter. As a rule, we destroyed none but kept our wagons full and fed our teams bountifully

The skill and success of the men in collecting forage was one of the features of this march. Each brigade commander had authority to detail a company of foragers, usually about fifty men, with one or two commissioned officers selected for their boldness and enterprise. This party would be dispatched before daylight with a knowledge of the intended day's march and camp, would proceed on foot five or six miles from the route traveled by their brigade, and then visit every plantation and farm within range. They would usually procure a wagon or family carriage, load it with bacon, cornmeal, turkeys, chickens, ducks, and everything that could be used as food or forage, and would then regain the main road, usually in advance of their train. When this came up, they would deliver to the brigade commissary the supplies thus gathered by the way. Often would I pass these foraging parties at the roadside, waiting for their wagons to come up, and was amused at their strange collections – mules, horses, even cattle, packed with old saddles and

Sherman's famous (or infamous) "bummers" scoured the countryside for food, booty, and contraband on the way to Savannah. (Library of Congress)

loaded with hams, bacon, bags of cornmeal, and poultry of every character and description. Although this foraging was attended with great danger and hard work, there seemed to be a charm about it that attracted the soldiers, and it was a privilege to be detailed on such a party. Daily they returned mounted on all sorts of beasts which were at once taken from them and appropriated to the general use, but the next day they would start out again on foot, only to repeat the experience of the day before. No doubt, many acts of pillage, robbery, and violence were committed by these parties of foragers, usually called bummers; for I have since heard of jewelry taken from women and the plunder of articles that never reached the commissary; but these acts were exceptional and incidental. I never heard of any cases of murder or rape, and no army could have carried along sufficient food and forage for a march of three hundred miles, so that foraging in some shape was necessary. The country was sparsely settled, with no magistrates or civil authorities who could respond to requisitions, as is done in all the wars of Europe, so that this system of foraging was simply indispensable to our success. By it our men were well supplied with all the essentials of life and health, while the wagons retained enough in case of unexpected delay, and our animals were well fed. Indeed, when we reached Savannah, the trains were pronounced by experts to be the finest in flesh and appearance ever seen with any army.

The *Richmond Examiner* took a less polite and altogether different view of Sherman's foraging campaign:

For a hundred miles Sherman left behind him a wreck of railroads. He had consumed the fat of the land, and he had strewn every mile of his march with the evidences of savage warfare. His army had been permitted to do whatever crime could compass and cruelty invent. Even crockery, bedcover-

ing, or clothes were fair spoils. As for plate, or jewelry or watches, these were things Rebels had no use for. If the spoils were ample, the depredators were satisfied and went off in peace; if not, everything was torn and destroyed and most likely the owner was tickled with sharp bayonets into confessing where he had his treasures hid. Furniture was smashed to pieces, music was pounded out of 400-dollar pianos with the ends of muskets. Rich cushions and carpets were carried off to adorn teams and war steeds. After all was cleared out, most likely some stragglers set the house and all the surroundings ablaze. This is the way Sherman's army lived on the country.

THE SIEGE OF PETERSBURG

While Sherman marched to the sea in Georgia, Grant continued his sidestepping campaign around Lee's Army of Northern Virginia in an effort to capture Richmond. In a grim ten-month struggle Grant's army gradually but relentlessly encircled the town of Petersburg and cut Lee's railroad supply lines from the south. For the Confederates it was ten months of rifle bullets, artillery, and mortar shells, relieved on by rear-area tedium: drill and more drill, salt pork and corn meal, burned beans and bad coffee.

To the individual soldier it added up to sloshing in steaming trenches in summer; shivering in ice, snow, and mud in winter. Somehow, most survived the coldest wartime winter they could remember.

After Cold Harbor, Grant abandonend, at least for the time being, his plan to capture Richmond by direct assault. Instead, he moved his army to the south side of the James River and on June 15 threw his forces against Petersburg. Except for a series of Union fumbles, the city might well have fallen in that attack. Federal commanders, perhaps shaken by the Cold Harbor disaster, failed to press home their assaults, allowing the few Confederate defenders to hold on until Lee transferred his army from Richmond.

On June 18, an all-out Union attempt to break the Confederate line also failed. In one assault, the 1st Maine Heavy Artillery, serving as infantrymen, went into battle 850 strong; it withdrew less than a half hour later with 632 casualties. Grant's abortive attempt to capture Petersburg cost him 10,000 men; but his efforts were not entirely wasted. Two of the railroads leading into the city had been cut, and several roads were in Union hands. Behind the northern troops was City Point (now Hopewell), which the Federals speedily converted into a huge supply base. Grant then settled down to a siege which lasted nearly ten months – the longest siege in American warfare – and took the lives of 70,000 Americans.

The editors of *Harper's Weekly*:

Petersburg itself was of little consequence to either army. Its military importance arose solely from its relations to the system of railroads which connected Richmond with the region from which its supplies were drawn. Had the Confederate capital been provisioned for a siege, Petersburg might safely have been abandoned. But at no time were full rations for a fortnight in advance ever accumulated – oftener there was not three-days' supply in depot. The possession of Petersburg would insure the capture of Richmond by giving to the assailants the absolute control of the Weldon and Southside Railroads, and rendering almost certain that of the Danville Railway: two certainly, and almost inevitably a third, of the five avenues of supply for the Confederate army.

Jefferson Davis:

General Grant now determined on the method of slow approaches and proceeded to confront the city with a line of earthworks. By gradually extending the line to his left he hoped to reach out toward the Weldon and Southside Railroads.

The line of General Lee conformed to that of General Grant. Besides the works east and southeast of Richmond, an exterior line of defense had been constructed against the hostile forces at Deep Bottom and, in addition to a fortification of some strength at Drewry's Bluff, obstructions were placed in the river to prevent the ascent of the Federal gunboats. The lines thence continued facing those of the enemy north of the Appomattox, crossing that stream, extending around the city of Petersburg, gradually moving westward with the works of the enemy. The struggle that ensued consisted chiefly of attempts to break through our lines.

Hardly had the siege of Petersburg begun when coal miners of the 48th Pennsylvania Infantry began digging a tunnel under the Confederates at Pegram's Salient (also known as Elliot's Salient). The Union plan was to blast a mighty gap in the Confederate line by exploding four tons of gunpowder planted directly beneath their position. A black infantry division belonging to Burnside's IX Army Corps was selected to lead the charge after the explosion. Other troops would follow to widen the gap, capture the city, and, presumedly, end the war.

On the eve of the battle, however, the Union high command decided against using the black troops. They feared that if anything went wrong they would be accused of purposely killing off black soldiers.

Burnide was forced to choose another untrained and weakened division to lead the assault, even though the black troops were more thoroughly trained for that important role. The result was a series of Union blunders.

On the morning of July 30, 1864, the powder was exploded underneath the salient, leaving a crater 170 feet long, 60 feet wide, and 30 feet deep. Union troops easily occupied the crater, but failed to penetrate further. Union forces, instead of going around the gap left by the explosion, plunged directly into the crater. More troops followed, crowding into the crater and creating confusion and chaos. The Confederates, led by Gen. William Mahone, counterattacked. When the fighting was over, the Union army had lost more that 4,000 casualties and the Confederates, 1,500. The Confederates had retaken the crater, but it little affected the outcome of the war. It meant

Sherman's troops tore up and destroyed Confederate railroads as the army advanced from Atlanta, depriving the Southern army in Virginia of vital supplies. The rails were heated on bonfires made from the ties, and then twisted into unusable junk. (Library of Congress)

only another nine months of siege before the surrender of Appomattox.

The irony of the whole story is that had the Union infantry attack been executed as planned with the trained black troops, Petersburg might well have been captured in the summer of 1864.

THE MARCH TO THE SEA

As Christmas 1864 approached, Sherman neared his goal, Savannah, Georgia. He recorded the last days of the campaign:

In approaching Savannah, General Slocum struck the Charleston Railroad near the bridge, and occupied the river-bank at his left flank, where he had captured two of the enemy's river-boats and had prevented two others (gunboats) from coming down the river to communicate with the city; while General Howard, by his right flank, had broken the Gulf Railroad. . . and occupied the railroad itself down to the Little Ogeechee. . . so that no supplies could reach Savannah by any of its accustomed channels.

We, on the contrary, possessed large herds of cattle, which we had brought along or gathered in the country, and our wagons still contained a reasonable amount of breadstuffs and other necessities, and the fine rice crops of the Savannah and Ogeechee rivers furnished to our men and animals a large amount of rice and rice-straw.

We also held the country to the south and west of the Ogeechee as foraging ground.

Still, communication with the [Union Atlantic] fleet was of vital importance, and I directed General Kilpatrick to cross the Ogeechee by a pontoon-bridge, to reconnoitre Fort McAllister, and to proceed to St. Catherine's Sound, in the direction of Sunbury or Kilkenny Bluff, and open communication with the fleet. General Howard had previously, by my direction, sent one of his best scouts down the Ogeechee in a canoe for a like purpose. But more than this was necessary. We wanted the vessels and their contents, and the Ogeechee River, a navigable stream close to the rear of our camps, was the proper avenue of supply.

The enemy had burned the road-bridge across the Ogeechee, just below the mouth of the Camochee, known as "King's Bridge." This was reconstructed in an incredibly short time in the most substantial manner by the Fifty-eighth Indiana, Colonel Buel, under the direction of Captain Reese, of the Engineer corps, and on the morning of the thirteenth December, the Second division of the fifteenth corps, under command of Brigadier-General Hazen, crossed the bridge to the west bank of the Ogeechee, and marched down with orders to carry by assault Fort McAllister, a strong inclosed redoubt, manned by two companies of artillery and three of infantry, in all about two hundred men, and mounting twenty-three guns, **en barbette**, *and one mortar.*

General Hazen reached the vicinity of Fort McAllister about one p.m., deployed his division about the place, with both flanks resting upon the river, posted his skirmishers judiciously behind the trunks of trees whose branches had been used for abattis, and about five p.m. assaulted the place with nine regiments at three points, all of them successfully. I witnessed the assault from a rice-mill on the opposite bank of the river, and can bear testimony to the handsome manner in which it was accomplished.

Once McAllister fell, the capture of Savannah was simple, according to Sherman:

Fort McAllister had been captured late in the evening of December 13. On the eighteenth I received General Hardee's letter declining to surrender [Savannah], and nothing remained but to assault. The ground was difficult, and I concluded to make one more effort to surround Savannah completely on all sides. But toward evening of December 21, a tug arrived, reporting that the city of Savannah had been found evacuated on the morning of that day and was then in our possession. General Hardee had crossed the Savannah River by a pontoon bridge, carrying off his men and light artillery, blowing up his ironclads and navy yard, but leaving for us all the heavy guns, stores, cotton, railway cars, steamboats and an immense amount of public and private property.

As 1864 came to an end, Sherman was on the coast in Georgia and Grant was knocking on the doors of Richmond. Soon Sherman would turn and march north through the Carolinas. Grant waited patiently for the spring campaign to begin. On December 26, President Lincoln wrote Sherman:

When you were about leaving Atlanta for the Atlantic coast, I was anxious if not fearful; but feeling that you were the better judge, and remembering "nothing risked, nothing gained," I did not interfere. Now the undertaking being a success, the honor is all yours; for I believe none of us went further than to acquiesce; and, taking the work of General Thomas into account, as it should be taken, it is indeed a great success. . . . But what next? I suppose it will be safer if I leave General Grant and yourself to decide.

CHAPTER 6

1865

APPOMATTOX COURT HOUSE

Ulysses S. Grant:

One of the most anxious periods of my experience during the Rebellion was the last few weeks before Petersburg. I felt that the situation of the Confederate army was such that they would try to make an escape at the earliest practicable moment, and I was afraid, every morning, that I would awake to hear that Lee had gone. He had his railroad by the way of Danville south, and I knew he could move much more lightly and more rapidly than I. If he got the start, the war might be prolonged another year.

I could not see how it was possible for the Confederates to hold out much longer where they were. Desertions were taking place throughout the whole Confederacy. It was my belief that the enemy were losing at least a regiment a day by desertions alone. It was a mere question of arithmetic to calculate how long they could hold out.

For these and other reasons I was naturally very impatient to commence the spring campaign.

There were two considerations I had to observe, however, which detained me. One was the fact that the roads were impassable for artillery and teams. The other was that I should have Sheridan's cavalry with me, and was therefore obliged to wait until he could join me.

Sheridan arrived at City Point on March 26, and Grant immediately launched his advance to drive Lee from Petersburg. He wrote of the move on the 29th:

. . . I moved out with all the army available, after leaving a sufficient force to hold the line about Petersburg. The next day, March 30, we had made sufficient progress to the south-west to warrant me in starting Sheridan with his cavalry by Dinwiddie, with instructions to come up by the road leading northwest to Five Forks, thus menacing the right of Lee's line.

My hope was that Sheridan would be able to carry Five Forks, get on the enemy's right flank and rear and force them to weaken their center to protect their right, so that an assault in the center might be successfully made.

Lee would understand my design to get up to the Southside Railroad and ultimately to the Danville Railroad. These roads were so important to his very existence while he remained in Richmond and Petersburg, and of such vital importance to him even in case of retreat, that naturally he would make most strenuous efforts to defend them. He did, and on the thirteenth sent Pickett with five brigades to reinforce Five Forks.

Pickett, who was still writing to his sweetheart:

Well, I made the best arrangements of which the ground admitted. About two o'clock in the afternoon Sheridan made a heavy demonstration with his cavalry, threatening also the right flank. Meantime Warren's corps swept around the left flank and rear of the infantry line, and the attack became general.

I succeeded in getting a sergeant and enough men to man one piece, but after their firing eight rounds the axle broke. One regiment fought hand to hand after all their cartridges had been used. The small cavalry force, which had got into place, gave way, and the enemy poured in. Charge after charge was made and repulsed, and division after division of the enemy advanced upon us. We were completely entrapped. Their cavalry enveloped us front and right and, sweeping down upon our rear, held us in a vise.

My darling, overpowered, defeated, cut in pieces, starving, captured, as we were, those that were left of us formed front north and south and met with sullen desperation their double onset. With the members of my own staff and the general officers and their staff officers we compelled a rally enabling many of us to escape capture.

The birds were hushed in the woods when I started to write, and now one calls to its mate, "Cheer up – cheer up." Let's listen and obey the birds, my darling.

During the night of April 2, General Lee withdrew the Army of Northern Virginia from Petersburg and headed for Danville, where he knew he could obtain supplies. But the flight was futile. Sheridan had swung around to the west and Lee was blocked. Near Appomattox on the 9th, Lee struck out at Sheridan and for a moment it looked as though he might break through, but reinforcements came and the Confederates had to withdraw. Joshua Chamberlain described the last moments of the battle:

Watching intently, my eye was caught by the figure of a horseman riding out between those lines, soon joined by another, and taking a direction across the cavalry front towards our position. They were nearly a mile away, and I curiously watched them, till lost from sight in the nearer broken ground and copses between.

Suddenly rose to sight another form, close in our own front – a soldierly young figure, a Confederate staff officer undoubtedly. Now I see the white flag earnestly borne, and its possible purport sweeps before my inner vision like a wrath of morning mist. He comes steadily on, the mysterious

Richmond, the capital of the Confederacy, was finally taken in April 1865, after Lee was forced to withdraw from Petersburg in a futile attempt to break out of Grant's grasp. The city's ruined buildings are seen from across the James River in this photo by one of the Matthew Brady photographers. The Confederate government had already fled. (Library of Congress)

form in gray, my mood so whimsically sensitive that I could even smile at the material of the flag, – wondering where in either army was found a towel, and one so white. But it bore a mighty message, – that simple emblem of homely service, wafted hitherward above the dark and crimsoned streams that never can wash themselves away.

The messenger draws near, dismounts; with graceful salutation and hardly suppressed emotion delivers his message: "Sir, I am from General Gordon. General Lee desires a cessation of hostilities until he can hear from General Grant as to the proposed surrender."

What word is this! so long so dearly fought for, so feverishly dreamed, but ever snatched away, held hidden and aloof; now smiting the senses with a dizzy flash! "Surrender?" We had no rumor of this from the messages that had been passing between Grant and Lee, for now these two days, behind us. "Surrender?" It takes a moment to gather one's speech. "Sir," I answer, "that matter exceeds my authority. I will send to my superior. General Lee is right. He can do no more." All this with a forced calmness, covering a tumult of heart and brain. I bid him wait a while, and the message goes up to my corps commander, General Griffin, leaving me amazed at the boding change.

Now from the right come foaming up in cavalry fashion the two forms I had watched from away beyond. A white flag again, held strong aloft, making straight for the little group beneath our battle-flag, high borne also, – the red Maltese cross on a field of white, that had thrilled hearts long ago. I see now that it is one of our cavalry staff in lead, – indeed I recognize him, Colonel Whitaker of Custer's staff; and hardly keeping pace with him, a Confederate staff officer. Without dismounting, without salutation, the cavalryman shouts: "This is unconditional surrender! This is the end!" Then he hastily introduces his companion, and adds: "I am just from Gordon and Longstreet. Gordon says 'For God's sake, stop this infantry, or hell will be to pay!' I'll go to Sheridan," he adds, and dashes away with the white flag, leaving Longstreet's aide with me.

I was doubtful of my duty. The flag of truce was in, but I had no right to act upon it without orders. There was still some firing from various quarters, lulling a little where the white flag passed near. But I did not press things quite so hard. Just then a last cannon-shot from the edge of the town plunges through the breast of a gallant and dear young officer in my front line, – Lieutenant Clark, of the 185th New York, – the last man killed in the Army of the Potomac, if not the last in the Appomattox lines. Not a strange thing for war, – this swift stroke of the mortal; but coming after the truce was in, it seemed a cruel fate for one so deserving to share his country's joy, and a sad peace-offering for us all.

Shortly comes the order, in due form, to cease firing and to halt. There was not much firing to cease from; but "halt," then and there? It is beyond human power to stop the men, whose one word and thought and action through crimsoned years have been but forward. They had seen the flag of truce, and could divine its outcome. But the habit was too strong; they cared not for points of direction, it was forward still, – forward to the end; forward to the new beginning; forward to the Nation's second birth!

Colonel Charles Marshall of Lee's staff described the surrender scene:

We struck up the hill towards Appomattox Court House. There was a man named McLean who used to live on the first battle field of Manassas, at a house about a mile from Manassas Junction. He didn't like the war, and having seen the first battle of Manassas, he thought he would get away where there wouldn't be any more fighting, so he moved down to Appomattox Court House. General Lee told me to go forward and find a house where he could meet General Grant, and of all people, whom should I meet but McLean. I rode up to him and said, "Can you show me a house where General Lee and General Grant can meet together?" He took me into a house that was all dilapidated and that had no furniture in it. I told him it wouldn't do.

Then he said, "Maybe my house will do!" He lived in a very comfortable house, and I told him I thought that would suit. I had taken the orderly along with me, and I sent him back to General Lee and Babcock, who were coming on behind. I went into the house and sat down, and after a while General Lee and Babcock came in. Colonel Babcock told his orderly that he was to meet General Grant, who was coming on the road, and turn him in when he came along. So General Lee, Babcock and myself sat down in McLean's parlour and talked in the most friendly and affable way.

In about an hour we heard horses, and the first thing I knew General Grant walked into the room. There were with him General Sheridan, General Ord, Colonel Badeau, General Porter, Colonel Parker, and quite a number of other officers whose names I do not recall.

General Lee was standing at the end of the room opposite the door when General Grant walked in. General Grant had on a sack coat, a loose fatigue coat, but he had no side arms. He looked as though he had had a pretty hard time. He had been riding and his clothes were somewhat dusty and a little soiled. He walked up to General Lee and Lee recognized him at once. He had known him in the Mexican war. General Grant greeted him in the most cordial manner, and talked about the weather and other things in a very friendly way. Then General Grant brought up his officers and introduced them to General Lee.

I remember that General Lee asked for General Lawrence Williams, of the Army of the Potomac. That very morning General Williams had sent word by somebody to General Lee that Custis Lee, who had been captured at Sailor Creek and was reported killed, was not hurt, and General Lee asked General Grant where General Williams was, and if he could not send for him to come and see him. General Grant sent somebody out for General Williams, and when he came, General Lee thanked him for having sent him word about the safety of his son.

After a very free talk General Lee said to General Grant: "General, I have come to meet you in accordance with my letter to you this morning, to treat about the surrender of my army, and I think the best way would be for you to put your terms in writing."

General Grant said: "Yes, I believe it will."

So a Colonel Parker, General Grant's Aide-de-Camp, brought a little table over from a corner of the room, and General Grant wrote the terms and conditions of surrender on what we call field note paper, that is, a paper that makes a copy at the same time as the note is written. After he had written it, he took it over to General Lee.

General Lee was sitting at the side of the room; he rose and went to meet General Grant to take that paper and read it over. When he came to the part in which only public property was to be surrendered, and the officers were to retain their side arms and personal baggage, General Lee said: "That will have a very happy effect."

General Lee then said to General Grant: "General, our cavalrymen furnish their own horses; they are not Government horses, some of them may be, but of course you will find them out – any property that is public property, you will ascertain that, but it is nearly all private property, and these men will want to plough ground and plant corn."

General Grant answered that as the terms were written,

As Lee rode away from the surrender, dignity intact, Alfred Waud was again on the spot to record the event for history with his pen and paper. (Library of Congress)

Genl Lee leaving the McLean house after the surrender &c

Orderlies holding horses all about

only the officers were permitted to take their private property, but almost immediately he added that he supposed that most of the men in the ranks were small farmers, and that the United States did not want their horses. He would give orders to allow every man who claimed to own a horse or mule to take the animal home.

General Lee having again said that this would have an excellent effect, once more looked over the letter, and being satisfied with it, told me to write a reply. General Grant told Colonel Parker to copy his letter, which was written in pencil, and put it in ink. Colonel Parker took the table and carried it back to a corner of the room, leaving General Grant and General Lee facing each other and talking together. There was no ink in McLean's inkstand, except some thick stuff that was very much like pitch, but I had a screw boxwood inkstand that I always carried with me in a little satchel that I had at my side, and I gave that to Colonel Parker, and he copied General Grant's letter with the aid of my inkstand and my pen.

There was another table right against the wall, and a sofa next to it. I was sitting on the arm of the sofa near the table, and General Sheridan was on the sofa next to me. While Colonel Parker was copying the letter, General Sheridan said to me, "This is very pretty country."

I said, "General, I haven't seen it by daylight. All my observations have been my night and I haven't seen the country at all myself."

He laughed at my remark, and while we were talking I heard General Grant say this: "Sheridan, how many rations have you?"

General Sheridan said: "How many do you want?" and General Grant said, "General Lee has about a thousand or fifteen hundred of our people prisoners, and they are faring the same as his men, but he tells me his haven't anything. Can you send them some rations?"

"Yes," he answered. They had gotten some of our rations, having captured a train.

General Grant said: "How many can you send?" and he replied "Twenty-five thousand rations."

General Grant asked if that would be enough, and General Lee replied "Plenty; plenty; and abundance;" and General Grant said to Sheridan "Order your commissary to send to the Confederate Commissary twenty-five thousand rations for our men and his men."

After a while Colonel Parker got through with his copy of General Grant's letter and I sat down to write a reply. I began it in the usual way: "I have the honor to acknowledge the receipt of your letter of such a date," and then went on to say the terms were satisfactory.

I took the letter over to General Lee, and he read it and said: "Don't say, 'I have the honor to acknowledge the receipt of your letter of such a date'; he is here; just say, 'I accept these terms,'"

Then I wrote:

HEADQUARTERS OF THE ARMY OF NORTHERN VIRGINIA

April 9, 1865

I received your letter of this date containing the terms of the surrender of the Army of Northern Virginia proposed by you. As they are substantially the same as those expressed in your letter of the 8th instant, they are accepted. I will proceed to designate the proper officers to carry the stipulations into effect.

Then General Grant signed his letter, and I turned over my letter to General Lee and he signed it. Parker handed me General Grant's letter, and I handed him General Lee's reply, and the surrender was accomplished. There was no theatrical display about it. It was in itself perhaps the greatest tragedy that ever occurred in the history of the world, but it was the simplest, plainest, and most thoroughly devoid of any attempt at effect, that you can imagine.

The story of General Grant returning General Lee's sword to him is absurd, because General Grant proposed in his letter that the officers of the Confederate Army should retain their side-arms. Why, in the name of common sense, anybody should imagine that General Lee, after receiving a letter which said that he should retain his side-arms, yet should offer to surrender his sword to General Grant, is hard to understand. The only thing of the kind that occurred in the whole course of the transaction – which occupied perhaps an hour – was this: General Lee was in full uniform. He had on the handsomest uniform I ever saw him wear; and he had on a sword with a gold, a very handsome gold and leather scabbard that had been presented to him by English ladies. General Grant excused himself to General Lee towards the close of the conversation between them, for not having his side arms with him; he told him that when he got his letter he was about four miles from his wagon in which his arms and uniform were, and he said that he had thought that General Lee would rather receive him as he was, than be detained, while he sent back to get his sword and uniform. General Lee told him he was very much obliged to him and was very glad indeed that he hadn't done it.

General Lee's farewell to his troops is one of the classic documents of the Civil War. Colonel Marshall:

On the night of April 9th after our return from McLean's house General Lee sat with several of us at a fire in front of his tent, and after some conversation about the army and the events of the day in which his feelings towards his men were strongly expressed, he told me to prepare an order to the troops.

The next day it was raining and many persons were coming and going, so that I was unable to write without interruption until about 10 o'clock, when General Lee finding that the order had not been prepared, directed me to get into his ambulance, which stood near his tent, and placed an orderly to prevent anyone from approaching us. I made a draft in pencil and took it to General Lee who struck out a paragraph, which he said would tend to keep alive the feeling

The end of the Confederate dream came at the unpretentious house of Wilmer McLean in rural Virginia, near Appomattox Courthouse. With no further hope, Lee asked Grant for terms of surrender at a meeting here on April 9. (Library of Congress)

existing between the North and South, and made one or two other changes. I then returned to the ambulance, recopied the order and gave it to a clerk in the office of the Adjutant General to write in ink.

After the first draft of the order had been made and signed by General Lee, other copies were made for transmission to the corps commanders and the staff of the army. All these copies were signed by the General and a good many persons sent other copies which they had made or procured and obtained his signature. In this way many of the orders had the General's name signed as if they were originals.

The full text of the order follows:

GENERAL ORDER NO. 9

HEADQUARTERS ARMY OF NORTHERN VIRGINIA, 10th April 1865

After four years of arduous service marked by unsurpassed courage and fortitude the Army of Northern Virginia has been compelled to yield to overwhelming numbers and resources.

I need not tell the survivors of so many hard fought battles, who have remained steadfast to the last, that I have consented to this result from no distrust of them. But feeling that valor and devotion could accomplish nothing that could

The war was over, the South shattered for generations, and Lincoln dead from the assassin's bullet when the triumphant Union Army staged one last Grand Review down Pennsylvania Avenue on May 24, 1865. (Library of Congress)

compensate for the loss that would have accompanied the continuance of the contest, I determined to avoid the useless sacrifice of those whose past services have endeared them to their country.

By the terms of the agreement Officers and men can return to their homes and remain there until exchanged. You will take with you the satisfaction that proceeds from the conciousness of duty faithfully performed and I earnestly pray that a merciful God will extend to you his blessing and protection.

With an unceasing admiration of your constancy and devotion to your country and a grateful rememberance of your kind and generous consideration of myself, I bid you all an affectionate farewell.

R.E. LEE

General